# *Sunset* Cook Book of
# Favorite
# Recipes I

By the Editors of Sunset Books and Sunset Magazine

A new, more colorful presentation, with larger type for easier reading, of material originally published in 1969 under the title *Sunset Cook Book of Favorite Recipes*.

# Lane Publishing Co. • Menlo Park, California

# How These Favorites Were Chosen

For 40 years, *Sunset Magazine* and *Sunset Books* have been publishing dependable, tested recipes, many of which have become favorites of those who cook to please family and friends. More than 20 years ago a book called "Favorite Recipes" was published and became the best-selling Sunset cook book. Several years ago the editors began plans for this new book, which contains all the new favorites from the last 20 years, as well as some recipes from the old book and earlier era which still are popular.

To make this selection, *Sunset Magazine* asked its readers to send a letter or card mentioning their favorite *Sunset* recipes. The response was overwhelming. Several staff members spent weeks tabulating the recipe "votes" and still more time locating the actual recipes which were leading contenders. Then the winners were selected, with the primary objective of presenting as useful a cook book as possible.

The result is an amazing variety of recipes. Nearly all the popular kinds and cuts of meat, poultry, and seafood are represented. Recipes for nearly all of the vegetables and fruits commonly sold are here. A wide choice of basic sauces, salad dressings, basic breads, and popular desserts is included. Yet most of the recipes incorporate some new twist or bit of originality.

This book is meant to be used daily, primarily for family meals. Yet you will find many relatively uncomplicated dishes to add sparkle to your entertaining.

Publications today abound with recipes for dishes that are good enough to eat, but not really great enough to bother making again. But this book is packed with recipes for exceptional dishes you will prepare time and time again. Here are recipes which will give you pleasure, save you time, and earn you praise. Here are the recipes destined to become *your* favorites.

*Edited by* Marjorie Ray Piper

*Special Consultant:* Annabel Post
HOME ECONOMICS EDITOR,
SUNSET MAGAZINE

*Illustrations:* Alice Harth
*Front Cover:* Beef-Vegetable Pie (page 27)
Photographed by Darrow M. Watt
Cover design by Zan Fox

Editor, Sunset Books: David E. Clark

Nineteenth printing October 1982

Copyright © 1969, 1949, Lane Publishing Co., Menlo Park, CA 94025. Second edition. World rights reserved. No part of this publication may be reproduced by any mechanical, photographic, or electronic process, or in the form of a phonographic recording, nor may it be stored in a retrieval system, transmitted, or otherwise copied for public or private use without prior written permission from the publisher. Library of Congress Catalog Card Number: 82-81373. ISBN 0-376-02177-2. Lithographed in the United States.

# Contents

# Appetizers & First Courses

## Simple Appetizers

All of the following are easy-to-prepare appetizer favorites.

**Crudités.** Fill a small straw basket with a "nosegay" of fresh, raw relish vegetables such as cauliflower, Chinese (edible pod) peas, baby carrots, radishes, artichoke hearts, cherry tomatoes, cucumber, asparagus spears, green beans, and celery. Cut large vegetables into sticks, slivers, or other easy-to-dip shapes. Serve with mayonnaise for a dip (preferably homemade).

**Edam Cheese Spread.** Carefully cut the top from a small Edam cheese and take out contents, leaving a thin wall. Add enough mayonnaise to cheese to make it of spreading consistency, mashing and stirring with a fork to blend well. Add 1 tablespoon Sherry, dash of liquid hot-pepper seasoning, few drops of Worcestershire, 1 tablespoon each chopped chives and pimiento, and 1 teaspoon dry mustard. Place mixture in cheese shell. Serve with crackers.

**Fresh Pineapple with Curry Mayonnaise.** Cut top off pineapple (a little of the pineapple with leaves attached). Cut off rind deep enough to remove eyes. Run a sharp, thin knife around the core, leaving a ½ to 1-inch tube of fruit around the cylindrical core. Inserting toothpicks as you work, make vertical, parallel cuts an inch or less apart all around the pineapple to the core. Then make horizontal cuts the same distance apart. This will make 1-inch (or smaller) cubes, each skewered to the core with a toothpick.

Place leafy top back on upright pineapple. Serve with a bowl of Curry Mayonnaise, recipe on page 115, to use as a dip.

**Melon with Meat.** Cut melon into bite-sized chunks and wrap with a paper-thin slice of one of the appropriate meats suggested. Fasten with toothpicks.

Or, for a first course, arrange meat-wrapped melon on small plates. Provide forks.

Persian, Crenshaw, and Casaba melons and honeydew or cantaloupe are all complemented by prosciutto, Westphalian ham, and baked ham. Other meats which match well with most melons are pastrami, corned beef, tongue, smoked beef, Canadian bacon, Genoa or dry salami, smoked Thuringer, Lebanon bologna, galantina, mortadella, and coppa.

**Coconut Chips.** Remove meat from 1 coconut (use easy-crack method—recipe on page 120). Peel off brown skin, and shave the meat in thin slices, using a vegetable peeler. Spread shavings on a baking sheet and toast in a 375° oven, turning occasionally, until crisp and lightly browned. Sprinkle lightly with salt, if you wish.

**Spiced Toasted Nuts.** Spread 1 cup of whole or halved nuts (pecans, walnuts, almonds, or filberts) in a shallow baking pan. Coat nuts with 1 teaspoon (or more) salad oil. Bake in a 300° oven about 20 minutes, or until nuts are a light brown in the center. Sprinkle with one of the following seasonings: 2 teaspoons paprika mixed with ½ teaspoon salt; 1 teaspoon chile powder with ½ teaspoon salt; ½ teaspoon (or more) curry powder with ½ teaspoon salt; or, ¾ teaspoon garlic *or* onion salt.

**Cocktail Cream Puffs.** Fill petite cream puff shells (recipe on page 88) with thick cheese sauce; chicken, tuna, or crab salad; or a well-seasoned mixture of cream cheese and deviled ham. Serve cold, or bake in a 425° oven until thoroughly hot.

**Cocktail Biscuits.** Make very tiny baking powder biscuits. While still hot, split and fill with deviled ham spread, or fried slices of Italian or chorizo sausage.

**Seafood Cocktail.** Provide a bowl of cooked shrimp, crab legs, or scallops; or arrange the seafood on a platter. Provide toothpicks or bamboo skewers and a bowl of Spicy Seafood Cocktail Sauce, recipe on page 116, for dipping.

**Avocado Dip with Red and Black Caviar.** Halve 1 large avocado and carefully scoop out flesh, preserving shell. Mash pulp with ¼ cup sour cream, 2 tablespoons lime juice, and ⅛ teaspoon salt. Spoon into half shells. Make a cavity in center of each mound of avocado. Fill one hollow with about 2 tablespoons black caviar, the other with about 2 tablespoons red caviar. Place avocado halves in a shallow basket and surround with tortilla chips or corn chips.

## Herb Olives

2 cups unpitted ripe or green olives
1 bay leaf
2 small hot, dried red chiles
2 tablespoons drained capers
2 cloves garlic
12 rosemary leaves
2 tablespoons finely chopped celery leaves
1 cup (or more) salad oil or olive oil

Press each olive gently between a nutcracker or the fingers so the marinade can penetrate the olives.

Place olives in a jar, interspersed with all the ingredients except oil. Pour in enough oil to cover olives. Cover jar and shake well. Refrigerate 3 or 4 days before using; shake jar several times during this time. Remove garlic if olives are stored for any length of time.

## Guacamole

This recipe gives you many seasoning choices.

2 large ripe avocados
2 or 3 tablespoons lemon or lime juice, or to taste
 Salt to taste, about ½ teaspoon
2 to 4 canned California green chiles (seeded and chopped); and/or cayenne, liquid hot-pepper seasoning, or minced hot green chiles to taste

Cut avocados in half, remove seeds, and scoop out pulp with a spoon, or peel. Mash pulp coarsely with a fork while blending in lemon or lime juice. (Or, for a smooth dip, whirl in a blender.) Season to taste with salt. Add the chopped chiles, cayenne, or pepper seasoning if you'd like a touch of heat. Makes about 1⅔ cups.

**Variations.** Add 1 clove of garlic, minced or mashed; 2 or 3 tablespoons minced onion, or both garlic and onion.

Blend in ½ teaspoon ground coriander or 2 teaspoons minced *cilantro* (sometimes called Chinese parsley or fresh coriander).

Blend mayonnaise into the mixture to give it a smoother consistency.

Mix in 1 pimiento, chopped, or as much as 1 tomato, chopped.

For a festive appearance, garnish with tomato wedges and *cilantro* or

parsley sprigs, or sprinkle pomegranate seeds over the top.

**Stuffed Celery Los Angeles.** Stuff celery stalks with Guacamole and dust lightly with paprika.

## Pickled Mushrooms à la Grecque

1 pound uniform mushrooms (preferably 1½ inches in diameter)
1½ cups water
¾ cup olive oil
2 tablespoons lemon juice
1 small clove garlic (put through the press)
1 stalk celery diced fine
1 tablespoon white wine vinegar
¼ teaspoon fennel seed
¼ teaspoon oregano
¾ teaspoon ground coriander
½ bay leaf
¼ teaspoon whole black peppers
1 teaspoon salt

Clean mushrooms. Cut off gritty ends of stems and discard. In a pan combine all ingredients except mushrooms. (If you wish, tie spices in a cheesecloth bag so they may be removed before serving.)

Simmer for 15 minutes, then add the whole mushrooms and cook another 5 minutes. Cool and chill for at least 24 hours. Serve at room temperature.

## Bagna Cauda

Crisp, raw vegetables are dipped in a hot anchovy-butter sauce of Italian origin.

½ cup (¼ lb.) butter
¼ cup olive oil
4 small cloves garlic, mashed
1 can (2 oz.) flat anchovy fillets, well drained and finely chopped
 Raw vegetables (see following suggestions)
 Thinly sliced French bread or sliced crusty rolls

Choose a heatproof container that will be only about half filled by the sauce. In it, combine the butter, olive oil, garlic, and chopped anchovies. Stir over moderate heat until mixture bubbles. This is enough for 8 to 10 servings.

To serve, set over candle or low

alcohol flame—mixture must not get hot enough to brown and burn. Accompany with baskets of prepared vegetables and bread.

To eat, swirl a piece of vegetable through the sauce (impaled on a skewer if you like). Hold a piece of bread under vegetable to catch the drip and eat the bread when it becomes tastily soaked.

**Raw Vegetables.** You'll need an equivalent of 1 to 2 cups vegetable pieces per person. But don't completely cut the vegetables in pieces. Leave whole, if small, or gash them almost through so they can be broken apart just before dipping—this preserves their attractive appearance. Sprinkle with water just before serving so they have a dewy-fresh appearance.

*Artichokes.* Break off small outer bracts; cut thorny tip from remaining bracts with scissors. Trim stem ends. Keep in acid water (1 tablespoon vinegar to 1 quart water) until ready to serve. To eat, bite off tender base with each bract.

*Cabbage.* Cut red or white cabbage in half. Cut vertical gashes in each half.

*Carrots.* Leave on an inch of stem; peel. Gash carrot not quite through in short sections.

*Cauliflower.* Cut out core, keeping head whole. Break off flowerets to eat.

*Cherry tomatoes.* Dip with stems.

*Green beans.* Snap off ends and remove strings.

*Green peppers.* Cut pepper vertically down to the stem in 8 to 12 sections around the seed center.

*Mushrooms.* Trim stem ends. Eat small mushrooms whole. Cut large ones through cap only, into 4 to 6 sections.

*Radishes.* Cut off root ends and all but one or two leaves to hold for dipping.

*Turnips.* Peel and cut not quite through in thick slices.

*Zucchini and yellow crookneck squash.* Trim ends; cut not quite through in short sections.

## Hasty Hots

You probably have all the ingredients on hand to make these quick hot appetizers. No wonder the recipe has become a favorite.

- 4 green onions
- ½ cup grated Parmesan cheese
- 6 tablespoons mayonnaise
  Toast rounds or sliced French rolls

Chop green onions fine. Add grated cheese and enough mayonnaise to make a spread of fairly firm consistency.

Toast one side of bread rounds or roll slices. Spread mixture on untoasted side and put under broiler just until bubbly. Makes 1½ to 2 dozen canapés.

## Olive-filled Cheese Balls

Bake these in the morning and reheat at party time in a 350° oven.

- 1 cup shredded sharp Cheddar cheese (about ¼ lb.)
- 2 tablespoons butter
- ½ cup flour
  Dash of cayenne
- 25 medium-sized olives (pitted ripe or stuffed green), well drained

Cream together cheese and butter. Blend in flour and cayenne. Drop teaspoonfuls of dough on waxed paper. Wrap each teaspoonful of dough around an olive, covering completely.

Bake in a 400° oven for 15 minutes. Makes about 25 balls.

## Potted American Cheese with Sherry

- 1 pound process American or Cheddar cheese
- 2 tablespoons butter or margarine
- 1 teaspoon sugar
- ⅛ teaspoon salt
- ½ teaspoon paprika
  Dash of cayenne
- ½ cup Sherry

Crumble cheese with a fork or pastry blender. Add butter, sugar, salt, paprika, and cayenne; blend well. Grad-

ually beat in Sherry, then continue beating until mixture is light and creamy. (An electric mixer is excellent here.) Pack into small jars. Cut a piece of waxed paper to fit and lay it over the top of the cheese, then cover the jar tightly. Store in the refrigerator. Makes about 1¾ cups.

**Blue Cheese with Port.** Substitute 1 pound of blue cheese, use ½ teaspoon Worcestershire instead of the sugar, and 6 tablespoons Port instead of Sherry.

## Cheese Fondue

You can melt the cheese in an earthenware fondue pot or heatproof dish directly over a denatured-alcohol or canned-heat flame. If you use a metal pan, place it over simmering water. (Use the water bath with a chafing dish, or a double boiler.) The heating unit should be designed so you can regulate the heat—a candle warmer won't do.

Only *imported* cheese will melt properly. Don't substitute domestic cheese.

- 1 clove garlic, cut in half
- 2 cups light dry white wine (such as Riesling, Chablis, or Traminer)
- ½ pound imported Swiss cheese (Emmental), shredded
- ½ pound imported Swiss or Danish Gruyère (Samsoe), shredded
- 1 tablespoon cornstarch
- 1 teaspoon dry mustard (optional)
- 3 tablespoons kirsch, brandy, or light white rum (optional)
  Freshly ground nutmeg and pepper, to taste
- 1 small loaf French bread, cut in 1-inch cubes with some crust on each

Rub fondue pot with garlic. Add wine, and heat slowly until bubbles form and slowly rise to the surface. Combine the cheeses, cornstarch, and mustard. Add cheese mixture, a spoonful at a time; stir slowly and continuously until blended into a smooth sauce. It should bubble *very* slowly; if it gets too hot, cheese will separate.

Stir in kirsch a tablespoon at a time, and again bring to a slow boil. Sprinkle with nutmeg and pepper, to taste. Take to the table with the bread cubes, and adjust heat so fondue keeps bubbling slowly. If fondue gets

too thick, thin with heated wine. To eat: each person spears bread with a fork, swirls it in the cheese. Makes 12 to 16 appetizer servings, or serves 4 as a main dish.

## Artichoke Appetizers

- 1 large artichoke
  Water and vinegar
- 1 teaspoon salad oil
- 1 bay leaf, crushed
- ½ teaspoon salt
- 1 package (3 oz.) cream cheese
- ¼ teaspoon liquid hot-pepper seasoning
- ½ teaspoon garlic powder
  Salt to taste
  About 2 tablespoons half-and-half (light cream)
  About ¼ pound small cooked shrimp
  Paprika

Cover the artichoke with water; add 1 tablespoon vinegar per quart of water, the oil, bay leaf, and salt. Simmer about 30 minutes, or until a leaf pulls away easily and its base is tender. Cool, then remove the leaves. Use the leaves that have a good edible portion on the ends.

Blend the cream cheese with hot-pepper seasoning, garlic powder, additional salt to taste, and half-and-half to make a smooth paste. Spread this filling on the base of each leaf. Place a small shrimp on top of the filling and sprinkle with paprika. Arrange on a round plate or tray in the shape of a sunflower so each leaf is easy to pick up. Makes about 18.

## Onion-Dill Dip for Vegetables

- 2½ cups plain yogurt
- 1 package (amount for 4 servings) dry onion soup mix
- 1 tablespoon minced parsley
- ¼ teaspoon garlic powder
- 1 teaspoon dill weed
  Dash pepper
  Crisp raw vegetables (see Bagna Cauda recipe on page 5 for suggestions)

Combine all ingredients except vegetables. Chill at least 1 hour. Serve with vegetables. If you like, you can cut the vegetables into smaller pieces than suggested in the preparation of the vegetables for Bagna Cauda. Makes 3 cups.

## Raw Mushrooms with Green-Chile Cheese

2 to 3 tablespoons minced canned California green chiles (seeds removed)
1 small package (3 oz.) cream cheese with chives
   About 8 fresh mushrooms
   Paprika or minced parsley

Blend the chiles and cheese, adding more chile if you want it hotter.

Slice the mushrooms lengthwise, through the stem and cap. Place about ½ teaspoon chile cheese on each slice. Sprinkle with paprika or minced parsley. Makes about 30 slices.

## Anchovy Turnovers

1 cup regular all-purpose flour
1 small package (3 oz.) cream cheese
½ cup (¼ lb.) butter or margarine
1 tube (2 oz.) anchovy paste

Sift flour, measure, and sift again into a mixing bowl. Cut in cream cheese and butter. Roll into a ball, and chill for about 2 hours.

Roll out dough ⅛ inch thick and cut into 2-inch rounds. Put about ¼ teaspoon anchovy paste in the center of each round. Moisten edges and press together, turnover fashion. Prick tops. Place on a baking sheet and chill until serving time.

Then bake in a 375° oven for 10 minutes. Serve at once. Makes about 5½ dozen.

## Clam-Cheese Dip

2 packages (3 oz. each) chive cream cheese
1 whole clove garlic, crushed
1 tablespoon mayonnaise
   Garlic salt to taste
1 can (7½ oz.) minced clams, drained
   Juice of 1 small lemon

Mash cheese with a fork; add crushed garlic, mayonnaise, and garlic salt;

mix well. Add clams and lemon juice to cheese mixture and beat until ingredients are well blended. Makes about 1 cup.

## Christmas Tree Cheese Spread

You need a styrofoam "tree" (cone with 12-inch base), which you cover with cheese spread and then decorate.

3 packages (8 oz. each) cream cheese
1 jar (5 oz.) bacon-flavored process cheese spread
1½ teaspoons prepared horseradish
1 teaspoon Worcestershire
¼ teaspoon each dry mustard and celery salt
½ small clove garlic, mashed (optional)
   Garnishes for trimming "tree" (see suggestions following)
   Crisp crackers

Beat together the cream cheese and bacon-flavored cheese with an electric mixer until smooth and creamy. Blend in the horseradish, Worcestershire, mustard, celery salt, and garlic, if used. Spread this mixture over the styrofoam cone, first wrapped in plastic film.

Decorate the tree with suggested garnishes and chill well. If you want to refrigerate it for several hours or overnight, wrap the chilled tree loosely with a towel or plastic film. Arrange crackers around base to serve.

**Garnish Suggestions.** Green or red pepper and pimiento "stars" cut with a knife or aspic cutters; tiny cooked shrimp; sliced pimiento-stuffed green olives, pitted ripe olives, or pickles; tiny pickled peppers; pickled onions; sprigs of parsley; and luncheon meats or cheese cut in fancy shapes.

## Cheese Pinwheels

Trim the crusts from a small, unsliced loaf of white bread; cut lengthwise into ¼-inch-thick slices. Spread slices thickly with any desired cheese spread. Roll lengthwise as for a jelly roll. Wrap rolls in waxed paper and chill thoroughly. Just before serving, cut rolls in ¼-inch thick slices. Arrange slices attractively on a tray; garnish if you like.

## Fettucine

A special first-course dish in many fine restaurants is the noodle, cream, and cheese concoction called Fettucine.

A particularly smooth and delicious version may be made with the recipe for Pasta with Sauce Suprême on page 72.

You can buy fresh Fettucine noodles in many stores, but a recipe for making egg noodles is on page 71.

## Spicy Bean Cocktail Dip

The smooth texture of this lively dip goes well with crisp vegetables.

1 small can (about 8 oz.) kidney beans, drained
1 clove garlic, minced or mashed
¼ teaspoon liquid hot-pepper seasoning
1 teaspoon Worcestershire
1 tablespoon mayonnaise
   Juice of ½ lemon
½ teaspoon minced chives or finely chopped green onions
   Dippers: potato wafers, thin crackers, or raw vegetable sticks

Put in blender the drained beans, garlic, liquid hot-pepper seasoning, Worcestershire, mayonnaise, and lemon juice. Blend until smooth, about 60 seconds (or press mixture through a wire strainer if you don't have a blender).

Turn into a serving bowl and sprinkle with chives. Serve with potato wafers or thin crackers, or try it with raw carrot and celery sticks. Makes 1 cup dip.

## Cocktail Wieners

Don't be deceived by the simplicity of this sauce. It is surprisingly delicious.

1 jar (6 oz.) prepared mustard
1 jar (10 oz.) red currant jelly
1 pound frankfurters, cut in bite-size pieces

Heat over hot water the prepared mustard mixed with red currant jelly. Add frankfurters and heat through. Serve hot from a chafing dish, electric frying pan, or shallow saucepan. Spear with toothpicks to eat. Makes 8 to 10 servings.

## Bacon-wrapped "Hot Bites"

These have been popular appetizers for many years, undoubtedly because they are so easy and so tasty.

**Hot Bites.** Cut thin-sliced bacon in half lengthwise, then in halves or thirds crosswise, depending on the size of the tidbit you will wrap it around. Wrap each piece around a stuffed green olive; pitted ripe olive; a small piece of sweet pickle or gherkin; or cubes of jack or American cheese spread with prepared mustard. Fasten bacon with a toothpick (not plastic).

Arrange 1 inch apart on a baking sheet; or, better yet, on a cake rack placed on the baking sheet. Broil, turning once, or bake in a 450° oven until bacon is crisp. Serve hot.

**Bacon-banded Olives.** This variation is especially popular. Fill the cavities of pitted ripe olives with very finely minced onion before wrapping with bacon (cut slices in half lengthwise, then in thirds crosswise). Fasten with toothpicks.

Arrange 1 inch apart on a baking sheet; or, better yet, on a cake rack placed on the baking sheet. Broil, turning once, or bake in a 450° oven until bacon is crisp. Serve hot.

**Water Chestnut Appetizers.** Use 1 can (5 oz.) water chestnuts, drained; ¼ cup soy sauce; ¼ cup sugar; and about 4 slices bacon, cut in half lengthwise and in half crosswise. Marinate water chestnuts in soy sauce for 30 minutes. Then roll each in sugar and wrap with bacon, fastening with a pick. Bake in a 400° oven about 20 minutes; drain on paper towels. To

reheat: bake in a 350° oven about 5 minutes. Makes about 16.

**Shrimp and Bacon Bits.** Cook 1 pound medium-large shrimp in boiling, salted water about 5 minutes. Drain, shell, and devein. Broil ½ pound thinly sliced bacon on one side only; drain, and cut each slice in half crosswise. Blend 1 clove of minced or mashed garlic into ½ cup chile sauce. Dip each shrimp into sauce to coat well, wrap in a bacon piece, and fasten with toothpick. (You can cover and refrigerate until ready to broil.)

Arrange 1 inch apart on a broiler rack and broil until bacon is crisp, turning to crisp both sides. Makes about 2 dozen.

**Tamale Tempters.** Cut Mexican-style canned tamales (remove any husks) in 1 to 1½-inch lengths; wrap each piece in a strip of bacon, and fasten with toothpicks. 'Broil, turning once, or bake in a 500° oven until bacon is crisp.

## Appetizer Meatballs in Sauce

For a large group you can easily prepare tiny meatballs to serve hot in your choice of sauce (Sweet and Sour, Curry, Stroganoff, or Teriyaki). These recipes are on pages 116 and 117.

Instructions for making these meatballs into a main dish also follow.

2 pounds ground chuck or lean ground beef
½ cup each fine dry bread crumbs and milk
2 eggs
1½ teaspoons salt (or part garlic salt)
Your choice of sauce:
Sweet and Sour Sauce
Curry Sauce
Stroganoff Sauce
Teriyaki Sauce
(sauce recipes on pages 116 and 117)

Combine the meat, crumbs, milk, eggs, and salt in a bowl. Mix lightly to blend.

Shape the meat into balls about the size of large marbles. Arrange on shallow baking pans. Put into a 500° oven for 4 to 5 minutes, or until lightly browned. Remove and add to the prepared sauce; include any pan juices. Cool, then refrigerate until time to serve.

Reheat meat and sauce together over low heat; keep warm in chafing dish or over candle warmer. Provide toothpicks or bamboo skewers for spearing the meatballs, and plenty of small paper napkins. Makes about 100 meatballs.

**Main-dish Meatballs Variation.** Shape the meat about the size of golf balls. Bake on shallow pans in a 500° oven for about 7 to 9 minutes. Remove and add to the sauce. Reheat as for appetizer meatballs. Makes about 3 dozen.

## Chicken Liver-Mushroom Pâté

¼ cup (⅛ lb.) butter
½ pound mushrooms
1 pound chicken livers
1 teaspoon each garlic salt and paprika
⅓ cup finely chopped green onion
⅓ cup dry white wine
Dash of dill weed
3 drops liquid-hot pepper seasoning
½ cup (¼ lb.) soft butter
Salt

In the ¼ cup butter, simmer for 5 minutes the mushrooms, livers, garlic salt, paprika, and onion. Add the wine, dill weed, and hot-pepper seasoning. Cover and cook slowly 5 to 10 minutes more.

Cool and press through a wire strainer or whirl smooth in a blender. Blend in the ½ cup butter and add salt to taste. Pack in a decorative jar or crock if you wish. Chill overnight. Makes 3 cups.

## Meat or Seafood Fondue

Use either meat or seafood—don't cook both in the same butter-oil mixture. Let guests do their own cooking.

To serve this as a main dish, allow about ½ pound meat per person.

**2 to 2½ pounds meat or seafood for each 12 to 16 people (see following suggestions)**
**Half butter and half salad oil**
**Choice of dipping sauces (see suggestions)**

*Meat suggestions:* boneless beef sirloin or tenderloin, chicken breasts, or boneless leg of lamb. Cut in bite-sized pieces.

*Seafood suggestions:* salmon or swordfish steaks (cut in ¾-inch squares); whole raw medium-sized shrimp (shelled and deveined); or scallops (halved if large).

Refrigerate prepared meat or seafood until about 15 to 20 minutes before serving time.

Put butter and salad oil in a Fondue Bourguignonne pot or an electric frying pan. Fill pan no more than ¼ full. Heat just below the smoking point (about 425° in electric frying pan). Spear a cube of meat or seafood with a fork and hold it in the hot butter-oil until cooked, about 1 to 2 minutes. Remove from the hot cooking fork to a plate. Use another fork to eat it.

Offer one or more of the following dipping sauces: Blender Béarnaise, recipe on page 115; Tomato Chutney, page 119; Mustard Mayonnaise, page 114; Anchovy Mayonnaise, page 114; Guacamole, page 5; or the following easily prepared sauces:

**Teriyaki Dipping Sauce.** Blend ⅓ cup *each* condensed consommé and Sherry; ¼ cup chopped green onions; 3 tablespoons *each* soy sauce, lime juice, and honey; 1 clove garlic, mashed; and 2 teaspoons grated fresh ginger. Heat to boiling; serve hot or cold.

**Seasoned Butters.** Combine ½ cup (¼ lb.) softened butter with one of the following: 1 package (4 oz.) blue cheese; or, ¼ cup prepared mustard; or 1 clove puréed garlic plus cayenne or Worcestershire to taste; or, 1 teaspoon toasted dried onion plus ¼ teaspoon *each* salt and Worcestershire. Let mixture sit several hours to blend flavors.

**Chutney Sauce.** Blend ¾ cup sour cream, 1 teaspoon curry powder, and ¼ cup finely chopped chutney.

**Sour Cream Sauce.** Mix 1 cup (½ pt.) sour cream with 1 teaspoon paprika or dill weed, and 2 tablespoons minced or grated onion. Add salt to taste.

**Quick Curry Sauce.** Blend 1 can (10½ oz.) undiluted cream of mushroom soup or beef gravy with 1 to 1½ tablespoons curry powder. Season with puréed garlic and lemon juice, if you wish. Heat, stirring constantly; serve hot.

## Spicy Grilled Shrimp

Generously baste these pink sea crescents with a minty marinade.

**2 pounds medium-sized shrimp**
**1 teaspoon chile powder**
**1 tablespoon vinegar**
**¼ teaspoon pepper**
**1 clove garlic, minced or mashed**
**1 teaspoon each salt and basil**
**1 tablespoon finely chopped fresh mint or 1 teaspoon dried mint**
**¾ cup salad oil**

Wash, shell, and devein the shrimp (or use about 1½ pounds frozen deveined large shrimp—they need not be thawed).

In a bowl or glass jar, blend the chile powder with the vinegar, pepper, garlic, salt, basil, and mint. Stir in the oil and shake or mix until well blended. Pour over the shrimp, cover the dish, and marinate in the refrigerator for 4 hours, or overnight.

Thread the shrimp on skewers and grill over charcoal for 6 to 10 minutes (depending on size), turning once and basting liberally with the marinade. (Or arrange unskewered shrimp on a broiler rack and broil in the oven, turning once and basting well.) Makes 50 appetizers, or 4 to 6 servings as a main dish.

## Avocado Cocktail with Grapefruit & Shellfish

Combine (in proportions to suit your taste) grapefruit sections with either avocado balls or cubes, or chunks of cold cooked lobster, crab meat, or whole shrimp. You can even combine grapefruit, avocado, *and* shellfish.

Serve very cold with the following sauce:

**Creamy Cocktail Sauce.** Mix ½ cup catsup, 1 cup whipping cream, 1 tablespoon olive oil, 1 tablespoon vinegar, ¼ teaspoon salt, 1½ teaspoons sugar, 2 teaspoons paprika, and a dash of liquid hot-pepper seasoning. Chill. Makes about 1½ cups, enough for 6 to 8 servings.

## Swedish Salmon

The flesh of fresh salmon is "cooked" without heat to a delicious state resembling lightly smoked salmon or kosher-style lox. Serve plain or with sour cream and a selection of thinly sliced white and dark bread.

Or serve Mustard Mayonnaise (page 114) or Mustard Sauce (page 116).

With this recipe you can make a pickled (vinegar) version or a cured version called "buried" salmon. Leave the skin on the fish if you use the vinegar; skin it for "burying."

**1 teaspoon each dried dill weed and dill seed (or 1 tablespoon finely chopped fresh dill weed)**
**2-pound salmon fillet (can be 1 or 2 pieces from a center or tail section)**
**3 tablespoons salt**
**4 teaspoons sugar**
**¼ teaspoon each freshly ground black pepper and allspice**
**¼ cup red or white wine vinegar**

Mix dill weed and seed (or use just the fresh dill) and sprinkle half in the bottom of a flat dish (such as a glass casserole) that the salmon almost fills. Set salmon skin-side-down in dish; sprinkle with remaining dill. Blend salt, sugar, pepper, and allspice and distribute evenly over salmon, patting lightly into flesh. Pour vinegar over fish if you want to make the pickled version.

Cover dish with clear plastic film and set a weight on the fish (such as a plate holding a pound or so of butter or a large bottle of fruit juice). Refrigerate at least 2 days; spoon juices over fish occasionally during this time. After a day, remove weights. The salmon keeps as long as a week in the brine, but gradually grows too salty to be enjoyable.

Slice fish thinly across the grain, on the diagonal. Makes 8 to 12 first-course servings.

# Hot & Cold Soups

## Ways to Alter Canned Soups

**Chicken Curry Soup.** Thin 1 can (10½ oz.) condensed cream of chicken soup with 1 can of milk instead of water. Add curry powder to taste when you heat the soup. Serves 3 or 4.

**Asparagus-Mushroom Soup.** Mix 1 can (10½ oz.) condensed cream of mushroom soup, 1 can (10½ oz.) condensed cream of asparagus soup, 1½ cups milk, and 1 cup half-and-half (light cream). Heat just to the boiling point, and add a dash of Sherry before serving. Serves 4 to 6.

**Chicken-Mushroom Soup.** Substitute 1 can (10½ oz.) condensed chicken with rice soup for the asparagus soup in the recipe for Asparagus-Mushroom Soup (see preceding recipe). Serves 4 to 6.

**Tomato Consommé.** Mix 2½ cups tomato juice and 1 can (10½ oz.) condensed consommé. Season to taste with salt and pepper, add ¼ teaspoon or more crumbled basil, and ¼ teaspoon sugar. Serve hot. Serves 3 or 4.

**Celery-Tomato Soup.** Blend 1 can (10½ oz.) condensed cream of celery soup, 1 can (10¾ oz.) condensed tomato soup, and 1½ soup cans water. Heat and garnish with salted whipped cream or sour cream. Serves 4.

**Russian Curry Soup.** Mix 1 can (11¼ oz.) condensed green pea soup, half a 10¾ oz.-can condensed tomato soup, 2 cups milk or broth, ½ teaspoon curry powder, ½ cup whipping cream or undiluted evaporated milk, and salt to taste. Heat. Garnish with croutons. Serves 4 or 5.

**Corn-Tomato Soup.** Combine 1 can (10¾ oz.) condensed tomato soup, 1 can (8 oz.) cream-style corn, and 1½ cups milk. Heat. Serves 3 or 4.

**Crab Soup Mongole.** Mix 1 can (11¼ oz.) condensed green pea soup, 1 can (10¾ oz.) condensed tomato soup, and 2 cups half-and-half (light cream); season to taste with Worcestershire, salt, and pepper. Add ¾ to 1 cup flaked crab meat and ⅓ cup Sherry. Heat. Serves 4.

**Golden Pea Soup.** To 1 can (11¼ oz.) condensed green pea soup, add water as directed. Add ½ cup grated raw carrot. Heat thoroughly. Sprinkle with grated Parmesan cheese. Serves 2 to 3.

**Spring Potato Soup.** Combine 1 can (10¼ oz.) frozen cream of potato soup, 2½ cups regular-strength chicken broth, and 1 cup milk. Whirl in blender and heat (or just combine ingredients and heat). Sprinkle each serving with thinly sliced green onion tops. Makes 4 to 6 servings.

**Egg Drop Soup.** In a pan, dissolve 4 chicken bouillon cubes in 4 cups hot water, or use 2 cans (10½ oz. each) condensed chicken broth plus 2 cans water. Add 1 cup diced raw tomato (optional) and simmer for 5 minutes. Beat 1 egg slightly; add to the soup and stir constantly 1 or 2 minutes, or until the egg separates in shreds. Serve at once. Makes 4 to 6 servings.

**Cold Cream of Shrimp Soup.** Blend 1 can (10 oz.) frozen cream of shrimp soup with ½ soup can *each* milk and water and 1 to 2 teaspoons lemon juice. Chill about 4 hours. Top with finely minced pimiento or a dash of paprika. Serves 3 to 4.

**Jellied Madrilène.** Chill 2 cans (13 oz. *each*) madrilène for 4 hours or until jelled. Turn into a bowl and break up with a fork; spoon into chilled cups or bowls. Top each portion with a dollop of sour cream, finely minced chives, and freshly ground black pepper. Center a small spoonful of red caviar in each mound of sour cream. Makes 4 to 6 servings.

**Chilled Tomato-Cucumber Soup.** Combine 1 can (10¾ oz.) condensed tomato soup, 1 can (10¾ oz.) condensed consommé, and 1 soup can water. Stir in ¼ cup finely grated cucumber. Chill about 4 hours. Top soup with a spoonful of sour cream or with chopped green onion tops. Serves 4.

## Orange-Beef Broth

This has a subtle flavor and aroma. It's clearly a winter winner.

2 large navel oranges
3 tablespoons butter or margarine
2 cans (10½ oz. each) condensed beef broth
1 soup can water
½ cup orange juice
1 teaspoon sugar
2 whole cloves

Using a vegetable peeler, cut thin strips about an inch long from the outer zest of the oranges—one for each serving of soup—and set aside to use for garnish.

With a sharp knife, cut all the remaining peel, including the white membrane, from the oranges. Lift out the orange sections (work over a pan to catch all the juices); discard the pulp and peel. Add butter to the orange sections in the pan and simmer for about 3 minutes.

Add the beef broth, water, orange juice, sugar, and cloves. Bring to a boil and simmer about 10 minutes. Press through a wire strainer; reheat.

Add a twist of the reserved orange peel to each serving bowl or cup. Pour in the piping hot soup. Makes 6 small servings.

## Gazpacho

This cold soup containing raw vegetables can double as a salad.

- 4 large very ripe tomatoes, peeled and chopped
- 1 large cucumber, peeled and diced
- 1 medium-sized onion, finely minced
- 1 green pepper, seeded and finely minced
- 1 cup tomato juice, cold water, or regular-strength chicken broth
- 1 tablespoon wine vinegar
- 3 tablespoons olive oil
- 1 small clove garlic, mashed or minced
  Salt and pepper to taste
  Lettuce leaves
  Ice cubes

Mix the tomatoes, cucumber, onion, green pepper, tomato juice, vinegar, oil, and garlic; add salt and pepper to taste. Chill soup until icy.

Serve in small glasses or bowls, lined with lettuce leaves if you like. Add an ice cube to each serving. Serves 6 to 8.

## Wine Consommé

- 4 cups regular-strength beef broth
- 1 egg white, slightly beaten
- 1 cup dry red wine
- 1 teaspoon sugar
  Dash lemon juice
  Salt and pepper
  Thin lemon slices

Heat broth to boiling. To clarify it, stir in the egg white, and bring mixture to a boil. Pour soup through a moistened muslin cloth; discard egg white and return clarified broth to the pan.

Bring again to a boil and add wine, sugar, and lemon juice. Add salt and pepper to taste. Serve hot, garnished with lemon slices. Makes 6 servings of about ¾ cup each.

**Jellied Wine Consommé.** Soften 2 envelopes unflavored gelatin in ½ cup water. Add gelatin mixture to boiling clarified broth, along with wine, sugar, and lemon juice; chill until set. Whip with a fork and serve with lemon wedges.

## Favorite Onion Soup

- 4 medium-sized onions, thinly sliced
- ¼ cup (⅛ lb.) butter or margarine
- 3 cups regular-strength beef broth
  Worcestershire, salt, and pepper to taste
- 4 slices French bread, toasted
  Butter or margarine
  Grated Parmesan cheese

Sauté onions in the butter over very low heat until they are a rich golden or caramel color. Add beef broth, Worcestershire, salt, and pepper to taste. Cover and simmer for 20 to 30 minutes, or until onions are very tender.

Spread bread with butter and sprinkle with cheese. Pour the soup into 4 individual heatproof casseroles, float a slice of cheese toast in each, and place under the broiler just until the cheese is nicely browned. Serves 4.

## Vichyssoise

- 4 leeks or 1 large bunch green onions, finely chopped (use white part only)
- 1 large onion, thinly sliced
- ¼ cup (⅛ lb.) butter or margarine
- 1 quart (4 cups) regular-strength chicken broth, or 6 bouillon cubes to 4 cups boiling water
- 3 large potatoes, peeled and thinly sliced
- 1 cup (½ pt.) whipping cream
  About 1 cup milk
  Salt and pepper
  Chopped chives or green onion tops

Over low heat, cook leeks or green onions and sliced onion in butter until soft, but not browned. Add chicken broth and potatoes and cook, covered, until potatoes are tender, about 20 minutes.

Press through a fine wire strainer, or blend smooth in an electric blender. Pour in cream and milk and season to taste with salt and pepper. If too thick, thin with additional milk. Chill thoroughly. Serve cold sprinkled with chopped chives or green onion. Makes 8 servings.

## Greek Lemon Soup

Enriched with eggs, this soup is slightly tart and velvety.

- 4 cups rich chicken broth, or 4 cups water plus 3 tablespoons chicken stock base
- 4 eggs
- ¼ cup lemon juice
- 1 whole lemon, thinly sliced

Heat chicken broth to boiling, then reduce heat to very low. Beat eggs until foamy and beat in the lemon juice. Gradually stir in part of the hot broth, beating constantly with a fork. Pour eggs into pan of broth and cook over *very* low heat, stirring constantly, *just* until thickened. Remove from heat at once. Pour into bowls and garnish each with a lemon slice. Makes 6 to 8 servings.

**Chicken-Rice Variation.** Add 3 tablespoons instant-cooking rice to the boiling broth; remove from heat and let stand 5 minutes. Pour part of the hot broth into the beaten eggs and lemon juice, and return to pan. Add 1 can (5 oz.) boned chicken, flaked; heat, stirring *just* until soup is thickened. Float a lemon slice in each serving.

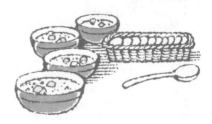

## Cream of Onion Soup

- 3 tablespoons butter or margarine
- 6 large onions, thinly sliced
- 1 tablespoon flour
- 1 quart (4 cups) milk, scalded
- 1 cup cream or undiluted evaporated milk, scalded
- 4 egg yolks, slightly beaten
  Salt and pepper to taste
  Croutons and grated Parmesan cheese (optional)

Melt butter in a saucepan; add onions; stir until onions begin to soften and liquid forms, then cover and simmer over low heat for 30 minutes. (Be careful that the onions do not burn.)

Sprinkle flour over onions and stir until smooth. Add onion mixture to hot milk; cook over low heat for 15 minutes, stirring frequently; force through a wire strainer or whirl in a blender. Gradually stir hot cream into egg yolks; add to soup mixture and cook 3 minutes, stirring constantly. (If soup should curdle, beat with a rotary beater until smooth.)

Serve at once. Croutons and a sprinkling of cheese may be added to serving bowls. Serves 6 to 8.

## Cream of Carrot and Potato Soup

- 4 medium-sized potatoes
- 3 large carrots
- 1 medium-sized onion
  Boiling, salted water
- 1 tablespoon butter or margarine
- 1 tablespoon flour
- 2 cups milk
  Salt and pepper to taste

Peel and slice the potatoes, carrots, and onion; cook in boiling, salted water to cover until very tender. Mash through a wire strainer, saving the cooking liquid; or whirl in a blender with the liquid.

Melt the butter in a large pan, stir in flour until bubbly, and then pour in milk. Cook, stirring constantly, until slightly thick. Add the vegetable pulp and liquid. Season with salt and pepper, beat with a rotary beater to make frothy. Serves 6.

## Fresh Mushroom & Parsley Cream Soup

- ½ pound fresh mushrooms, thinly sliced
- ¼ cup (⅛ lb.) butter or margarine
- ¾ cup finely chopped parsley
- 1 can (10½ oz.) condensed beef broth (bouillon)
- ½ cup half-and-half (light cream)
- 2 egg yolks
- 1 cup (½ pt.) sour cream
  Salt
- ½ cup whipping cream

Sauté mushrooms in the butter until lightly browned. Add parsley and cook, stirring, for a few minutes more. Add beef broth and half-and-half; simmer for about 3 minutes.

Beat 2 egg yolks with ¾ cup of the sour cream, stir in some of the hot soup, then return all to pan. Remove from heat. Add salt to taste.

Whip heavy cream and stir in the remaining ¼ cup sour cream. Heat soup just to boiling point (do not boil) and pour into individual heatproof bowls. Spoon whipped cream mixture onto soup. Set under broiler until topping browns. Serve at once. Makes 4 to 6 servings.

## Cream of Spinach

- 1 bunch (about ¾ lb.) fresh spinach, or 1 package (10 oz.) frozen chopped spinach
- 2 tablespoons butter
- 2 cups half-and-half (light cream) or milk
- 2 tablespoons flour
- ⅛ teaspoon thyme
  Dash nutmeg
- ½ teaspoon salt
  Sour cream
  Croutons

Cut root ends off fresh spinach and wash well. Or partially thaw frozen spinach.

Melt butter in a large pan, add the spinach, cover, and steam over high heat for 5 minutes or until spinach is limp.

Turn into an electric blender with 1 cup of the half-and-half and whirl until smooth, or press through wire strainer to make a purée. Mix the remaining cream or milk into the flour and add to the spinach. Return spinach to pan; add the thyme, nutmeg, and salt. Cook over medium heat, stirring, until thickened. Serve hot with sour cream and croutons. Makes 4 servings.

## Fresh Tomato Soup

- 2 cups peeled, diced ripe tomatoes
- 3 tablespoons butter
- 2 tablespoons flour
- 1 teaspoon salt
  Dash pepper
- ¼ teaspoon soda
- 1 cup half-and-half (light cream)
- ½ cup dry white wine or regular-strength chicken broth

Simmer the tomatoes in butter for about 5 minutes; rub through a wire strainer or whirl smooth in a blender. Sprinkle in flour, salt, and pepper, blending. Bring to a boil; reduce heat and cook for 2 to 3 minutes, stirring constantly.

Add soda and half-and-half; cook until slightly thickened. Stir in wine or chicken broth and heat to simmering. Makes 4 to 6 servings.

## Lentil Soup

- 2 cups lentils
- 2 quarts water
- 2 slices uncooked bacon, cut in pieces
- 1 medium-sized onion, sliced
- ¼ cup chopped carrots
- ½ cup chopped celery
- 3 tablespoons chopped parsley
- 1 clove garlic, minced or mashed (or 1 teaspoon garlic juice)
- 2 teaspoons salt
- ¼ teaspoon pepper
- ½ teaspoon oregano
- 1 can (1 lb.) tomatoes
- 2 tablespoons wine vinegar

Wash the lentils and place them in a pan with the water, bacon, onion, carrots, celery, parsley, garlic, salt, pepper, and oregano. Cover pan and simmer for 1½ hours.

Add the tomatoes and break them up with a spoon; add the vinegar and simmer 30 minutes longer. Taste, and add more salt if needed. Makes about 10 servings.

## Baked Split Pea Soup

- 1 cup dried split peas
  Water
- 1 lamb shank
- 1 carrot, diced
- 1 onion, sliced
- 1 stalk celery, sliced
- 1 teaspoon salt
  Pepper to taste
- ⅛ teaspoon thyme
- ½ bay leaf, crumbled fine

Soak peas overnight in cold water; drain and reserve water. (Or cover peas with water, bring to a boil, cover, and let sit 2 hours.) Remove meat from lamb shank and cut in cubes. Combine all ingredients (including lamb bone) in a large casserole or bean pot. Add a total of 8 cups water, including water used for soaking peas.

Cover and bake in a 300° oven for 3 to 4 hours. Serves 6.

## Minestrone

With this recipe you can use vegetables in season, or substitute frozen ones wherever you wish. It is also easy to cut the recipe to make less.

- 1 package (1 lb.) dried pinto, pink, or cranberry beans, washed
- 3½ to 4 quarts water
- 1 teaspoon salt
- 10 or 12-inch long prosciutto bone, or ½ pound salt pork cut in thick slices
- ½ cup tomato sauce
- ¼ teaspoon allspice
  Salt and pepper to taste
- 1 cup each of six of the following: peas, diced carrots, diced boiling or new potatoes, diced zucchini, chopped onions or chopped leeks, coarsely chopped savoy cabbage or spinach, green or wax beans cut in small pieces

In a large kettle place dried beans, water, salt, and prosciutto bone or salt pork. Bring to a boil, cover, and simmer for 3 hours. Drain and save stock.

Force half the beans through a wire strainer (or whirl in a blender with some of the broth). Combine beans, bean purée, broth (including salt pork), tomato sauce, allspice, and additional salt and pepper to taste. Add vegetables, bring to a boil, cover, and simmer 1½ hours. Serve hot. Makes 6½ quarts, about 16 servings.

## Vegetable Soup with Basil

The basil mixture which seasons this soup is called *pistou* in the French Riviera where the dish originated; the soup is *Soupe au Pistou*.

- 2 large, ripe tomatoes, peeled and coarsely chopped
- 1 pound green beans, cut in 1-inch lengths
- 3 medium-sized potatoes
- 2 quarts (8 cups) water
- 1 tablespoon salt
- ⅛ teaspoon pepper
- ¼ pound vermicelli, broken in half
  Pistou Mixture (recipe follows)
- ¾ cup finely shredded, aged, natural Swiss cheese

Place tomatoes and their juices and green beans in a large saucepan (at least 4-quart size). Peel potatoes and cut into ½-inch cubes (you should have about 3½ cups), add to tomato mixture along with water, salt, and pepper. Bring mixture to a boil, reduce heat, cover, and simmer for 1 hour. Add vermicelli and cook until tender, about 15 minutes longer; taste and add more salt if needed.

Stir about ½ cup of the simmering liquid into the pistou mixture in serving bowl. Then ladle in about two-thirds of the hot vegetables, vermicelli, and broth remaining in pan. Gradually add cheese, about 2 tablespoons at a time, stirring well after each addition. Blend in as much of the remaining soup as bowl will hold; serve immediately. Makes 6 servings.

**Pistou Mixture.** In a soup tureen or large deep bowl (at least 3-quart size) from which you can serve the soup, mix 1 package (⅜ oz.) whole sweet basil leaves; 4 cloves garlic, minced or mashed; and ¼ cup olive oil.

Stir mixture well so that oil coats the basil thoroughly. Then cover and let stand while you prepare the soup.

## Instant Borsch

If you keep your canned-goods shelf stocked with the necessary ingredients, you can prepare this soup in about 10 minutes.

You could also add leftover cooked beef, cut in chunks or strips.

Other possible additions would be a tablespoon or so of tomato paste or catsup, and a can of celery hearts, diced (including liquid).

- 1 jar (1 lb.) sweet-sour red cabbage, well drained
- 1 can (1 lb.) shoestring beets, including liquid
- 1 can (10½ oz.) condensed onion soup
- 1 can (10½ oz.) condensed beef broth (bouillon)
- 1 soup can water
- 1 teaspoon freeze-dried parsley
  Dash pepper
- 1 tablespoon (or more) lemon juice
  Sour cream

If you want to remove excess sweetness from the cabbage, put it in a wire strainer, run cold water over it, and press liquid out (discard liquid).

Combine cabbage, beets and liquid, onion soup, broth, water, parsley, pepper, and lemon juice. Bring to a boil, simmer 5 minutes. Serve with a spoonful of sour cream in each bowl. Serves 8.

## Oxtail-Tomato Vegetable Soup

If you usually use beef bones for making vegetable soup, you may enjoy this change taking advantage of the rich flavor of oxtails.

Other kinds of vegetables you enjoy in soup can be added or substituted.

*(Continued on next page)*

2 oxtails (about 3 pounds), cut in
    pieces
    Flour
2 tablespoons bacon drippings or
    salad oil
2¼ cups tomato juice
3 cups water
1 teaspoon lemon juice
½ cup each diced carrots, turnips,
    onions, and celery
1 cup diced potatoes
1 teaspoon salt
⅛ teaspoon pepper
1 teaspoon Worcestershire

Sprinkle meat with flour. Heat drippings in a large pan which has a cover, add oxtails, and slowly brown them on all sides; add tomato juice, water, and lemon juice.

Cover and simmer gently for about 3 hours. Remove bones; add vegetables, salt, pepper, and Worcestershire. Cover and simmer 30 to 45 minutes longer, or until vegetables are as tender as you like. Add more salt if necessary. Serves 6 to 8.

# Hamburger Soup

Serve this meaty soup as a main dish.

2 pounds ground beef
2 tablespoons olive oil or salad oil
½ teaspoon salt
¼ teaspoon each pepper, oregano,
    and basil
⅛ teaspoon seasoned salt
1 package onion soup mix (for 3 or 4
    servings)
6 cups boiling water
1 can (8 oz.) tomato sauce
1 tablespoon soy sauce
1 cup celery, sliced crosswise
¼ cup celery leaves, torn in large
    pieces
1 cup sliced carrots
⅓ cup dried split peas
1 cup elbow macaroni
    Grated Parmesan cheese

In a large saucepan or kettle having a tight fitting lid, brown meat in oil. Add salt, pepper, oregano, basil, seasoned salt, and onion soup mix. Stir in boiling water, tomato sauce, and soy sauce. Cover and simmer for about 15 minutes.

Meanwhile, prepare celery, celery leaves, and carrots; then add to simmering mixture with split peas and continue to cook for 30 minutes. Add macaroni and simmer for 30 minutes longer, adding more water if necessary.

Pass grated Parmesan cheese to be sprinkled over individual servings. Makes 6 to 8 servings.

# Clam Chowder Perfection

Clam, potato, and onion bits marry with milk in this rich chowder.

About 15 to 20 small clams in the
    shell, or 2 cans (7½ oz. each)
    minced clams
    Water
5 medium-sized potatoes, diced
1 large onion, diced
2 slices bacon, diced
    Clam liquid
¼ cup (⅛ lb.) butter or margarine
¼ cup flour
1½ cups milk
    Salt and pepper to taste

If fresh clams are used, scrub them well and place in a pan with about 1 cup water in the bottom. Cover and bring to a simmer; steam about 5 minutes, or until shells open and clams are just tender. Pull clams from shells; strain liquid through a fine-mesh wire strainer lined with cloth and reserve. Cut clams into small pieces. Measure; you should have about 2 cups.

If canned clams are used, drain them, reserving the liquid.

Place the potatoes, onion, and bacon in a saucepan and nearly cover them with clam liquid and water; cover and simmer until potatoes are just tender.

Meanwhile, make a thick white sauce by melting the butter over low heat in a pan large enough to hold the chowder; add flour and stir until bubbly and blended. Add milk and cook, stirring constantly, until thick.

Add the clams and potato mixture with its liquid to the sauce. Thin

to consistency you like with water; season with salt and pepper. Heat, stirring, just to the boiling point before serving. Makes 6 to 8 servings.

# Oyster Bar Stew

Unexpected company will enjoy this savory and easy-to-make stew.

¼ cup (⅛ lb.) butter or margarine
18 medium-sized oysters and juices
1 cup bottled clam juice
1 quart milk or half-and-half (light
    cream), scalded
¼ teaspoon paprika
    Salt, pepper, cayenne, celery salt,
    and Worcestershire to taste

Melt butter, add oysters, and cook over low heat until edges curl. Add remaining ingredients; heat thoroughly. Serves 4.

# Crab Stew

Crab meat hides under a pretty green and white garnish in this Sherry-laced soup.

2 tablespoons soft butter or
    margarine
1 tablespoon flour
2 hard-cooked eggs
½ teaspoon dry mustard
1 teaspoon salt
½ teaspoon black pepper
    Dash of cayenne
1 quart milk, scalded
6 to 12 ounces fresh or canned crab
    meat
2 tablespoons Sherry
1 lemon, sliced
    Chopped parsley

Cream butter with flour, mashed hard-cooked egg *yolks* (reserve whites and chop), mustard, salt, pepper, and cayenne, beating until mixture is smooth. Slowly add enough hot milk to make a thin paste. Pour paste into the remaining hot milk and bring just to the boiling point, stirring constantly.

Add crab meat and heat 1 minute longer. Remove from heat and add Sherry. Place a slice of lemon in each soup bowl. Pour in stew and garnish with chopped hard-cooked egg white and parsley. Serves 4 or 5.

# Salads & Salad Dressings

## Caesar Salad

Several chefs and restaurateurs claim to have originated this salad. No one seems to know whether it was created by, or for, a "Caesar." *Sunset Magazine* discovered the salad in a small Coronado, California, restaurant and first published a recipe in 1945.

This recipe calls for eggs which have been boiled briefly. However, many cooks make Caesar Salad with raw eggs (be sure to beat them thoroughly before pouring over the salad).

You can turn this salad into a main dish by adding cooked meat, poultry, seafood, or salami cut in chunks or long, thin strips.

1   clove garlic
¾   cup olive oil or other salad oil
2   cups cubes of dry French bread
2   large heads romaine
½   teaspoon salt
    Freshly ground pepper
2   eggs, boiled 1 minute and cooled
    Juice of 1 large lemon
6   to 8 anchovy fillets, chopped
½   cup grated Parmesan cheese

Crush garlic in a small bowl, pour over the oil, and let stand several hours. Make croutons by browning the bread cubes in ¼ cup of the garlic oil in a frying pan over medium heat, stirring often. (If you prefer, you can coat the bread cubes with the oil and toast them in a 325° oven.)

Tear romaine into a large salad bowl, sprinkle with salt, and grind over a generous amount of pepper.

Pour over the remaining ½ cup garlic oil and mix until every leaf is glossy.

Break the eggs into salad; squeeze over the lemon juice, and mix thoroughly. Add chopped anchovies and grated cheese, and mix again. Lastly, add the croutons, mix gently, and serve immediately. Serves about 12.

## Spinach with Pine Nut Dressing

½   cup chopped pine nuts
¼   cup salad oil or olive oil
3   tablespoons tarragon vinegar
¼   teaspoon grated lemon peel
½   teaspoon salt
    Dash nutmeg
6   cups small spinach leaves torn into pieces

If you want to toast the nuts for this dressing, spread on a baking sheet and place in a 350° oven for about 5 minutes.

Mix pine nuts, oil, vinegar, lemon peel, salt, and nutmeg for a dressing. Pour over spinach and mix gently. Makes 6 servings.

## Green Goddess Salad

The Palace Hotel in San Francisco created this salad in 1915 in honor of an actor starring in a play called "The Green Goddess."

The salad soon became a western favorite. Then cooks began to experiment with other uses for the delicious dressing.

After dips became a popular party food, some realized how good the dressing is for this purpose—especially with pieces of raw vegetables.

You will undoubtedly find many types of salads enhanced by its flavor.

8   to 10 anchovy fillets, minced
1   green onion, minced
¼   cup minced parsley
2   tablespoons minced fresh tarragon, or 1 tablespoon crumbled dried tarragon
¼   cup minced chives
3   cups mayonnaise (or 2 cups mayonnaise and 1 cup sour cream)
¼   cup tarragon vinegar
1   clove garlic
1   large head romaine
1   pound cooked lobster, shrimp, crab meat, or chicken

*(Continued on next page)*

Combine anchovies, green onion, parsley, tarragon, and chives in a bowl; mix lightly. Stir in mayonnaise and vinegar; mix thoroughly.

*Note:* If you have a blender, add vinegar and mayonnaise, then *unchopped* anchovies, onion, parsley, tarragon, and chives. Whirl to both chop and blend.

Rub a salad bowl with the garlic and break romaine into bite-sized pieces into the bowl. Pour over enough dressing to moisten (about 2 cups), toss lightly, spoon on salad plates, and garnish with desired shellfish or chicken. Serves 6.

Recipe makes about 1 quart dressing, or enough for 12 servings. (You can store dressing in the refrigerator for at least a week.)

## Pico de Gallo

This salad of Mexican origin is good with steak or favorite Mexican dishes.

- 2 quarts crisp, broken pieces of romaine
- 1 medium-sized orange, peeled and thinly sliced
- ½ cucumber, thinly sliced
- ½ sweet onion, slivered
- ½ green pepper, diced
- ½ to 1 cup raw, peeled, and chopped jícama (a Mexican root vegetable), optional
- Small romaine leaves for garnish, optional
- ½ cup salad oil or olive oil
- ⅓ cup wine vinegar
- ½ teaspoon salt

Place romaine in a salad bowl. Arrange on the greens the orange, cucumber, onion, green pepper, and jícama if available. Garnish rim of the salad with tips of inner romaine leaves, if you desire.

Blend oil with wine vinegar and salt. Pour dressing over salad and mix lightly to serve. Makes 8 servings.

## Creamy Lettuce Salad

- 6 slices bacon
- 1 tablespoon flour
- 1 cup (½ pt.) sour cream
- 2 tablespoons vinegar
- 2 teaspoons sugar
- 1 teaspoon salt
- 2 small heads iceberg lettuce, broken in bite-sized pieces, or 2 quarts of torn leaf lettuce

Cut the bacon into small pieces and fry until crisp. Add flour to the bacon and drippings, and stir over low heat until flour is well blended. Add sour cream, vinegar, sugar, and salt. Stir constantly, being careful not to let mixture boil, just until hot.

Immediately pour over the lettuce in a bowl. Mix lightly and serve at once. Makes 6 to 8 servings.

(Or let dressing cool to room temperature before adding to lettuce if you do not like a "wilted-lettuce" type of salad. Don't chill the dressing or the bacon fat will coagulate.)

## Avocado Ring Mold

You can make this into a fruit or vegetable salad depending on your choice of garnish.

- 1 package (3 oz.) lemon-flavored gelatin
- 1 cup hot water
- 3 tablespoons lemon juice
- 1 teaspoon salt
- ½ cup mayonnaise
- 1 cup mashed avocado
- ⅔ cup heavy cream, whipped
- 2 to 3 cups fruit or vegetables for garnish (see suggestions following)
- Mayonnaise or French dressing

Dissolve gelatin in hot water; chill until slightly thickened. Combine remaining ingredients except garnish and dressing; fold into gelatin mixture. Pour into a 1½-quart ring mold and chill until firm.

Unmold on a large chilled plate and garnish with orange and grapefruit sections or vegetables such as cooked green beans, carrot strips, cherry tomatoes, or sliced beets which have been marinated in French dressing for an hour or more. Dressing may be passed in a bowl. Serves 6.

## Jellied Avocado-Tomato Salad

- 1 package (3 oz.) lemon-flavored gelatin
- 1 cup hot water
- 1 can (10¾ oz.) condensed tomato soup
- Juice of ½ lemon
- Salt and Worcestershire to taste
- 1 cup finely diced celery
- 1 avocado, finely diced
- Salad greens
- French dressing or mayonnaise

Dissolve gelatin in the hot water. Add tomato soup, lemon juice, and salt and Worcestershire to taste; chill.

When mixture is slightly thickened, fold in celery and avocado. Pour into a ring mold or individual molds; chill until firm. Unmold on crisp greens and serve with French dressing or mayonnaise.

*Note:* You may fill center of ring-molded salad with cottage cheese, mixed green salad, seafood salad, or any desired combination of salad vegetables. Serves 6.

## Avocado with Hot Sauce Piquant

- 2 tablespoons catsup
- 2 tablespoons Worcestershire
- 2 tablespoons vinegar
- 2 tablespoons butter or margarine
- 2 tablespoons sugar
- Avocados, cut in half lengthwise and seeded

Combine catsup, Worcestershire, vinegar, butter, and sugar in a saucepan. Stir over low heat just long enough to dissolve the sugar and melt the butter. Serve warm, spooned into the center hollows of halved avocados.

This makes ½ cup sauce, enough for 2 to 4 avocados.

## Cucumber Salad

- 3 or 4 small cucumbers, peeled and thinly sliced
- Ice water
- 1 cup (½ pt.) whipping cream or sour cream
- 1½ tablespoons vinegar
- 1 small onion, grated
- Salt and pepper to taste

Cover cucumbers with ice water and refrigerate 30 minutes to 2 hours. Mix cream, vinegar, and onion; season with salt and pepper.

Drain cucumbers and pat dry with paper towels. Place in a bowl and pour the dressing over them. Serves 6 to 8.

## Celery Victor

Chef Victor Hirtzler of the St. Francis Hotel in San Francisco originated this salad in the early 1900's.

2 hearts of celery
1 medium-sized onion, sliced
   About 2½ cups regular-strength beef or chicken broth
1 cup garlic French dressing
   Watercress or shredded lettuce
   Coarsely ground black pepper
   Anchovy fillets and pimiento strips
   Tomatoes and ripe olives (optional)

Trim the root ends of the celery and cut off all but the smallest leaves. Put in a saucepan with the onion and cover with broth. Cover and simmer until tender, about 15 minutes. Let cool in broth. Remove hearts, cut in half lengthwise, and place in shallow dish. Pour over the French dressing, and chill several hours.

To serve, drain off most of dressing and place celery on watercress or lettuce. Sprinkle with pepper and garnish with anchovy fillets and pimiento strips. Quartered tomatoes and ripe olives may be used for garnish. Serves 4.

## California Cole Slaw

4 cups finely shredded cabbage
½ cup thinly sliced celery
½ cup chopped cucumber
2 tablespoons chopped green pepper
2 tablespoons sliced green onions
1 tablespoon chopped parsley
1 tablespoon lemon juice
¼ cup each mayonnaise and sour cream
½ teaspoon salt
½ teaspoon sugar
   Dash each pepper and paprika
1 avocado

Combine the cabbage with the celery, cucumber, green pepper, onions, and

parsley. You may do this ahead; cover and chill.

For the dressing combine the lemon juice, mayonnaise, sour cream, salt, sugar, pepper, and paprika; mix until smooth. If you make the dressing ahead, cover and refrigerate until serving time.

Just before serving, peel the avocado and dice it. (You might save out a few avocado slices, brush them with additional lemon juice, and use to garnish the top of the salad.) Add diced avocado and dressing to the salad and mix in lightly. Makes about 6 servings.

## Sweet-Sour Slaw with Kidney Beans

1 can (about 1 lb.) red kidney beans, drained
3 cups shredded cabbage
¼ cup chopped sweet pickles
¼ cup sliced green onions (including tops)
½ cup golden raisins
⅓ cup chile sauce
½ cup mayonnaise
½ teaspoon celery seed

Combine beans, cabbage, pickles, onions, and raisins; mix. Combine chile sauce, mayonnaise, and celery seed for dressing. Pour over salad, and mix to coat evenly. Serves 6.

## Cauliflower Salad with Black Olives

Although cauliflower has never led the vegetable popularity parade, it has made a hit in this salad.

Readers of *Sunset Magazine* voted it one of the top-favorite salads.

1 medium-sized head cauliflower
   Boiling, salted water
6 tablespoons olive oil or salad oil
3 tablespoons white wine vinegar
1 tablespoon each chopped capers, minced parsley, and chopped pimiento
1 green onion, chopped
½ teaspoon salt
⅛ teaspoon each dry mustard and pepper
½ cup sliced pitted black olives

Cut apart the cauliflower carefully, keeping the flowerets fairly large. Drop into boiling, salted water; boil 4

to 5 minutes, until just slightly tender. Pour into a colander and cool in running cold water.

Drain well and reassemble by arranging top-side-down in a bowl (one about the same shape on the bottom as the cauliflower). Combine the oil, vinegar, capers, parsley, pimiento, onion, salt, mustard, and pepper; spoon over the cauliflower. Cover bowl and refrigerate for at least 2 hours or overnight.

To serve, hold cauliflower in bowl with one hand and drain off the marinade into another bowl. Flip cauliflower over onto a serving plate. Add olives to the marinade and spoon over top of cauliflower. Makes 6 servings.

## Krisp Kraut Salad

1 can (1 lb.) sauerkraut
1 can (2 oz.) sliced pimientos, drained
½ cup chopped sweet onion or green onions
¾ cup sliced celery
1 cup coarsely shredded carrots
1 green pepper, seeded and sliced
¼ cup vinegar
½ cup sugar
¾ teaspoon salt
⅛ teaspoon pepper
   Iceberg lettuce (optional)
   Chopped parsley (optional)

Empty the sauerkraut into a wire strainer and drain, pressing out all the liquid.

Combine in a bowl the kraut, pimiento, onion, celery, carrots, and green pepper. In a small bowl combine the vinegar, sugar, salt, and pepper; stir until the sugar is dissolved, then pour over the sauerkraut mixture. Mix together lightly. Cover and refrigerate at least 30 minutes, or up to about 6 hours.

To serve you might turn the salad into a lettuce-lined bowl and sprinkle the top with chopped parsley. Makes about 8 servings.

## Savory Potato Salad

2½ pounds potatoes (about 7 medium)
    Boiling, salted water
2 tablespoons French dressing
½ teaspoon pepper
    Salt to taste
3 hard-cooked eggs, chopped
2 stalks celery, chopped
1 small onion, chopped
1 large dill or sweet pickle, chopped
1 tablespoon chopped parsley
1 tablespoon celery seed
½ cup mayonnaise

Cook unpeeled potatoes in boiling, salted water until tender, but firm. Peel when cool enough to handle, and slice or dice them into a bowl. Sprinkle with the French dressing, pepper, and salt to taste.

Add the eggs, celery, onion, and pickle. Sprinkle with the chopped parsley and celery seed. Mix ingredients lightly and evenly. Add mayonnaise and mix until all ingredients are coated. Chill before serving. Serves 8.

## Mustard Ring

Alone, this molded ring is good with baked ham. It pairs well with cole slaw.

4 eggs
¾ cup sugar
1 envelope unflavored gelatin
1½ tablespoons dry mustard
½ teaspoon turmeric
¼ teaspoon salt
1 cup water
½ cup cider vinegar
1 cup (½ pt.) whipping cream
    Cole slaw (optional)
    Curly endive, watercress, or parsley

Beat eggs in top of double boiler. Mix together thoroughly the sugar and gelatin; stir in mustard, turmeric, and salt. Add the water and vinegar to the eggs, stir in the sugar mixture, and cook over boiling water until slightly thickened, stirring continuously. Cool until thick.

Whip cream and fold in. Turn into a 1½-quart ring mold. Chill until firm. Unmold and, if desired, fill center with cole slaw. Garnish with greens. Serves 8.

## Marinated Bean Salad

1 can (1 lb.) red kidney beans, drained
1 can (8 oz.) cut green beans, drained
1 can (1 lb.) garbanzo beans, drained
1 can (1 lb.) black-eyed peas, drained
2½ cups chopped celery
1 cup finely minced parsley
1 bunch green onions, chopped
1 small jar (3 oz.) stuffed green olives, halved
1 can (4½ oz.) chopped black olives
½ cup salad oil or olive oil
½ cup red wine vinegar
1 teaspoon salt
⅛ teaspoon pepper
2 tablespoons brown sugar
1 clove garlic, mashed
    Romaine

Combine beans and peas; rinse with water. Drain and mix in a bowl with celery, parsley, green onions, green olives, and black olives.

Combine salad oil, vinegar, salt, pepper, brown sugar, and garlic. Pour over bean mixture. Mix lightly, cover, and refrigerate overnight.

Toss mixture well and arrange in bowl lined with crisp romaine. Makes about 8 servings.

## Tomato Paste Salad

1 can (6 oz.) tomato paste
1½ cups water
1 package (3 oz.) lemon-flavored gelatin
1 cup (½ pt.) cottage cheese
½ cup finely chopped green onions
½ cup mayonnaise or salad dressing
1 tablespoon Worcestershire
1 cup flaked crab meat (optional)
    Salad greens

In a saucepan combine tomato paste and water; bring to a boil. Remove from heat; add gelatin to hot liquid and stir until dissolved. Chill until mixture begins to congeal.

Using a rotary beater, beat in cottage cheese, green onions, mayonnaise, and Worcestershire. Fold in crab meat. Pour into a 1½-quart mold or individual molds. Chill until firm. Unmold on a bed of crisp greens. Serves 8.

## Easy Seafood Mold

1 package (3 oz.) lemon-flavored gelatin
1 cup hot water
1 can (8 oz.) tomato sauce
½ cup thinly sliced celery
¾ cup chopped or flaked cooked seafood (fish, crab, or shrimp)
    Lettuce leaves, mayonnaise, paprika

Dissolve gelatin in hot water. Add tomato sauce, and stir well.

Chill until mixture begins to thicken, then fold in the celery and seafood. Pour into a shallow pan; chill until set.

Cut into squares and serve on lettuce with mayonnaise and a dash of paprika. Serves 6.

## Crab Louis

Which Louis originated this remains a point of debate; but Solari's Grill in San Francisco was among the first restaurants to serve it, around 1911.

1 cup mayonnaise
¼ cup heavy cream, whipped
¼ cup chile sauce
¼ cup chopped green pepper
¼ cup chopped green onion
    Salt to taste
    Lemon juice to taste
2 heads iceberg lettuce
2 large Dungeness crabs, cracked and shelled, or 1½ to 2 pounds crab meat
4 large tomatoes
4 hard-cooked eggs

Mix together the mayonnaise, whipped cream, chile sauce, green pepper, and green onion. Season with salt and lemon juice to taste.

Arrange outer leaves of lettuce on 4 large plates; shred the heart of the lettuce and arrange a bed of shredded lettuce in the center of the leaves. Place the body meat of the crab on the shredded lettuce. Cut tomatoes and eggs in sixths and arrange symmetrically around the crab.

Pour over the Louis dressing, and garnish with crab legs. Serves 4.

## Baked Crab Salad

2 tablespoons minced green pepper
1 small onion, finely chopped
¾ to 1 cup chopped celery
1 cup flaked fresh or canned crab meat
½ cup cooked shrimp
2 hard-cooked eggs, chopped
¾ cup fine soft bread crumbs
½ cup mayonnaise
    Pepper to taste
1 teaspoon Worcestershire
    Fine cracker or dry bread crumbs

Mix the green pepper, onion, celery, crab meat, shrimp, eggs, and soft bread crumbs. Season mayonnaise with pepper and Worcestershire; combine with first mixture.

Spoon into 6 greased scallop shells or a 1½-quart casserole. Sprinkle with cracker or bread crumbs. Bake in a 350° oven for 30 minutes. Serves 4 to 6.

## Salade Niçoise

¾ cup olive oil
¼ cup red wine vinegar
¼ teaspoon salt
    Freshly ground pepper
2 tablespoons each finely chopped chives and parsley
4 large boiling potatoes
    Boiling, salted water
1½ pounds green beans
2 large tomatoes
2 or 3 hard-cooked eggs
10 to 12 anchovy fillets
½ cup pitted extra-large ripe olives
1 tablespoon capers (optional)
    Butter lettuce
1 can (7 oz.) solid-pack white albacore tuna, drained (optional)
    Watercress (optional)

For dressing, shake together oil, vinegar, salt, pepper, chives, and parsley; chill.

Cook unpeeled potatoes in boiling, salted water 20 minutes, or until tender; cool immediately under cold water; peel and slice. Pour over just enough dressing to coat slices, mix lightly. Cover; chill at least 2 hours.

Cut off ends of beans and cut into 1½-inch lengths; cook in boiling, salted water about 15 minutes or until crisp-tender; drain and cool immediately with cold water. Drain well again, then turn into a bowl and coat lightly with dressing. Cover and chill at least 2 hours.

Select a rimmed platter or large, shallow bowl and mound potato salad down the center. Arrange marinated green beans on each side. Peel tomatoes and cut in wedges. Quarter the hard-cooked eggs and alternate the egg quarters and tomato wedges beside the green beans. Criss-cross the anchovy fillets across the top of the potatoes.

Garnish with olives and sprinkle with capers. Cover with foil or clear plastic film and chill until serving time. When ready to serve, add a border of the inside leaves of butter lettuce and pour remaining dressing over them. Arrange tuna (in a round chunk, just as it comes from the can) on a side plate with watercress. Makes 4 main-dish servings.

## Chicken Loaf

1 envelope unflavored gelatin
¼ cup cold water
1 cup regular-strength chicken broth
2 egg yolks, well beaten
2 cups diced cooked chicken or turkey
½ cup chopped pecans
1 cup heavy cream, whipped
    Salt and paprika to taste
    Lettuce leaves, tomato quarters, olives
    Mayonnaise or Old-fashioned Boiled Dressing (recipe on page 22)

Soak gelatin in the cold water for at least 5 minutes to soften.

Heat the broth to boiling and pour a little into the beaten egg yolks, stirring constantly. Pour egg mixture into broth and cook over very low heat, stirring constantly, until smooth and thick. (Do not let mixture boil or it will separate.) Stir gelatin mixture to be sure all is dissolved and pour into thickened broth.

Chill until practically congealed; then fold in the chicken, nuts, and whipped cream. Turn into a mold and chill. Unmold on a chilled platter and garnish with lettuce, tomatoes, and olives, as desired. Serve with mayonnaise or boiled dressing. Serves 8.

## Exotic Luncheon Salad with Turkey

This is one of the top-favorite *Sunset* salads, perhaps because it elicits "ooh's" and "ah's" at ladies' luncheons.

Litchi nuts can usually be purchased at gourmet shops or Oriental food shops. They look and taste somewhat like Royal Anne cherries, which you might consider as a substitute. However, litchi nuts help make the salad exotic.

2 quarts bite-sized pieces of cooked turkey breast meat (about 2½ to 3 pounds)
1 large can (20 oz.) water chestnuts, drained and sliced or diced
2 pounds seedless grapes, stems removed
2 cups sliced celery
2 to 3 cups toasted slivered almonds
3 cups mayonnaise
1 tablespoon curry powder
2 tablespoons soy sauce
2 tablespoons lemon juice (optional)
    Boston, Bibb, or butter lettuce
1 large can (20 oz.) litchi nuts, or 1 large can (1 lb. 13 oz.) pineapple chunks

Combine the turkey, water chestnuts, grapes, celery, and 1½ to 2 cups of the toasted almonds. Mix the mayonnaise with the curry powder, soy sauce, and lemon juice if used. Combine with the turkey mixture; chill for several hours.

Spoon onto a bed of lettuce leaves arranged on individual serving plates. Sprinkle with the remaining almonds and garnish with litchi nuts or pineapple chunks. Serves 12 generously.

## Ruby Salad

If you don't want to use wine in this molded salad, increase the boiling water to 1⅓ cups and the lemon juice to 3 tablespoons.

- 1 package (3 oz.) raspberry-flavored gelatin
- 1 cup boiling water
- ½ cup Port or dry red wine
- 1 tablespoon lemon juice
- 1 can (1 lb.) whole cranberry sauce
- 1 teaspoon grated orange peel
- 1 cup halved, seeded red grapes
  Salad greens
  Mayonnaise or sour cream (optional)

Add gelatin to boiling water and stir until dissolved. Add wine and lemon juice and stir until blended.

Set dish in a pan of ice water and stir until mixture of consistency of un-beaten egg white, about 20 minutes (or chill until partly set). Add cranberry sauce, orange peel, and halved grapes; mix until blended. Turn into a 1-quart mold or into 4 to 6 individual molds. Chill until firmly jelled.

Unmold on salad greens. Pass mayonnaise or sour cream as a dressing. Makes about 4 to 6 servings.

## Cranberry Salad Mold

This salad, a Thanksgiving favorite, can substitute for the traditional cranberry sauce.

- 1 can (about 8 oz.) crushed pineapple, drained (reserve syrup)
  Water
- 2 packages (3 oz. each) lemon-flavored gelatin
- ½ cup sugar
- 1 cup finely chopped celery
- 1 pound raw cranberries, ground or very finely chopped
- ½ cup finely chopped walnuts, almonds, or pecans
  Lettuce leaves
  Mayonnaise

Add water to the pineapple syrup to make 3 cups. Heat and pour over the lemon gelatin, add the sugar, and stir until thoroughly dissolved; chill.

When mixture is slightly thickened, fold in the pineapple, celery, cranberries, and nuts; pour into a shallow pan. Chill until firm.

Cut in squares and serve on lettuce with mayonnaise as a dressing. Serves 12.

## Low-calorie Pineapple Salad

- 2 packages (3 oz. each) lemon-flavored gelatin
- 2 cups boiling water
- 1 can (1 lb.) grapefruit sections, drained
- 1 can (about 8 oz.) crushed pineapple, drained
- 2 cups (1 pt.) plain or pineapple-flavored low-fat yogurt
  Salad greens for garnish

Combine the gelatin with the boiling water and stir until completely dissolved. Add the drained grapefruit and the drained pineapple; mix until well blended. Chill until the mixture is thick and syrupy.

Add the yogurt and beat with a rotary beater just until the yogurt is mixed smoothly into the gelatin. Turn into a 1½-quart ring mold or other mold and chill until firm. To serve, unmold and garnish with salad greens. Serves 8.

## 24-Hour Salad

- 2 cups pineapple chunks, well drained
- 2 or 3 large oranges, peeled and diced
- 1 pound Thompson seedless grapes, halved
- 1 package (about 10 oz.) miniature marshmallows
- 1 cup chopped walnuts or pecans
- ½ cup heavy cream, whipped
- 1 cup Old-fashioned Boiled Dressing (recipe on page 22)
  Lemon juice to taste
  Lettuce leaves

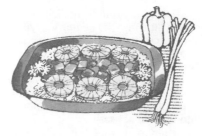

Combine fruit, marshmallows, and nuts. Fold the whipped cream into the boiled dressing and season to taste with lemon juice. Pour over the fruit and mix lightly. Chill 24 hours. Spoon onto crisp lettuce. Serves 16.

## Mandarin Mold with Fruited Cream

- 2 packages (3 oz. each) lemon-flavored gelatin
- 1 cup hot water
- 1 cup cold water
- 2 tablespoons lemon juice
- 1 large can (12 oz.) frozen orange juice concentrate, undiluted
- 2 cans (11 oz. each) mandarin oranges, drained
- 1 banana
- 1 small can (about 8 oz.) crushed pineapple, well drained
- 1 cup mayonnaise
- 1 cup (½ pt.) whipping cream
  Salad greens

Dissolve gelatin in the hot water. Stir in cold water, lemon juice, orange juice, and the oranges. Turn into a 1½-quart mold and chill until firm.

For dressing, mash the banana and mix with the drained pineapple and mayonnaise. Whip cream and fold in.

Unmold salad on salad greens, and pass the dressing separately. Makes about 8 servings.

## Molded Ginger Ale & Pear Salad

- 1 package (3 oz.) lime-flavored gelatin
- ½ cup hot water
- 1½ cups ginger ale
- 4 large pears
  Lemon juice
  Lettuce leaves
  Mayonnaise

Dissolve gelatin in the hot water; add ginger ale. Chill until thick and syrupy.

Peel, halve, and core pears. Immediately dip pears in lemon juice. Arrange in a mold. Pour the thickened gelatin over the pear halves. Chill until firm.

Unmold on crisp lettuce and garnish with mayonnaise. Serves 8.

## Unusual Apple Salad

This can be a dessert as well as salad if served with sweetened whipped cream. It also is attractive molded and served in a large goblet.

 3 cups water
    Red or green food coloring
 6 large cooking apples, peeled and
    cored
 1 cup sugar
 1 can (about 8 oz.) crushed pine-
    apple, drained
 ¼ cup chopped walnuts
 1 package (3 oz.) lemon-flavored
    gelatin
    Water
    Lettuce or curly endive
    Mayonnaise or sour cream

Pour 3 cups water into a wide sauce-pan or deep frying pan and tint with food coloring. Place apples in water side by side and sprinkle with the sugar. Cover and simmer over low heat just until the apples are tender, about 15 minutes. Cool in the liquid, remove apples, and reserve liquid.

Put each apple into a deep cup, straight-sided tumbler, or goblet (you won't be able to unmold apples if goblet curves inward at the top). Mix the pineapple and nuts; stuff the apple cavities with the mixture.

To the liquid drained from the apples, add water if necessary to make 2 cups. Heat the liquid and dissolve gelatin in it. Cool slightly.

Pour gelatin mixture over apples to cover the tops. Chill until firm.

To serve, unmold (unless you serve in goblets) onto a bed of greens and dress with mayonnaise or sour cream. Serves 6.

## Minted Melon Salad

 2 envelopes unflavored gelatin
 ¼ cup cold water
 1 cup sugar
 1 cup water
 ⅓ cup finely chopped fresh mint
 1½ cups orange juice
 ⅓ cup lemon juice
    Dash of salt
 1½ to 2 cups melon balls (one kind of
    melon or an assortment)
    Lettuce leaves
    Mayonnaise

Soften gelatin in the ¼ cup cold water about 5 minutes.

Combine sugar and 1 cup water, and boil for 5 minutes; remove from heat. Dissolve softened gelatin in this hot syrup; add mint; cool to room temperature. Strain this mixture through a fine wire strainer (discard mint); then add orange juice, lemon juice, and salt; chill.

When slightly thickened, fold in melon balls. Turn into individual molds or a 1-quart ring mold; chill until firm. Unmold on crisp lettuce. Serve with mayonnaise. Serves 6 to 8.

---

## Salad Dressings

---

## French Dressing

 ¼ cup vinegar
 ¾ cup salad oil or olive oil
 1 teaspoon salt
 ¼ teaspoon pepper
 ¼ teaspoon (or more) paprika

Combine all ingredients in a bottle which will hold at least 1 cup. Shake well before using. Makes 1 cup.

**Optional Seasonings.** You can add 1 or more of the following: 1 clove of garlic, split lengthwise or puréed; ¼ teaspoon dry mustard or ½ teaspoon prepared mustard (Dijon-style is preferred); ¼ teaspoon or more Worcestershire or soy sauce; minced onion, minced shallots, chopped chives, or minced parsley in varying quantities.

Herbs can be added in varying amounts. Try ¼ teaspoon of such herbs as marjoram, thyme, rosemary, dill weed, or tarragon. Basil, oregano, and chopped fresh mint can be used in larger amount—½ teaspoon. (All can be used in larger quantity on salads containing pungent ingredients or onion.) Follow bottle directions for the various herb blends now marketed. Let the herbs marinate in the dressing for flavor to develop—you can always add more later.

Sugar or honey can be added to taste or to suit the type of salad. Lemon juice can be substituted for part of the vinegar.

**Optional Variations.** Add ¼ cup or more crumbled blue cheese. Or ¼ cup very finely chopped watercress and 2 tablespoons catsup. Or 1 tablespoon drained capers. Or 3 minced anchovy fillets (or 2 teaspoons anchovy paste). Or ½ small avocado, diced.

## Tomato Soup French Dressing

 1 can (10¾ oz.) condensed tomato
    soup
 1 cup salad oil
 1 cup vinegar
 1 tablespoon Worcestershire
 2 tablespoons sugar
 1 teaspoon dry mustard
 1 teaspoon salt
 1 teaspoon paprika
 1 small whole onion, peeled
 2 small cloves garlic, split lengthwise

Combine ingredients in a quart jar. Shake well and refrigerate several hours to allow onion and garlic flavors to permeate. Makes about 4 cups.

## Russian Dressing

Here's a creamy dressing to serve with vegetable or seafood salads, or with hearts of lettuce.

 1 cup mayonnaise
 3 tablespoons chile sauce
 1 tablespoon each finely chopped
    green pepper and finely chopped
    pimiento
 1 teaspoon minced chives
 1 hard-cooked egg yolk, sieved
 ½ teaspoon paprika
 1 teaspoon vinegar
    Salt to taste

Blend all ingredients and chill thoroughly. Makes about 1⅓ cups.

## Mayonnaise

Because mayonnaise is more than just a salad dressing (a sauce of many uses), the recipes for making it by hand or in a blender are on pages 114 and 115. Once you discover how fool-proof these are, you may make mayonnaise often.

A number of ways to vary and season mayonnaise are also given on pages 114 and 115. Many of them are suitable for a variety of salads.

## Thousand Island Salad Dressing

Blend minced onion and green pepper into this thick dressing.

2 cups mayonnaise
½ cup chile sauce
1 tablespoon minced onion
1 pimiento, minced
2 tablespoons minced green pepper
2 hard-cooked eggs, finely chopped
  Salt and pepper to taste

Blend all ingredients and thin with a little cream, if desired. Chill before serving. Makes about 2¾ cups.

## Poppy Seed Dressing

This favorite is most delicious on a green salad containing oranges and onion, or grapefruit sections with avocado slices.

⅓ cup honey
1 teaspoon salt
2 tablespoons vinegar
1 tablespoon prepared mustard
¾ cup salad oil
1 tablespoon finely chopped onion
2 to 3 teaspoons poppy seed

In a pint jar, blend the honey, salt, vinegar, and mustard. Gradually add the salad oil, stirring to blend thoroughly. Stir in onion and poppy seed.

Cover and chill for several hours to blend flavors. Shake well before using. Makes about 1¼ cups.

## Sour Cream Dressing with Blue Cheese

If you want a plain sour cream dressing, omit the cheese.

3 ounces blue cheese, crumbled
1 cup (½ pt.) sour cream
1 cup mayonnaise
  Juice of one lemon
2 teaspoons soy sauce
1 egg, beaten
¼ teaspoon each mixed salad herbs, coarsely ground pepper, and garlic powder
  Salt to taste

Combine all ingredients and mix. Chill, preferably several hours to blend flavors. Makes about 2½ cups.

## Old-fashioned Boiled Dressing

Many cooks insist that boiled dressing makes the best cole slaw or potato salad.

1 tablespoon flour
1 tablespoon sugar
1 teaspoon dry mustard
1 teaspoon salt
  Dash of cayenne
2 eggs, well beaten
¾ cup milk
⅓ to ½ cup vinegar, heated
1 tablespoon butter or margarine

In the top of a double boiler mix together the flour, sugar, mustard, salt, cayenne, eggs, and milk; add heated vinegar. Place over boiling water and cook, stirring constantly, about 10 minutes, or until thickened. Remove from heat and add butter. Beat briefly with a rotary beater to ensure perfect smoothness. Chill.

Thin dressing with fruit juice, lemon juice, milk, or cream before using. Or fold in whipped cream. Makes 1⅓ cups.

## Orange & Lemon Cream Dressing

Serve with fruit salads.

1 egg
  Grated peel and juice of 1 orange
  Grated peel and juice of 1 lemon
½ cup sugar
1 teaspoon flour
½ cup whipping cream

Beat egg in the top of a double boiler; add orange and lemon peel and juice, sugar, and flour. Place over boiling water and cook, stirring constantly, until mixture is smooth and thickened.

Remove from heat; chill. Whip cream and fold into dressing just before using. Makes 1½ cups.

## Blender Caesar-style Salad Dressing

Here's an easy-to-make Caesar dressing flavored with egg, lemon juice, garlic, and Parmesan cheese—and it all goes together quickly in a blender. You can make the dressing up to 5 days in advance; just before serving, mix it well with romaine lettuce leaves to create a salad that tastes like the more complicated Caesar. Garnish the salad with tomatoes and seasoned croutons, if you like.

1 egg
½ cup grated Parmesan cheese
¼ cup lemon juice
2 cloves garlic, minced or pressed
1 teaspoon Worcestershire
½ teaspoon each salt and pepper
½ cup salad oil

In a blender container, combine egg, Parmesan cheese, lemon juice, garlic, Worcestershire, salt and pepper; whirl until well blended. Remove lid of blender container. With motor on lowest speed, gradually pour in oil in a thin stream and continue to whirl until dressing is thick and creamy.

Pour into a jar; cover and refrigerate for at least 1 hour or up to 5 days. Let stand at room temperature for 15 minutes before using. Shake well. Makes about 1¼ cups.

# *Varied Main Dishes*

## *Beef*

### *Beefsteak Jalisco*

A squeeze of orange juice brightens up this easy entrée.

    About 3 pounds beef top round
    Salt
1   orange

Have your meatman make the first cut of beef top round about 2 inches thick (this is the part next to the sirloin); this should make about 3 pounds or more.

Trim off all fat and gash the surface of the steak in a diagonal pattern, making ⅜-inch-deep cuts about 1 inch apart. Rub the meat lightly with salt. Grill about 5 to 6 inches over medium-hot coals for about 10 minutes on a side for rare meat; or cook longer.

Transfer meat to carving board and squeeze the juice of the orange over the meat. Slice meat vertically and make sure some juice moistens each piece. Makes 8 to 10 servings.

### *Bake-Broil Steaks*

This method assures a medium-rare steak.

For tender steaks such as porterhouse, sirloin, or rib: stand a 2-inch-thick steak on edge in a V-shaped rack in a roasting pan. Place in a 200° oven for 2 hours. Then place flat on a rack and broil or grill 3 to 5 minutes on each side, until well browned.

For less-tender steaks such as chuck, sirloin tip, or top round: brush lightly with water on each side. Sprinkle with unseasoned meat tenderizer according to package directions. Bake as for tender steaks, allowing 45 minutes per pound of meat; broil the same way.

### *Flank Steak with Mushrooms & Peas*

Serve this one-dish meal with steamed rice or Chinese noodles.

1¼  pounds flank steak
 ½  pound mushrooms, sliced (about 3 cups)
  1  cup diagonally sliced celery
  1  package (10 oz.) frozen peas
     Water
  1  tablespoon cornstarch
  2  tablespoons dry Sherry
1½  tablespoons soy sauce
  2  teaspoons grated fresh ginger (or ½ teaspoon ground ginger)
 ¼  teaspoon garlic powder
  3  tablespoons salad oil
     Steamed rice or Chinese noodles

Cut flank steak in half lengthwise; slice each half, on the diagonal, into ¼-inch-thick strips.

Place mushrooms, celery, and frozen peas in a large, heavy frying pan that has a cover. Add 1 cup water. Cover, bring to a boil, and cook over medium-high heat for about 5 minutes or until celery is tender but still crisp. Drain, reserving liquid, and place vegetables in bowl.

Blend ½ cup water and cornstarch; stir in Sherry, soy sauce, ginger, and garlic powder. Brown meat quickly in the very hot salad oil; reduce heat, return vegetables to pan with soy sauce mixture, and cook for about 1 minute longer, stirring constantly, until sauce becomes quite thick.

Blend in about ⅓ cup of the reserved vegetable liquid, if you prefer a thinner sauce. Serve with rice or noodles. Makes 4 servings.

## Flank Steak Barbecue

¼ cup soy sauce
3 tablespoons honey
2 tablespoons vinegar
1½ teaspoons each garlic powder and ground ginger (or 1 tablespoon minced fresh ginger)
¾ cup salad oil
1 green onion, finely chopped
1 flank steak, approximately 1½ pounds

Mix together soy sauce, honey, and vinegar; blend in garlic powder and ginger. Add oil and chopped green onion.

Place meat in a small pan and pour the mixture over it; let stand 4 hours or longer (turn meat occasionally).

Barbecue over glowing coals, about 5 minutes on each side for medium rare, or until done to your liking. Or broil in your oven, allowing about 2 minutes on each side for medium rare. Baste occasionally with the marinade. Slice on the diagonal to serve. Makes 4 servings.

## Savory Swiss Steak

½ cup all-purpose flour
1 tablespoon dry mustard
Salt and pepper
1½ pounds round steak, cut 1 inch thick
2 tablespoons salad oil, shortening, or bacon fat
1 can (1 lb.) tomatoes
1 cup sliced onions
½ cup diced celery
2 to 3 carrots, diced
2 tablespoons Worcestershire
1 tablespoon brown sugar

Mix flour, mustard, salt, and pepper. Sprinkle meat with the mixture and pound it into the steak with a meat pounder, a potato masher, or the edge of a plate. Cut pounded steak into individual portions. Heat the oil in a heavy frying pan or Dutch oven over medium-high heat; brown meat on both sides in the oil.

Pour remaining ingredients over meat; add salt and pepper to taste. Cover and bake in a 350° oven, or simmer on top of the stove, for about 1½ hours. Serves 4.

## Roast Beef

You can roast beef in the oven or in a barbecue with a spit.

To oven-roast, place meat on a rack in a shallow uncovered pan with fat side up; roast in a 325° oven.

To cook on a rotisserie, insert spit through the center of the roast, securing it with holding forks and balancing it evenly. Follow rotisserie directions.

For best results, insert a meat thermometer in the center of the roast (not touching bone, fat, or the spit).

For rare meat, the meat thermometer temperature should be 130° to 135°. Medium doneness is 140° to 145°. Well done is 150° to 155°.

## One Rib for Two

At last, here is a way just two people can enjoy a meal of roast beef without any leftovers.

1 rib of standing rib roast (about 2½ lbs.)
1 tablespoon salad oil or olive oil
1 small clove garlic, mashed
2 large baking potatoes

Wrap the meat well and freeze until solid. Rub the mixture of the oil and garlic evenly over the frozen meat. Stand, rib bone down, on a rimmed baking sheet between the 2 potatoes, placed like book ends. (Roast frozen; do not thaw.)

Roast in a 400° oven 1 hour and 15 minutes for rare, 1 hour and 25 minutes for medium rare, 1 hour and 35 to 40 minutes for well done.

If you wish, insert a meat thermometer through the fat layer into the center of the roast after it has cooked for about 1 hour, and continue cooking until meat is done to your liking.

Let stand about 5 minutes before carving. Serves 2.

## Oven Rump Roast

Basted with a red wine sauce, this roast is a dinner party delight.

6 pound boneless rump roast
2 teaspoons salt
1 teaspoon dry mustard
¼ teaspoon each garlic salt and pepper
Unseasoned meat tenderizer (optional)
1 tablespoon catsup
1 teaspoon Worcestershire
½ cup dry red wine (or ½ cup water and 1 tablespoon lemon juice)
Sour Cream-Mushroom Sauce (recipe follows)

Rub roast with salt, mustard, garlic salt, and pepper. If you wish, use meat tenderizer according to directions on the package. Insert a meat thermometer into the center of the thickest part of the roast, and place meat on a rack in a shallow baking pan.

Mix together catsup, Worcestershire, and wine; brush meat with this basting sauce. Roast in a 325° oven until the meat thermometer registers 130° for rare meat, or about 1 hour 45 minutes. (Figure on about 18 minutes per pound. If temperature is allowed to go past 130°, meat will be past the prime pink and juicy stage.) Baste with the wine sauce several times during roasting.

Let the meat stand at room temperature 10 minutes to set the juices, then slice and serve with the mushroom sauce. Makes 10 servings.

**Sour Cream-Mushroom Sauce.** Wash and slice 2 pounds mushrooms. Cream together 6 tablespoons butter or margarine, 3 tablespoons all-purpose flour, 2 teaspoons *each* salt and prepared mustard, ¼ teaspoon *each* nutmeg and pepper, 2 cups (1 pint) sour cream, and ¼ cup *each* minced parsley and instant minced onions.

Alternate the layers of sliced mushrooms and sour cream sauce in a buttered 2½-quart casserole. Bake uncovered in a 325° oven for 1 hour, stirring once or twice. (If you wish, stir some of the meat juices into the sauce.)

## Steak & Navy Bean Casserole

2 pounds round steak, cut in 1-inch cubes
2 tablespoons shortening or salad oil
2 cups cooked (but still firm) navy beans
1 can (1 lb.) tomatoes (2 cups)
  Salt and pepper to taste
2 cups sliced onions
½ cup brown sugar, firmly packed
5 slices bacon

In a large frying pan, cook round steak in shortening until browned on both sides. Add beans, tomatoes, and salt and pepper to taste. Cover and simmer for 10 minutes.

Spoon half of this mixture into a 2-quart casserole. Spread onions over the bean mixture; then sprinkle with half the brown sugar. Add remaining half of bean mixture; sprinkle with remaining sugar. Lay strips of bacon over the top.

Bake uncovered in a 325° oven for about 1 hour. Makes 6 servings.

## Fruited Corn Beef

You can easily double this recipe to serve a large group.

  About 5 pounds corned beef round
  Cold water
  Whole cloves
½ cup brown sugar firmly packed
¼ cup fine dry bread crumbs
½ teaspoon dry mustard
  Grated peel and juice of 1 medium-sized orange
  Grated peel and juice of 1 lemon
1 cup cider or Sherry

Cover meat with cold water, bring to a boil, and remove scum. (If beef seems very salty, pour off water and add fresh.) Simmer slowly 3 hours, or until just barely tender. Cool in the cooking liquid.

Place drained corned beef in baking pan; score fat and stud with cloves. Combine brown sugar, crumbs, mustard, and grated orange and lemon peels. Pat meat with crumb mixture.

Place in a 350° oven to brown slightly. Baste frequently with a mixture of the orange and lemon juices and cider. Continue baking 30 minutes or until heated through. Slice to serve. Serves 8 to 10.

## Beef Stroganoff

This version is baked, making it much more convenient to serve for a guest dinner.

2½ pounds round steak, cut in strips ½-inch thick
¼ cup salad oil
1 teaspoon salt
½ teaspoon pepper
¼ cup dry red wine
1 cup small whole onions, peeled, or 1 large onion, sliced
2 cups sliced fresh mushrooms
¼ cup tomato paste
3 tablespoons flour
1 can (10½ oz.) condensed consommé
1 bay leaf, crumbled
1 clove garlic, mashed or minced
½ cup sour cream
  Hot buttered noodles

Brown meat quickly in oil, then transfer to a 3-quart casserole; add salt, pepper, and wine.

In the drippings in the frying pan, sauté onions until golden brown; add mushrooms and cook 5 minutes. Mix tomato paste, flour, and consommé; add to onions and mushrooms along with bay leaf and garlic. Mix well, then pour over meat.

Cover and bake in a 350° oven for 1 hour, or until meat is tender. Remove casserole from oven and slowly stir in sour cream. Serve with noodles. Makes about 6 servings.

## Flemish Pot Roast

4 to 5-pound beef chuck roast
1 tablespoon salad oil
4 medium-sized onions, sliced
2 tablespoons butter or margarine
2 tablespoons flour
1 can (12 oz.) beer
1 tablespoon each brown sugar and vinegar
1 bay leaf
2 cloves garlic
1½ teaspoons salt
2 tablespoons parsley

Using a heavy Dutch oven, brown meat in oil, turning to brown both sides. In a separate pan, sauté onions in butter until pale golden color. Sprinkle with flour and cook 2 minutes. Pour in beer and bring to a boil, stirring. Then pour over meat. Add brown sugar, vinegar, bay leaf, garlic,

and salt. Cover and simmer 2 hours, or until meat is tender.

Lift meat onto a hot platter, sprinkle with parsley, and keep warm. Cook down pan juices with onions until juices are slightly thickened. Strain juices into a sauce bowl. Spoon onions into a vegetable bowl. Carve meat. Pass gravy and onions at the table. Makes 8 servings.

## Beef Burgundy

16 small white onions, peeled (about 1 pound)
6 slices lean bacon, diced
¼ cup (⅛ lb.) butter or margarine
4 pounds beef chuck, cut in 1½-inch cubes, fat trimmed off
¼ cup brandy (optional)
1½ teaspoons salt
¼ teaspoon freshly ground pepper
2 cups Burgundy or other dry red wine
2 whole cloves garlic, peeled
2 cups small whole, or sliced, fresh mushrooms
1½ cups water
  Bouquet garni: Tie in a piece of cheesecloth 1 or 2 sprigs parsley, 1 celery top, 1 quartered carrot, a bay leaf, and a sprig of thyme (or 1 teaspoon dried thyme)
6 tablespoons flour
½ cup cold water

Brown onions with bacon and butter in a Dutch oven; remove onions and bacon with a slotted spoon; reserve.

Add meat to the pan and brown well on all sides. If desired, pour brandy over the beef and set aflame, tilting pan to keep the flame going as long as possible. Sprinkle meat with the salt and pepper. Add the Burgundy, garlic, mushrooms, the 1½ cups water, bouquet garni, onions, and bacon. Cover and simmer about 1½ hours, or until the meat is tender.

*(Continued on next page)*

Lift the beef, mushrooms, and onions out of the pan with a slotted spoon; arrange in a covered 3-quart casserole or baking dish, or in a serving dish if you plan to serve at once.

Strain the liquid through a sieve, discarding bouquet garni, garlic, and bacon. Mix the flour to a smooth paste with the ½ cup cold water; stir into the meat stock and cook, stirring, until gravy is thick and smooth.

Pour gravy over the meat and serve immediately; or refrigerate and reheat, covered, in a 350° oven for about 35 minutes, or until hot and bubbly. Makes 8 servings.

## Italian Pot Roast

1 ounce dried mushrooms (about 5 large ones)
1 cup hot water
2 tablespoons olive oil or salad oil
2 large onions, chopped
3 to 4-pound chuck roast
½ teaspoon salt
¼ teaspoon each pepper and ground ginger
4 cloves garlic, minced or mashed
1 can (8 oz.) tomato sauce
1 cup pitted ripe olives

Wash the mushrooms and soak them in 1 cup hot water for at least 30 minutes (or as long as overnight in the refrigerator). Drain, discarding soaking liquid, and slice in ¼-inch strips, removing any hard stems.

Heat 2 tablespoons oil in a large frying pan which has a cover, or a Dutch oven. Add onions and cook, stirring, until golden; remove with a slotted spoon and reserve. Sprinkle meat with salt, pepper, and ginger. Brown slowly on both sides in the oil remaining in the pan. Distribute the onion and garlic around the meat, cover, and cook over very low heat for 1 hour.

After 1 hour, add the mushrooms, tomato sauce, and olives. Cover and simmer 1 to 2 hours longer (the meat probably will be tender after about 1 hour, but will improve in flavor with further cooking). Skim off any excess oil. Serves 6 to 8.

*Note:* After onions and garlic have been added to browned meat, the covered pan may be baked in a 325° oven instead of simmered on the range. Add mushrooms, sauce, and olives after 1 hour. Total cooking time is the same.

## Hungarian Goulash

3 large onions, thinly sliced
1 tablespoon salad oil
1 teaspoon caraway seed
½ teaspoon marjoram
1 teaspoon (or more) salt
2 to 4 teaspoons paprika
1 teaspoon vinegar
2 pounds boneless beef chuck, cut in 1-inch cubes
1 cup dry red wine

Sauté onions in oil until tender and golden; add caraway seed, marjoram, salt, and paprika moistened with vinegar; mix well. Add meat and brown nicely on all sides.

Add wine, cover tightly, and simmer very slowly for about 2 hours, or until meat is tender. Add water during cooking, if necessary. Makes 4 to 6 servings.

## Barbecued Chuck with Mushroom Stuffing

3 to 4-pound chuck roast, sliced through the center
⅔ cup dry red wine
⅓ cup salad oil
3 cloves garlic, minced or mashed
⅛ teaspoon each rosemary, marjoram, and thyme
Freshly ground pepper to taste
½ pound fresh mushrooms, sliced, or 2 cans (4 oz. each) sliced mushrooms
6 tablespoons butter
3 green onions, finely chopped
¼ cup finely chopped parsley

Ask your meatman to saw a 2-inch-thick chuck roast through the center to make 2 chuck steaks, each 1 inch thick. (If possible, have it cut from the chuck section close to the rib end so the bones will be smaller and the meat more tender.) Or you can start with 2 chuck steaks of the same size. With a sharp knife, cut out the long, slender blade bone in each steak, but leave the other large bone that is on the side of each steak.

For marinade, mix together wine, oil, garlic, rosemary, marjoram, thyme, and pepper. Turn into a large, shallow baking dish, add meat, and let marinate overnight, turning occasionally.

For stuffing, sauté fresh mushrooms in butter until golden brown, or drain canned mushrooms. Mix in chopped green onions and chopped parsley. Spoon mushroom mixture over 1 chuck steak and arrange the second steak on top. Tie securely with string.

Barbecue over medium coals about 45 minutes, allowing 20 to 25 minutes on each side for medium rare. To serve, cut away string and slice slightly on the diagonal into strips about ⅛ inch thick. Serve mushroom stuffing on the side. Makes 4 servings.

## Oven Beef Stew

Lots of carrots, mushrooms, and onions go into this no-worry stew. Serve with crusty rolls.

2 pounds beef stew meat
2 teaspoons salt
   Flour
1½ cups water
6 carrots, cut in large pieces
½ pound mushrooms, whole or large pieces
10 small onions, whole
½ cup chopped parsley
   Chopped parsley for garnish

Sprinkle meat with salt, then dust with flour, shaking off excess. Arrange pieces in an ungreased baking pan, keeping them slightly separated. Bake in a 500° oven for 20 minutes.

Remove from oven and pour water into pan, stirring to scrape free the browned particles. Add carrots, mushrooms, onions, and the ½ cup chopped parsley.

Cover pan tightly with lid or foil, and bake in a 375° oven for 2½ hours, or until meat is very tender; stir once or twice while cooking. Garnish with more chopped parsley. Serves 4 or 5.

## Beef-Vegetable Pie

Simmer meat and chill pastry up to a day ahead. Add vegetables just before baking so they will retain the crispness typical of Oriental dishes.

This dish is pictured on the front cover.

1½ pounds beef stew meat, cut in 1-inch pieces
3 tablespoons salad oil
1 medium-sized onion, finely chopped
3 cloves garlic, minced
¼ teaspoon salt
2 tablespoons Sherry or ½ teaspoon sugar
¼ teaspoon black pepper
¼ cup soy sauce
1 cup water
Pastry for single-crust 9-inch pie
2 small carrots, sliced ¼ inch thick
1 small green pepper, seeded and cut in 1½-inch squares
2 medium-sized firm tomatoes
3 tablespoons each cornstarch and cold water
1 small can (11 oz.) small white onions, drained

Brown meat in the oil in a frying pan (one that can be tightly covered), stirring over high heat. Add onion and garlic; stir until they begin to turn golden. Then add salt, Sherry or sugar, pepper, soy, and the 1 cup water. Cover and simmer 1¼ hours, or until meat is tender, adding a little more boiling water if necessary.

While meat is cooking, make the pastry and roll to the size needed for a top crust on a 9-inch pie pan. Cover with clear plastic film and chill.

Cook carrots 5 minutes in boiling, salted water; drain immediately. Cook green pepper in boiling water for 1 minute only; drain immediately, rinse with cold water, and chill. Peel tomatoes if you wish and cut each into 6 wedges; remove seed pockets; set aside.

When meat is tender, drain off liquid and measure. Add enough water to make 1¼ cups (or reduce to 1¼ cups by boiling if necessary). Transfer meat to a bowl. Bring meat juices to a boil and stir in a smooth paste of the cornstarch and cold water. Stirring, cook until clear and thickened. Add meat and let cool slightly. Then add onions, carrots, and green pepper. Pour meat and veg-etables into a 9-inch pie pan and arrange tomato wedges evenly over the top.

Cover with chilled pastry, flute trim, and cut slits in the center. Bake in a 450° oven for 25 to 30 minutes, or until crust is golden brown. Serve at once (do not reheat). Makes 6 servings.

## Favorite Brown Stew

2 pounds beef stew meat, cut in 1½ or 2-inch cubes
½ cup all-purpose flour
3 tablespoons chopped suet or other fat
1 medium-sized onion, sliced
1 clove garlic
2 bay leaves
1 teaspoon salt
1 teaspoon sugar
½ teaspoon pepper
½ teaspoon paprika
Dash of cloves or allspice
1 teaspoon lemon juice
1 teaspoon Worcestershire or bottled brown gravy sauce
4 cups boiling water
5 or 6 carrots, sliced
6 or 8 whole, small boiling onions
4 or 5 stalks celery, sliced

Put meat and flour in a paper bag; shake until all pieces of meat are coated with flour. Melt suet or other fat in a heavy frying pan or Dutch oven; add meat and any extra flour remaining in bag; sauté until meat is nicely browned, turning to brown all sides.

Add onion, garlic, seasonings, and boiling water; cover tightly and cook over low heat for 1½ to 2 hours, or until meat is tender. Add vegetables; continue cooking 15 to 30 minutes longer, or until vegetables are tender. Serves 6.

## Family-style Tostadas

If you prefer, let members of the family assemble their own tostadas.

1 can (1 lb.) refried beans
Dash liquid hot-pepper seasoning
6 green onions, sliced (use part of the green tops)
4 ounces sliced jack cheese, cut in strips
Salad oil
6 corn tortillas
Salt
Meat Sauce (recipe follows)
Salad Mixture (recipe follows)
1 medium-sized avocado, sliced
1 cup shredded sharp Cheddar cheese
Taco sauce (optional)

Blend beans with hot-pepper seasoning and ¼ cup of the onions; reserve remaining onions for salad mixture. Place a third of the bean mixture in a greased 1-quart casserole; top with a third of the jack cheese. Make 2 more layers each of remaining beans and cheese.

Just before serving, cover and bake in a 350° oven for about 30 minutes, until heated through.

Heat about ½ inch of oil in a frying pan over medium-high heat (to about 350°–375°). Fry tortillas, one at a time, until crisp and lightly browned (about 1 minute). Drain on paper towels; sprinkle with salt. (If prepared ahead, reheat in oven, uncovered, on a baking sheet during last 5 to 10 minutes the beans are heating.)

To serve, top warm tortilla with hot bean mixture, then meat sauce, and salad mixture. Garnish with avocados, Cheddar cheese, and taco sauce. Serves 6.

**Meat Sauce.** Cut 1 pound beef stew meat into ½-inch cubes. Brown in 1 tablespoon salad oil. Add 1 small onion, finely chopped, and 2 cloves garlic, minced or mashed; cook until soft. Blend in 1 canned California green chile, seeded and chopped, ½ teaspoon salt, 1 can (10 oz.) enchilada sauce, and ¼ cup tomato juice. Cover and simmer until meat is very tender, 1½ to 2 hours. Serve hot.

**Salad Mixture.** Lightly mix remaining sliced green onions, 6 pitted ripe olives, sliced, 1 tomato, peeled and chopped, 2 tablespoons chopped parsley, and ¼ teaspoon salt. Top with 3 cups shredded lettuce; cover with clear plastic film and chill. To serve, mix in 2 tablespoons Italian-style salad dressing (or homemade French dressing seasoned with garlic and oregano).

## Beefsteak Pie or Steak & Kidney Pie

With this recipe you can make either an all-steak pie or the classic English beef and kidney version.

2½ teaspoons salt
¼ teaspoon pepper
1 teaspoon fines herbes (combination of thyme, oregano, sage, rosemary, marjoram, and basil)
6 tablespoons flour
2½ pounds top sirloin, cut in 1½-inch cubes (or 1½ lbs. sirloin and 1 lb. lamb kidneys, trimmed and cut in 1½-inch cubes)
1 pound mushrooms, sliced
4 tablespoons butter
¼ cup dry red wine
Egg Pastry (recipe follows)
1 beaten egg

Combine the 2½ teaspoons salt, pepper, herbs, and 6 tablespoons flour; dredge the meat cubes in the mixture. Brown the mushrooms in the 4 tablespoons butter over medium heat, stirring, until limp. Arrange half the meat cubes in a 2-quart casserole and half the mushrooms over the beef. Then add the remaining meat and finish with an even layer of the remaining mushrooms on top. Pour the red wine evenly over.

On a floured board, roll the pastry (recipe follows) to make a thick round about ½ inch thick and trim to fit the casserole top. Roll out the pastry trimmings and cut a long strip of dough about ¾ inch wide to fit the rim of the casserole. Moisten the edges of the casserole and press the pastry strip onto the rim. Arrange the pastry round over the filling and rim,

moisten edges and press to flute, and fasten firmly onto the dough-topped casserole rim.

Roll out scraps of dough and cut leaf-shaped ovals to use for decoration. Prick pastry top, brush with the beaten egg, arrange leaf shapes on pastry, and brush again with egg.

Bake in a 350° oven for about 60 minutes or until meat is tender. You can test the meat with a long wooden skewer or knitting needle carefully probed through the pastry. If the top begins to brown too much, cover with brown paper or foil. Serves about 6.

**Egg Pastry.** Measure 1½ cups unsifted flour into a bowl; stir in ½ teaspoon salt. Cut in ½ cup (¼ lb.) butter until mixture resembles fine crumbs. Add 1 egg, slightly beaten, and 4 to 5 tablespoons milk, mixing with a fork until dough holds together in a ball. Chill.

## German Short Ribs

Prepare these tangy ribs, cooked slowly in a Dutch oven, a day ahead.

2½ to 3 pounds beef short ribs, cut
2 tablespoons flour
1 teaspoon salt
⅛ teaspoon pepper
2 tablespoons shortening
2 medium-sized onions, sliced
1 cup dry red wine
½ cup chile sauce or catsup
3 tablespoons each brown sugar and vinegar
1 tablespoon Worcestershire
½ teaspoon each dry mustard and chile powder
1½ tablespoons flour with ½ cup water

Roll the short ribs in 2 tablespoons flour, combined with salt and pepper, to coat all sides. Melt shortening in a Dutch oven, add short ribs and cook slowly until well browned all over. Add onions and brown lightly. Then add the wine, chile sauce, brown sugar, vinegar, Worcestershire, mustard, and chile powder.

Cover and cook over low heat until the meat is tender, about 2 hours. Remove from heat, cool, and refrigerate.

Then lift off all the fat, which will be congealed on top. Stir in the 1½ tablespoons flour blended with water. Cook until thickened and meat is heated through. Makes about 4 servings.

## Forgotten Short Ribs

About 1½ teaspoons salt
About ½ teaspoon pepper
3 to 4 pounds beef short ribs
1 can (8 oz.) tomato sauce
2 tablespoons molasses
2 tablespoons cider vinegar
1 teaspoon liquid smoke flavoring
1 tablespoon instant minced onion

Sprinkle salt and pepper on all sides of the shortribs and put into a Dutch oven or 3-quart casserole. In a small pan, combine the tomato sauce with the molasses, vinegar, liquid smoke, and instant minced onion; bring to a boil and simmer for 5 minutes.

Pour over the short ribs; cover and bake in a 275° oven for 3 to 4 hours, or until very tender. Just before serving, spoon off any excess fat. (If you prepare this dish a day ahead, refrigerate it, and then lift off the solidified fat before you reheat it.) Makes 4 servings.

## Beef Tongue with Raisin Sauce

1 beef tongue (about 4 lbs.) fresh, corned, or smoked
Water
1 onion, sliced
1 sprig parsley
1 bay leaf
5 or 6 whole black peppers
1 tablespoon salt (for fresh tongue)
½ cup vinegar
½ cup corn syrup
¼ teaspoon each allspice, cloves, and cinnamon
½ cup seeded raisins

Wash tongue. If corned or smoked tongue is used, soak in cold water for several hours before cooking. Place in a large kettle with boiling water to cover; add onion, parsley, bay leaf, black peppers, and salt; cover and simmer for 2½ to 3 hours, or until meat is tender.

Allow to remain in the liquid until cool enough to handle, then remove skin and trim the base to remove excess fat and any bones.

An hour or so before serving, put tongue in a Dutch oven or heavy frying pan. Pour vinegar, syrup, spices, and raisins over tongue; cover. Simmer very slowly for 45 minutes, turning the tongue several times during cooking and basting frequently with the sauce. Slice to serve. Serve sauce spooned on top or separately in a bowl. Serves 6 to 8.

## Beef Liver in Lemon Butter

This has become a favorite because those who normally don't care for liver enjoy it prepared this way.

¼ cup all-purpose flour
½ teaspoon salt
⅛ teaspoon pepper
1 pound beef liver, thinly sliced
1 egg, slightly beaten
½ cup salted soda cracker crumbs
6 tablespoons butter or margarine
3 tablespoons lemon juice
1 teaspoon sugar

Combine the flour, salt, and pepper; dredge the liver slices to coat lightly all over with the flour. Dip each floured liver slice into the beaten egg, then into the cracker crumbs until evenly coated with the crumbs.

Heat 4 tablespoons of the butter in a wide frying pan over medium high heat. Sauté the liver slices quickly until nicely browned on both sides and juicy-pink inside, about 3 to 4 minutes.

Remove liver to a serving plate, cover with foil, and keep warm on a hot tray or in a warm oven. Melt remaining 2 tablespoons butter in the pan, add the lemon juice and sugar, and stir until sugar is dissolved. Pour the sauce over liver and serve. Makes about 4 servings.

## Liver with Green Onion Sauce

2 bunches green onions
4 tablespoons butter, margarine, or salad oil
2 tablespoons flour
¼ teaspoon salt
⅛ teaspoon pepper
Dash nutmeg
1 cup milk
1 pound calf liver or baby beef liver, cut ¼-inch thick

Thinly slice green onions, including about 3 inches of the green tops. In a medium-sized frying pan that has a cover, sauté the onions in 2 tablespoons of the butter over medium heat until tender, but not browned. Stir in the flour, salt, pepper, and nutmeg.

Remove from heat and gradually stir in the milk. Cook, stirring, until slightly thickened. Reduce heat to warm and cover pan while you cook liver.

Arrange liver on a greased broiler pan, brush with remaining 2 tablespoons butter, melted; broil 3 to 4 inches from heat in a preheated broiler. Cook about 2 minutes on each side, until browned, but still slightly pink inside.

Cut liver slices into strips; add liver and all the pan juices to the onion sauce. Reheat quickly; serve. Serves 3 to 4.

# Ground Beef

## Meatballs in Sauce

A recipe for tiny appetizer meatballs in a choice of four popular sauces (Sweet and Sour, Curry, Stroganoff, or Teriyaki) appears on page 8.

You can easily adapt this recipe to make larger meatballs for a main dish—see the last paragraph of the recipe for instructions. The recipe will make about 3 dozen main-dish-sized meatballs.

## Yummy Balls

Reasons why Yummy Balls have become one of the top-ranking, all-time favorites: they're simple to make, inexpensive, savory with the sauce that forms from the soup and meat fat, and reheatable if dinner is late.

1 pound ground beef
½ pound ground lean pork
1 small onion, minced
½ cup uncooked rice
½ cup cracker crumbs
1 egg
½ teaspoon salt
Pepper to taste
1 can (10¾ oz.) condensed tomato soup
1 soup can water

Mix ground meats, onion, rice, cracker crumbs, egg, and seasonings. Shape into balls about the size of golf balls, and place in a greased casserole. Pour over tomato soup diluted with water.

Bake in a 375° oven for 1 hour. Makes 6 servings.

## Norwegian Meatballs

The secret of the rich flavor and color of these meatballs is adequate browning. First you brown the meatballs well. Then you brown flour in butter to make the gravy. Take the time to make sure the flour changes color without burning.

2 pounds ground beef
¼ pound ground pork
1 egg
Salt and pepper to taste
¼ teaspoon each mace and ground ginger
2 slices bread, or 2 tablespoons flour or cornstarch
Butter or margarine
1 medium-sized onion, sliced (optional)
¼ cup flour
Hot water

Combine beef, pork, egg, salt, pepper, mace, and ginger. Remove and discard crusts from bread if used (bread makes lighter meatballs); moisten slices with water, tear in pieces, and add to meat. Or sprinkle meat with the flour.

Knead the mixture thoroughly with your hands, about 5 or 10 minutes. Wash hands and wet them with cold water; roll meat mixture in walnut-sized balls, or even smaller ones if you like.

Melt a small amount of butter in a large frying pan over medium-high heat; add meatballs and brown them on all sides. Remove with a slotted spoon and place in a casserole. If onions are used, cook them in the drippings, adding more butter if necessary and stirring frequently, until they are golden brown; remove with slotted spoon and distribute over meatballs in the casserole.

Make a brown gravy by adding flour to the butter remaining in the pan; cook, stirring, over low heat until the flour has turned golden brown. Pour in hot water gradually

*. . . Norwegian Meatballs (cont'd.)*

and stir until gravy is thick and smooth (scrape all browned particles from pan into gravy). Season with salt and pepper.

Pour gravy over meatballs, cover, and bake in a 350° oven for about 45 minutes. Serves 6.

# Hamburger Soup

On page 14 is a recipe for Hamburger Soup, a meaty concoction of ground beef, vegetables, split peas, macaroni, and grated cheese.

This is one of those soups that can serve as a main dish with nothing more to accompany it than French bread and a simple salad.

# Family Meat Loaf

Serve this moist and well-seasoned meat loaf for a warm-me-up meal.

1½  pounds ground beef chuck
⅔  cup quick-cooking rolled oats, or 1 cup fine dry bread crumbs
1  cup milk
1  teaspoon salt
⅛  teaspoon pepper
¼  teaspoon poultry seasoning
2  eggs
1  teaspoon Worcestershire
1  small onion, finely chopped
¼  cup catsup
1½ to 2 tablespoons brown sugar
1  teaspoon prepared mustard
¼  teaspoon nutmeg (or less)

In a large mixing bowl, combine the ground chuck, rolled oats or crumbs, milk, salt, pepper, poultry seasoning, eggs, Worcestershire, and chopped onion. Put in a loaf pan (4½ by 8½ inches).

Combine the catsup, brown sugar, mustard, and nutmeg. Spread over the meat loaf. Bake in a 350° oven for about 1 hour and 15 minutes. Makes 6 to 8 servings.

# Joe's Special

No one is quite sure of the origin of the one-dish meal called Joe's Special. A staple of several San Francisco restaurants, it has been popular in that city for at least two generations.

2  pounds ground beef chuck, crumbled
2  tablespoons olive oil or salad oil
2  medium-sized onions, finely chopped
2  cloves garlic, minced or mashed
½  pound mushrooms, sliced (optional)
1¼  teaspoons salt
¼  teaspoon each nutmeg, pepper, and oregano
1  package (10 oz.) frozen chopped spinach, thawed and well drained; or ½ pound fresh spinach, washed, drained, and chopped (about 4 cups)
4  to 6 eggs

Brown ground beef well in oil in a large frying pan over high heat. Add onions, garlic, and mushrooms (if used); reduce heat and continue cooking, stirring occasionally, until onion is soft. Stir in seasonings and spinach; cook for about 5 minutes longer.

Add eggs; stir mixture over low heat just until eggs begin to set. Makes 4 to 6 servings.

# Beef Casserole, Chinese Style

1  pound ground beef
1  package (10 oz.) frozen peas, thawed
2  cups finely sliced raw celery
1  can (10½ oz.) condensed mushroom soup
2  tablespoons half-and-half (light cream)
¾  teaspoon salt
¼  teaspoon pepper
1  small onion, finely chopped
1  cup crushed potato chips

Cook ground beef in a frying pan until brown and crumbly, adding some fat if necessary; turn into a 1½-quart casserole. Arrange thawed peas over browned meat, then cover with the sliced celery. Mix together the mushroom soup, cream, salt, pepper, and onion; pour over celery. Sprinkle potato chips over the top of the casserole.

Bake in a 375° oven for 30 minutes, or until hot and bubbly. Serves 6.

# Enchilada Pie

1  pound ground beef
1  onion, chopped
1  teaspoon salt
¼  teaspoon pepper
1  tablespoon chile powder
1  can (8 oz.) tomato sauce
6  corn tortillas, spread with butter
1  can (4½ oz.) chopped ripe olives
1½  cups shredded sharp Cheddar cheese
½  cup water

Brown ground beef and onion; add seasonings and tomato sauce. In a 2-quart casserole alternate layers of buttered tortillas, meat sauce, olives, and cheese.

Add water, cover, and bake in a 400° oven for 20 minutes. Serves 4 to 6.

# Beef-Bean Enchiladas

Mexican-style food is especially relished by *Sunset Magazine* readers. This recipe has proved to be the most popular version of enchiladas.

1½  pounds ground beef, crumbled
1  medium-sized onion, chopped
1  can (1 lb.) refried beans
1  teaspoon salt
⅛  teaspoon garlic powder
⅓  cup canned or bottled taco sauce
1  cup quartered pitted ripe olives
2  cans (10 oz. each) enchilada sauce
    Salad oil
12  corn tortillas
3  cups shredded Cheddar cheese (about 12 oz.)
    Sliced pitted ripe olives for garnish
    Sour cream
    Canned or bottled green chile salsa

In a frying pan sauté ground beef and onions until meat is browned and onions are soft. Stir in beans, salt, garlic powder, taco sauce, and olives; heat until bubbly.

Heat enchilada sauce; pour about half into an ungreased, shallow 3-quart baking dish. Pour oil to a depth of about ¼ inch in a small frying pan; heat. Dip tortillas, one at a time, in hot oil to soften; drain quickly. Place about ⅓ cup of the ground beef filling on each tortilla, and roll to enclose filling. Place, seam sides down, in sauce in baking dish. Pour remaining enchilada sauce evenly over tortillas; cover with cheese.

Bake, uncovered, in a 350° oven for about 15 minutes or until thoroughly heated. (Or cover and refrigerate for up to 1 day; if taken directly from refrigerator, increase baking time to 45 minutes.)

Garnish with olive slices. Spoon sour cream and chile sauce over each serving to taste. Makes 6 servings.

## Spoonbread Tamale Pie

It's amusing to trace the evolution of tamale-pie cookery throughout the 40 years that *Sunset Magazine* has been publishing recipes. Cooks keep changing these popular dishes so that every few years "new" recipes appear which closely resemble old ones.

Spoonbread Tamale Pie, printed in 1966, is quite similar to Fiesta Tamale Pie, which became a favorite in the '30s. However, there are some changes. The new recipe uses all beef instead of part beef and part pork, and the filling contains some cornmeal and green pepper not in the old recipe.

1½ pounds ground lean beef or chuck
1 large onion, chopped
1 small green pepper, chopped
1 clove garlic, minced or mashed
¼ cup shortening or salad oil
1 can (about 15 oz.) pear-shaped tomatoes
1 can (12 oz.) whole-kernel corn
2 teaspoons salt
4 to 6 teaspoons chile powder
¼ teaspoon pepper
½ cup yellow cornmeal
1 cup water
1 cup pitted black olives
   Cornmeal Topping (directions follow)

Sauté the meat, onion, green pepper, and garlic together in heated shortening until onions are golden, about 10 minutes. Stir in tomatoes, corn, salt, chile powder, and pepper; cover and simmer 5 minutes. Stir in the cornmeal blended with the water; simmer 10 minutes more. Add olives and turn

into a 9 by 13-inch baking dish.

Spread topping mixture over meat. Bake uncovered in a 375° oven for 40 minutes. Makes about 8 servings.

**Cornmeal Topping:** Scald 1½ cups milk with ½ teaspoon salt and 2 tablespoons butter. Gradually add ½ cup cornmeal; cook, stirring until thickened. Remove from heat; stir in 1 cup shredded Cheddar cheese and 2 beaten eggs.

## Tangy Tortilla-Beef Casserole

No doubt this has become a great favorite because you can make it a day ahead and bake just before serving.

1½ pounds ground chuck, crumbled
1 medium-sized onion, chopped
1 can (1 lb.) tomatoes
1 can (10 oz.) enchilada sauce
1 can (2¼ oz.) sliced ripe olives, including liquid
1 teaspoon salt
¼ teaspoon garlic powder
⅛ teaspoon pepper
¼ cup salad oil
8 corn tortillas
1 cup small-curd cottage cheese
1 egg
½ pound jack cheese, thinly sliced
½ cup each shredded Cheddar cheese and finely crushed, packaged tortilla chips

Brown ground chuck and onion in a large frying pan. Blend in tomatoes, enchilada sauce, ripe olives with liquid, salt, garlic powder, and pepper. Bring mixture to a boil, reduce heat, and simmer, uncovered, for about 20 minutes, stirring occasionally.

Meanwhile, heat salad oil in a small frying pan; in it sauté tortillas one at a time for a few seconds on each side or just until softened. Drain tortillas on paper towels; cut drained tortillas in half. Beat cottage cheese with egg.

Spread ⅓ of the meat sauce in a greased, shallow, 3-quart casserole; top with half the jack cheese, half the cottage cheese mixture, and half of the tortilla halves, arranging each in an even layer. Repeat layering, using ⅓ more of the meat sauce and the remaining jack cheese, cottage cheese mixture, and tortilla halves. Spread

with remaining meat sauce; top with Cheddar cheese and a border of crushed tortilla chips.

Bake, uncovered, in a 350° oven for about 20 minutes (about 35 minutes if cold), or until casserole is thoroughly heated and Cheddar cheese is melted. Cut in squares or wedges to serve. Makes 6 servings.

## Ground Beef Tacos

You can prepare the taco filling and toppings ahead. Then just fry the tortillas until light brown.

1 pound lean ground beef
1 or 2 tablespoons salad oil
1 medium-sized onion, chopped
½ cup canned Mexican red chile sauce or enchilada sauce
8 corn tortillas
   Salad oil for deep frying
2 to 3 cups shredded lettuce
1 cup shredded mild Cheddar or jack cheese
   Canned or bottled taco sauce

In a frying pan, break apart and brown the meat, adding oil if necessary. Add onion and cook until soft. Add sauce and simmer slowly about 10 minutes, stirring constantly until liquid has evaporated. Keep warm, or reheat.

Fry one tortilla at a time in about ½-inch of hot oil (365°), until it becomes soft (just a few seconds). Then fold it in half and hold slightly open with tongs or two forks so that there is a space between the halves for filling to be added later. Fry the tortilla until crisp and light brown, turning as necessary to cook all sides. The process takes about 1 minute *only*. Drain on paper towels.

Fill each tortilla with meat sauce, lettuce, and cheese; top with sauce. Makes 8 tacos (about 4 servings).

## Lasagne Belmonte

    1  medium-sized onion, chopped
    3  tablespoons olive oil or salad oil
 1½  pounds lean ground beef
    1  clove garlic, minced or mashed
    2  cans (8 oz. each) tomato sauce
    1  can (6 oz.) tomato paste
 ½  cup each dry red wine and water
        (or 1 cup water)
    1  teaspoon each salt and oregano
 ½  teaspoon each pepper and sugar
  12  ounces lasagne noodles
        Boiling, salted water
    1  pound (2 cups) ricotta cheese or
        small-curd cottage cheese
 ½  pound mozzarella cheese, thinly
        sliced
 ½  cup shredded Parmesan cheese

In a large frying pan that has a cover, sauté onion in oil until soft; add beef and garlic, and cook, stirring, until meat is brown and crumbly. Stir in tomato sauce, tomato paste, wine, and water. Add salt, oregano, pepper, and sugar, stirring until mixed. Cover pan and simmer slowly about 1½ hours.

Meanwhile cook noodles in boiling, salted water as directed on the package, until tender, about 15 minutes. Drain thoroughly, rinse with cold water, and drain again.

Arrange about ⅓ of the noodles in the bottom of a 9 by 13-inch shallow casserole dish. (Lay one layer of noodles lengthwise in the dish and the next layer crosswise. Alternate this way as you continue to arrange the dish.) Spread ⅓ of the tomato sauce over the noodles; top with ⅓ of the ricotta and mozzarella cheese. Repeat this layering two more times. Top with the Parmesan.

Bake uncovered in a 350° oven for 30 minutes. Makes 6 to 8 servings.

**Spicy Lasagne Variation.** Substitute ½ pound Italian sausage for ½ pound of the beef. Remove the sausage casing, chop, and brown with the beef.

## More

    1  pound ground beef
 ¼  pound salt pork
    1  tablespoon butter or margarine
    1  small onion, minced
 1½  cups broken spaghetti (cooked in
        boiling, salted water)
    1  can (1 lb. 12 oz.) tomatoes
    1  can (1 lb.) peas
    1  can (4 oz.) pimientos, chopped
    1  can (4½ oz.) chopped ripe olives
    2  cups (½ lb.) shredded American
        cheese

Have your meat dealer grind the beef and salt pork together.

Melt the butter in a large frying pan over medium-high heat, add onion, and cook, stirring occasionally, until lightly browned. Add the meat and cook, stirring frequently, until well browned.

Add spaghetti to the meat with the tomatoes and peas, half the pimientos and olives, and half the cheese. Mix lightly with a fork. Pour into a greased 3-quart baking dish; sprinkle the remaining cheese, olives, and pimientos over the top.

Bake in a 400° oven for about 20 minutes, or until the cheese is melted. Serves 6 to 8.

## Noodle Medley

    1  package (8 oz.) thin noodles
        Boiling, salted water
 1½  pounds ground beef
    2  tablespoons salad oil (if neces-
        sary)
    3  large onions, ground or minced
    1  green pepper, ground or minced
    1  can (6 or 8 oz.) sliced mushrooms
    1  can (1 lb. 12 oz.) tomatoes
    1  tablespoon Worcestershire
        Salt and pepper to taste
 ½  cup or more shredded American
        or Cheddar cheese

Cook noodles in boiling, salted water until almost tender (they should be firm because you will cook them further); drain. Brown meat quickly, in hot oil if the meat does not contain much fat. Add onions, green pepper, mushrooms, tomatoes, Worcestershire, salt, and pepper; bring to a boil.

Combine noodles and meat mixture; simmer gently 15 to 20 minutes, stirring frequently; mix in cheese. Serve at once; or prepare in advance,

turn into a greased casserole, and reheat in a 350° oven. Serves 8.

## Italian-style Macaroni Casserole

A version of this called Mock Ravioli (because it tastes like ravioli) became popular at least three decades ago. Later the recipe was revised to take advantage of the convenience of frozen spinach. The dish still has its original virtue: It can be made ahead.

**GROUND BEEF FILLING:**
    2  pounds ground beef
    2  medium-sized onions, chopped
    1  clove garlic, minced or mashed
    1  can (3 or 4 oz.) sliced mushrooms,
        drained
    1  can (8 oz.) tomato sauce
    1  can (6 oz.) tomato paste
    1  cup water
 1½  teaspoons mixed Italian herbs
 1½  teaspoons salt
 ½  teaspoon pepper

**SPINACH FILLING:**
 ½  cup salad oil
    2  packages (10 oz. each) frozen
        chopped spinach, thawed
    2  cups soft bread crumbs
 ½  cup minced parsley
 ½  cup grated Romano cheese
    1  teaspoon rubbed sage
 1½  teaspoon salt
    1  package (1 lb.) butterfly or sea-
        shell macaroni, cooked in boil-
        ing, salted water

**Beef Filling.** Sauté ground beef, onions, and garlic in large frying pan (with a cover) over medium heat until crumbly. Add mushrooms, tomato sauce, tomato paste, water, herbs, salt, and pepper. Stir mixture to blend. Cover and simmer gently for 1½ hours.

**Spinach Filling.** In a large bowl, mix together the salad oil, spinach, soft bread crumbs, parsley, cheese, sage, and salt. Stir mixture until it is well-blended.

Grease a 9 by 13-inch baking pan and place half the cooked macaroni in the bottom. Top with half the spinach mixture and then half the ground beef mixture. Repeat the layers, ending with the meat mixture on top. Bake, uncovered, in a 350° oven for 30 minutes (if refrigerated, 50 minutes). Makes 10 to 12 servings.

# Western Meal-in-One

1 pound ground beef
1 tablespoon salad oil or bacon drippings
1 clove garlic, minced or mashed
1 teaspoon salt
1 large onion, finely chopped
1 green pepper, seeded and chopped
1 teaspoon chile powder
1 can (1 lb.) tomatoes
1 can (1 lb.) kidney beans
¾ cup uncooked rice
¼ cup chopped ripe olives
¾ cup shredded Cheddar cheese

Brown the ground meat in oil until crumbly. Add garlic, salt, onion, green pepper, and chile powder, and sauté for 5 minutes, or until vegetables are limp. Mix in tomatoes, kidney beans, and rice, and turn into a greased 2-quart casserole.

Bake, uncovered, in a 350° oven for 45 minutes. Sprinkle with olives and cheese, and continue baking for 15 minutes longer, or until cheese is melted. (If you assemble the casserole in the morning and refrigerate it, allow 1½ hours for baking.) Makes 8 servings.

# Rolled Meat Pancakes

When this recipe first was printed, in 1950, it served a small number of people. Later the editors discovered it was especially good to make ahead for serving large groups, so a recipe to serve 18 to 27 people was devised. Here are both the small and large-quantity versions.

½ pound ground beef
¼ pound bulk pork sausage
½ medium-sized onion, finely chopped
1 clove garlic, minced or mashed
1 package (10 oz.) frozen chopped spinach, cooked and well-drained
 Salt to taste
2 eggs
¼ teaspoon salt
1 cup milk
⅔ cup regular all-purpose flour
 Butter or margarine
2 cans (8 oz. each) tomato sauce
¾ cup shredded sharp Cheddar cheese

Brown meats with onion and garlic until crumbly. Mix in spinach; salt to taste.

Beat eggs with salt and milk. Sift flour, measure, and beat into egg mixture.

Pour about 2 tablespoons batter into buttered, hot 5 or 7-inch frying pan; tilt pan so batter covers bottom. When brown on one side, remove. Continue until batter is used, buttering pan as needed.

Divide filling between pancakes, and roll each. Place 2 or 3 in individual baking dishes, or arrange in a 9 by 13-inch baking pan. Pour tomato sauce over rolls; sprinkle with cheese. Bake in a 350° oven for 30 minutes. Serves 6 to 9.

**For 18 to 27 Servings.** Following preceding instructions, use this quantity of ingredients: 2 pounds ground beef, 1 pound bulk sausage, 2 medium-sized onions, 3 cloves garlic, 4 packages frozen spinach, salt to taste, 6 eggs, ¾ teaspoon salt, 3 cups milk, 2 cups flour, butter or margarine as needed, 3 large cans (15 oz. *each*) tomato sauce, and 2 cups shredded sharp Cheddar cheese. Bake in three 9 by 13-inch pans.

# Simplified Lahmajoun

What has been simplified is an old Middle Eastern snack, which is something like pizza but more meaty.

In the Middle East, lahmajoun is often sold by strolling street vendors, who carry their wares in some kind of container which has a strap to sling over the shoulder.

They shout "lahmajoun" in much the same tone of voice that Americans use to sell hot dogs at football games.

However, whoever buys lahmajoun gets a big green onion on top of it—not mustard.

1 package (8 oz.) refrigerated biscuits
 Beef or Lamb Filling (recipes follow)
1 cup shredded jack cheese

Roll out each biscuit on a lightly floured board to a thin round, about 5 inches in diameter. Arrange rounds slightly apart on 2 large greased baking sheets. Divide the filling into 10 portions; spread evenly over the surface of each biscuit. (Be sure to spread the meat clear to the edge of the biscuit, as the meat will shrink while baking.) Sprinkle cheese over the meat.

Bake in a 450° oven for 10 to 12 minutes, or until meat is cooked and biscuits are crisp. Serve hot—as they are or rolled up and fastened with wooden picks. Makes 10.

**Beef Filling.** Mix together 1½ pounds lean ground beef, 3 chopped green onions, ¼ cup chopped parsley, 1 teaspoon salt, ½ teaspoon oregano, and ½ can (8 oz. size) tomato sauce.

**Lamb Filling.** Mix together 1½ pounds lean ground lamb, 3 chopped green onions, 2 tablespoons chopped fresh mint (*or* 1½ teaspoons dried), 1 teaspoon salt, and ½ can (8 oz. size) tomato sauce.

# Beef & Cheese Pie

1 pound ground beef
⅔ cup undiluted evaporated milk
¼ cup fine dry bread crumbs
1 teaspoon garlic salt
⅓ cup catsup
1 can (2 or 3 oz.) sliced mushrooms, drained
1 cup (¼ lb.) shredded Cheddar cheese
¼ teaspoon crumbled oregano
2 tablespoons grated Parmesan cheese

Combine meat, milk, bread crumbs, and garlic salt in a 9-inch pie pan; pat mixture against sides and bottom of pie pan. Spread catsup over the meat mixture; sprinkle with mushrooms, Cheddar cheese, oregano, and Parmesan cheese.

Bake in a 450° oven for 20 minutes or until meat is done to your taste. Cut into wedges to serve. Makes 4 servings.

## Ground Beef Yeast Knishes

A half-pound of chicken fat, cut in pieces and melted in a pan over low heat, will yield about 1 cup melted fat. Strain the fat before using.

You do not have to use chicken fat, but should use it if you want these to be authentically Jewish.

- 1 tablespoon sugar
- ¾ cup warm water (lukewarm for compressed yeast)
- ½ teaspoon salt
- ¼ cup melted chicken fat, salad oil, or melted butter (cooled)
- 1 package yeast, active dry or compressed
- 2 eggs, slightly beaten
- 3¾ cups unsifted regular all-purpose flour
- Melted chicken fat or butter
- Beef Filling (recipe follows)

Dissolve sugar in the water. Add salt, melted (cooled) fat, and yeast, and let stand until yeast is softened, about 5 minutes. Stir in the eggs, then flour, blending in the flour a little at a time to make a soft dough.

Turn dough out on a lightly floured board and knead until smooth and elastic, about 10 minutes, adding more flour as necessary. Place the dough in a greased bowl, cover, and let rise in a warm place until doubled, about 1 hour.

Punch the dough down, then roll out very thinly on a lightly floured board to form a large rectangle about 15 by 24 inches and about ⅛ inch in thickness. Brush the dough with melted chicken fat.

Place a row of filling about 1 inch from the edge of the dough, using about 2 cups of the filling. (For appetizer-sized knishes, use only 1 cup of the filling for each row.)

Roll up the dough as for a jelly roll, making three complete turns. Cut off dough parallel with the roll, and repeat the filling process twice more until all dough is used.

Cut each filled roll into 1-inch pieces. Stretch dough up over cut edges on both sides of each piece and seal in center to enclose filling.

Brush knishes with melted fat; place on greased baking sheets about ¾ inch apart. Let rise 30 minutes.

Bake in a 375° oven for about 25 minutes, or until golden. Makes about 4 dozen 2-inch or 8 dozen 1¼-inch knishes.

To reheat frozen foil-wrapped knishes, take directly from freezer and place in a 350° oven about 45 minutes.

**Beef Filling.** Sauté 2 cups chopped onions in 2 tablespoons melted shortening or salad oil until soft and golden.

Blend cooked onions with 2½ cups mashed cooked potatoes, 1 tablespoon salt, ¼ teaspoon pepper, 5 cups ground cooked beef, and 1 egg, blending well. Makes about 6 cups filling.

# Veal

## Saltimbocca

To make this Italian dish authentically, you will probably have to go to a delicatessen for the prosciutto (salt-cured ham) and the proper cheese.

- 4 veal round steaks, each cut ½-inch thick (about 2 lbs.)
- 24 very thin slices prosciutto (about 6 oz.)
- ¼ pound Fontina (or Swiss) cheese, cut in 12 sticks
- ¼ cup (⅛ lb.) butter
- ¼ teaspoon each sage and basil
- ½ teaspoon Dijon-style or English mustard
- ⅓ cup dry white wine
- Hot boiled egg noodles, buttered

Trim fat, bone, and connective tissue from steaks. Place meat between sheets of waxed paper and pound with a flat-surfaced mallet until ¼ to ⅜ inch thick. Divide meat into 12 pieces of fairly equal size (join scraps into larger pieces by overlapping edges and pounding between sheets of waxed paper; handle gently).

Top each piece of veal with several slices prosciutto and a piece of cheese. Roll meat to enclose filling completely, turning in the sides; secure with small skewers.

Melt butter in a frying pan, and blend in sage, basil, and mustard. Add meat rolls and brown quickly on all sides, turning frequently; takes 4 to 5 minutes. Remove rolls; add wine to pan. Boil rapidly until reduced by half, scraping meat particles free. Pour over veal; serve with noodles. Serves 6.

## Veal Paprika

- 2 pounds boneless veal steak, cut in 2-inch cubes
- 2 tablespoons butter or margarine
- 1 can (3 or 4 oz.) whole mushrooms, drained (reserve liquid)
- 2 tablespoons flour
- 1 teaspoon (or more) paprika
- 1 cup sour cream (or 1 cup whipping cream and 1 tablespoon lemon juice)
- 1 tablespoon onion juice
- Salt to taste

In a frying pan, brown veal in butter. Remove to a casserole.

Blend 3 tablespoons of the mushroom liquid, flour, and paprika in the frying pan to make a smooth paste. Slowly add the sour cream and cook, stirring constantly, over very low heat (do not boil) until thickened and smooth. Remove from the heat; add the mushrooms, onion juice, and salt; pour over the veal.

Cover and bake in a 350° oven for about 1 hour, or until tender. Serves 6.

## Wiener Schnitzel

- 2 to 3 pounds boneless veal cutlets, ⅓-inch thick
- Salt and pepper
- About ¾ cup flour
- 2 eggs, well beaten
- 1½ cups fine dry bread crumbs, sifted to remove large crumbs
- Half butter and half salad oil for frying
- 1 lemon cut in thin slices and 2 lemons cut in wedges
- Parsley

Trim skin and fat from outside of meat. Leave cutlets whole if small, or divide following natural divisions of meat. Put each between waxed paper and gently pound with a smooth mallet to about ¼-inch thickness. Make very small cuts along the edges to prevent curling. Lightly sprinkle with salt and pepper.

Dust each piece with flour and shake to remove excess. Draw the cutlet through the beaten egg to coat, then hold up until excess drips off. Coat in bread crumbs and shake to remove excess. Then lay cutlet flat and pat in crumbs so they won't fall off in the frying.

Fry cutlets *just* before serving. Have ready a shallow pan lined with paper towels in a warm oven for keeping cutlets hot. Also warm a serving platter.

In a large frying pan over medium-high heat, melt enough butter with oil to cover the pan bottom completely. Heat until fat shows ripples when you tip the pan. Add a few cutlets (don't crowd pan), which should turn golden brown in about 1 minute; turn to brown other side. Remove cutlets to pan in oven and add more butter and oil as needed.

Decorate each cutlet with a thin slice of lemon topped with a tiny parsley sprig. Arrange on heated platter and garnish platter with lemon wedges and parsley. Makes 6 to 8 servings.

# Veal Picatte

2 boned veal round steaks (about 1 lb.), skin removed
   Flour
¼ cup (⅛ lb.) butter
   Salt and pepper
   Juice of 1 lemon (about 3 tablespoons)
   Lemon wedges

Place veal between waxed paper and pound with a flat wooden mallet until about ¼-inch thick. Cut into serving-sized pieces and coat with flour, shaking off the excess.

Heat butter in a wide frying pan until sizzling. Add veal without crowding and brown quickly (about 30 seconds) on each side. Place on a hot serving platter, pour the pan drippings over meat; sprinkle with salt and pepper and the lemon juice. Garnish with lemon wedges. Makes 4 servings.

# Veal Scallopini

¼ cup (⅛ lb.) butter or margarine
½ pound mushrooms, thinly sliced
1½ tablespoons lemon juice
1½ pounds veal, cut for scallopini
¼ cup flour
1 teaspoon salt
¼ teaspoon pepper
¾ cup Marsala, dry Sherry, or dry white wine
1 teaspoon beef stock base, or 1 bouillon cube
1 tablespoon minced parsley

Melt half the butter in a large frying pan, add mushrooms, sprinkle with lemon juice, and sauté for a few minutes, just until mushrooms are tender. Turn out of pan and set aside.

Cut veal into 1-inch-wide strips and dust in the flour seasoned with the salt and pepper. Melt remaining butter in the frying pan and brown meat quickly on both sides. Pour in wine, add beef stock base, and cook rapidly for a few minutes, stirring constantly. Return mushrooms to the pan and heat thoroughly.

Serve at once; garnish with minced parsley.

Makes 4 generous servings.

# Veal Sweetbreads with Bacon

1 pound veal sweetbreads
   Salt, lemon juice, and water
6 slices bacon
2 tablespoons butter or bacon drippings
¼ cup chopped onion
5 medium-sized mushrooms, sliced
¼ teaspoon each salt and tarragon
2 tablespoons dry white wine
½ cup whipping cream

Wash sweetbreads well in cool water. Cover with water, adding 1 teaspoon salt and 1 tablespoon lemon juice per quart of water. Bring to a boil and simmer about 15 minutes. Drain and plunge sweetbreads immediately into cold water to stop cooking; drain again.

With your fingers and the point of a sharp knife, remove as much of the white connecting membrane as possible and break sweetbreads into bite-sized pieces. (If you are not going to finish cooking them immediately, place them in a bowl of cold water and

refrigerate; use within 36 hours.)

Fry bacon until crisp; drain, crumble, and set aside for garnish. Melt butter (or use drippings) in a frying pan and sauté onion and mushrooms just until tender. Add sweetbreads, salt, tarragon, wine, and cream. Boil rapidly, stirring occasionally, over high heat until sauce is reduced by half and slightly thickened.

Spoon into warm serving dish and garnish with bacon. Serve at once. Makes about 4 servings.

# Lamb

# Roast Lamb

Roasts—such as leg, shoulder, or rack—profit by seasonings such as garlic, lemon juice, thyme, or oregano.

Place meat, fat side up, on a rack in a shallow uncovered pan. Insert meat thermometer in a central meaty portion, not touching bone. Many cooks prefer to brown lamb in a 400° oven for a few minutes and then continue roasting at 325° or 350°.

Lamb sold now is tender at a lower meat thermometer temperature than formerly—about 145° (medium rare) to 165° (medium well done).

# Roast Leg of Lamb with Artichokes

1 clove garlic, minced or mashed
1 teaspoon each salt and whole oregano
¼ teaspoon pepper
1 large leg of lamb, 6 to 8 pounds
1 cup water
1 or 2 packages (8 oz. each) frozen artichoke hearts, thawed
1 can (8 oz.) tomato sauce
3 tablespoons lemon juice
   Rice pilaf (optional)

Combine garlic, salt, oregano, and pepper; rub all over the lamb and into the natural seams in the meat. Set into an open roasting pan (not on a rack); pour ½ cup of the water into pan. Insert a meat thermometer into the thickest part of the meat.

Roast in a 400° oven for 20 minutes; reduce heat to 325° and roast about 45 minutes longer.

Arrange artichokes in the pan around the roast, then pour into the pan the tomato sauce and remaining ½ cup water. Continue to roast for 20 to 25 minutes, or until internal temperature registers 145° to 150° for medium rare (or 160° to 165° for medium well done); baste several times.

Remove meat to serving plate and drizzle with lemon juice. Serve with artichokes and sauce and rice pilaf, if you wish. Makes about 8 servings.

## Barbecued Breast of Lamb

2  pounds breast of lamb, cut in serving-sized pieces
   Salt and pepper to taste
1  lemon, thinly sliced
1  large onion, finely chopped
1  cup each catsup and water
3  tablespoons each vinegar and brown sugar
1  teaspoon chile powder
2  tablespoons Worcestershire

Spread lamb in a wide, shallow casserole or baking pan which has a cover. Season generously with salt and pepper. Place a slice of lemon on each piece of meat; sprinkle onion over all. Bake uncovered in a 450° oven 30 minutes to brown well.

While meat is browning, combine remaining ingredients in a small saucepan; bring to boil and cook about 5 minutes. Pour sauce over browned meat; cover pan. Reduce oven to 350° and bake about 1 hour longer, or until tender. Serves 4.

## Shish Kebab

To prepare this popular dish cooked on skewers ("shish" means skewer), buy the following amounts for 6 to 8 people.

8  to 9-pound leg of lamb
6  small tomatoes, or 1 basket cherry tomatoes
24  small boiling onions, or 6 small onions
1  pound small mushrooms, cleaned and stems trimmed
4  large green peppers

Have your meatman bone the leg of lamb and remove fat and gristle—or do this yourself. To obtain the most uniform-sized pieces, you may want to cut the meat into cubes yourself. In America, the meat is usually cut in about 1½-inch cubes. But in the Middle East, much smaller pieces are used—about 1 inch or less; these broil quicker and may be more tender and juicy.

Cut unpeeled tomatoes into quarters; if cherry tomatoes are used, just remove stems and skewer whole.

Peel and parboil boiling onions until almost tender. Cut regular onions in large wedges, then cut each wedge in half for easiest skewering.

Mushrooms can be destemmed if you want only caps, but whole stemmed ones are most easily skewered—through the center of the stem.

Green peppers should be cut in wide strips which can be skewered through both ends, or in squares.

Because meat and vegetables have different cooking times, most cooks prefer to skewer each kind separately rather than alternating all the ingredients on one skewer.

Some cooks prefer to marinate the ingredients before cooking, particularly the meat so that it will be well-flavored. (Marinating is not required for tenderizing.) Other cooks just brush the skewers with flavorful ingredients while they are cooking.

Olive oil, either in the marinade or as a baste, is a good idea to prevent the foods from drying and to give a glossy, attractive appearance.

You do not need definite measurements for marinade ingredients. Some of the things often used in addition to olive oil are lemon juice or pieces of whole lemon including peel, a small amount (you don't want too liquid a marinade) dry red or white wine, garlic, and onion (either cut in large pieces or in the form of onion juice).

Greeks use oregano in copious amounts as a seasoning, the Turks sometimes use marjoram or thyme, and Arabs often like coriander or cumin. Bay leaves are another good seasoning—either in the marinade or inserted between pieces of food on the skewers; wedges of unpeeled lemon may also be cooked this way.

Meat may be marinated as long as overnight in the refrigerator, but probably 1 or 2 hours will be enough to flavor it well. Cherry tomatoes, onions, mushrooms, and peppers should not be marinated more than 2 or 3 hours or they will get limp. Don't marinate quartered tomatoes—they will lose their juices and dilute the marinade.

You may skewer the foods and then marinate them, or marinate first and skewer just before cooking.

The skewered meat and vegetables may be broiled over charcoal, or placed in a broiler pan or on a broiler rack and cooked under the oven broiler (be sure it is thoroughly preheated).

Cooking times will vary, depending upon the size of the pieces of food. Strive for a medium rate of cooking —you don't want the kebabs to cook so slowly the food dries nor so fast it is charred on the outside and still raw inside. Lamb should not be overcooked—it is best when juicy and slightly pink inside.

Baste occasionally with oil or the marinade and salt the food as it cooks.

## Baked Lamb Chops with Rice

4  shoulder or loin lamb chops
   Salt and pepper to taste
   Flour
2  tablespoons salad oil
½  cup uncooked long-grain rice
4  medium-sized onions, peeled and halved
1  bouillon cube dissolved in 1 cup boiling water
½  cup Sherry
1  teaspoon rosemary
¼  teaspoon curry powder
1  clove garlic, minced or mashed
   Boiling water
½  cup finely chopped parsley

Season chops with salt and pepper and lightly coat with flour. Brown slowly in hot oil in a large, heavy frying pan or casserole which has a cover and can be put in the oven.

While chops are browning on the second side, add rice to the oil; let rice brown along with the chops, stirring frequently to prevent burning; lay onion halves on top of rice. Mix dissolved bouillon cube, Sherry, rosemary, curry powder, and garlic; pour over chops.

Cover frying pan and bake in a 325° oven for about 50 minutes. From time to time, if liquid cooks away, add a small amount of boiling water. Add salt if necessary and parsley, mixing it in lightly. Bake about 10 minutes more, or until liquid is cooked away, leaving the rice fluffy and the chops tender. Serves 4.

## L'Ambrosia

4 whole lamb shanks (about 4 to 5 pounds)
2 cloves garlic, slivered
½ teaspoon salt
¼ teaspoon pepper
7 tablespoons flour
1 medium-sized onion, finely chopped
2½ cups water, or regular-strength beef or chicken broth (½ cup dry white wine may be substituted for part of the liquid)
2 teaspoons Worcestershire
2 bay leaves

Cut small gashes in the lamb at intervals and insert slivers of the garlic. Sprinkle meat with salt and pepper; coat heavily with part of the flour.

Place the shanks in a close-fitting roasting pan. Place uncovered in a 500° oven for about 45 minutes, turning several times, until well browned. Add the onion and remaining flour to the pan during about the last 15 minutes of browning so that it also can be lightly browned. Remove pan from oven and lower temperature to 350°.

Mix the water or other liquid and Worcestershire and slowly blend into the onion, flour, and pan juices. Add bay leaves.

Cover the roasting pan and bake in the 350° oven for about 1 to 1½ hours, or until the shanks are tender. Turn the shanks in the pan gravy several times while they cook. Add more salt to gravy if necessary. Serves 4.

## Lamb Shanks with Curried Rice

4 lamb shanks, each cut in two pieces
2 tablespoons salad oil
½ teaspoon salt
⅛ teaspoon pepper
½ envelope (3 to 4-serving size) dried onion soup mix
⅔ cup condensed beef consommé, or 1 teaspoon beef stock base in ⅔ cup boiling water
1 teaspoon Worcestershire
½ cup Major Grey chutney, chopped
About 2 cups cooked, curried rice, prepared according to your favorite recipe or with a mix

In a heavy pan with a cover, brown lamb shanks in salad oil. Add salt, pepper, onion soup mix, consommé, and Worcestershire. Cook over low heat about 2 to 2½ hours, or until lamb is tender.

Cool, refrigerate, and skim off fat. Add chutney. Heat just until simmering. Serve over the curried rice. Serves 4.

## Lamb Meatballs in Sour Cream Sauce

1½ pounds ground lamb
½ pound ground beef chuck
⅓ cup fine dry bread crumbs
1½ teaspoons salt
¼ teaspoon pepper
1½ teaspoons Worcestershire
2 eggs, slightly beaten
2 tablespoons butter or margarine
2 red bell peppers, seeded, cut in strips (or green peppers if not available)
½ cup chopped onion
1 tablespoon water
1 cup sour cream

In a bowl combine the lamb, beef, bread crumbs, salt, pepper, Worcestershire, and eggs. Mix well and shape into balls about 1½ to 2 inches in diameter. Place balls in a single layer in

a shallow baking pan. Bake in a 500° oven for 8 to 10 minutes.

Meanwhile heat the butter in a frying pan; add pepper strips, onion, and water; and sauté, stirring often, for about 15 minutes, or until vegetables are tender. Add sour cream and stir until heated through—do not boil.

Add the hot, cooked meatballs, including any juices, and stir just until well coated with the sauce. Remove from heat. Makes 6 to 8 servings.

## Irish Lamb Stew

2½ pounds boneless lamb shoulder, cut in cubes
¼ cup flour
2 teaspoons each salt and dry mustard
2 tablespoons bacon drippings or butter
8 small onions, peeled
2 stalks celery, sliced
2 carrots, peeled and sliced diagonally
2 turnips, peeled and cut in wedges
¼ teaspoon each crumbled dried marjoram and thyme
2 cups water
½ package (9 oz. package) frozen peas
2 tablespoons each sugar and vinegar
2 cups hot mashed potatoes (optional)
1 tablespoon melted butter (optional)

Roll meat in flour seasoned with salt and 1 teaspoon of the mustard. Using a large heavy pan, brown meat in bacon drippings, turning to brown all sides. Add onions, celery, carrots, turnips, marjoram, thyme, and water. Cover and simmer for 1½ hours, or until the meat is tender. Add peas and cook 5 minutes.

Mix together the sugar, vinegar, and remaining teaspoon of mustard and blend into the sauce. (If necessary, thicken with a flour and water paste.)

At this point you can serve the stew. Or do this to decorate:

Turn stew into baking dish. Push mashed potatoes through a cake decorator, making a wreath around the edge of the baking dish. Brush potatoes with melted butter and place in a 450° oven for 10 minutes, or until potatoes are lightly browned. Makes 8 servings.

# Lamb Curry

Serve with rice and a selection of condiments, such as chutney, toasted coconut, raisins, chopped nuts, minced onion, chopped hard-cooked egg, sliced green onion including tops, a bowl of yogurt, or Tomato Chutney (recipe on page 119).

 2 tablespoons butter or margarine
 2 pounds boneless, lean lamb stew
     meat, cut in 1-inch cubes
 1 teaspoon curry powder (or as
     much as 2 tablespoons, depend-
     ing on taste)
   Dash pepper
 ¼ teaspoon ground ginger or 1 tea-
     spoon minced fresh ginger
 1 medium-sized onion, finely
     chopped
 1 clove garlic, minced or mashed
 ½ green pepper, seeded and
     chopped
 1 stalk celery, chopped
 1 teaspoon salt
 1½ cups regular-strength chicken
     broth
 2 tablespoons each flour and water
 ¼ cup yogurt or sour cream
 ½ teaspoon paprika

Heat butter in a large frying pan or saucepan. Add lamb and brown thoroughly. Add curry powder, pepper, and ginger. Cook, stirring, about 1 minute. Add onion, garlic, green pepper, and celery; cook, stirring, about 5 minutes, or until vegetables are limp. Add salt and chicken broth.

Simmer, covered, until meat is tender, about 45 minutes or longer. Dissolve flour in water, blend into meat mixture, and continue cooking about 15 minutes, stirring often.

Remove from heat; stir in the yogurt or sour cream and paprika. If you reheat, do not boil. Makes about 6 servings.

# Pork

## Roast Pork

Various fresh pork roasts can be roasted, fat side up, on a rack in an uncovered shallow pan in a 300° to 325° oven. They are done when a meat thermometer inserted in a meaty center portion, not touching bone, reaches 170° (or 185° in the case of bone-in picnic shoulders, Boston shoulders, or whole bone-in *fresh* hams).

The glaze in the following recipe can be used to baste roasts during the last hour of cooking.

## Glazed Pork Loin Roast

You'll relish the flavor of this roast, marinated for 12 hours in a soy, honey, and red wine sauce.

 ½ cup each soy sauce, honey, and
     water
 ¼ cup dry red wine
 2 tablespoons sugar
 ½ teaspoon ground ginger, or 2 tea-
     spoons minced fresh ginger
 1 teaspoon dry mustard
 1 teaspoon salt
 2 or 3 cloves garlic, cut in large
     pieces
 4 to 6-pound pork loin roast

Mix together soy sauce, honey, water, wine, sugar, ginger, mustard, salt, and garlic. Place roast in a close-fitting pan, fat side down, and pour the liquid over it. Cover and place in the refrigerator for at least 12 hours.

Place meat on a rack in a pan and roast in a 325° oven for about 30 to 35 minutes for each pound, or until a meat thermometer inserted in a thick meaty portion registers 170°. Baste frequently with marinade. Makes 8 to 12 servings.

## Baked Ham

Hams sold now are confusing in variety of processing and cuts. Although it occasionally is possible to find an old-fashioned smoked ham complete with bone and rind, almost all the hams on sale have been processed in some way. Nearly all have been trimmed and most have been boned.

These come in two forms—fully cooked (including canned hams) and cook-before-eating. The fully cooked hams can be eaten without further cooking, but are greatly improved by further baking to heat them throughout (to 130° on a meat thermometer). The cook-before-eating hams *must* have further cooking, to an internal temperature of at least 160°.

Any kind of ham you bake in the oven, whether merely to heat it or to cook it, can be improved and beautified by a glaze. Follow label instructions for length of time to bake the ham, usually at 300° or 325°. Remove the ham to glaze 30 to 45 minutes before it is supposed to be done.

Before you glaze it, you can score the surface (fat if there is any) in a diamond pattern and stud each diamond with a whole clove. Then spread surface with one of the following glazes and finish baking.

**Orange Glaze.** Spread surface with a mixture of 1 cup orange juice, 1 tablespoon grated orange peel, ¾ to 1 cup brown sugar, and 1 teaspoon dry mustard. Baste frequently with the pan juices. Garnish with thin slices of unpeeled orange.

**Sherry Glaze with Apricots.** Spread surface with a mixture of 1 teaspoon dry mustard, ½ cup each fine dry bread crumbs and brown sugar, and a sprinkling of black pepper. Baste during baking with Sherry. Fifteen minutes before removing from the oven, surround with drained canned apricot halves, dotted with butter, and baste these with the pan juices to glaze.

**Pineapple Glaze.** Spread with a mixture of 1 teaspoon dry mustard, 1 cup brown sugar, and a sprinkling of black pepper. Lay pineapple slices over the top and insert a maraschino cherry on a toothpick in the center of each. Baste with a mixture of Sherry and the canned pineapple syrup. Before serving, add ½ cup currant or grape jelly to the pan juices; blend well and bring to a boil. Serve this sauce separately.

**Peanut-Honey Glaze.** Spread with a mixture of chunk-style peanut butter, enough honey to give a spreadable consistency, and a sprinkling of ground cloves. This makes a wonderfully flavored, crunchy crust.

# Eggs Benedict

2 English muffins, split
  Butter or margarine
4 slices boneless cooked ham or
  Canadian bacon, ⅛ to ¼-inch
  thick
4 eggs
  Hollandaise Sauce (recipe on page
  115), warmed
  Paprika and parsley

Toast the muffin halves, butter them, and keep them warm. Broil or pan-fry the slices of ham. Keep them hot, also. Poach the eggs.

To serve, place a slice of ham on each muffin half, top with a poached egg, and cover with warm Hollandaise. Sprinkle with paprika and garnish with parsley. Serve at once to 2 or 4 people.

# Bruncho Relaxo

No more Mexican than the water chestnuts it contains, this easily prepared dish is a California man's formulation for a relaxed brunch or an informal meal at any time. Try serving it with fresh fruit.

½ pound cooked ham, cut in thin
  strips
2 green onions, sliced
1 can (4 or 5 oz.) water chestnuts,
  drained and sliced
1 can (10½ oz.) condensed cream
  of mushroom soup
1¼ teaspoons Dijon-style mustard
1 cup shredded Swiss or Gruyère
  cheese
6 hard-cooked eggs, sliced
3 slices white bread, crusts cut off,
  spread on both sides with butter or margarine, then cubed

Arrange the ham strips in a layer on the bottom of a greased 8 by 8 by 2-inch casserole. Top the ham with a layer of half the green onions and water chestnuts. Combine the mushroom soup, mustard, and cheese; spread a third of the mixture over the onions and water chestnuts. Arrange egg slices evenly on soup mixture; sprinkle with the remaining onions and water chestnuts.

Cover with the remaining soup mixture. Put buttered and cubed bread on top. Bake uncovered in a 350° oven for about 40 minutes, or until heated through. Makes 4 to 6 servings.

# Bauernfrühstück (German Omelet)

¼ cup (⅛ lb.) butter or margarine
2 cups diced uncooked potatoes
¼ cup finely chopped onion
1 cup diced ham
¼ cup chopped parsley
6 eggs
¾ teaspoon salt
  Dash pepper
2 tablespoons half-and-half (light
  cream) or milk
½ cup shredded jack cheese

Melt butter in a 9 or 10-inch frying pan. Add potatoes and onion; cover and cook over medium-high heat, stirring occasionally to brown evenly, for about 20 minutes or until potatoes are tender and golden. Add ham and cook a few minutes longer until lightly browned. Sprinkle mixture with parsley. Reduce heat.

Beat together eggs, salt, pepper, and light cream until well blended. Pour egg mixture over potatoes and ham. Cover and cook until eggs are almost set (about 10 minutes), slipping spatula around edge of pan occasionally to allow egg mixture to run down. Sprinkle with cheese and cover again until cheese melts.

Cut in wedges to serve. Makes 4 to 6 servings.

# Caramelized Ham with Walnuts

2 ham slices, about 1 pound each
2 teaspoons vinegar
2 tablespoons dark brown sugar
½ cup chopped walnuts
2 tablespoons salad oil
2 cups boiling water
½ cup Sherry

Rub ham-slice surfaces with vinegar and sugar. Let stand 15 minutes. Lightly toast walnuts in oil in a large frying pan; remove with a slotted spoon.

Over high heat, quickly brown ham on both sides in the hot oil. (The caramelizing of the sugar is important to the color and flavor.) Add toasted walnuts, boiling water, and Sherry. Cook slowly uncovered until liquid has almost evaporated and ham is tender. Serve with nuts atop ham slices. A citrus salad makes a nice companion. Serves 6.

# Ham Hocks with Lima Beans

You make this ham-bean dish in a casserole, but it is really a thick soup.

2 cups dry lima beans
  Water
4 ham hocks
2 bay leaves
1 large onion, chopped
½ green pepper, sliced in rounds
1 can (1 lb.) tomatoes
1 can (8 oz.) tomato sauce
1 tablespoon salt
¼ teaspoon each pepper and ground
  cloves

Soak the beans in water to cover overnight (or if your time is limited, cover with water, boil briskly 2 minutes, remove from heat, and soak only 1 hour).

Without draining the beans, add ham hocks, bay leaves, and water—if needed to cover the beans again. Simmer about 1 hour or until beans are tender. Add the onion, green pepper, tomatoes, tomato sauce, salt, pepper, and cloves. Mix until blended and pour into a large (4-quart) casserole.

Cover and bake in a 350° oven about 1 hour, or until the meat is tender. Remove meat from beans; chop meat and return to soup before you serve it. Makes 6 servings.

# Sausage Oven Dinner

Any dinner as easy to prepare as this is sure to be a favorite. Cole slaw would be a compatible salad.

4 medium-sized apples
16 whole cloves
¼ cup each granulated sugar and
  brown sugar, firmly packed
1 cup water
¼ teaspoon each cinnamon and
  nutmeg
1 can (1 lb. 13 oz.) hominy, drained
16 to 20 (1 to 1½ lbs.) pork link
  sausages

Slice ends off apples and cut in half crossways. Core and stick 2 whole cloves in each half. Place in 9-inch-square baking pan. Combine the sugars, water, cinnamon, and nutmeg. Bring to a boil, stir 3 minutes until sugar is dissolved, and pour over apples. Place in a 400° oven 15 minutes before putting in the sausages and hominy.

Place hominy in a 9-inch-square pan. Set a wire cake rack over the pan and lay the sausages on the rack. Place in oven. Turn apples over in syrup.

Reduce oven to 350° and bake 1 hour, or until sausages are brown. (Sausages and apples should be turned about every 15 minutes.)

Drain hominy well. Mound in center of a platter, top with sausages, and ring with apples. Serves 4.

## Tourtière (Pork Pie)

The recipe is of French-Canadian origin. The name comes from the French word for a large tart pan; the pie has resemblance to the rich English meat pies.

3 pounds ground lean pork, crumbled
1 small onion, finely chopped
1 cup finely chopped celery
1 clove garlic, minced or mashed
¼ cup each chopped parsley and celery leaves
1 bay leaf
1 teaspoon salt
¼ teaspoon each mace and marjoram
⅛ teaspoon cloves
Dash cayenne
Tourtière Pastry (recipe follows)
2 slices French bread, crusts removed
2 tablespoons all-purpose flour
1 cup regular-strength beef broth

Sauté pork with onion, celery, and garlic until meat is browned and vegetables are soft, stirring occasionally. Blend in parsley, celery leaves, and seasonings. Simmer, uncovered, for about 30 minutes.

Meanwhile, line a 10-inch pie pan with half of the pastry. Whirl bread in blender to make fine crumbs; spread in bottom of pastry.

Remove bay leaf and drain fat from pork mixture. Stir in flour; add broth, stirring until well blended. Cook until thickened and bubbly. Spread meat mixture in pastry-lined pan.

Roll out remaining pastry for top crust; place over filling. Trim and flute edge of pastry; prick or slash in several places.

Bake in 425° oven for 15 minutes, reduce heat to 350°, and bake 25 to 30 minutes longer or until crust is well browned. Makes 8 servings.

**Tourtière Pastry.** Sift together 2 cups unsifted all-purpose flour and ¾ teaspoon salt. Cut in ½ cup lard and 2 tablespoons butter. Stir in 1 egg beaten with 3 tablespoons cold water; shape dough into ball. Chill at least 30 minutes; roll out.

## Ginger Pork Chops with Prunes

4 pork chops, about ½ inch thick
Salad oil or shortening
2 medium-sized onions, chopped
½ teaspoon ground ginger
1 teaspoon brown sugar
1 clove garlic, minced or mashed
¾ cup regular-strength beef broth
1 stick whole cinnamon
1 tablespoon soy sauce
4 teaspoons Worcestershire
12 large pitted prunes
1 tablespoon flour blended with ¼ cup cold water
Lemon wedges

Score the edges of the pork chops. In a frying pan that has a tight cover, lightly coat the bottom with oil, and brown the chops on both sides. Add the onion and sauté until lightly browned. Then add the ginger, brown sugar, garlic, broth, cinnamon, soy, and Worcestershire. Stir.

Set the prunes on top of chops, cover, and simmer very slowly for about 35 to 40 minutes, or until tender.

Remove the meat and prunes to a warm serving plate. Stir the flour and water paste into gravy and bring to boiling; cook, stirring, until thickened. Serve the gravy in a bowl. Garnish meat with lemon wedges. Makes 4 servings.

## Sweet-Sour Smoked Pork Chops

8 thick smoked pork chops
2 tablespoons butter or salad oil
1½ cups regular-strength chicken broth
¼ cup each cornstarch, soy sauce, and brown sugar
2 tablespoons vinegar
1 green pepper, sliced
8 small white onions, quartered
1 can (15 oz.) pineapple chunks, drained

Brown chops on both sides in butter. Add broth, cover, and simmer 20 to 30 minutes, or until tender. Blend together the cornstarch, soy sauce, brown sugar, and vinegar; add to pan juices with the chops, stirring until thickened. Add the green pepper, onions, and pineapple.

Cover and cook about 10 minutes, until vegetables are tender. Serves 8.

## Portuguese Spareribs in Garlic Wine

4 pounds country-style spareribs
1 cup cider vinegar
3 cups water
½ cup dry white wine
2 teaspoons each crushed whole coriander and crushed whole cumin
5 to 6 cloves garlic
¼ teaspoon cayenne
2 teaspoons salt
½ cup water
4 to 6 tablespoons water

Put spareribs in a deep non-metal bowl. Blend together vinegar, 3 cups water, wine, coriander, cumin, garlic cloves (slightly broken), cayenne, and salt. Pour liquid over pork. Cover and refrigerate for 4 days; turn meat in marinade several times during this period.

On the fourth day, remove meat from marinade and let drain for about 30 minutes. Discard all liquid. Arrange meat in a single layer in a roasting pan and add ½ cup water.

Bake uncovered in a 350° oven for 2 hours. Remove to a serving platter. Skim as much fat as possible from drippings, then add 4 to 6 tablespoons water to pan and bring to a boil, scraping free all the browned particles. Serve separately in a sauce dish. Makes 4 servings.

## Finger-lickin' Spareribs

6 pounds country-style spareribs
½ cup each Sherry and water
1 teaspoon salt
⅛ teaspoon pepper
¼ lemon, sliced thin
½ cup finely chopped onion
1 teaspoon each chile powder and celery seed
¼ cup each vinegar and Worcestershire
1 cup catsup
½ cup brown sugar
2 cups water

In a large frying pan, brown spareribs (without flour). Then add Sherry and ½ cup water and cook, covered, for 1 hour. In another pan, combine all sauce ingredients and cook for 1 hour.

Let spareribs cool in liquid long enough so you can skim off fat. Then remove spareribs and drain.

Lay drained spareribs in large shallow casserole or roaster. Cover with the sauce and bake 1 hour in a 300° oven. Makes 6 servings.

---

# Poultry

---

## Lemon Chicken

6 to 8 pieces of broiler-fryer chicken (breasts, legs, thighs)
1 whole lemon
⅓ cup flour
1½ teaspoons salt
½ teaspoon paprika
¼ cup salad oil or shortening
2 tablespoons brown sugar
1 lemon, thinly sliced
1 cup regular-strength chicken broth
2 sprigs fresh mint

Wash chicken and drain on paper towels. Grate the peel from the lemon and set aside; cut lemon in half and squeeze the juice over the pieces of chicken, rubbing each piece with the juice. Shake in a paper bag with the flour, salt, and paprika. Brown chicken slowly in the salad oil. Arrange in casserole or baking pan.

Sprinkle grated lemon peel over the chicken, add the brown sugar, and then cover with the thinly sliced lemon. Pour in the broth and place the mint over the top of the chicken.

Cover and bake in a 375° oven until chicken is tender (40 to 45 minutes). Remove mint before serving. Serves 6 to 8 if chicken pieces are large.

## Almond Chicken Baked in Cream

1 large broiler-fryer chicken (about 3½ lbs.), cut up
Flour
1 teaspoon each celery salt, paprika, and salt
½ teaspoon each curry powder, crushed oregano, and freshly ground pepper
6 tablespoons melted butter or margarine
¾ cup sliced almonds
1½ cups half-and-half (light cream)
½ cup sour cream
3 tablespoons fine dry bread crumbs blended with 1 tablespoon melted butter

Coat chicken pieces with flour. Blend celery salt, paprika, salt, curry powder, oregano, and pepper with butter; coat chicken pieces in seasoned butter. Arrange in a single layer in a baking dish.

Sprinkle evenly with almonds. Pour half-and-half between pieces.

Bake, covered, in a 350° oven for 45 minutes. Uncover; spoon about ½ cup sauce from the pan into the sour cream and mix. Pour evenly over chicken. Sprinkle evenly with buttered crumbs. Bake uncovered about 15 minutes longer, or until tender. Makes 6 servings.

## Chicken Armenian

A similar recipe from an Armenian restaurant was printed in *Sunset Magazine* in the early 1940's. Since then chickens have changed—they are fatter and more tender. The recipe has been revised to produce the same delicately flavored results.

¼ to ⅓ cup butter
2 broiler-fryer chickens (about 2⅓ pounds each), each cut in 4 pieces
1 large onion, thinly sliced
1 clove garlic, minced or mashed
1 cup tomato juice
½ cup Sherry
1 teaspoon paprika
1¼ teaspoons salt
Pepper to taste
Armenian Pilaf (recipe on page 69)

Melt ¼ cup (⅛ lb.) butter in a large frying pan and fry the chickens on both sides until light brown. Place skin side down, side by side, in a large shallow baking pan or broiler pan.

Fry the onion in the remaining butter, adding more if necessary, until limp and golden; add the garlic, tomato juice, Sherry, and paprika to the pan; and heat just to the boiling point. Pour over the chicken. Sprinkle the chicken with the salt and pepper.

Bake uncovered in a 400° oven for 45 minutes or until light reddish-brown, turning the chicken at the end of the first 20 minutes. Baste with pan juices several times during last 25 minutes of cooking. Serve with Armenian Rice Pilaf, spooning some of the pan juices over the chicken and rice. Serves 4 generously.

## Chicken Sauté

3½ pound broiler-fryer chicken, cut in serving-sized pieces
Flour
About ¼ cup olive oil or salad oil
1 clove garlic, minced or mashed
½ pound mushrooms, thinly sliced, or 1 can (6 or 8 oz.) sliced mushrooms, drained
2 tablespoons chopped parsley
1 cup dry white wine
Salt and pepper to taste
½ teaspoon crumbled rosemary or marjoram (optional)

Coat chicken pieces with flour. Heat the oil in a large frying pan and sauté chicken in it until golden brown on all sides. Remove chicken to a baking pan.

Sauté garlic and mushrooms in the remaining oil until limp. Add parsley, wine, salt and pepper to taste, and herbs if desired. Pour over chicken. (At this point you may re-frigerate and bake later.)

Bake uncovered in a 350° oven for about 45 minutes or until tender, basting frequently. Serves 4.

## Chicken, Artichoke & Mushroom Casserole

- 1 broiler-fryer chicken (about 3 lbs.), cut up
- 1½ teaspoons salt
- ¼ teaspoon pepper
- ½ teaspoon paprika
- 6 tablespoons butter or margarine
- 1 can (1 lb.) artichoke hearts, drained
- ¼ pound mushrooms, sliced
- 2 tablespoons flour
- ⅔ cup regular-strength chicken broth
- 3 tablespoons Sherry
- ¼ teaspoon dried rosemary

Sprinkle chicken with salt, pepper, and paprika. Brown in 4 tablespoons of the butter and remove to a cas-serole, which has a cover. Arrange artichoke hearts in between the chicken pieces.

Melt the remaining butter in the pan and sauté sliced mushrooms until barely tender. Sprinkle flour over the mushrooms and stir in broth, Sherry, and rosemary. Cook, stirring, until slightly thickened, then pour over chicken and artichokes.

Cover and bake in a 375° oven for 40 minutes or until chicken is tender. Serves 4.

## Chinese Five-spice Chicken

- 3 to 4 pound broiler-fryer chicken, cut into serving pieces
- ½ cup soy sauce
- ¼ cup chopped onion
- 1 clove garlic, crushed
- 1 teaspoon minced fresh ginger
- ½ teaspoon cinnamon
- ¼ teaspoon each ground allspice and crushed anise seed
- ⅛ teaspoon ground cloves
  Dash black pepper

Marinate the chicken pieces in the soy sauce mixed with the onion, garlic, and ginger for 3 to 4 hours.

Drain and arrange chicken in a shallow greased baking pan. Mix re-maining ingredients, sprinkle over chicken, and bake in a 325° oven about 1 hour, or until tender, turning once. Makes 4 servings.

## Pollo alla Cacciatora (Chicken Cacciatora)

- 2 broiler-fryer chickens (about 3 lbs. each), cut up
  Flour
- ¼ cup each butter and olive oil
- 2 small cloves garlic, mashed
- 2 medium-sized onions, chopped
- 1 can (1 lb. 12 oz.) Italian-style pear-shaped tomatoes, drained and chopped (reserve juice)
- 1 large green pepper, thinly sliced
- 2 tablespoons each chopped pimiento and chopped parsley
- 1½ teaspoons salt
- ½ teaspoon each crumbled thyme and oregano
- ¼ teaspoon pepper
- 1 bay leaf
- ⅔ cup dry red wine (or ½ cup chicken broth plus 2 table-spoons vinegar)
- 2 cups thinly sliced fresh mush-rooms
  Chopped parsley for garnish
  Hot buttered spaghetti (optional)

Dry the chicken and dredge lightly with flour. Heat the butter and oil in a large frying pan. Lightly brown the chicken on all sides, a few pieces at a time, removing the browned pieces to a plate.

Sauté the garlic and onion in the pan drippings just until tender. Return the chicken to the frying pan; add the tomatoes, green pepper, pimiento, 2 tablespoons parsley, salt, thyme, oregano, pepper, bay leaf, wine, and ⅓ cup of reserved tomato juice.

Cover and simmer gently over medium heat about 45 minutes, or until chicken is almost tender (or bake, covered, in a 350° oven about 45 minutes). Add the sliced mushrooms. Spoon some of the liquid around the chicken over the mushrooms.

Cover and continue cooking 10 to 15 minutes or until mushrooms are just tender. Remove chicken and veg-etables to a warm platter. Rapidly boil liquid until slightly reduced and thick-ened; pour over chicken. Garnish with parsley and serve with spaghetti. Makes 8 to 10 servings.

## Sesame Chicken

- 1 egg, slightly beaten
- ½ cup milk
- ½ cup flour
- ¼ cup sesame seed
- 1 teaspoon salt
- ¼ teaspoon freshly ground pepper
- ¼ cup (⅛ lb.) butter
- 1 broiler-fryer chicken (about 2½ lbs.), cut in pieces

Combine the egg and milk. In another small bowl, mix the flour, sesame seed, salt, and pepper. Melt butter in a baking pan. Dip chicken parts in milk mixture; then dip them in flour. Put chicken in pan, turning so that butter coats all sides well.

Bake uncovered in a 350° oven for 1 to 1¼ hours, or until tender, brown, and crisp. Makes about 4 servings.

## Baked Chicken in Mushroom Sauce

- 4 broiler-fryer chicken thighs and drumsticks, joined (or 8 thighs or drumsticks)
  Seasoned pepper or pepper
- 1 can (10½ oz.) condensed cream of mushroom soup
- 1 cup shredded mild Cheddar cheese
- 1 teaspoon whole sage, crushed
- 1 bunch green onions

Line a shallow baking dish (about 9 by 13 inches) with foil. Arrange chicken pieces in dish with skin side up. Sprinkle lightly with pepper.

Combine soup with cheese and sage. Finely chop green onion bulbs (save the tops) and add to soup mixture, stirring until well blended. Spoon over the chicken to coat all pieces.

Bake uncovered in a 400° oven for about 55 minutes, or until tender, basting several times with sauce in the pan.

To garnish, thinly slice some of the reserved onion tops and sprinkle over the chicken. Makes 4 servings.

## Chicken Divan

3 pounds chicken breasts
2 cups water
1 tablespoon salt
   Celery leaves
1 medium-sized onion, quartered
2 pounds fresh broccoli, or 2 packages (10 oz. each) frozen broccoli
2 cups white sauce (recipe on page 116), made with half milk and half chicken broth
½ cup Hollandaise sauce (canned or made by recipe on page 115)
¾ teaspoon salt
3 tablespoons Sherry
1 teaspoon Worcestershire
1 cup (¼ lb.) grated Parmesan cheese
½ cup whipping cream

Simmer chicken in water with the 1 tablespoon salt, celery leaves, and onion until tender, about 25 minutes. Let cool. Remove skin and bones and slice. Separate broccoli into flowerets, and cook in boiling salted water until tender, about 15 minutes.

Combine the white sauce, Hollandaise sauce, the ¾ teaspoon salt, Sherry, and Worcestershire. Butter a large, shallow casserole (about 3-quart size), and arrange broccoli, spoke-fashion, around the edge; place the remainder in the center of the dish. Sprinkle with half the grated cheese. Arrange sliced chicken on top.

Whip cream and fold into combined sauces; spoon over chicken. Sprinkle with remaining cheese.

Bake uncovered in a 400° oven for 20 minutes (be careful not to overcook). Then place about 5 inches under broiler and broil until lightly browned and bubbly. Makes 6 to 8 servings.

## Chicken Livers Lorraine

This is much tastier than a reading of the ingredient list might indicate. It's good for breakfast or brunch with scrambled eggs, and for other meals served with buttered egg noodles dressed up with toasted sesame seed.

½ pound chicken livers
¼ cup flour
   Salt
   Pepper
   Butter or margarine
⅔ cup mayonnaise
2 tablespoons Worcestershire

Coat livers generously with flour seasoned with salt and pepper. Sauté gently in butter for not more than 3 minutes on each side. Remove pan from heat and transfer chicken livers to warm serving dish.

Mix mayonnaise and Worcestershire in pan and scrape all bits of meat into it, then spoon it over chicken livers and toss gently so all are coated.

Put dish in oven that has been heated to 200° and then turned off. Keep in oven at least 15 minutes or up to 45 minutes. Makes 2 to 3 servings.

## Curried Chicken

Look for the frozen coconut milk called for in this recipe in Oriental food stores, if your supermarket doesn't carry it.

3 tablespoons each salad oil and curry powder
2 large mild onions, chopped
3 tart apples, peeled and chopped
3 cloves garlic, minced or pressed
2 tablespoons dry mustard
½ teaspoon ground ginger
1½ teaspoons salt
¼ teaspoon liquid hot pepper seasoning
1½ cups regular-strength chicken broth
1 can (12 oz.) frozen coconut milk
4 whole chicken breasts, skinned, split, boned, and cooked
   Condiments (suggestions follow)

Heat the oil in a 5-quart Dutch oven over medium heat. Add curry powder, onion, apple, and garlic; cook and stir until onion is limp. Stir in the mustard, ginger, salt, hot pepper seasoning, broth, and coconut milk.

Cover and simmer 30 minutes or until apples are tender.

Add cooked chicken breasts, cover, and simmer until chicken is heated. Transfer to a serving platter. Pass your choice of condiments. Makes 6 to 8 servings.

**Condiments.** Sliced green onions, shredded coconut, chopped peanuts, sliced bananas, and finely chopped chutney.

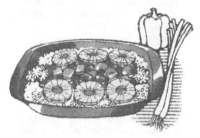

## Chicken in Casserole with Grapes

2 whole chicken breasts (about 2 lbs.), cut in halves
4 thighs
4 drumsticks
   Salt and pepper
   Flour
½ cup (¼ lb.) butter or margarine
¼ cup minced onion
¼ cup regular-strength chicken broth
¾ cup dry white wine
½ pound mushrooms, sliced
2 cups seeded Muscat grapes or Thompson seedless grapes

Sprinkle chicken with salt and pepper and coat lightly with flour. Heat 5 tablespoons of the butter in a frying pan and quickly brown chicken on all sides.

Arrange pieces closely together in a single layer in a large shallow baking pan. Add onion to butter in frying pan; cook until soft. Add chicken broth and wine; bring to a boil, then pour over chicken. Bake, covered, in a 375° oven for 40 minutes.

Meanwhile, sauté mushrooms in the remaining 3 tablespoons butter until tender. When chicken has cooked for 40 minutes, add mushrooms and grapes; continue baking, covered, for 8 minutes more, or until grapes are just heated. Arrange on a platter or serve from a chafing dish. Makes 6 to 8 servings.

## Chicken & Corn Casserole

2 tablespoons salad oil
1 large onion, chopped
1 large red bell or green pepper, seeded and diced
½ pound mushrooms, sliced
1 tablespoon chile powder
2 cans (1 lb. each) cream-style corn
1 can (8 oz.) tomato sauce
1 package (8 oz.) egg noodles, cooked and drained according to package directions
4 cups cooked chicken or turkey, torn into large pieces
½ cup grated Parmesan cheese
Chopped parsley

Heat oil in a wide frying pan over medium heat. Add onion, red or green pepper, mushrooms, and chile powder. Cook, stirring often, until onion is limp.

In a shallow 3-quart casserole, combine cooked onion mixture, corn, tomato sauce, cooked and drained noodles, and chicken. Stir gently until well blended. Evenly sprinkle Parmesan cheese over top. If made ahead, cover and refrigerate as long as 24 hours.

Bake, uncovered, in a 350° oven for 35 minutes (45 minutes, if chilled) or until hot throughout. Sprinkle with parsley. Makes 10 to 12 servings.

## Tetrazzini

Luisa Tetrazzini, considered the greatest coloratura soprano of the turn-of-the-century era, was the toast of San Francisco. The chef of the Palace Hotel, responsible for several other great classic dishes, created a chicken dish in her honor which has become popular.

Cooks have since adapted the dish to turkey and seafood.

6 tablespoons butter or margarine
5 tablespoons flour
2½ cups regular-strength chicken broth
1¼ cups half-and-half (light cream)
½ cup dry white wine
¾ cup shredded Parmesan cheese
¾ pound mushrooms, sliced
Salted water
8 ounces noodles (spaghetti or tagliarini)
3 to 4 cups slivers of cooked chicken or turkey

*Note:* A 3-pound chicken, stewed, will provide enough meat and broth.

Melt 2 tablespoons of the butter, mix in flour and gradually blend in the chicken broth, cream, and wine. Cook, stirring, for about 3 minutes after mixture starts to simmer. Stir in ½ cup of the Parmesan cheese. Measure out 1 cup of the sauce and blend in remaining cheese.

Melt the remaining 4 tablespoons butter in a pan, add mushrooms, and cook quickly, stirring, until lightly browned. Bring a quantity of salted water to boiling, add noodles and cook until just tender to bite, but not soft; drain.

Combine the large portion of sauce, mushrooms (save a few slices for garnish), hot noodles, and chicken; salt to taste. Turn into a large shallow casserole or individual casseroles. Spoon the 1 cup of sauce evenly over the surface and top with reserved mushroom slices.

Bake in a 375° oven until bubbling; allow 15 minutes for large casserole and about 8 minutes for individual ones. Broil tops until lightly browned. Makes 6 to 8 servings.

## Baked Chicken, Rice & Almonds

4 to 5-pound stewing chicken
Salt to taste
12 whole black peppers
1 bay leaf
1 large onion, quartered
1 stalk celery, sliced
Boiling water
1 cup uncooked long-grain rice
¼ cup (⅛ lb.) butter or margarine
¼ cup flour
1 cup milk
1 cup whipping cream or evaporated milk
Salt and pepper to taste
1 can (4 oz.) pimientos, chopped
1 cup slivered, blanched almonds
1 can (3 or 4 oz.) sliced mushrooms
⅓ cup fine dry bread crumbs blended with 2 tablespoons melted butter

Put chicken in a large kettle; add salt, black peppers, bay leaf, quartered onion, and celery. Barely cover with boiling water; cover and simmer for

2½ to 3 hours, or until chicken is tender. Let cool in the broth.

Remove chicken and cut into fairly large pieces. Strain broth and reserve.

Put 2 cups of the broth in a saucepan and heat to boiling; slowly sprinkle in rice. Cover tightly and cook over very low heat for about 25 minutes, or until all broth is absorbed.

Make a cream sauce by melting the butter in a saucepan, stirring in the flour until well blended, then gradually stirring in milk and cream. Cook, stirring constantly, until thickened. Season with salt and pepper.

In a greased large casserole put first a layer of rice, then a layer of chicken, then a layer of sauce; sprinkle with part of the pimiento, almonds, and mushrooms. Repeat until all ingredients are used, ending with rice.

Cover with crumbs and bake in a 375° oven 45 to 60 minutes, until browned.

If desired, chicken gravy may be made by thickening the remaining broth with a flour and water paste, cooking until thickened. Serves 8 to 10.

## Roast Chicken

A chicken of any size can be roasted.

To prepare, rinse with cold water, pat dry. Lightly salt the cavity.

If you use stuffing, spoon it lightly into the wishbone cavity. Fasten neck skin to back with a skewer; shape wings akimbo style (bring tips onto back).

Then spoon stuffing into body cavity. Close cavity by inserting skewers across the opening and lacing around them with cord.

Place chicken on a rack in a shallow uncovered pan; brush skin with oil. See following instructions for temperature and time.

The chicken is done when breast meat near the wing joint is fork-tender.

**Roasting Temperatures and Times.** Chickens 2 pounds and under take about 1 hour to cook in a 400° oven. Chickens over 2 pounds but less than 4 pounds take about 30 minutes per pound in a 375° oven. Chickens over 4 pounds take 25 minutes per pound in a 350° oven.

## Rice Pilaf Turkey Stuffing

½ cup pine nuts or slivered almonds
½ cup (¼ lb.) butter or margarine
1 cup finely chopped onion
3 cups uncooked long-grain rice
½ cup chopped parsley
¼ teaspoon each cinnamon and allspice
2 teaspoons salt
¼ teaspoon pepper
5 cups regular-strength chicken broth

Lightly toast the nuts in a 350° oven for 5 to 10 minutes. In a wide frying pan, heat butter and sauté onion about 5 minutes. Add rice and cook, stirring, over medium-high heat for about 4 minutes. Blend in parsley, cinnamon, allspice, salt, pepper, and toasted nuts.

In another pan boil broth and pour over rice mixture; stir lightly. Reduce heat to low, cover, and simmer until moisture is absorbed (25 minutes). Makes about 9 cups stuffing.

## Bread Stuffing for Poultry

This amount is sufficient for a large chicken. Make three times the recipe for a 12 to 14-pound turkey.

4 cups bread crumbs (see instructions)
1 small onion, minced
   Chicken giblets, minced (optional)
½ cup (¼ lb.) butter or margarine, melted
1 teaspoon salt
¼ teaspoon pepper
½ teaspoon marjoram, sage, or poultry seasoning
½ cup thinly sliced or diced celery
   Regular-strength chicken broth or milk

You can use white or whole wheat bread (crusts removed) or corn bread. The bread should be slightly dry— leave it out uncovered a few hours or dry in a 175° oven. Using a fork, tear it into coarse crumbs.

Sauté the onion and giblets in the butter until onion is limp and golden.

Sprinkle bread with the salt, pepper and herbs; add celery. Pour over the onion-butter mixture and toss lightly with a fork until ingredients are evenly distributed. Sprinkle the mixture with broth or milk, tossing with the fork, *just* until barely moistened.

Stuff the bird lightly. At no time mash the stuffing—keep it fluffy. Extra stuffing can be baked in a separate greased pan during the last 45 minutes the bird is roasting.

**Optional Ingredients.** ½ cup or more coarsely chopped walnuts, cooked sliced mushrooms, or chopped oysters; 1 cup chopped raw apple and ½ cup seedless raisins.

## Roast Turkey

Frozen birds should be completely thawed. To defrost in the refrigerator (recommended method), partially open or puncture the plastic wrapping. Allow about 24 hours for each 6 pounds for it to thaw. When the turkey is pliable, remove wrapping and giblets, and cover with a damp towel.

To thaw at room temperature, allow about 1 hour per pound of weight. When the turkey is pliable, proceed as for turkey thawed in the refrigerator.

To prepare thawed bird, remove any pinfeathers and wash inside and out. Dry inside and out.

If turkey is to be roasted *without* stuffing, rub the inside with salt, about ¼ teaspoon per pound. Don't salt otherwise, or salt very lightly

Allow about ½ to ¾ cup of stuffing per pound. Don't stuff the bird until just before you roast it. (See Bread Stuffing and Rice Pilaf Stuffing recipes on this page.)

Fill the neck cavity lightly with stuffing, then fasten the neck skin to the back of the turkey with a skewer.

Lightly stuff the body cavity (stuffing expands with cooking). Fasten opening with skewers and lace shut with cord. Leave legs free. Fasten wings to the body with skewers.

Brush or rub all over with salad oil, shortening, butter, or margarine. Place the turkey, breast up, on a rack in a shallow roasting pan. Insert a meat thermometer into the thickest part of the thigh. Put into a 325° oven (300° if over 24 pounds). Lay a sheet of foil (or cheesecloth dipped in oil) loosely over the bird when it starts to turn golden. The turkey is done when the thermometer in the thigh registers 185°. If you do not have a thermometer, test by moving the drumstick up and down. The turkey is done if the leg joint moves easily and the fleshy part of the drumstick feels soft.

**Approximate Roasting Time.** 6 to 8 pounds (ready to cook), 2 to 2½ hours; 8 to 12 pounds, 2½ to 3 hours; 12 to 16 pounds, 3 to 3¾ hours; 16 to 20 pounds, 3¾ to 4½ hours; 20 to 24 pounds, 4½ to 5 hours; and 24 pounds or more, about 14 minutes per pound.

## Turkey Leftovers

Two recipes elsewhere in this book make excellent use of leftover turkey.

Tetrazzini, on opposite page, can use meat from any part of the bird. Exotic Luncheon Salad, page 19, specifies white meat, but dark meat can be used.

## Turkey Enchiladas with Sour Cream

2 cans (4 oz. each) California green chiles
1 large clove garlic, minced
2 tablespoons olive oil or salad oil
1½ pounds fresh, ripe tomatoes
2 cups chopped onions
2 teaspoons salt
½ teaspoon oregano
½ cup water
3 cups shredded cooked turkey
2 cups sour cream
2 cups (½ lb.) shredded Cheddar cheese
⅓ cup salad oil or lard
12 corn tortillas

Rinse seeds from the chiles and chop; sauté with the garlic in the 2 tablespoons oil, heated. Peel and chop the tomatoes and add with the onions, 1 teaspoon of the salt, oregano, and water. Simmer slowly, uncovered, until thick, about 30 minutes; set aside.

Meanwhile combine the turkey with the sour cream, cheese, and remaining 1 teaspoon salt. Heat the ⅓ cup oil and dip the tortillas, one at a time, in the hot oil just until they become limp.

Fill them with the turkey mixture, roll up, and arrange them side by side and with seam sides down in a large shallow baking pan. Pour the chile sauce over the top and bake in a 350° oven until heated through, about 20 minutes. Makes 6 servings.

# Braised Turkey Legs

4 turkey legs, or 2 each legs and
   thighs (3 to 3½ lbs.)
¼ cup (⅛ lb.) butter or margarine
1 clove garlic, minced or mashed
1 large onion, sliced and separated
   into rings
1½ cups each diagonally sliced celery
   and carrots
½ cup each regular-strength chicken
   broth and dry white wine (or 1
   cup broth)
1 teaspoon seasoned salt
⅛ teaspoon pepper
1 tablespoon flour

Brown turkey in butter in a large frying pan. Add garlic, onion, celery, and carrots. Sauté until onions are soft. Stir in broth, wine, seasoned salt, and pepper.

Bring to a boil, reduce heat, cover, and simmer for about 2 hours or until turkey is very tender.

Remove turkey and vegetables to a warm serving dish with a slotted spoon. Stir a little pan liquid into flour to make a smooth paste. Over high heat, quickly reduce sauce in pan by about ⅓; blend in flour mixture and cook, stirring constantly, until thickened. Pour sauce over turkey and vegetables. Serve immediately. Makes 4 to 6 servings.

# Honey-glazed Roast Duckling

A bit of the tropics sneaks into this duckling, served with hot fruit, lime wedges, and mint sprigs.

4½ to 5-pound duckling
1 teaspoon salt
   Celery tops
   Quartered onion
   About ¼ cup water
¼ cup honey
1 tablespoon soy sauce
1 small papaya (optional)
4 slices fresh or canned pineapple
   Hot buttered rice
1 lime, cut in wedges
   Mint for garnish (optional)

Rinse duckling inside and out and pat dry; strip off all extra fat. Season the inside with salt and insert celery tops and quartered onion into the cavity. Tie legs and tail together; skewer neck skin to the back and tuck the

wing tips underneath. Prick the skin on the thighs, back, and lower breast with a knife.

Place, breast down, on a rack in an open roasting pan. Roast in a 375° oven for 30 minutes; turn breast up and continue roasting 1 hour longer. Pour off the fat in the roasting pan (or remove with bulb baster) and add about ¼ cup water to the pan to keep the drippings from sticking.

Reduce oven temperature to 325°. Blend together honey and soy and baste duckling; repeat basting and roast 30 minutes longer or until tender.

Peel papaya, halve, and scoop out seeds; cut into wedges. Arrange papaya and pineapple on a foil-lined baking pan and brush with the honey-soy glaze. Place under the broiler and heat until hot through.

Spoon hot steamed rice onto a large platter and arrange the duckling, cut into quarters, on top. Garnish with the hot fruit, lime wedges, and mint. Makes 4 servings.

# Roast Goose

Rinse goose with cold water; remove any large layers of fat from the body cavity. Wipe dry. Sprinkle inside with salt and pepper. Stuff the wishbone cavity with one or more of the following flavoring ingredients:

These can be very simple and should not be fatty. You can use quartered onions, sliced celery, toasted bread cubes, apple wedges, unpeeled orange wedges, pitted prunes, or combinations for flavoring.

Then, bring neck skin over back and fasten with a skewer. Turn bird over.

Also fill the body cavity with more flavoring ingredients. Insert skewers or toothpicks across the

opening and lace shut with cord. Loop cord around ends of drumsticks and draw them slightly in toward the body. Place, breast down, on a rack in an uncovered pan. Roast in a 325° oven. Prick skin from time to time to release accumulated fat.

Spoon or siphon off the fat in the pan during roasting. When it is about two-thirds done, as figured by the following roasting timetable, turn the bird breast up and finish roasting.

Basting is unnecessary; but you can use some non-fat glaze such as fruit juice, honey, soy sauce, or wine such as Sherry or Port. Baste during last 30 minutes of roasting only.

The drumstick meat should feel soft when the bird is done. An 8 to 12-pound bird will serve 6 to 8.

**Approximate Roasting Times.** Ready-to-cook weight 4 to 6 pounds, 2¾ to 3 hours; 6 to 8 pounds, 3 to 3½ hours; 8 to 10 pounds, 3½ to 3¾ hours; 10 to 12 pounds, 3¾ to 4¼ hours; 12 to 14 pounds, 4¼ to 4¾ hours.

# Roast Rock Cornish Game Hens

Season the cavity of each bird with salt, pepper, and a piece of butter. Insert giblets if you wish.

Skewer shut the neck and abdominal openings. Place in a shallow baking pan and tuck wing tips behind shoulders. Leave several inches between the birds.

Roast in a 350° oven for about 50 minutes, or until leg joint moves easily.

Baste as needed with melted butter; you will need about ¼ cup for 2 birds. You can season each ¼ cup butter with one or more of the following: ¼ teaspoon chile powder, ⅛ teaspoon ground ginger, ¼ teaspoon dry or ½ teaspoon prepared mustard, 1 teaspoon minced parsley, ½ teaspoon crushed tarragon or rosemary, or ¼ teaspoon rubbed sage. Allow 1 bird per person.

*To make a sauce,* for every 2 birds blend 1 to 1½ tablespoons flour with pan drippings; blend in 1 cup regular-strength chicken broth or half-and-half (light cream), or part broth and part cream. Cook, stirring, until thickened.

# Seafood

## Fish Baked in Wine

White fish, such as sole, halibut, and sea bass, and salmon are good this way. In fact, most fish can be used.

- 2 pounds fish fillets or slices
  Salt and pepper
- 1 large onion, sliced
- 1 cup dry white wine
- 3 tablespoons butter or margarine
- 2 large tomatoes, peeled and thinly sliced, or 1 can (8 oz.) tomato sauce
- ½ green pepper, sliced
- 2 teaspoons Worcestershire

Sprinkle fish with salt and pepper; cover with sliced onion; pour wine over all and marinate 30 minutes.

Melt butter in a large, shallow baking pan; remove fish and onion from wine and place in pan. Cover with tomatoes and green pepper; sprinkle with salt.

Bake uncovered in a 375° oven about 35 minutes, or until fish flakes with a fork and no longer is translucent in the center. Baste frequently with a mixture of the wine in which the fish was soaked and the Worcestershire. Serves 4 to 6.

## Baked Fish Fillets

This olive and caper-capped dish can be made with thick fillets of rockfish or turbot, or boneless chunks of sea bass or sturgeon.

- ¼ cup chopped onion
- 2 tablespoons olive oil
- 1 can (1 lb.) stewed tomatoes
- 2 teaspoons sugar
- ⅛ teaspoon ground cloves
- 2 pounds fillets or boneless chunks of rockfish, sea bass, sturgeon, or turbot (thaw if frozen)
  About 3 tablespoons melted butter or margarine
- ½ cup pimiento-stuffed Spanish olives, sliced
- 1 tablespoon capers, drained
- 1 tablespoon minced parsley

In a heavy saucepan or frying pan, sauté onion in olive oil until soft.

Add tomatoes, sugar, and cloves. Simmer, uncovered, stirring often, until thickened (about 15 minutes).

Pat fish dry. Brush all sides of fish pieces with melted butter and arrange in a shallow baking pan. Bake, uncovered, in a 400° oven until fish flakes when tested with a fork, about 10 to 12 minutes, depending on the fish used.

Lift fish to a warm serving platter and keep warm. Pour any fish juices into sauce. Remove from heat, stir in olives and capers, and spoon sauce over fish. Garnish with parsley. Makes 6 servings.

## Halibut Baked in Cream

Baked in a cup of cream along with sliced onion and tomato, halibut acquires a special flavor. Try serving with green beans and rice.

- 2-pound slice of halibut, or halibut steaks
  Salt and pepper
- 1 cup (½ pt.) whipping cream
- 1 can (1 lb.) sliced tomatoes, drained; or 2 thoroughly ripe tomatoes, peeled and sliced
- 1 medium-sized onion, thinly sliced
- 3 tablespoons butter

Lay halibut in a close-fitting, buttered, shallow baking dish or high-rimmed ovenproof platter. Sprinkle with salt and pepper and pour cream over it. Cover with canned tomatoes or with salted slices of fresh tomatoes; and top with onions. Dot with butter.

Cover dish tightly with foil. Bake in a 375° oven 20 minutes. Remove foil and spoon cream over fish. Continue baking about 15 minutes, basting occasionally with the cream, until fish flakes easily. Serves 4 to 6.

## Oven-crisp Trout

- 6 pan-dressed trout
  Salt and pepper
- ¼ cup (⅛ lb.) soft butter
- ½ cup finely chopped parsley
- 1 egg
- ¼ cup milk
- 1 teaspoon salt
- ¾ cup fine dry bread crumbs, toasted
- ½ cup shredded Swiss cheese
- 2 tablespoons butter

Thaw the fish if frozen, or clean fresh trout; wash and pat dry with paper towels. Sprinkle inside the fish lightly with salt and pepper.

Combine the butter and parsley and spread the mixture inside the cavity of each fish. Beat the egg together with the milk and salt. Also have ready the bread crumbs combined with the cheese.

Dip each fish in the egg mixture and then roll in the crumb-cheese mixture to coat each side well. Arrange the fish on a generously buttered shallow baking pan. If any of the crumb mixture is left, sprinkle it over the tops of the fish; dot with the 2 tablespoons butter.

Bake in a 500° oven for 15 to 20 minutes, or until fish are tender and browned. Serves 6.

## Best Baked Salmon

- 2-pound salmon fillet
  Salt and pepper
  Juice of ½ lemon
- 1 cup (½ pt.) sour cream
- 1 teaspoon grated onion

Place salmon in a shallow baking pan. Season well with salt and pepper; sprinkle with lemon juice. Mix the sour cream and onion, and spread over fish.

Bake uncovered in a 375° oven for 35 to 45 minutes, or until the fish flakes without being translucent in the center and the sauce in the pan has become rich and slightly brown. Serves 4 to 6.

## Salmon Supreme

A little bit of paprika and Worcestershire sauce accent the color of salmon in this simple recipe.

*(Continued on next page)*

¼ cup (⅛ lb.) butter or margarine
  Juice of 1 lemon
1 teaspoon Worcestershire
½ teaspoon salt
¼ teaspoon paprika
  Pepper
  About 2 pounds salmon steaks
  Minced parsley (optional)

In a shallow close-fitting baking pan, melt the butter and then add the lemon juice, Worcestershire, salt, paprika, and pepper. Coat the salmon in the butter and place the steaks side by side.

Bake in a 400° oven for 15 minutes; turn fish over and spoon some of the butter on top. Bake about 15 minutes more, or until fish flakes with a fork and no longer is translucent in the center. Serve sprinkled with parsley, if you like. Makes 3 to 4 large servings.

# Salmon Delight

1 egg
¾ cup milk
1 cup soft bread crumbs
1 can (1 lb.) salmon
1 cup shredded American or process Cheddar cheese
1 teaspoon grated green pepper
1 tablespoon lemon juice
½ teaspoon each celery salt and garlic salt
½ cup fine dry bread crumbs mixed with 2 tablespoons melted butter

Beat egg and milk together; add soft bread crumbs. Flake salmon, removing bones and skin. Combine bread-milk mixture, salmon, cheese, pepper, lemon juice, celery salt, and garlic salt.

Place in a 9-inch-square baking pan and top with buttered crumbs. Bake in a 350° oven for about 30 minutes. Serve plain, or with tomato sauce or white sauce containing chopped hard-cooked eggs (recipes on pages 119 and 116). Serves 4 to 5.

# Mushroom-baked Sole

1 medium-sized onion, finely chopped
¼ cup chopped parsley
1 cup sliced mushrooms (about 4 large)
¼ cup (⅛ lb.) butter or margarine
6 to 8 sole fillets (about 1½ lbs.)
  Salt and pepper
¼ cup dry white wine
½ cup half-and-half (light cream)
1 tablespoon flour
  Paprika and chopped parsley

Sauté onion, parsley, and mushrooms in 3 tablespoons of the butter for about 10 minutes, until onions are soft, stirring occasionally.

Place half the sole fillets, flat, in a greased baking dish (about 9 by 13 inches); sprinkle lightly with salt and pepper. Spread sautéed mixture evenly over sole; top with remaining fillets, and sprinkle with salt and pepper. Pour on wine; dot with remaining 1 tablespoon butter.

Bake uncovered in a 350° oven for 15 minutes. Remove from oven. Drain off pan liquid; reserve.

Gradually stir half-and-half into flour in a small pan; blend in fish liquid. Cook, stirring constantly, until thickened. Pour over fish. Bake for 5 minutes longer, until fish flakes easily with a fork. Serve sprinkled with paprika and parsley. Serves 4.

# Sole with Grapes

1 to 1½ pounds fillet of sole (4 to 6 medium-sized)
  Flour
  Nutmeg
  Salt
2 to 3 tablespoons butter
1 cup Thompson seedless grapes
½ cup whipping cream

Coat sole fillets with flour and shake off the excess. Sprinkle each fillet lightly with ground nutmeg and salt.

Melt 2 tablespoons butter in a wide frying pan over moderately high heat, and cook the fillets until a rich golden color on each side. Do not crowd pan—cook fillets in sequence, if necessary. Add 1 more tablespoon butter, if required. Transfer fillets to a warm dish; keep hot.

Add grapes to pan and swirl

about over high heat just until grapes are warm and a brighter green. Pour over the fish. Then stir the cream into pan and boil over highest heat, stirring, until a light golden color; drizzle over fish and serve at once. Makes 4 servings.

# Shellfish Casserole

1 cup vegetable-juice cocktail or tomato juice
1 cup mayonnaise
1 can (7 or 8 oz.) crab meat or 1 to 1½ cups fresh crab meat
1 can (about 5 oz.) shrimp or 1 cup small fresh shrimp (shelled and deveined)
2 cups cooked rice
⅓ cup finely chopped green pepper
  Salt and pepper to taste
2 tablespoons butter, melted
1 cup soft bread crumbs
½ cup slivered almonds

In a bowl, combine the vegetable juice and mayonnaise; mix until well blended. Stir in crab meat, shrimp, rice, green pepper, and salt and pepper to taste; mix just until ingredients are well distributed. Spoon into greased 2-quart casserole.

In small pan, add to butter the fresh bread crumbs and almonds. Mix with fork until crumbs are coated with butter. Spoon evenly over mixture in the casserole.

Bake in a 375° oven until bubbly and top is lightly browned. Serve immediately. Makes about 6 to 8 servings.

# Seafood Newburg

2 tablespoons butter or margarine
1 tablespoon each minced onion, minced parsley, and minced green pepper (optional)
1 cup sliced fresh mushrooms
2 tablespoons flour
2 cups (1 pt.) half-and-half (light cream)
  Salt, pepper, paprika, cayenne, and nutmeg
2 cups diced cooked lobster, crab legs, or whole shrimp
2 egg yolks
¼ cup Sherry

Melt the butter in a saucepan; add the onion, parsley, green pepper (if used), and mushrooms; cover and cook gently, stirring frequently, for 10 minutes. Blend in the flour and gradually stir in half-and-half. Cook, stirring constantly, until mixture is thickened and smooth. Add salt, pepper, spices as desired, and seafood. Heat, stirring constantly.

Beat egg yolks with the Sherry, blend in some of the hot cream sauce, and stir mixture into the pan. Cook, stirring constantly, about 1 minute or until thickened and hot (do not boil). Serve at once to 4 or 6 people.

Newburg may be served on toast, in patty shells, on toasted English muffins, or with steamed rice.

## Tuna & Noodles

¼ cup (⅛ lb.) butter or margarine
¼ cup flour
2 cups milk
2 packages (3 oz. each) cream cheese, or 1 cup shredded American cheese
  Salt, pepper, and Worcestershire to taste
1 package (8 oz.) thin noodles, cooked in salted water and drained
1 can (about 7 oz.) tuna, drained and flaked
1 can (6 or 8 oz.) sliced mushrooms (optional)
2 tablespoons minced pimiento (optional)

Make a sauce by melting the butter in a saucepan over low heat, stirring in the flour until blended, and gradually stirring in milk. Cook, stirring constantly, until thick. Crumble cream cheese and stir to melt in and blend (American cheese may just be mixed in). Season with salt, pepper, and Worcestershire.

Combine sauce, noodles, tuna, drained mushrooms, and pimiento. Turn into individual casseroles. Bake in a 375° oven about 20 minutes. Serves 4 to 6.

## Cracked Crab

Cold cracked Dungeness crab is a simple entrée that never fails to please when accompanied with mayonnaise (preferably homemade) or melted butter. For those times you want a change from the classic, a recipe follows for hot cracked crab in a spicy tomato sauce you can prepare from ingredients on hand.

Instructions follow for cooking a live crab, cleaning a cooked one, and cleaning a live one.

For each person, provide a Dungeness crab of 1¾ to 2¼ pounds, with perhaps 1 extra for every 5 hearty eaters.

*To Cook Live Crab:* Bring to boiling about 2 gallons water and 2 tablespoons salt in a large kettle. Immerse 2 or 3 crabs at a time, head first, in the water, pushing down. Cover and simmer about 20 minutes. Remove with tongs and drain well. Cook additional crab in the same water.

*To Clean Cooked Crab:* Remove the legs by twisting them to break free. Break off appendages on the bottom side of the crab body and then pull off the shell back.

Scoop out and save the crab butter, if desired. The butter is the creamy fat inside the back shell. In an uncooked crab it is mustard-colored, but pale yellow after cooking. Some or all of the butter may be mixed into the mayonnaise you serve with the crab, if you like.

Remove and discard all soft material and gills from body. Rinse well and drain. Tap back of knife with a mallet to cut body cavity into several chunks. Crack legs with a mallet or nutcracker.

*To Clean Live Crab:* Caution and courage are necessary, plus a heavy knife or cleaver and a mallet or hammer. Rubber gloves can protect you from cuts and scratches. Work on a board.

Grasp the crab from the rear by the last 1 or 2 legs of either side (beware of the front claws). Place crab with back on cutting board. Place the knife in the direct center of the crab between the legs. Hit the back of the knife a hard, quick blow to kill the crab instantly.

Twist off each of the legs, scrub, and rinse well. Pull off the back shell and clean as described above for a cooked crab.

**Cracked Crab in Spicy Tomato Sauce.** In a large pan (at least 5 quarts) combine 2 cups tomato catsup with 1 cup water, 3 whole cloves, 1 teaspoon seasoned salt, ½ teaspoon thyme, ½ teaspoon sugar, 1 tablespoon Worcestershire, 1 teaspoon prepared horseradish, and 1 bay leaf. Heat slowly, stirring occasionally, until it simmers.

Clean and disjoint either live or boiled crabs (2 large ones, about 2 pounds each). Crack the shells of each piece (or ask the fish dealer to do it). Rinse well in cool water.

Add the crab pieces to the simmering sauce; bring back to simmering, reduce heat and cook about 25 minutes if the crab was uncooked to start. (If boiled crab is used, cook just until heated through.) Serve with the sauce that clings to shells and extra sauce in small bowls at each place. Makes 2 to 4 servings.

## Crab Casserole with Artichoke Hearts

3 tablespoons butter or margarine
3 tablespoons flour
1 cup milk
½ cup dry white wine or regular-strength chicken broth
½ cup shredded medium-sharp Cheddar or Swiss cheese
2 teaspoons Worcestershire
2 packages (8 oz. each) frozen artichoke hearts, cooked and drained
4 hard-cooked eggs, sliced
¾ pound crab meat
2 tablespoons grated Parmesan cheese

Melt butter in saucepan, blend in flour, and gradually stir in 1 cup milk. Cook over low heat until thickened, stirring constantly. Slowly blend in wine or broth. Add cheese and Worcestershire; cook until cheese melts.

Spoon a little sauce in the bottom of 1½-quart casserole. Alternate layers of artichoke hearts (reserving a few for garnish), eggs, and crab meat. Make a middle layer of half the sauce, and top casserole with remaining sauce. Sprinkle with cheese.

At this point you can refrigerate the casserole if you like. Bake uncovered in a 350° oven for about 30 minutes, or until thoroughly heated. Garnish with artichoke hearts just before serving. Makes 4 or 5 servings.

## Scalloped Crab

- 12 to 16 ounces crab meat (about 2 to 2½ cups)
- 1½ cups soda cracker crumbs
- 2 tablespoons butter or margarine
  Salt, pepper, and paprika to taste
  About 1 cup milk
  Lemon wedges

Arrange a layer of crab in the bottom of a greased 1½-quart casserole or 9-inch-square baking pan. Sprinkle generously with cracker crumbs; dot with butter and season with salt (if crumbs are salted, salt sparingly), pepper, and paprika.

Repeat layers until all crab meat and crumbs are used, then add enough milk to moisten well. Bake in a 375° oven about 30 minutes. Serve with lemon wedges. Serves 5.

## Broiled Crab Sandwiches

- 1 pound (about 2 cups) fresh crab meat, or 2 cans (about 7 oz. each) crab meat
- 1 bunch green onions (include part of green tops), thinly sliced
- 3 tablespoons lemon juice
- ¼ cup chile sauce or catsup
- 5 tablespoons mayonnaise
- 8 slices toast or 8 English muffin halves, lightly buttered
- 2 eggs, separated
- ⅓ cup shredded mild Cheddar or Swiss cheese

Turn the crab meat into a bowl; pick over and discard any pieces of shell.

Add the onions, 2 tablespoons of the lemon juice, chile sauce or catsup, and 1 tablespoon of the mayonnaise. Mix with a fork until blended.

Spread on the buttered toast or English muffins.

In another bowl, blend together the remaining 4 tablespoons mayonnaise and 1 tablespoon lemon juice; blend in egg yolks and cheese. Beat egg whites until they hold firm peaks; fold into mayonnaise mixture. Spread over sandwiches, covering crab filling.

Arrange sandwiches on broiler rack set about 5 inches below a preheated broiler; broil until browned, 3 to 4 minutes. Makes 8 sandwiches.

## Scallops La Jolla

Prepared with lots of sliced mushrooms, these scallops are a treat. Cream and cheese give them an irresistible appeal.

- 3 pounds raw scallops
- 1½ cups dry white wine (or ⅓ cup lemon juice with 1¼ cups water)
- 2 tablespoons lemon juice
- ¾ pound fresh mushrooms, sliced
- 1 green pepper, diced
- ¼ cup (⅛ lb.) butter or margarine
- ½ teaspoon salt
  Dash pepper
- ¼ cup flour
- 1 cup diced Swiss cheese
- ½ cup grated Romano or Parmesan cheese
- 1 cup heavy cream, whipped
  About 2 tablespoons butter for topping
  Paprika

Wash and drain scallops. Bring wine and the 2 tablespoons lemon juice almost to boiling; add scallops, mushrooms, and green pepper; simmer slowly for 8 minutes. Drain, saving liquid.

Melt the butter; blend in salt, pepper, and flour until bubbly; gradually stir in liquid in which scallops were cooked; cook until thickened. Add Swiss cheese and ¼ cup of the grated cheese; stir over low heat until blended. Remove from heat and fold in whipped cream; stir in scallop mixture.

Divide among 6 or 10 buttered individual baking dishes. Sprinkle with rest of grated cheese, dot with butter; sprinkle with paprika. Broil until browned. Makes about 6 main-dish servings, or 10 appetizer servings.

## Shrimp Bordelaise

- 1 large carrot, minced
- 1 medium-sized onion, minced
- 2 stalks celery, minced
- ¼ cup (⅛ lb.) butter
  Pinch thyme
- ½ bay leaf
  Salt and pepper to taste
- 2 pounds (about 30) large raw shrimp in shells
- ¼ cup brandy
- 2 cups dry white wine
- 3 egg yolks

Put carrot, onion, and celery in a heavy pan with the ¼ cup butter, thyme, and bay leaf. Simmer until the vegetables are tender. Discard bay leaf and season with salt and pepper.

Wash shrimp. Split shells down the back with scissors; remove sand veins. Loosen shells, but do not remove. Put unshelled shrimp in a saucepan. Warm brandy, pour over shrimp, and set aflame. When flame dies, add vegetables and wine. Cover and cook 10 minutes.

Remove shrimp with slotted spoon to a rimmed platter; keep warm. Beat egg yolks with a little of the hot sauce in a cup; then stir into the sauce. Cook, stirring constantly, over very low heat just until thick (don't boil). Pour over shrimp. Makes 4 to 6 servings.

## Shrimp Casserole

- 1 pound mushrooms, sliced
- ¼ cup (⅛ lb.) butter or margarine
- 1 pound cooked shrimp, shelled and deveined
- 2 cups cooked white or brown rice
- 1 cup whipping cream or undiluted evaporated milk
- ⅓ cup catsup
- 1 teaspoon Worcestershire
  Salt, pepper, and onion juice to taste
- ½ cup to ¾ cup shredded American or mild Cheddar cheese

Sauté mushrooms slowly in butter for about 10 minutes, or until tender. Mix mushrooms, shrimp, and rice. Combine cream, catsup, Worcestershire, salt, pepper, and onion juice; add to first mixture, mix lightly but well.

Turn into a greased casserole, sprinkle with cheese, and bake in a 350° oven about 45 minutes. Serves 8.

## Hawaiian Shrimp Curry

You don't have to go to the Islands to capture their flavor—just reach for the curry and some condiments. You can use cream or milk instead of coconut milk.

6 tablespoons butter or margarine
1 tablespoon curry powder
2 teaspoons ground ginger
  Pepper to taste
¼ cup finely minced onion
¼ cup water
7 tablespoons flour
2 cups milk
1 cup unsweetened coconut milk (recipe on page 120), or use frozen coconut milk
1½ tablespoons lemon juice
  Salt
1½ pounds cooked, peeled, and deveined shrimp
1½ cups rice, steamed
  Curry Condiments (suggestions follow)

Melt butter in a large saucepan; add curry powder, ginger, and pepper. Cook, stirring constantly, over low heat until the spice gives off a nutty odor and darkens slightly in color. Be careful not to scorch the spice, or it will ruin the curry.

Add onion and cook, stirring often, until it is soft and begins to turn golden. Add water and simmer uncovered until moisture has evaporated and onion is very soft. Remove pan from heat.

Dissolve the flour in the milk, pour into pan. Also add coconut milk. (At this point, if you want a smooth sauce, you can pour the mixture into a blender and whirl until smooth.) Return pan to low heat and cook, stirring often, until sauce thickens.

Add lemon juice, salt to taste, and shrimp. Heat, stirring, just until the shrimp are thoroughly hot. Serve with the steamed rice and a selection of the suggested Curry Condiments in small bowls. Serves 5 to 6.

**Curry Condiments.** Chopped peanuts, chopped crisp bacon, mango chutney or chopped preserved ginger, chopped green pepper or onion (or a mixture of the two), melon balls, papaya chunks, diced banana (coated with lemon juice), and toasted coconut (sprinkle shredded coconut thinly over a baking sheet and place in a 350° oven for 2 or 3 minutes).

## Clam Pudding

12 square salted soda crackers
1 cup milk
1 can (7 or 8 oz.) minced clams, including liquid
¼ cup (⅛ lb.) butter or margarine, melted
1 tablespoon each minced onion and minced green pepper (optional)
⅛ teaspoon salt
  Pepper to taste
2 eggs, well beaten

Crumble the crackers into a bowl; add milk, clams, and their liquid. Soak crackers until very soft, 10 or 15 minutes. Add the melted butter, onion, green pepper, salt, pepper to taste, and beaten eggs. Mix thoroughly.

Pour into a buttered 1-quart baking dish or 9-inch-square baking pan. Bake in a 325° oven 30 to 40 minutes until center is firm and the top delicately browned. Serves 4.

## Clam & Spinach Ring

Stiffly beaten egg whites give this molded entrée its lightness.

3 tablespoons butter or margarine
3 tablespoons flour
1 cup undiluted evaporated milk
1 can (7 to 8 oz.) minced clams, drained (reserve liquid)
  Salt and pepper to taste
3 eggs, separated
1 cup finely chopped, cooked spinach (well drained)
  Hot, buttered, steamed rice
  Paprika

Melt butter and stir in flour; add milk and clam liquid and cook, stirring constantly, until mixture is thickened and smooth; season with salt and pepper. Remove from heat and add beaten egg yolks. Let cool for 10 minutes.

Beat egg whites stiff. Add spinach and clams to cooled sauce; fold in stiffly beaten egg whites. Pour into a well-greased ring mold. Set in a pan of hot water and bake in a 350° oven about 1 hour, or until set. Remove from oven and let stand about 5 minutes.

Turn out on a platter and fill center with buttered rice. Dust with paprika. Serves 6.

## Clamcakes

These little cakes can also be served as a hot or cold appetizer.

2 eggs
½ cup cottage cheese with chives
¼ cup sour cream
⅓ teaspoon salt
1 tablespoon melted shortening or oil
2 tablespoons dried sweet pepper flakes
1 can (about 7 to 8 oz.) minced clams, with juice
  About ⅔ cup flour
  Sour cream or yogurt for topping

In a bowl stir all ingredients, except sour cream or yogurt for topping, until completely mixed.

Pour dollar-sized patties on a greased griddle and cook on each side until brown. Serve hot or cold, with sour cream or yogurt. Makes 36 dollar-sized clamcakes.

## Savory Fried Oysters

Roll each oyster in flour, coat with mayonnaise, and roll in fine soda cracker crumbs. Sauté in butter until a golden brown. Sprinkle with salt and pepper to taste, and serve with lemon wedges.

## Oysters à la Osage

About 2 cups oysters (cut if large)
⅛ teaspoon freshly grated nutmeg
⅛ teaspoon salt
¼ teaspoon pepper
6 slices bacon, cooked crisp and crumbled
1 cup shredded Swiss cheese
1 cup whipping cream
½ cup coarsely broken salted soda crackers
2 tablespoons butter

Grease a shallow 1½-quart baking dish. Arrange the oysters and their juices in the dish, grate nutmeg over them, and sprinkle on salt and pepper. Sprinkle on the bacon and cheese, pour the cream over all, then cover with cracker crumbs and dot with butter.

Bake uncovered in a 400° oven for 20 minutes. Makes about 4 servings.

## Hangtown Fry

12 to 18 medium-sized oysters,
    drained
    Salt and pepper
    Fine soda cracker crumbs
1 egg, beaten
2 to 4 tablespoons butter or mar-
    garine
6 eggs
¼ cup milk
    Fried ham, crisp bacon, or
      browned link sausages
    French-fried potatoes

Season oysters with salt and pepper. Dip them in cracker crumbs, then in the beaten egg, and again in cracker crumbs. Fry to a golden brown on one side in 2 tablespoons of the butter in a large frying pan.

While oysters are browning, beat the 6 eggs with the milk and season with salt and pepper. Turn the browned oysters over, add more butter if necessary, and pour in the egg mixture. Cook slowly until eggs are set and lightly browned. During the cooking, lift the cooked eggs with a spatula to let the uncooked part run underneath.

To serve, fold in half and slip onto a hot platter. Garnish with meat and accompany with French-fried potatoes. Serves 4.

## How to Prepare a Whole Abalone

Bring live abalone home in a sack soaked with salt water. They will live 2 or 3 days if kept in a cool, damp environment. Leave the abalone in the shells overnight, if freshly gathered, to let the muscles relax. Then shuck and trim according to the instructions which follow.

Most of the body is a large muscle-mass called the foot—the edible portion. The sole is the side of the foot that attaches to a rock. The front end of the shell is where you see the respiratory holes. The other end is the heel.

*To Shuck:* Pull back abalone foot and force an abalone iron, stout knife tip, or wooden wedge between the meat and shell. Move the tool around until the muscle falls free. Grasp foot firmly and carefully pull from heel of shell, leaving viscera (including stomach) attached to shell. Stomach

should remain attached; but, if not, cut it loose from the foot, being careful not to break the sac. Wash foot meat in cold water.

Trim lacelike dark portions off around the edges of meat and trim ¼ inch off the sole (trimmings may be used for chowder or fritters). Let meat stand until muscle relaxes.

Hold meat down firmly and cut across grain in about ¾-inch slices. Pound each slice evenly and lightly with the smooth side of a wooden mallet until limp and velvety.

*To Cook:* Slash edges of pounded steaks to prevent curling; sprinkle with salt and pepper. Dust each with flour, dip in beaten egg, and then coat in fine dry bread crumbs. Fry in butter or olive oil over medium-high heat *just* 30 seconds to 1 minute on each side, turning only once. It is important to cook the abalone very briefly, or it will toughen. Serve with lemon wedges and a sprinkling of minced parsley if you wish.

## Fried Squid

Quite a few *Sunset Magazine* readers really go for squid. They mentioned this recipe as their favorite way to turn that ugly animal into a tender delicacy.

1 to 2 pounds fresh or thawed frozen
    squid
    Garlic salt
    Equal portions fine dry bread
      crumbs and flour (about 1 cup
      total for 1 lb. squid)
    Salad oil for frying

To clean each squid, hold under running water and pull off and discard the speckled membrane that covers the mantle or hood. Pull the transparent shell or sword out from inside the hood and discard it. Pull the body from the hood; strip off and discard the material that easily separates from the body (including the ink sac). Squeeze out and discard contents of the hood, and rinse hood inside.

Pop out parrot-like beak from between the legs (all eight of them). Slice hood crosswise in ¼ to ½-inch-wide strips, forming rings.

Drain squid on paper towels, then sprinkle with garlic salt. Coat squid with mixture of crumbs and flour; shake off excess.

In a medium-sized deep sauce-

pan, heat 1½ inches salad oil to 375°. Cook rings a spoonful at a time for about 30 seconds or until lightly browned. *Squid gets excessively tough if overcooked.*

Drain rings on paper towels, keeping warm. Bring oil back to 375° before each addition. Cook body with legs last, also for about 30 seconds; it tends to spatter fat so have a lid handy to cover pan loosely. Serve at once.

One pound of squid makes 2 or 3 main-dish servings or appetizers for 6.

## Other Main Dishes

## Cheese Boraks

These turnovers of flaky pastry are served throughout the Middle East as appetizers or main dishes. The recipe has been adapted to cheese readily available in America and to the convenience of freezing.

2 cups flour
1 teaspoon each salt and baking
    powder
½ cup milk
1 egg
¼ cup melted butter, margarine, or
    shortening
½ cup each thinly sliced green onion
    tops and minced parsley
1 tablespoon melted butter or mar-
    garine
½ teaspoon salt
⅛ teaspoon white (or black) pepper
1 pound soft jack or Swiss cheese,
    coarsely shredded (about 4 cups)
    Shortening or salad oil for frying

To make pastry, sift and measure flour; sift again, into a bowl, with salt and baking powder. Make a well in center of dry ingredients. Beat together milk and egg; pour into well and stir with a fork until thoroughly mixed. Stir in melted butter, 1 tablespoon at a time; turn dough onto a lightly floured board and knead until smooth, about 3 or 4 minutes. Shape dough into a ball, cover with a bowl or waxed paper, and let rest on floured board for 30 minutes.

To make filling, sauté onion and parsley in butter until soft. Season with salt and pepper. Remove from heat and mix in cheese.

To assemble, roll dough on floured board until ⅛ inch thick. Cut in 14 to 16 rounds, each 5 inches in diameter (use a 1-pound coffee can as a cutter); reroll dough as necessary to use scraps.

Spoon equal amounts of cheese mixture in center of each round and pack cheese down slightly. Moisten rim of each round of dough with water, fold dough over cheese filling, and press edges together, forcing out any air pockets inside the boraks. Seal edges by pressing together with a fork or your fingers.

Heat shortening or salad oil (about 1 inch deep) to 375°; fry the boraks until golden on each side. Drain on paper towels. (Be careful not to pierce boraks—cheese will leak out if you do.)

Serve immediately, or refrigerate and reheat in a 350° oven for 10 to 15 minutes. If you freeze them, allow to stand at room temperature about 30 minutes, then reheat in oven. Makes 14 to 16.

## Cheese Soufflé

    3  tablespoons each butter or mar-
         garine and flour
    1  cup milk
         Dash cayenne
    ¼  teaspoon dry mustard
    ½  teaspoon salt
    1  cup shredded Cheddar cheese
         (mild to sharp) or Swiss cheese
    4  to 5 eggs, separated

In a saucepan melt butter and stir in flour. Blend in milk, cayenne, dry mustard, and salt; cook, stirring, until thickened. Add cheese and continue stirring until melted. Remove from heat and beat in egg yolks.

Whip whites until they hold short distinct peaks. Fold about half the whites thoroughly into the sauce; fold in remaining whites as thoroughly as you like.

Pour into well-buttered 1½-quart soufflé dish (or 4 to 6 dishes of 1-cup size). Draw a circle on surface an inch or so in from rim with tip of knife or spoon. Bake in a 375° oven; a 1½-quart soufflé takes 35 minutes; individual 1-cup soufflés take 20 minutes. Makes 4 servings as an entrée, 6 as a first course.

## Stuffed Finger Rolls

    4  hard-cooked eggs, chopped
    1  can (4½ oz.) chopped ripe olives,
         drained, or ½ cup chopped ripe
         olives
    2  tablespoons each minced green
         pepper and minced parsley
    2  tablespoons shredded mild Cheddar
         cheese
    2  tablespoons minced onion
         (optional)
         Mashed garlic or garlic powder to
         taste (optional)
    2  tablespoons each catsup and salad
         oil
         Salt to taste
    8  finger rolls, soft French rolls, or
         hot-dog buns
         About ⅓ cup shredded mild Ched-
         dar cheese

Place in a bowl the eggs, olives, green pepper, parsley, the 2 tablespoons cheese, and onion and garlic if used. Add catsup and oil. Blend well.

Cut off the tops of the finger rolls or French rolls. Scoop out the centers with a fork. (If hot-dog buns are used, they will already be split. Scoop some of the center out of both halves.)

Fill the rolls with the egg mixture and sprinkle the filling of each with part of the ⅓ cup cheese. Replace tops. Wrap each stuffed roll with foil. The rolls may be prepared as much as 3 hours ahead and refrigerated until 15 minutes before you plan to heat them.

To heat, place rolls on a baking sheet and put in a 375° oven for about 25 or 30 minutes. Serve immediately. Makes 8 snack servings or 4 servings if a main-dish sandwich.

## Cheese Custard

    ½  cup (¼ lb.) butter or margarine
   12  slices white bread (crusts re-
         moved, lightly toasted)
    2  packages (8 oz. each) sliced proc-
         ess Cheddar cheese
    3  eggs, well beaten
    2½ cups milk
    ¾  teaspoon salt
    ½  teaspoon Worcestershire
    ¼  teaspoon dry mustard

Set oven at 325°. Place butter in a 9 by 9-inch baking pan or 2½-quart casserole and put in oven until butter melts. Remove from oven and quickly dip sliced bread in butter to coat one side of each. When all slices are coated and butter is mostly used up, cut the bread into 1-inch cubes. Spread remaining butter up sides of pan to grease thoroughly.

Place a layer of sliced cheese in the bottom of the pan; sprinkle with buttered bread cubes. Repeat two more times.

Mix beaten eggs, milk, salt, Worcestershire, and mustard. Pour over the cheese and bread. Bake in the 325° oven for about 1 hour. Makes 6 to 8 rich servings.

## Classic Omelet

This will make one omelet, which is enough for one person as a main dish.

    3  eggs
    1  tablespoon water
    ¼  teaspoon salt
         Dash pepper
    1  tablespoon butter

Break eggs into a bowl; add water, salt, and pepper. Beat vigorously with a fork or a wire whip for about 30 seconds, or until yolks and whites are blended.

In an omelet pan (an 8-inch pan is best), heat butter on medium-high heat until it bubbles, browns ever so slightly, and gives off a rich, nutlike odor. Pour beaten eggs all at once into heated pan. They should begin to set and turn opaque around the edges almost immediately.

Slide pan rapidly back and forth on the burner, keeping omelet in motion and free from the bottom of the pan to avoid browning and sticking.

As soon as bottom of the omelet

begins to set, slip a thin spatula under the edges and let the uncooked eggs flow into the center of the pan. Don't worry about tearing; the liquid egg mends the damage. Your omelet is done when the egg no longer runs freely but the top still looks liquid and creamy.

Hold omelet pan with your left hand and tilt pan sideways, lifting left side off the heat. With your right hand, use spatula to guide omelet as you fold the left side (about ⅓) over the center. Holding the omelet over a hot serving dish, shake the pan and ease with the spatula until the omelet beings to slip out. With a quick downward flick of the left wrist, let the folded section of the omelet fall over its extended edge on the hot plate.

## Stuffed Eggs au Gratin

6  hard-cooked eggs
¼  cup (⅛ lb.) butter or margarine, melted
½  teaspoon Worcestershire
¼  teaspoon prepared mustard
2  or 3 green onions, minced (including part of the green tops)
1  teaspoon minced parsley
3  slices boiled ham, minced
   Salt and pepper to taste
2  cups white sauce (recipe on page 116)
   Chopped parsley or chives
1  cup shredded American or mild Cheddar cheese

Cut the eggs in half lengthwise and slip out the yolks into a bowl. Mash the yolks with the butter, Worcestershire, and mustard. Mix in minced onion, parsley, and ham; season to taste with salt and pepper.

Fill the egg whites with this mixture, and arrange in the bottom of a buttered casserole or deep pie pan.

Pour white sauce over the eggs (add chopped parsley or chives to the sauce for color) and sprinkle cheese over the top. Bake in a 325° oven for 25 to 30 minutes. Serves 3 or 4.

## Corn Tamale Pie

This not only is one of the oldest *Sunset* recipes (from the early 1930's), but one of the most simple to make.

2  cans (15 oz. each) tamales in sauce
1  can (1 lb.) whole-kernel corn
1  can (8 oz.) tomato sauce
2  tablespoons chopped ripe olives (optional)
2  eggs, beaten
   Salt and pepper to taste
½  cup shredded mild Cheddar cheese

Drain sauce from tamales; remove wrappers (discard sauce and wrappers). Drain corn in a wire strainer, pressing lightly to remove excess moisture.

Place tamales in a bowl; break apart and mash with a fork. Add corn, tomato sauce, olives if used, and beaten eggs. Mix thoroughly and add salt and pepper to taste.

Pour into a buttered 9-inch-square baking pan or 9-inch pie pan, sprinkle with the cheese, and bake in a 350° oven for about 1 hour, or until the center of the pie is firm and the top golden brown. Makes 5 to 6 servings.

## Chiles Rellenos

This is the traditional version with simple cheese filling and the puffy coating restaurants often use.

2  cans (4 oz. each) California green chiles
½  pound jack cheese
   Flour
   Coating (recipe follows)
   Tomato Sauce (recipe follows) or canned Mexican red chile sauce, heated
   Garnish of shredded jack cheese or sliced green onion tops

Drain chiles, rinse, and cut a slit down the side of each; gently remove seeds and pith inside.

Stuff chiles with sticks of cheese (about ½ inch wide, ½ inch thick, and 1 inch shorter than the chile). Have flour ready in a shallow pan. Roll each

chile in flour to coat all over; gently shake off excess. Prepare coating (batter) just before you want to fry the chiles. Coat and fry according to the instructions with the coating recipe.

Top with heated sauce and garnish with cheese or onion. Makes 3 or 4 servings.

**Coating.** Separate 3 eggs. Beat the whites until they form soft peaks. Beat yolks with 1 tablespoon water, 3 tablespoons flour, and ¼ teaspoon salt until thick and creamy; fold into whites.

Heat about 1½ inches of oil in a wide frying pan over medium heat. Dip stuffed chiles into the fluffy batter, place on a saucer, and slide into the hot oil. When the bottoms are golden brown, gently turn using a spatula and fork, and cook other side—3 to 4 minutes per side. Drain on paper towels.

**Tomato Sauce.** Sauté 3 tablespoons finely chopped onion and 1 minced clove of garlic in 1 tablespoon butter until golden. Stir in 1 can (15 oz.) Spanish-style tomato sauce, ⅓ cup water, ¼ teaspoon salt, and ¼ teaspoon crumbled oregano. Simmer for 15 minutes. Makes 2½ cups.

## Baked Chiles Rellenos

This is not the traditional Mexican dish. It is a simple casserole which puffs up something like a soufflé. Undoubtedly it has become a favorite because it provides the good traditional flavors with much less work.

6  eggs, separated
1  tablespoon flour
¼  teaspoon salt
¼  teaspoon pepper, or to taste
1  can (4 oz.) California green chiles, seeded and rinsed
½  pound mild Cheddar or jack cheese, sliced
   Canned or bottled green chile salsa or hot Mexican tomato sauce (optional)

Beat egg whites until stiff. Mix flour, salt, and pepper with egg yolks; then fold in beaten egg whites and pour half of this mixture into a greased 2 by 9 by 13-inch baking dish.

Slit each chile lengthwise down one side and lay flat over egg batter and then cover with cheese slices. Pour rest of egg mixture over cheese. Bake 25 minutes in a 325° oven. Cut in 3-inch squares and serve with sauce if desired. Serves 4.

## Green Chile & Cheese Pie

Quiche Lorraine Pastry Shell (recipe on this page)
1½ cups shredded jack cheese
1 cup shredded mild Cheddar cheese
1 can (4 oz.) California green chiles, seeded, pith removed, and chopped
1 cup half-and-half (light cream)
3 eggs, slightly beaten
¼ teaspoon salt
⅛ teaspoon ground cumin (optional)

Partially bake pastry shell prepared according to recipe for about 12 minutes, or until pale gold. Sprinkle all of the jack cheese and half the Cheddar over the bottom. Distribute chiles over cheese. Beat half-and-half with eggs, salt, and cumin until blended; pour into the shell. Sprinkle remaining Cheddar lightly over pie filling.

Bake in a 325° oven for 40 minutes or until center of pie is set; shake gently to test. Let stand about 15 minutes before cutting. Serve hot or cold. Makes 6 main-dish servings.

## Sour Cream Enchiladas

Salad oil
1 can (10 oz.) enchilada sauce
12 corn tortillas
2 cups (1 pt.) sour cream
1 cup chopped green onions (including some tops)
½ teaspoon ground cumin
4 cups (about 1 lb.) shredded long-horn Cheddar cheese
Sour cream
Chopped green onions

In a small frying pan heat about ½ inch salad oil over high heat. Have ready a pad of paper towels, the enchilada sauce in a shallow pan (pie pan), and an empty shallow pan. Fry the tortillas one at a time, turning once, just until soft; it takes 15 seconds or less. Transfer immediately to paper towels to drain briefly, then dip on all sides in the enchilada sauce,

and then put in the empty shallow pan.

Repeat procedure for each tortilla, using an assembly-line technique. When all the tortillas are sauced, blend the 2 cups sour cream, 1 cup chopped onion, the cumin, and 1 cup of the shredded cheese.

In a casserole about 8 by 10 inches (or 9 by 9 inches) overlap two tortillas at one end of the pan, allowing part of the tortillas to extend over the edge of the pan. Spread about 6 tablespoons of the filling down the center of the tortillas, and fold the extending section down over the filling.

Repeat this technique to fill remaining tortillas, placing them side by side and completely covering the pan bottom; use all the filling. Sprinkle the remaining 3 cups cheese evenly over the top.

You can cover and chill the casserole for 3 or 4 hours if you want to make it ahead. Bake casserole uncovered in a 375° oven for 20 minutes.

Garnish with more sour cream spooned down center of enchiladas and sprinkle with more chopped green onions. Makes 6 servings (8 to 12 as a side dish).

## Quiche Lorraine

Pastry Shell (recipe follows)
10 slices cooked bacon, chopped
1¼ cups (about 6 oz.) diced or thinly sliced Swiss cheese
4 eggs
1¼ cups whipping cream
½ cup milk
Freshly grated (or ground) nutmeg

Evenly distribute bacon and cheese over the bottom of the baked pastry shell. Beat eggs until blended, then mix well with cream and milk. Pour over cheese and bacon. Grate nutmeg over the filling.

Bake in a 325° oven for about 40 minutes or until custard appears firm when pan is gently shaken. Makes 6 servings.

Pastry Shell. Measure 1½ cups unsifted all-purpose flour into a bowl. Add ⅛ teaspoon salt and ½ cup (¼ lb.) butter, cut in small pieces. With pastry blender or fingers, break the butter into very small particles, no larger than small peas. Beat 1 egg and add to flour mixture, blending well with a fork. Shape mixture into a compact ball.

Roll dough out on a well-floured board to fit a deep 9-inch or a 10-inch pie pan; turn to prevent sticking. Gently fit into pan (if it tears, just press broken edges together) and flute the rim decoratively. If you use a 9-inch pan, build up a high rim so that the shell can hold all the filling. Prick bottom in about 12 places with a fork.

Bake in a 425° oven for 10 minutes or until lightly browned. Cool. (Wrap airtight if it is to stand any length of time.)

## Italian Mushroom Sauce for Spaghetti

1 cup dried mushrooms (about 4 or 5 large ones)
1 cup water
½ cup minced parsley
1 medium-sized onion, finely chopped
1 small dried, hot, red chile, crumbled
5 large cloves garlic, minced or mashed
¼ pound ground beef chuck (optional)
½ cup olive or salad oil
½ teaspoon thyme
1 cup regular-strength beef broth
1 large can (1 lb. 12 oz.) solid-pack tomatoes
1½ teaspoons salt
½ teaspoon pepper
1 package (8 to 12 oz.) spaghetti or macaroni, any type, cooked
Grated Parmesan or Romano cheese

Rinse mushrooms, and soak in water until soft (about 20 minutes). Meanwhile cook parsley, onion, chile, garlic, and meat (if used) in oil until onion is transparent. Drain mushrooms, reserving liquid, and chop fine, discarding tough portions. Add to mushrooms and liquid the sautéed mixture along with thyme, broth, tomatoes (break up whole tomatoes), salt, and pepper.

Cover and cook slowly for 1½ hours. Add additional beef broth if needed, to give sauce desired consistency. Adjust salt and pepper to suit taste.

Serve over hot, cooked, and thoroughly drained spaghetti. Sprinkle with cheese. Makes 6 to 8 servings.

# Spaghetti Francisco

This baked dish is especially popular because it is one of those meal-in-one combinations you can assemble ahead and heat when time to serve.

Undoubtedly this dish has been encountered at many a church social and fund-raising event. Quantities to use for serving large groups are included.

1 package (8 oz.) spaghetti, cooked in salted water and drained
¼ cup salad oil
1 can (1 lb.) cream-style corn
2 slices bacon, diced
1 small onion, chopped
½ medium-sized green pepper, chopped
½ can (8 oz.) tomato sauce
½ can (10¾ oz.) condensed tomato soup
1 can (8 oz.) mushrooms, drained
Salt and pepper to taste
½ pound American or mild Cheddar cheese, shredded

Mix cooked spaghetti, oil, and corn.

Sauté bacon, onion, and green pepper until bacon is crisp. Add sauce, soup, mushrooms, and salt and pepper to taste. Bring to a boil. Pour over spaghetti mixture and mix.

Sprinkle a 9 by 13-inch baking pan with a little cheese, pour in spaghetti mixture, and top with remaining cheese. Bake in a 350° oven until thoroughly hot and bubbly. Serves 6 to 8.

**Quantities for 10 to 15 people.** Use 1 package (1 lb.) spaghetti; ½ cup oil; 2 cans (1 lb. each) cream-style corn; 4 slices bacon; 2 small onions; 1 green pepper; 1 can (8 oz.) tomato sauce; 1 can (10¾ oz.) condensed tomato soup; 2 cans (8 oz. each) mushrooms;

salt and pepper to taste; and 1 pound American or mild Cheddar cheese.

**Quantities for 35 to 40 people.** Use 3 pounds spaghetti; 1 cup oil; 4 cans (1 lb. each) cream-style corn; 12 slices bacon; 3 medium-sized onions; 3 green peppers; 3 cans (8 oz. each) tomato sauce; 2 cans (10¾ oz. each) condensed tomato soup; 3 cans (8 oz. each) mushrooms; salt and pepper to taste; and 2 pounds American or mild Cheddar cheese.

# Potato Gnocchi with Veal Sauce

You make little dumpling-like pasta called *gnocchi* for this Italian dish and top them with sauce.

3 cups finely mashed unseasoned potatoes (directions follow)
1½ cups unsifted regular all-purpose flour
1½ teaspoons salt
1 tablespoon olive oil
2 eggs, beaten slightly
Flour
Boiling, salted water
2 to 3 tablespoons melted butter
Veal Sauce (recipe follows)
1½ cups shredded Parmesan or dry jack cheese, or ¾ pound thinly sliced teleme cheese

Cook peeled potatoes until tender in unsalted water and drain thoroughly, then rub through a fine wire strainer. Or, prepare instant dehydrated mashed potatoes by heating the amount of water called for to make 6 to 8 servings; stir in potatoes as directed.

Measure the mashed potatoes into a bowl and add the 1½ cups flour, salt, and oil; blend with a fork. Add eggs and blend thoroughly. Turn dough out onto a moderately well-floured board and knead gently about 15 times.

Cut off a piece of dough and roll on a very lightly floured board into a cord ⅜ inch thick. Cut in 1¼-inch lengths. Roll each in the center lightly with your forefinger to give a bow shape. Set gnocchi, not touching, on a lightly floured pan.

When all are shaped, cook by dropping about ⅓ at a time into about 3 quarts of boiling, salted water. Cook for 5 minutes after they return to surface of water (stir gently if they

haven't popped up in about 1 minute). Keep water at a slow boil.

Remove with a slotted spoon, draining well. Place in a shallow-rimmed pan and mix gently with the melted butter. Cover tightly with foil and keep in a warm place while you cook the remaining gnocchi.

You can hold the gnocchi in a slightly warm oven (150° or lower) for as long as 3 hours, if well covered. Flavor is best if they don't cool after cooking.

To serve, arrange about half in a wide, shallow, rimmed, ovenproof dish and top with about half the hot veal sauce and half the cheese. Top with remaining gnocchi, sauce, and cheese. Heat in a 375° oven for about 10 minutes until piping hot. Broil top lightly if desired. Makes 6 main-dish or about 8 first-course servings.

**Veal Sauce.** Combine ½ cup dried mushrooms with 1 cup cold water and let stand at least 30 minutes. Mince pork fat or bacon to make ¼ cup and place in a large frying pan with 3 tablespoons olive oil. Finely chop ¾ pound fat-free, boneless veal. Mince 1 medium-size onion, finely dice 1 carrot, and finely chop 2 stalks celery. Add meat and vegetables to pan. Cook over medium heat, stirring, until vegetables are soft.

Rinse mushrooms and cut in pieces if large; add to meat mixture. Also add 1 can (8 oz.) tomato sauce, 1 can (1 lb.) whole tomatoes (break apart in pan), 1 cup dry red wine, 1½ teaspoons salt, ¼ teaspoon allspice, and dash of pepper.

Simmer about 2 hours uncovered, or until reduced to about 4 cups.

# Other Main Dishes Using Pastas

Elsewhere in this book are other main-dish pasta recipes.

Those containing ground beef are all on page 32: Italian-Style Macaroni Casserole, More, Lasagne Belmonte, and Noodle Medley.

On pages 71 and 72 are dishes you will usually serve as starchy accompaniments, but which can be light main dishes: Noodles Romanoff, Macaroni Mousse, Macaroni & Cheese, Tomato Sauce for Spaghetti (to which you can add seafood), and Pasta with Sauce Suprême.

# Vegetables & Other Accompaniments

## Vegetables

### Butter-steamed Fresh Vegetables

Boiling vegetables is out of favor with knowing cooks. The butter-steaming method (using very little liquid) is quicker and preserves more of the natural flavor, color, and food value.

A few simple rules must be observed: Use a frying pan at least 10 inches wide. Slice or chop vegetables in small pieces—so they will cook quickly. Cook no more than 5 cups of prepared vegetables at a time over the highest possible heat.

To cook most of the vegetables, you use only butter or margarine, water, and the usual salt-and-pepper seasoning. However, in a few cases other fat (such as bacon drippings) is used and broth may be substituted for the water.

Cooks who get accustomed to butter-steaming their vegetables say they no longer would cook them any other way.

Butter, margarine, or other fat
  suggested in specific directions
  following
Vegetables, cut or chopped according
  to specific directions
Water (unless broth is specified)
Salt and pepper to taste

**BASIC INSTRUCTIONS.** Use a wide electric frying pan set at highest heat or a wide frying pan over direct high heat. (Pan should be *at least* 10 inches in diameter and have a cover.) Melt butter (it will begin to brown slightly almost as it melts). Add vegetables, then add water. Stir and cover. Cook at high heat, stirring occasionally, until vegetables are cooked and liquid is gone. Season with salt and pepper, and serve immediately.

*Note:* See quantities and cooking times for each vegetable following, plus seasoning variations. Use preceding basic instructions *unless* changes are suggested in the following recipes.

**Artichokes.** Use 2 tablespoons butter and 5 cups frozen, thawed artichoke hearts or very small fresh artichokes prepared this way: Cut off top half of fresh artichoke, peel off tough outer leaves, trim stem end, cut in quarters, and scoop out any fuzzy choke. Add 6 tablespoons water. Total cooking time is 6 minutes for frozen artichokes or 8 minutes for fresh. Makes about 5 servings.

*Artichokes with Tarragon.* Add ½ teaspoon tarragon along with the vegetable. Add 2 tablespoons lemon juice with the salt and pepper.

**Asparagus.** Use 2 tablespoons butter, 1 pound asparagus (snap off tough ends and cut in thin slices), and 2 tablespoons water. Total cooking time is 2 to 3 minutes. Makes about 3 servings.

*Asparagus with Pine Nuts and Cheese.* Add ¼ cup pine nuts (toasted if you like) along with the salt and cook, stirring, for about 30 seconds more. Pour into serving bowl, and sprinkle with ½ cup shredded Swiss cheese; stir until blended.

**Beets.** Use 2 tablespoons butter, 4 cups thinly sliced beets, and 6 tablespoons water (add 2 or 3 tablespoons more if needed during cooking). Total cooking time is 5 to 6 minutes. Makes 4 to 6 servings.

*Beets with Orange and Sour Cream.* Add 2 tablespoons orange juice and ¼ teaspoon grated orange peel during the last 2 minutes of cooking. Season with salt and pepper and blend in ½ cup sour cream.

**Beet Tops with Bacon.** In the wide frying pan, cook 4 slices diced bacon until browned; drain off all but 2 tablespoons of the drippings. Add 4 cups cleaned, slightly damp, chopped

beet tops; ¼ cup regular-strength beef broth; and ¼ cup half-and-half (light cream). Cover and cook over medium heat for about 5 minutes, stirring occasionally. Add 2 to 3 teaspoons tarragon vinegar and simmer rapidly, uncovered, until liquid is slightly reduced. Season with salt and pepper. Makes 3 servings.

**Broccoli.** Trim tough ends from 1½ pounds broccoli. Slice stems and leaves thinly; set aside the small blossoms. Follow basic directions using 2 tablespoons butter, the broccoli stems and leaves, and 4 tablespoons water. Cover and cook, stirring occasionally, for 4 minutes. Stir in the broccoli blossoms and 3 more tablespoons water. Cover and cook 3 minutes longer, stirring frequently. Season and serve. Makes 4 or 5 servings.

*Broccoli with Cream Cheese Sauce.* Just after cooking and seasoning with salt, add 1 package (3 oz.) cream cheese, diced, and stir until melted. Sprinkle with 1 tablespoon lemon juice.

**Cabbage.** Use 2 tablespoons butter, 5 cups finely sliced cabbage (1 small head), and ¼ cup water. Total cooking time is 3 to 4 minutes. Makes 4 or 5 servings.

*Dilled Cabbage.* Add ¼ teaspoon dill weed along with the cabbage. Just before serving stir in ¼ cup mayonnaise. Sprinkle with more dill weed.

**Carrots.** Use 2 tablespoons butter, 3 cups thinly sliced carrots (10 or 12 slender carrots), and 3 tablespoons water. Total cooking time is 5 minutes. Makes 4 or 5 servings.

*Cream-glazed Anise Carrots.* Add ¼ teaspoon anise seed along with carrots. After 5 minutes cooking, add 3 tablespoons whipping cream and cook uncovered, stirring, until liquid is almost gone.

**Cauliflower.** Use 3 tablespoons butter, 4 cups thinly sliced cauliflower, and 6 tablespoons water. Total cooking time is 5 minutes. Makes 4 to 6 servings.

*Cauliflower with Egg Sauce.* Cook as directed and pour into serving bowl; blend with 2 finely chopped hard-cooked eggs and ½ cup warm Hollandaise sauce (canned or freshly made). Makes 4 to 6 servings.

**Celery.** Use 2 tablespoons butter, 4 cups thinly sliced celery, and 2 tablespoons water. Total cooking time is 3 minutes. Makes 4 to 6 servings.

*Parmesan Celery.* Just before serving, sprinkle with 4 tablespoons shredded Parmesan cheese.

**Corn.** Use 2 tablespoons butter, 4 cups corn cut from cob (or frozen whole kernel corn, thawed), and 4 tablespoons water. Total cooking time is 3 minutes for frozen corn and 4 minutes for fresh. Makes 4 to 5 servings.

*Cream-glazed Spiced Corn.* Add ¾ teaspoon ground coriander or ¼ teaspoon ground cloves along with the vegetable. After corn is cooked, remove cover and add ¼ cup whipping cream, stirring until liquid is almost gone.

**Crookneck Squash.** Use 2 tablespoons butter, 4 cups thinly sliced crookneck squash (about 8 or 10 small squash), and 6 tablespoons water. Cooking time is 4 minutes. Makes 5 servings.

*Cream-glazed Crookneck Squash.* After cooking, remove cover, salt to taste and add 5 tablespoons whipping cream. Cook, stirring, until liquid is almost gone. Sprinkle with coarse ground pepper.

**Dandelion Greens with Ham.** Lightly brown 1 tablespoon butter or margarine in the wide frying pan. Stir in 4 cups cleaned, chopped dandelion greens and 2 tablespoons regular-strength beef broth; cover and cook over medium-low heat for about 10 minutes, stirring occasionally. Add 2 tablespoons whipping cream and ¼ cup diced cooked ham. Simmer rapidly uncovered until liquid is almost gone. Salt and pepper. Makes 3 or 4 servings.

**Green Beans.** Use 2 tablespoons butter, 1 pound green beans cut in 1-inch lengths, and 5 tablespoons water. Total cooking time is 7 minutes. Makes 4 or 5 servings.

*Cream-glazed Green Beans.* After cooking for 7 minutes, remove cover, salt to taste, and add 5 tablespoons whipping cream. Cook, stirring, until liquid is almost gone.

**Kale with Sausage.** Break apart 1 pound sausage and brown in the wide frying pan. Drain off all but 2 tablespoons of the drippings. Stir in 1 bunch (about 1¼ pounds) chopped kale and ½ cup regular-strength beef broth. Cover; cook over medium-low heat for about 15 minutes, adding more broth if needed. Makes 6 to 8 servings.

**Leeks.** Use 2 tablespoons butter, 3 cups thinly sliced leeks (white part only), and ¼ cup water. Total cooking time is 3 minutes. Makes 4 to 5 servings.

*Leeks with Bacon.* Add 4 slices cooked and crumbled bacon just before serving.

**Mustard Greens with Bacon.** In a wide heavy pan cook 4 slices diced bacon until browned. Drain off all but 2 tablespoons of the drippings; stir in 4 cups chopped mustard greens and 2 tablespoons regular-strength beef broth. Cover and cook over medium heat, stirring occasionally, for about 10 minutes. Makes 4 servings.

**Parsnips.** Use 4 tablespoons butter, 4 cups thinly sliced parsnips, and 6 tablespoons water (add 2 more tablespoons during cooking if necessary). Total cooking time is 6 minutes. Makes 4 to 6 servings.

*Caraway Parsnips.* Add ½ teaspoon caraway seed during the last 3 minutes of cooking time.

**Peas.** Use 2 tablespoons butter, 4 cups freshly shelled peas (or frozen peas, thawed), and ¼ cup water. Total cooking time is 2 minutes for frozen peas and 3 minutes for fresh ones. Makes 5 or 6 servings.

*Peas with Bacon.* Follow basic directions for butter-steaming, with this change: Cook 4 slices chopped bacon in pan until meat browned; set meat aside. Add to drippings 4 cups freshly shelled peas and 6 tablespoons water. Cover and cook, stirring frequently, for 3 minutes. Season with salt and pepper, and sprinkle with bacon.

**Fruited Rhubarb (or Red) Chard.** Immerse in boiling salted water 1 pound cleaned rhubarb chard; cook until water returns to a vigorous boil. Drain thoroughly, and chop. Melt 2 tablespoons butter or margarine in a wide heavy pan. Add ¼ cup raisins and ½ cup diced tart apple. Sauté, stirring, until apples are lightly glazed. Add chard and 3 tablespoons water or meat broth; cover and cook over medium heat, stirring, for about 7 minutes. Blend in 2 tablespoons raspberry jelly and 1 to 1½ teaspoons prepared horseradish. Makes 4 servings.

**Piquant Spinach.** Melt 2 tablespoons butter in a wide, heavy pan. Add 2 pounds washed and slightly damp spinach; stir well. (No liquid is necessary if spinach is damp.) Cover and cook over medium heat just until wilted. Blend in 2 teaspoons sugar and 3 tablespoons whipping cream. Simmer rapidly, stirring, until liquid is almost gone. Add 1 to 2 tablespoons vinegar and salt. Sprinkle with nutmeg. Makes 5 or 6 servings.

**Swiss Chard.** Melt 2 tablespoons butter or margarine in a wide heavy pan. Add the thinly sliced stems from 1 pound cleaned Swiss chard. Cover and cook, stirring occasionally, for 3 or 4 minutes. Stir in the chopped leaves and cook, covered, for 3 or 4 minutes more. Season with salt and pepper. Makes 3 or 4 servings.

*Swiss Chard with Eggs (Main Dish).* Add 4 beaten eggs and cook until set.

**Turnips.** Use 2 tablespoons butter, 4 cups thinly sliced turnips, and 5 tablespoons water. Total cooking time is 4 to 5 minutes. Makes 5 or 6 servings.

*Turnips with Soy.* Season with 1½ teaspoons soy sauce instead of salt.

**Turnip Tops with Bacon.** In a wide, heavy pan cook 4 slices diced bacon until browned. Drain off all but 2 tablespoons of the drippings; stir in 4 cups chopped turnip tops and 2 tablespoons regular-strength beef broth. Cover and cook over medium heat, stirring occasionally, for about 10 minutes. Makes 4 servings.

*Turnip Tops with Cheese.* Just before serving, stir in 2 tablespoons shredded sharp cheese until melted.

**Zucchini.** Use 2 tablespoons butter, 4 cups thinly sliced zucchini (about 8 small zucchini), and 6 tablespoons water. Total cooking time is 5 minutes. Makes about 5 servings.

*Zucchini with Cheese.* After cooking, remove cover and sprinkle on 3 tablespoons crumbled blue cheese or 4 tablespoons shredded Parmesan cheese; stir until cheese is melted. Season with salt and pepper.

## Golden Medley

¼ cup (⅛ lb.) butter or margarine
1 medium-sized onion, finely chopped
¼ cup chopped green pepper
3 tablespoons flour
2 cups milk
1 tablespoon finely chopped pimiento
1 teaspoon salt
¼ teaspoon pepper
1 cup shredded Cheddar cheese (about ¼ lb.)
1½ cups diced cooked potatoes
1½ cups thinly sliced cooked carrots

Melt butter in a saucepan. Add onion and green pepper; sauté until onion is golden brown. Blend in flour until smooth. Add milk, and cook, stirring, until smooth and thickened. Remove from heat; stir in pimiento, salt, pepper, and ½ cup of the cheese.

Arrange alternate layers of potatoes and carrots in a lightly greased 1½-quart casserole; add sauce; stir lightly; top with the remaining ½ cup cheese. Bake in a 350° oven for 30 minutes. Serves 6.

## Ratatouille

Even beyond its rich flavor yet relatively low caloric content, Ratatouille has other qualities which account for its popularity: It tastes better made ahead (even a day or more old) and is just as good cold as reheated.

About ½ cup olive oil
2 large onions, sliced
2 large cloves garlic, minced or mashed
1 medium-sized eggplant, cut in ½-inch cubes
6 medium-sized zucchini, thickly sliced
2 green or red bell peppers, seeded and cut in chunks
About 2 teaspoons salt
1 teaspoon basil
½ cup minced parsley
4 large tomatoes, cut in chunks
Parsley
Sliced tomato (optional)

Heat ¼ cup of the oil in a large frying pan over high heat. Add onions and garlic and cook, stirring, until onions are soft but not browned. Stir in the eggplant, zucchini, peppers, 2 teaspoons salt, basil, and minced parsley; add a little of the oil as

needed to keep the vegetables from sticking.

Cover pan and cook over moderate heat for about 30 minutes; stir occasionally, using a large spatula and turning the vegetables to help preserve their shape. If mixture becomes quite soupy, remove cover.

Add the tomatoes to the vegetables and stir to blend. Also add more oil if vegetables are sticking. Cover and cook over moderate heat for 15 minutes; stir occasionally. Again, if mixture becomes soupy, remove cover. Ratatouille should have a little free liquid, but still be of a good spoon-and-serve consistency. Add more salt if required. Serve hot, chilled, at room temperature, or reheated. Garnish with parsley and tomato. Serves 8 to 10.

**Ratatouille in the Oven.** Using the vegetables and seasonings in the above recipe, layer all ingredients into a 6 quart casserole, pressing down to make fit if necessary. Drizzle only 4 tablespoons of the olive oil over top layer. Cover casserole and bake in a 350° oven for 3 hours. Baste top occasionally with some of the liquid. Uncover during last hour if quite soupy. Mix gently and salt to taste. Garnish with parsley and tomato.

## Vegetable Moussaka

3 medium-sized eggplants (about 1 lb. each)
Salt
Flour
About 1¼ cups salad oil or olive oil
3 large onions, chopped
2 tablespoons butter or margarine
½ pound ground beef chuck
3 medium-sized tomatoes, peeled and chopped
About 3 large green peppers
Water
About 3 large tomatoes, peeled and cut in thick slices
¼ cup regular-strength beef broth

Peel eggplant, if you wish, and cut in crosswise slices that are ⅜ inch thick. Cut each in half. Sprinkle lightly with salt; let stand 20 minutes. Pat slices dry with paper towels. Dust lightly with flour, shake off excess.

Heat enough oil in a wide frying pan to coat bottom. Fry eggplant on both sides until very lightly browned and tender, keeping a layer of oil in pan. Do not crowd slices. Drain on paper towels.

While eggplant browns, prepare sauce. Cook onion in butter until soft, stirring occasionally. Add chuck; crumble and cook until no longer pink. Add chopped tomatoes and cook rapidly, stirring occasionally until most of the liquid has evaporated. Season with about 1 teaspoon salt.

Line a shallow 3-quart casserole with the eggplant, overlapping to make all fit. Spread sauce over eggplant.

Cut peppers in eighths; discard seeds, pith, and stem. Drop into rapidly boiling water to cover. Keep heat high, and cook for 2 minutes after boiling resumes. Drain immediately.

Top casserole with alternating and overlapping rows of pepper chunks and tomato slices. Sprinkle lightly with salt, and pour beef broth over the vegetables. Cover and bake in a 375° oven for 25 to 30 minutes. Serve hot or cold. Serves 6 to 8.

## Stuffed Artichokes

1 cup ground cooked meat or chicken
½ cup finely minced onion
2 tablespoons each finely chopped almonds and parsley
1 egg, beaten
⅛ teaspoon nutmeg
  Salt and pepper to taste
6 large artichokes
1 tablespoon lemon juice
6 slices tomato
1½ cups boiling water

Combine meat, onion, almonds, parsley, egg, nutmeg, salt, and pepper; mix well. Wash artichokes well and remove stems; cut off about 1 inch of the tops. Using a spoon, scoop out all the fuzzy choke and tiny leaves. Stuff meat mixture into center of the artichokes.

Place in a deep casserole or baking pan; sprinkle lemon juice over the artichoke leaves and top each with a tomato slice. Pour boiling water in pan. Cover and bake in a 375° oven for 1 to 1½ hours, or until artichoke leaves pull away easily and are soft at the ends. Serves 6.

To eat, pull leaves away, and bite or scrape off soft part. Eat stuffing and artichoke heart with a fork.

## Asparagus Parmesan

2½ pounds fresh asparagus
  Boiling, salted water
¼ cup (⅛ lb.) butter or margarine
2 to 3 tablespoons chopped green onions
¼ teaspoon curry powder
½ teaspoon salt
⅓ cup all-purpose flour
2 cups milk (or 1⅔ cups milk with ⅓ cup dry white wine)
⅓ cup shredded Parmesan cheese

Snap off tough ends of asparagus and cut tips into diagonal slices (about ⅔ inch long). Cook in boiling, salted water until tender-crisp. Drain.

In a saucepan, melt butter; add onion, curry powder, and salt; cook, stirring, until onion is limp. Blend in flour. Slowly add the milk, and cook, stirring constantly, until mixture thickens. Add asparagus. Turn into a shallow ungreased baking dish or into individual baking dishes. Sprinkle with the cheese and bake in a 400° oven for 15 to 20 minutes. Makes 5 or 6 servings.

*Note:* For quick meals, serve without baking—stir the cheese into the cream sauce and serve in sauce dishes.

## Lima Beans with Curry Sauce

2 packages (10 oz. each) frozen lima beans
  Boiling salted water
2 slices bacon, diced
1 medium-sized onion, minced
1 small clove garlic, mashed
1 teaspoon curry powder
1 can (10½ oz.) condensed cream of mushroom soup
2 tablespoons dry white wine, Sherry, or milk
½ cup sour cream
1 can (3½ oz.) French-fried onions

Cook the lima beans in the boiling water until just tender, about 15 minutes; drain well. In a frying pan, fry the bacon until crisp; remove with a slotted spoon. In the drippings, sauté onion, garlic, and curry until onion is soft, about 5 minutes. Stir in the soup, wine, and sour cream; heat to just under boiling point. Stir in the beans and bacon; heat through again.

Turn into a serving bowl, cover,

and keep warm in oven for as long as an hour; heat onions in a shallow pan, then sprinkle over beans just before serving. (Or put beans in greased 1½-quart casserole and top with onions; reheat, uncovered, in a 325° oven for about 15 minutes.) Makes 6 to 8 servings.

## Green Beans Oriental

2 packages (9 oz. each) frozen French-cut green beans
  Boiling, salted water
2 tablespoons butter or margarine
2 tablespoons minced onion
1 package (7 or 8 oz.) fresh bean sprouts or 1 can (1 lb.) bean sprouts, well drained
1 can (12 oz. drained wt.) water chestnuts, drained and sliced
1 can (10½ oz.) condensed cream of mushroom soup
½ soup can milk
½ cup shredded sharp Cheddar cheese
1 can (3½ oz.) French-fried onions

Cook green beans in boiling, salted water as directed on the package. Drain and set aside. Melt butter in a frying pan. Add onion, bean sprouts, and sliced chestnuts; cover pan and cook for 3 to 4 minutes.

Arrange half of green beans in a buttered 2½-quart casserole; spread with half the bean sprout mixture. Combine the soup with milk; spoon half of it over vegetables.

Repeat layers of beans, bean sprouts, and soup. Sprinkle with cheese.

Bake, uncovered, in a 400° oven for about 25 minutes. Remove from oven and cover with onion rings. Return to oven for about 5 minutes, until thoroughly hot. Serves 8 to 10.

## Green Beans Supreme

2 cans (1 lb. each) green beans, drained, or 2 packages (9 oz. each) frozen cut green beans
1½ cans (can is 10½ oz.) condensed cream of mushroom soup
¼ teaspoon oregano (optional)
1 can (3½ oz.) French-fried onions

If frozen beans are used, cook in boiling, unsalted water until tender;

drain. Mix the green beans, undiluted mushroom soup, and oregano in a 9-inch-square or round baking dish.

Bake uncovered in a 350° oven for 20 minutes. Sprinkle with onions, and bake 5 more minutes. Serves 5 to 6.

## Deviled Green Beans

1 medium-sized onion, chopped
1 clove garlic, minced
½ green pepper, chopped
1 jar (2 oz.) sliced pimientos, drained and chopped
3 tablespoons butter or margarine
2 teaspoons prepared mustard
1 can (8 oz.) tomato sauce
1 cup (about ¼ lb.) shredded long-horn or process Cheddar cheese
2 cans (1 lb. each) cut green beans, drained, or 2 packages (9 oz. each) frozen cut green beans, cooked in boiling, salted water

Sauté onion, garlic, green pepper, and pimientos in butter until onions are limp. Remove from heat. Stir in mustard, tomato sauce, and cheese.

Combine beans and sauce; turn into a 1½-quart casserole. Bake covered in a 350° oven for 20 minutes; uncover and bake 20 minutes more, or until cheese is melted. Serves 5 to 6.

## Basque Beans

1 meaty ham hock
1 large onion, peeled and sliced
Water
5 carrots, peeled and diced
1 green pepper, seeded and chopped
3 cloves garlic, peeled
3 or 4 sprigs parsley
2 cans (1 lb. 12 oz. each) tomatoes
2 cans (8 oz. each) tomato sauce
2 teaspoons chile powder
1 or 2 small (about 2″) yellow hot wax peppers or hot green peppers
3 teaspoons garlic salt
9 to 10 cans (about 1 lb. each) pink or red beans

Cook the ham hock and onion in water to cover until meat is tender. Cool. Remove the meat from the bone and chop into bite-size pieces.

Put the carrots, green pepper, garlic, parsley, tomatoes, tomato sauce, chile powder, peppers, and garlic salt into a blender until vegeta-bles are finely chopped. (Or put the carrots, peppers, garlic, and parsley through the meat chopper with a fine blade and then combine with the remaining ingredients.) Simmer 20 to 25 minutes.

Add ham to vegetable sauce along with drained beans. Simmer over low heat about ½ hour. Some of the drained bean liquor or liquid from cooking the ham can be added to make a thinner sauce on the beans, if you wish. Serves about 25.

## Fiesta Frijoles

2 pounds dried pink or red beans
Water
1 pound salt pork, diced
2 cloves garlic, minced
4 slices bacon, chopped, or 2 or 3 tablespoons bacon drippings
1 large or 2 small onions, sliced
4 cups (two 1-lb. cans) canned tomatoes
4 or 5 small dried chiles
3 tablespoons vinegar
1 tablespoon Worcestershire
3 tablespoons sugar
2 teaspoons (or more) chile powder
1 tablespoon finely chopped parsley
Salt to taste
2 tablespoons grated Parmesan or Romano cheese

Soak beans overnight in water to cover (or cover beans with water, bring to a boil, boil 2 minutes, let stand 1 hour).

Add pork and garlic, cook slowly in the soaking water for about 1 hour, or until pork is tender. Add more water, if necessary. Meanwhile, fry bacon (or melt bacon fat) in a large frying pan; add onion and cook until tender; add all remaining ingredients except salt and cheese. Cook, stirring frequently until thickened.

When pork is tender, add the tomato sauce to the bean mixture, and add salt to taste.

Cook slowly about 1 hour longer, or until beans are soft, but not mushy. Stir in grated cheese. Serves 10 to 12.

## Baked Beans Supreme

½ pound sliced bacon, diced
2 medium-sized onions, chopped
2 cans (about 1 lb. 4 oz. each) pork and beans
1½ teaspoons dry mustard
1 can (about 8 oz.) crushed pineapple
¼ cup chile sauce
¼ teaspoon salt

Sauté bacon and onions slowly until onions are soft; drain off fat. Combine bacon and onions with beans, mustard, pineapple, chile sauce, and salt; put into a casserole or bean pot (about 1½-quart size). Cover and bake in a 275° oven for 1½ to 2 hours. Makes 6 servings.

## Dutch Beets

2 tablespoons butter or margarine
1 tablespoon all-purpose flour
1 cup boiling water
1 tablespoon sugar
¼ teaspoon salt
2 tablespoons vinegar
2 teaspoons minced onion
Dash of pepper
2 cups sliced or diced cooked beets

In a saucepan, melt butter and stir in flour; add boiling water and cook, stirring constantly, until mixture is thick and smooth. Add sugar, salt, vinegar, onion, pepper, and beets; heat slowly for 10 to 15 minutes. Serves 4.

## Broccoli Casserole

1 package (10 oz.) frozen chopped broccoli or about 1½ pounds fresh broccoli
Salted water
2 tablespoons each butter and flour
¼ teaspoon salt
Dash pepper
1 cup milk
1 tablespoon grated onion
¾ cup mayonnaise
3 eggs, well beaten

Cook frozen broccoli in boiling, salted water just until thawed and bright green, then drain. Or trim fresh broccoli, cook until tender but still slightly crisp, then drain and coarsely chop.

In another pan, melt the butter.

*(Continued on next page)*

Blend in flour, salt, and pepper and cook until bubbly. Gradually stir in the milk, and cook, stirring, until thickened and smooth. Remove from heat and stir in the onion, mayonnaise, and beaten eggs. Carefully mix in the broccoli.

Turn into a 2-quart casserole. Set the casserole, uncovered, in a pan of hot water. Bake in a 350° oven about 30 minutes, or until the custard sauce has set. Makes 6 servings.

*Note:* For a short-cut, substitute 1 can (10½ oz.) white sauce (heated) for the butter, flour, salt, pepper, and milk.

## Broccoli & Bacon

- **1  pound broccoli**
- **4  slices bacon**
- **¼  cup minced green onions**
- **¾  cup dry bread crumbs**

Peel and split broccoli stems; cook whole branches in boiling, salted water just until tender. Drain.

While broccoli is cooking, fry bacon until crisp; drain on paper toweling and crumble. Cook green onions in the bacon drippings until wilted; stir in bread crumbs; mix well. Arrange hot broccoli on a hot platter; sprinkle with crumbled bacon, onion, and crumbs. Serves 3.

## Deviled Brussels Sprouts

A moderately hot and tangy sauce made with butter and seasonings accents these tender sprouts.

- **2  pounds Brussels sprouts**
  **Boiling, salted water**
- **⅓  cup butter or margarine**
- **2  teaspoons prepared mustard**
- **1  teaspoon Worcestershire**
- **1  tablespoon chile sauce or catsup**
  **Salt and pepper to taste**

Cook Brussels sprouts, covered, in a small amount of boiling, salted water for about 15 minutes, or just until tender. Drain well.

While the sprouts are cooking, prepare this sauce: Melt butter in a small saucepan. Add remaining ingredients and stir until smooth. Pour over the drained Brussels sprouts, or pass in a bowl. Makes 6 to 8 servings.

## Cauliflower with Crumb Topping

- **1  medium-sized cauliflower**
  **Boiling, salted water**
- **¼  cup (⅛ lb.) butter or margarine**
  **Salt and pepper**
- **1  or 2 hard-cooked eggs, chopped**
  **Crumb-Butter Topping (recipe on page 115)**

Separate cauliflower into large flowerettes and cook in boiling, salted water until the stems are just barely tender. Drain well. Melt the butter in a wide pan and sauté the flowerettes in it over low heat just until they are hot and well coated with the butter. Season with more salt, if necessary, and pepper. Place in serving dish.

Mix the hard-cooked eggs with the Crumb-Butter Topping and sprinkle over the hot cauliflower. Serve at once. Makes 5 to 6 servings.

## Sweet-Sour Spiced Red Cabbage

- **1  medium-sized head red cabbage, shredded**
- **3  tablespoons bacon drippings or butter**
- **2  small apples, thinly sliced**
- **5  whole cloves**
- **1  teaspoon caraway seed (optional)**
  **Salt to taste**
- **¼  cup vinegar**
- **2  tablespoons sugar**

Rinse shredded cabbage with cold water. Melt the bacon drippings or butter in a large, heavy frying pan; add the cabbage, apples, cloves, caraway seed, and salt.

Cover and cook slowly for 20 to 25 minutes, or until cabbage is tender. Add vinegar and sugar (or more vinegar and sugar to taste); simmer 5 minutes. Makes 6 servings.

## Butter-crisp Cabbage

- **3  to 4 tablespoons butter or margarine**
- **1  large head cabbage (about 2 pounds), shredded**
- **2  tablespoons lemon juice**
- **½  teaspoon caraway seed**
  **Salt and pepper to taste**

Melt butter in a large, heavy frying pan; add cabbage. Cover and cook, stirring occasionally about 8 to 10 minutes, or just until tender. Add lemon juice, caraway seed, salt, and pepper. Serves 6.

## Gingered Carrots

- **1  teaspoon olive oil**
- **4  cups sliced carrots (sliced diagonally ⅛-inch thick)**
- **1  cup water**
- **⅛  teaspoon garlic powder**
- **1  tablespoon each brown sugar and finely chopped crystallized or preserved ginger**
- **2  tablespoons white wine vinegar**
- **¼  teaspoon salt**
- **2  teaspoons chopped parsley**

Heat oil in a wide frying pan. Stir in carrots, water, garlic powder, brown sugar, ginger, vinegar, and salt. Cover and simmer over moderately high heat for 12 to 15 minutes, or until carrots are just tender. Sprinkle with parsley. Makes 6 servings.

## Carrots & Apples

- **8  to 10 medium-sized carrots**
  **Boiling, salted water**
- **4  cooking apples**
- **½  cup brown sugar, firmly packed**
  **Salt and pepper**
- **1½  tablespoons butter or margarine**

Simmer carrots in salted water for 10 minutes; drain and cut crosswise in thin slices. Peel, core, and quarter apples; slice thinly. Arrange alternate layers of carrots and apples in a greased baking dish, sprinkling each layer with sugar, salt, and pepper, and dotting with butter.

Cover and bake in a 350° oven for 45 minutes to 1 hour, or until carrots and apples are tender. Uncover baking dish during last 10 minutes of baking. Serves 6 or more.

## Celery Root Ring

3 large celery roots
  Boiling, salted water
3 eggs, separated
¾ cup whipping cream
  Salt and pepper to taste

Trim celery roots and cook in boiling, salted water about 45 minutes, or until tender. Drain, cool, and peel; force through a wire strainer.

Beat egg whites stiff. In another bowl, beat egg yolks, add cream, and stir into the puréed celery root; add salt and pepper to taste; fold in the beaten egg whites.

Pour into a greased ring mold, set in a shallow pan of hot water, and bake in a 375° oven 30 to 45 minutes, until firm.

Remove from oven, loosen edges with a sharp knife, and shake gently; then place a large plate over the mold, invert the mold quickly, and rap sharply to loosen the baked ring. Serves 6.

## Celery with Water Chestnuts

1 bunch celery
1 can (14 oz.) regular-strength
  chicken broth (1¾ cups)
½ teaspoon sweet basil
½ teaspoon salt
¼ teaspoon pepper
2 tablespoons each cornstarch and
  cold water
1 can (12 oz.) water chestnuts
⅓ cup sliced almonds
½ cup fine dry bread crumbs
3 tablespoons melted butter or
  margarine

Trim the celery, then slice into 1-inch pieces. Put into a large saucepan, add the chicken broth, basil, salt, and pepper. Cover and cook until the celery is almost tender but still slightly crisp, about 10 minutes.

Blend the cornstarch with cold water and gradually stir into the hot stock; cook, stirring, just until thickened. Drain and slice water chestnuts; add to sauce along with almonds. Turn into a 2-quart casserole. Mix the bread crumbs with the melted butter and sprinkle over top of vegetable.

Bake uncovered in a 350° oven for 30 minutes. Makes about 6 servings.

## Baked Fennel

Fennel looks something like a bunch of celery, but has wider stalks and feathery green leaves. It has a very delicate licorice-like flavor.

The Italians call it *finocchio* and the French *fenouil*.

Fennel is good raw—in salads or plain, as you would eat celery.

2 heads fennel, trimmed
  Boiling, salted water
¼ cup (⅛ lb.) butter or margarine,
  melted
2 tablespoons fine dry bread crumbs
1 tablespoon grated Parmesan
  cheese
1 hard-cooked egg, chopped
1 tablespoon finely chopped fennel
  leaves
  Dash of paprika

Cut the fennel heads lengthwise into quarters and drop into the boiling water; cook until just tender, about 8 to 10 minutes. Drain and arrange in a well-greased shallow baking dish.

Spoon 2 tablespoons of the melted butter over the fennel. Combine the bread crumbs, cheese, egg, fennel leaves, and remaining 2 tablespoons melted butter; sprinkle over top. Add a sprinkling of paprika.

Place in a 450° oven just until the crumbs have browned, about 10 minutes. Makes about 4 servings.

## Baked Corn au Gratin

6 ears corn, or 1 can (12 oz.) whole-
  kernel corn, well drained
1 small onion, finely chopped
1 green pepper, finely chopped
3 tablespoons butter or margarine
3 tablespoons all-purpose flour
2 cups milk
1 cup shredded American or mild
  Cheddar cheese
  Salt and pepper to taste
1 teaspoon sugar
2 eggs, well beaten
  Crushed cornflakes or Crumb-
  Butter Topping (see recipe on
  page 115)

If fresh corn is used, cut kernels from cob. In a saucepan, sauté onion and green pepper in butter until tender; stir in flour; add milk and cook, stirring constantly, until mixture is thick and smooth. Remove from heat, stir

in the cheese, salt, pepper, sugar, corn, and then the eggs.

Turn into a greased casserole and top with crushed cornflakes or Crumb-Butter Topping. Set in a shallow pan of hot water and bake in a 350° oven about 45 minutes. Serves 6.

## Western Succotash

2 cups cooked whole-kernel corn
1½ cups cooked lima beans or green
  beans
¼ cup finely chopped green onion
3 tablespoons butter
½ cup whipping cream
  Seasoned or garlic salt

In a saucepan combine corn, beans, onion, butter, and cream; heat slowly. Season to taste with salt. Serves 4 or 5.

## Baked Eggplant

1 medium-sized eggplant
  Salt and pepper to taste
1 to 2 eggs, well beaten
  About ¾ cup fine dry bread crumbs
  Butter

Slice unpeeled eggplant crosswise into ¼-inch-thick rounds. Sprinkle with salt, then dip each slice first into beaten egg and then into bread crumbs.

Lay slices flat (not overlapping) on a baking sheet well greased with oil or butter. Sprinkle lightly with salt and pepper; dot each slice with butter. Bake in a 450° oven about 20 minutes, or until browned. Serves 5 or 6.

## Stuffed Eggplant (Imam Bayildi)

2 medium-sized eggplant (1 lb. each)
  Salt
5 tablespoons olive oil
2 medium-sized onions, thinly
  sliced
3 large cloves garlic, minced or
  mashed
⅓ cup minced parsley
1 teaspoon sugar
1½ teaspoons salt
2 large tomatoes, peeled, seeded,
  and diced, or 1 can (1 lb.)
  whole tomatoes, drained and
  diced

*(Continued on next page)*

Cut eggplant in halves lengthwise and scoop out center seed sections, leaving a firm ½-inch-thick shell; reserve pulp. Sprinkle shells lightly with salt. Drizzle 2 tablespoons of the oil in a shallow baking pan; arrange eggplant in the pan.

In the remaining 3 tablespoons oil, sauté onion until limp. Stir in about 2 cups diced unseeded portions of the eggplant pulp, the garlic, parsley, sugar, the 1½ teaspoons salt, and tomatoes.

Distribute filling inside the eggplant shells. Cover the pan with foil and bake in a 350° oven until tender, about 1½ hours. Cool in pan and serve at room temperature (bring to room temperature, if cold); spoon pan juices over eggplant. Makes 4 large servings (or cut each in half for 8 modest servings).

# Greens with Onions

10 cups coarsely chopped Swiss chard, mustard greens, or kale (lightly packed)—about 1¼ lbs.
 2 medium-sized onions, thinly sliced
 2 tablespoons salad oil, butter, or bacon drippings
 ½ cup water
 Salt and pepper to taste

*Note:* If you use Swiss chard, include some of the stems when you chop greens.

Heat oil or butter in a wide pan over moderate heat; add onions and cook, stirring occasionally, until they are golden brown. Add greens and the water. Cover and cook, stirring occasionally, for about 10 minutes, or until greens are tender. Season with salt and pepper. Makes 4 to 6 servings.

# Amber Onions

2 cans (1 lb. each) small whole onions, or 2 pounds small onions
2 tablespoons butter
1½ tablespoons honey
2 tablespoons tomato juice
½ teaspoon salt
1 teaspoon paprika
⅛ teaspoon pepper

Drain the canned onions thoroughly and turn them into a shallow 1½-quart baking dish that has a cover. If you use fresh onions, peel them and cook in boiling, salted water until barely tender, about 15 minutes.

In a small pan, melt the butter; add the honey, tomato juice, salt, paprika, and pepper. Pour over the onions in the casserole.

Cover and bake in a 325° oven for about 1½ hours. Baste the onions several times with the sauce, but do not stir. Remove cover for the last 45 minutes of baking. Makes 6 to 8 servings.

# Party Onions

This delightful way of turning onions into a dish worthy of guests has been a favorite for years.

 Boiling water
 1 pound small onions
 1 cup water
 1 tablespoon brown sugar
 1 teaspoon salt
 ¼ teaspoon paprika
 Pepper to taste
 2 tablespoons chopped or slivered blanched almonds
 ¼ cup (⅛ lb.) butter
 2 tablespoons flour
 1 teaspoon Worcestershire

Pour boiling water over onions, let stand a few minutes, then drain and peel. Combine the 1 cup water, brown sugar, salt, paprika, and pepper, and bring to a boil. Add onions; cover and simmer for 30 minutes, or until onions are tender. Drain off liquid and save.

Place onions in a greased 1½-quart casserole. Brown almonds in the butter; add flour and brown lightly. Stir in the liquid left from cooking the onions, cook until slightly thickened, then add Worcestershire. Pour over onions. Cover and bake in a 375° oven for 25 minutes. Serves 6.

# Peas and Celery Medley

2 tablespoons butter or margarine
2 cups diagonally sliced celery
3 tablespoons water
2 packages (10 oz. each) frozen peas
1 can (10½ oz.) condensed cream of mushroom soup
1 can (3 or 4 oz.) sliced mushrooms
1 can (5 oz.) water chestnuts, drained and sliced
1 tablespoon butter, melted
¾ cup fresh bread crumbs

Melt the 2 tablespoons butter in a pan; add celery and water. Cover tightly; cook, stirring occasionally until tender-crisp, about 4 minutes. Add peas, simmer 5 more minutes. Heat soup with the mushrooms (including the liquid), and water chestnuts.

Layer vegetables alternately with creamed mixture into a buttered 1½-quart casserole. Mix the 1 tablespoon butter with bread crumbs; sprinkle over top. Bake in a 350° oven for 20 minutes, or until bubbly. Makes 8 servings.

# Pea Pods Piper

This dish makes unique use of those delicious-looking, crisp fresh pea pods you hate so to throw away. They are edible and taste much like Chinese peas—if the tough lining is stripped off.

 2 tablespoons butter or margarine
 ¼ cup slivered blanched almonds
 ¼ pound mushrooms, thinly sliced
 2 cups shelled fresh green peas
 1 cup stripped pea pods, coarsely chopped in 1-inch pieces (see following instructions for stripping off tough lining)
 ½ teaspoon salt
 ⅓ cup regular-strength chicken or beef broth

Melt butter in a frying pan over medium heat and sauté almonds until golden; remove almonds with slotted spoon and set aside. Add mushrooms to pan and cook, stirring occasionally, until juices have evaporated and mushrooms are golden; remove from pan and set aside.

Add peas, pea pods, salt, and broth to the pan; cover and simmer for 3 to 5 minutes, or until tender. Return mushrooms and almonds to pan; heat about 1 minute more. Makes 4 servings.

**To Strip Pea Pods.** Shell peas. Hold each half of the pod about 1 inch from its stem end. Fold the pod in toward the lining. This will break the crisp, edible outside portion, but not the tough inside membrane. Holding onto the stem end with one hand and the pod with the other, gently pull the membrane down and away from the pod. It usually will come off in one sheet.

With practice, you will acquire the knack of preparing the pods very quickly. If they break or do not strip easily, throw them away. You only need 1 cup.

# Honey Parsnips

6 medium-sized parsnips, peeled (about 1½ pounds)
   Boiling water
1 teaspoon salt
¼ cup (⅛ lb.) butter or margarine
¼ cup honey
   Lemon juice
   Cinnamon (optional)

Cut parsnips lengthwise in thin slices, then cut slices into pieces about 1½ inches long. Place in medium-sized pan and cover with boiling water. Add salt and cook for 20 minutes, or just until tender.

Melt butter in a large frying pan; add honey, and cook, stirring, until bubbly. Add parsnips, cover, and cook over low heat for 5 minutes.

Just before serving, sprinkle with lemon juice and cinnamon if you like. Makes about 6 servings.

# Fresh Mushrooms with Cheese

1 pound fresh mushrooms, sliced lengthwise
1 cup shredded Cheddar cheese (about ¼ lb.)
1 can (about 8 oz.) pitted black olives, drained and sliced or chopped
1½ tablespoons flour
½ teaspoon salt
⅛ teaspoon pepper
⅓ cup half-and-half (light cream)
1½ tablespoons butter
1 cup fresh bread crumbs

In a greased 2-quart casserole, arrange the mushrooms, cheese, and olives in alternate layers. Blend together flour, salt, pepper, and half-and-half; pour over the mushrooms.

In a small pan, melt the butter; add the bread crumbs and mix with a fork. Sprinkle the crumbs over casserole. Bake uncovered in a 350° oven until bubbly and golden brown, about 30 minutes. Makes about 8 servings.

# Fresh Mushrooms with Herbs

The French herb blend called *fines herbes*, sold by spice companies, may be replaced by your own mixture of thyme, oregano, sage, rosemary, marjoram, and basil.

½ pound fresh mushrooms (medium to large)
½ teaspoon seasoning salt
½ teaspoon fines herbes
¼ teaspoon dry mustard
2 tablespoons butter
1 tablespoon red wine vinegar

Wash and dry mushrooms, cut off ends of stems without separating them from the caps, and slice ⅛-inch thick lengthwise. Sprinkle with seasoning salt, fines herbes, and dry mustard.

Brown in butter, adding more if necessary to keep mushrooms moist. When nearly done, add vinegar; reheat, and serve hot. Serves about 4.

# Potato Casserole

2 cups hot or cold mashed potatoes
1 large package (8 oz.) cream cheese, at room temperature
1 small onion, finely chopped
2 eggs
2 tablespoons all-purpose flour
   Salt and pepper to taste
1 can (3½ oz.) French-fried onions

Put the potatoes into the large bowl of your electric mixer. Add the cream cheese, chopped onion, eggs, and flour. Beat at medium speed until the ingredients are blended, then beat at high speed until light and fluffy. Taste, and add salt and pepper, if needed.

Spoon into a greased 9-inch-square baking dish. Distribute the canned onions evenly over the top. Bake, uncovered, in a 300° oven for about 35 minutes. (If you prepare this dish ahead, add the onions just before putting it in the oven.) Makes 6 to 8 servings.

# Kartoffelrösti

2 pounds large new potatoes
5 tablespoons butter
¼ teaspoon salt
2 teaspoons water

Cook potatoes in boiling, salted water 25 to 30 minutes, or just until tender; drain, peel, and finely dice.

Melt butter in a 10 or 11-inch heavy frying pan, add potatoes and ¼ teaspoon salt; stir to distribute butter evenly. Press potatoes into an even layer in the pan. Sprinkle with 2 teaspoons water, cover tightly, and cook over medium-low heat until crusty and golden at the bottom, about 15 minutes.

Slip spatula under potatoes to loosen all the way around. Invert onto serving plate. Makes about 6 servings.

# Favorite Colorful Scalloped Potatoes

4 medium-sized potatoes, peeled and thinly sliced
1 green pepper, shredded
1 carrot, shredded
1 medium-sized onion, chopped
2 tablespoons butter or margarine
2 tablespoons flour
2 cups milk
   Chopped parsley
   Salt and pepper to taste
⅓ cup shredded American or mild Cheddar cheese

In a well-greased 1½ quart casserole, arrange layers of potato slices, sprinkling each layer with green pepper, carrot, and onion.

*(Continued on next page)*

In a saucepan, melt butter and blend in flour; add milk and cook, stirring constantly, until mixture is thickened and smooth. Add parsley; season with salt and pepper; pour over potatoes. Sprinkle with cheese.

Bake, covered, in a 350° oven about 45 minutes; uncover and bake 45 minutes longer, or until potatoes are tender and cheese is delicately browned. Serves 4.

## Scalloped Potatoes with Mushrooms

5 or 6 medium-sized potatoes, peeled and thinly sliced
Salt and pepper to taste
1 can (10½ oz.) cream of mushroom soup
1 soup can water

Put the sliced potatoes in a greased casserole in layers, sprinkling each layer lightly with salt and pepper. Blend the soup with water; pour over the potatoes.

Bake, covered, in a 350° oven for 45 minutes; uncover, and bake about 45 minutes longer, or until potatoes are tender and brown on top. Serves 6.

## Browned Potato Loaf

3 tablespoons butter or margarine
3 tablespoons all-purpose flour
1 cup milk
4 or 5 medium-sized potatoes (cooked, peeled, and diced or thinly sliced)
1 tablespoon minced parsley
1 teaspoon salt
¼ teaspoon pepper
¾ cup shredded sharp Cheddar cheese
Parsley sprigs for garnish

In a saucepan melt butter, add flour, and cook, stirring, until well blended and bubbly. Pour in milk all at once and cook, stirring constantly, until thick.

Add potatoes and minced parsley to the sauce. Cook on low heat, stirring occasionally, for about 5 minutes, or until mixture is fairly stiff. Season with salt and pepper.

Turn into a well-greased 5 by 9-inch loaf pan, press down firmly, and refrigerate several hours or overnight. Half an hour before serving, turn loaf out onto an oven-proof platter or pan and sprinkle with the cheese. Bake in a 375° oven until golden brown, about 30 to 40 minutes. Garnish with parsley sprigs; serve very hot. Makes 6 servings.

## Mashed Rutabaga & Potato Combination

1 large rutabaga, peeled and diced
Boiling, salted water
4 medium-sized potatoes
Butter or margarine
Salt and pepper to taste
Hot milk if necessary
Chopped parsley for garnish

Cook diced rutabaga, covered, in as small amount of boiling, salted water as possible about 30 minutes, or until tender; drain. Boil potatoes in their jackets for about 30 minutes, or until very tender; drain and slip off skins.

Combine hot rutabaga and hot potatoes. Mash or beat together with butter, salt, and pepper to taste. If the mixture is dry, beat in a little hot milk to obtain the consistency you like. Serve sprinkled with chopped parsley. Serves 6 to 8.

## Savory Sauerkraut

1 medium-sized onion, chopped
3 tablespoons bacon drippings
1 can (1 lb.) sauerkraut, drained
1 can (1 lb.) tomatoes
½ teaspoon caraway seed
½ teaspoon sugar

Fry the chopped onion in the bacon fat until soft. Add sauerkraut, tomatoes, caraway seed, and sugar; mix thoroughly.

Turn into a 1½-quart casserole and bake uncovered in a 350° oven for 30 to 40 minutes to blend flavors. Serves 6.

## Acorn Squash with Filberts or Pecans

This squash soaks up a sweet sauce of butter, brown sugar, cinnamon, and orange.

3 medium-sized acorn (Danish) squash
¼ cup (⅛ lb.) soft butter or margarine
¼ cup brown sugar, firmly packed
½ teaspoon salt
½ teaspoon cinnamon
1 tablespoon grated orange peel
Juice of 1 orange
½ cup coarsely chopped filberts or pecans
Water

Cut squash in half lengthwise; scoop out seed and stringy portion. Whip butter with a fork and cream in the brown sugar, salt, cinnamon, and orange peel. Beat in the orange juice; mix in the nuts.

Pour ½ inch of water in a large baking pan and arrange the squash cut side up in it. Divide the butter mixture evenly among the squash cavities. Cover the pan (with foil if it has no lid).

Bake in a 375° oven for 40 minutes; uncover, spread sauce around inside of squash, and continue baking uncovered for 40 minutes more, or until brown and tender. Makes 6 servings.

## Butter-sautéed Winter Squash

2 pounds winter squash (butternut, banana, turban, or Hubbard)
Boiling, salted water
¼ cup (⅛ lb.) butter or margarine
1 small onion, chopped
Salt
Pepper
Granulated or brown sugar to taste
Minced parsley

Cut unpeeled squash in 2-inch pieces and cook in boiling, salted water for 15 minutes. Drain, peel, and slice or dice.

Melt the butter in a frying pan; add squash and onion. Sauté over medium-high heat until browned. Sprinkle with salt, pepper, and a little sugar, if you like. Serve sprinkled with minced parsley. Makes 5 to 6 servings.

# Crookneck Squash in Cream

2 pounds crookneck squash
1 cup (½ pt.) whipping cream
1 tablespoon butter
  Salt and pepper

Trim away ends of squash and dice into ½-inch cubes. Combine in a saucepan with cream and butter. Bring to a gentle boil, cover, and simmer over low heat, shaking pan occasionally, until squash is tender (about 5 minutes).

Season with salt and pepper to taste. Makes 6 servings.

# Squash Turbans

4 large scallop (pattypan) squash
  Boiling, salted water
2 to 3 tablespoons butter or margarine
  Salt and pepper to taste
2 medium-sized tomatoes
8 slices (6 oz.) American cheese

Cut squash in half crosswise; cook in boiling, salted water until tender (about 15 minutes); drain. Season with butter, and salt and pepper to taste. Keep hot.

Cut each tomato in 4 thick slices (don't use ends); lay the slices on a broiling pan. Season with salt and pepper and place a slice of cheese on each slice of tomato. Broil slices 6 inches from broiler for 2 to 3 minutes, or until cheese is melted and begins to brown.

Place one tomato slice on each half of hot squash, and serve immediately. Serves 4.

# Creamed Purée of Spinach

Here's a simple way of preparing puréed spinach so that all of the fresh flavor and bright green color are retained. If you have a blender, you may use frozen spinach and make this much faster.

1⅓ pounds spinach
 ¼ cup (⅛ lb.) butter or margarine
 ¼ cup flour
1⅓ cups milk
1¼ teaspoons salt
  Pepper and nutmeg to taste

Remove any tough stems from spinach; wash well and drain thoroughly; put through meat chopper, using the finest blade. (Be sure to catch any juice and mix with the spinach.)

In the top part of a double boiler, melt butter and blend in flour. Add milk gradually and cook, stirring constantly, until mixture is a thick, smooth cream sauce.

Combine spinach with sauce; season to taste with salt, pepper, and nutmeg; cook over hot water for 10 to 15 minutes. Makes 4 to 6 servings.

**Blender Method.** Partially thaw 2 packages (10 oz. each) frozen chopped spinach. After you have made the cream sauce, pour half into the blender. Break one package of the spinach up into chunks and add to sauce. Set the blender at "chop." Switch blender on and *off* immediately until spinach is chopped as fine as you like. Pour into top of a double boiler. Process other half of sauce and spinach the same way. Season with salt, pepper, and nutmeg. Cook over hot water 10 to 15 minutes.

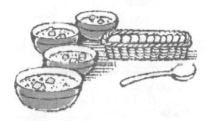

# Spinach with Sour Cream Sauce

3 packages (10 oz. each) frozen chopped spinach
  Boiling, salted water
1 cup (½ pt.) sour cream
1 package (1½ oz.) dehydrated onion soup mix
½ teaspoon salt
  Nutmeg (optional)

Cook spinach in boiling, salted water until tender; drain thoroughly. Turn into a blender the sour cream, soup mix, and salt, and blend until smooth (or beat with a mixer until well blended).

Mix together the cooked spinach and sour cream mixture, and turn into a greased casserole. Sprinkle with nutmeg if desired. Bake in a 325° oven for 20 minutes, or until hot. Serves 6 to 8.

# Sweet Potatoes & Apples Caramel

¼ cup granulated sugar
½ teaspoon salt
¼ teaspoon nutmeg
¼ cup (⅛ lb.) butter or margarine
  About 4 medium-sized sweet potatoes, cooked and peeled
3 tart, crisp apples, peeled
¼ cup hot water
⅔ cup brown sugar, firmly packed

Combine the granulated sugar, salt, and nutmeg; blend in butter with a fork. Thinly slice potatoes to make 4 cups, and thinly slice the apples.

In a 2-quart casserole or 9-inch square baking pan, make a layer of potatoes, then apples, then sugar mixture, using about ⅓ of each. Repeat making two more layers. Pour over the hot water. Cover and bake in a 350° oven for 1 hour, or until the apples are tender. Remove from oven, uncover, and press the brown sugar through a wire strainer onto the top of the casserole to make an even layer.

Set under the broiler for about 2 or 3 minutes, or until the topping melts and bubbles—watch closely to prevent its scorching. Makes 8 to 10 servings.

# Pecan-topped Sweet Potatoes

Crunchy pecan halves decorate this delightful sweet potato casserole.

2½ to 3 pounds sweet potatoes or yams, cooked and peeled
2 eggs
¾ cup brown sugar
½ cup (¼ lb.) butter, melted
1 teaspoon each salt and cinnamon
  Orange juice (up to 1 cup)
1 cup pecan halves

Mash sweet potatoes (you should have about 6 cups). Beat in eggs, ¼ cup of the brown sugar, ¼ cup of the melted butter, salt, and cinnamon. (If potatoes seem dry, beat in orange juice until moist and fluffy.)

Put in a 1½ or 2-quart casserole. (Refrigerate if you wish.) Before baking, arrange pecan halves on top; sprinkle with the remaining ½ cup brown sugar and drizzle with remaining ¼ cup melted butter. Bake, uncovered, in 375° oven for 20 minutes, or until heated. Makes 8 to 10 servings.

## Sweet Potatoes with Sherry or Orange Juice

- 3 pounds sweet potatoes (about 9 small or 6 large)
- ½ cup (¼ lb.) butter or margarine, melted
- ½ cup Sherry or orange juice
- ¼ teaspoon nutmeg
  Cinnamon
- ½ teaspoon grated orange peel
  Salt and pepper to taste
  Brown sugar

Boil sweet potatoes in their jackets for 20 to 30 minutes, or until tender; peel and mash well. Add butter, Sherry, nutmeg, ¼ teaspoon cinnamon, orange peel, salt, and pepper; whip until fluffy. (Add a little water or orange juice if the mixture seems too dry.)

Pile in a greased shallow baking dish; sprinkle lightly with brown sugar and cinnamon. Bake in a 400° oven until top is lightly browned. Serves 8.

## Broiled Tomatoes with Cheese

- 1 large, firm tomato
  Salt and pepper to taste
- ¼ teaspoon crumbled basil (optional)
- 2 teaspoons mayonnaise
- 4 teaspoons grated Parmesan cheese

Halve unpeeled tomato crosswise; sprinkle with salt and pepper. Sprinkle each half with ⅛ teaspoon basil, spread with 1 teaspoon mayonnaise, and sprinkle with 2 teaspoons cheese.

Broil 7 to 8 minutes about 10 inches from the broiler. (Although the cheese will not brown as nicely, you may also bake these in a 450° oven for about 10 minutes.) Each tomato makes a serving of 2 halves; 1 half can garnish·a steak or fish plate.

## Tomato Pudding

Some people prefer these old-fashioned scalloped tomatoes made with canned tomatoes and no spice. Others like the richer purée version.

- 1 can (1 lb. 12 oz.) tomatoes or tomato purée
- 1 cup brown sugar, firmly packed
- ¼ teaspoon each allspice and cinnamon (optional)
- ½ teaspoon dry mustard (optional)
- 7 slices dry bread, cut in ½-inch cubes
- ½ cup (¼ lb.) butter or margarine, melted

If canned tomatoes are used, press them through a wire strainer or whirl in a blender until puréed. Mix tomato purée with the brown sugar and spices, if used.

Sprinkle bread cubes in a shallow 2-quart ungreased casserole and dribble melted butter over them. Lightly mix in the tomato mixture.

Bake uncovered in a 350° oven for about 45 minutes, or until crusty and lightly browned on top. Makes about 8 servings.

## Zucchini Casserole

- 4 to 6 medium-sized zucchini
- 1 teaspoon salt
- 1 cup shredded Cheddar cheese
- ⅛ teaspoon pepper
- ⅛ teaspoon garlic powder
- ¼ cup chopped parsley
- ¼ cup packaged biscuit mix
- 4 eggs, well beaten
  About 1 tablespoon butter or margarine
  Sliced pimiento-stuffed olives for garnish

Shred enough of the unpeeled zucchini to make 4 cups, lightly packed into the cup. Turn into a bowl and mix in the salt; let stand 1 hour. Turn into a colander or strainer and press out liquid. Combine zucchini, cheese, pepper, garlic powder, parsley, and biscuit mix. Stir in the beaten eggs until well blended.

Turn into a well-greased 9-inch-square baking pan (or 12 medium-sized muffin pans). Dot the top with butter. Bake uncovered in a 350° oven for 25 minutes (20 minutes if in muffin pans), or until the custard is set. Serve hot. Garnish with olive slices. Makes about 6 servings.

## Broiled Zucchini

- 6 large zucchini
  Salt and pepper to taste
  About ¼ cup all-purpose flour
  Salad oil
- 1 large clove garlic

Slice the unpeeled zucchini lengthwise into ¼-inch-thick slices. Sprinkle the slices with salt and pepper; dredge very lightly with flour and sprinkle generously with salad oil.

Rub a baking sheet with the cut clove of garlic and then oil it lightly with the salad oil. Place the slices of zucchini side by side on the baking sheet. Bake in a 450° oven for about 20 to 30 minutes, or until as tender as you like. If you want the zucchini browner, broil just before serving. Makes 4 to 6 servings.

## Stuffed Zucchini

- 2 pounds small zucchini
  Boiling, salted water
- 2 eggs, slightly beaten
- ⅓ cup fine dry bread crumbs
- ⅓ cup grated Parmesan cheese
- ¼ cup salad oil
- 1 small onion, minced
  Few sprigs of parsley, minced
  Salt, garlic salt, pepper, and thyme

Parboil whole zucchini in boiling, salted water for about 15 minutes, until barely tender. Drain, trim ends, cut lengthwise in halves. Carefully scoop out the pulp.

Arrange shells in a greased shallow baking dish. Mash the scooped-out pulp; add the eggs, crumbs, cheese, oil, onion, parsley, and seasonings; mix well. Sprinkle zucchini shells with salt and pepper, and fill with the pulp mixture. Bake uncovered in a 350° oven for 25 to 30 minutes. Serves 6.

## Zucchini Patties

- 5 medium-sized zucchini
- 3 eggs
- 1 tablespoon grated Parmesan cheese
- 1 to 2 cloves garlic, minced or mashed
- 2 tablespoons flour
- ½ cup finely chopped parsley
- 1 teaspoon each salt and pepper
  About ½ cup olive oil or salad oil

Thoroughly scrub the zucchini; remove both ends, but do not peel. Coarsely shred the zucchini into a bowl; press out and remove the water. Mix the dry zucchini with the unbeaten eggs, Parmesan, garlic, flour, parsley, salt, and pepper.

Meanwhile heat a small amount of olive oil in a frying pan. Use a tablespoon to shape heaping spoonfuls of the zucchini mixture into patties. Sauté in the hot oil until lightly browned on both sides. Makes 6 servings.

# Rice, Grains & Pastas

## Armenian Pilaf

  ¼ cup (⅛ lb.) butter or margarine
1½ cups uncooked long-grain rice
  3 cups hot regular-strength chicken, beef, or lamb broth
     Salt (if broth is not very salty)

Melt butter in a heavy frying pan or a Dutch oven. Add rice and cook, stirring frequently, until butter bubbles. Add broth, cover tightly, and bake in a 400° oven for 30 minutes. Remove cover, stir rice carefully with a fork, and bake uncovered about 10 minutes longer, or until liquid is absorbed. Serves 6.

## Chinese Rice

Chinese rice is quite firm and dry, but the grains stick together enough to manage with chopsticks. Long-grain rice (tapered, oval grains) is the type markets ordinarily carry. Medium-

grain (shorter, more rounded grains) may be found in many larger stores.

  1 cup long or medium-grain rice
  ½ teaspoon salt (optional)
1½ to 2 cups cold water

Put rice in a heavy pan which has a tight lid. Add salt if desired (Chinese wouldn't use it), and cold water. (The exact measure isn't very important. The Chinese use the finger to judge a height of water about 1 inch above the rice—about the length to the first joint.)

Set pan over high heat and boil rapidly, uncovered, until most of the water has been absorbed; stir often (with fork or chopstick) while it is boiling to prevent sticking.

Turn heat to lowest setting, put on lid, and allow the rice to steam undisturbed for 20 to 30 minutes, depending upon how soft you like rice. Makes 4 or 5 servings.

## Japanese Rice

The secret of Japanese rice is the use of short or medium-grain rice, proper water measurement, and "no peek" cooking.

Either short or medium-grain rice has a fat, blunt shape different from the tapered oval shape of long-grain (the ordinary rice sold everywhere). Most large groceries also sell the short or medium-grain kind.

  1 cup short or medium-grain rice
1¼ cups cold water
  ½ teaspoon salt (optional)

Put rice in a heavy, deep pan which has a tight-fitting lid. Add cold water and salt (Japanese don't use it), cover, and soak for 1 to 2 hours.

Set over high heat and bring quickly to a full boil. Reduce heat to lowest setting and let rice simmer exactly 12 minutes for 1 to 3 cups rice, 15 minutes if more is used. Turn off heat and let rice stand 5 minutes or longer. Never take the lid off during cooking. It is best not to remove the lid until ready to serve. Makes 4 or 5 servings.

## Almost Wild Rice

A California man invented this rice dish which tastes much like the very

expensive wild rice. He added vermicelli, mushrooms, and onion.

  ¼ cup (⅛ lb.) butter
  1 twist vermicelli (figure "8" bundle)
  1 cup uncooked long-grain rice
  1 can (10½ oz.) condensed beef broth (bouillon)
  1 small can (2 or 3 oz.) sliced mushrooms
  ½ medium-sized onion, grated
  ½ teaspoon salt
  ½ teaspoon freshly ground black pepper
  2 cups water

Melt butter in a frying pan. Break vermicelli into very small pieces (about the size of rice grains) or crush. Add to butter and cook over medium heat, stirring often, until a rich brown. Add the rice, broth, mushrooms, grated onion, salt, pepper, and 1 cup water; stir.

Cover and simmer for about 45 minutes, adding the additional water during cooking process. Makes 6 servings.

## Golden Toasted Rice

If your cooktop is busy—or even if it isn't—you'll want to try this oven method for cooking rice. The savory nuttiness of the grains makes this a very popular recipe.

  1 cup uncooked long grain rice
  2 tablespoons butter
  1 can (10¾ oz.) condensed consommé, heated
  ½ cup hot water
  3 or 4 green onions, thinly sliced including green tops
  1 to 3 tablespoons soy sauce

Toast the rice by spreading the grains in a heavy pan and heating in a 350° oven until lightly browned.

Melt butter over medium heat in a 1½-quart heavy pan or flameproof casserole with a tight-fitting cover; add rice and cook it slightly, stirring constantly. Pour in hot consommé and water, stir once, cover. Turn heat to the lowest possible point and let rice steam for 25 minutes. (Or bake covered casserole in a 350° oven for 30 minutes.)

Stir in onions and soy sauce. Remove from heat, cover again, and let stand a few minutes to partially cook the onion. Serves 4.

## Rice-Mushroom Delight

¼ cup (⅛ lb.) butter or margarine (or half butter and half salad oil)
2 cups uncooked long-grain rice
1 can (10¾ oz.) condensed consommé
1 soup can water
1 can (8 oz.) sliced mushrooms (including liquid)
1 tablespoon chopped parsley
2 teaspoons salt
  Dash of thyme and/or marjoram

Melt butter in a large, heavy frying pan or a Dutch oven which has a lid. Add rice and sauté, stirring constantly, until golden brown. Stir in remaining ingredients and bring to a boil.

Then, cover *tightly* and cook over very low heat for about 30 minutes, or until rice is tender, and all liquid has been absorbed. Makes about 8 servings.

## Fruited Rice Ring for Curry

Serve curry in the center of this ring. You won't need to bother with condiments, because the marmalade and the raisins lend just the right amount of flavor contrast.

½ cup orange marmalade
¼ cup seedless or seeded raisins
  Salt to taste
4 cups cooked brown or white rice, cooled

Using a fork, fold marmalade and raisins into the rice (be careful not to mash rice grains). Add salt if necessary.

Pack firmly into a well-greased 1-quart ring mold. Set mold in a shallow pan of hot water and bake in a 350° oven just long enough to heat thoroughly. Unmold. Serves 6.

## Cheese-Almond Rice

1 can (6 or 8 oz.) sliced mushrooms, drained, liquid reserved
2 teaspoons instant chopped onions
⅓ cup chopped or sliced almonds
1 cup (¼ lb.) shredded Cheddar cheese
1¼ cups uncooked long-grain rice
⅛ teaspoon pepper
  Water
3 beef bouillon cubes
4 teaspoons soy sauce
2 tablespoons chopped parsley
2 tablespoons chopped pimiento

Combine drained mushrooms with onions, almonds, cheese, rice, and pepper; turn into a greased 2-quart casserole.

Add water to the liquid from mushrooms to make 3½ cups liquid; heat to the simmering point. Add the bouillon cubes and soy sauce to the hot liquid and stir until bouillon cubes are dissolved. Pour over rice mixture.

Cover and bake in a 375° oven for 45 minutes to 1 hour, or until liquid has been absorbed. Stir in the parsley and pimiento just before serving. Add salt to taste, if needed. Serves 6 to 8.

## Chinese Fried Rice

2 eggs, beaten
3 tablespoons salad oil
1 cup finely shredded or diced cooked shrimp, ham, pork, or beef (optional)
6 green onions, thinly sliced or chopped
4 cups cold cooked rice
2 tablespoons soy sauce
½ teaspoon sugar
  Pepper and salt if needed

**Method 1:** Fry beaten eggs until firm in the oil and cut into shreds. Return to frying pan with meat (cut into shreds to match eggs). Add onion. Cook over medium heat, stirring constantly, for 3 or 4 minutes. Add the rice. Mix the soy sauce, sugar, pepper, and salt if needed; dribble over the rice. Stir until rice is hot. Serves 6.

**Method 2:** Sauté rice in oil over medium heat about 15 minutes, or until it is golden brown. Add meat if desired. Pour beaten eggs over rice. Cook, stirring often, until the egg is set. Sprinkle with the onion and soy sauce

mixed with the sugar, pepper, and salt. Stir just until blended. Serves 6.

## Green Rice

1 cup rice, steamed
1 cup shredded American or mild Cheddar cheese
¼ teaspoon salt
1 cup milk
½ cup finely chopped fresh parsley
1 egg, beaten
¼ cup (⅛ lb.) butter or margarine, melted
½ medium-sized onion, chopped

Combine cold cooked rice and remaining ingredients. Turn into a well-greased 2-quart casserole and bake uncovered in a 350° oven about 45 minutes, or until set and slightly browned. Serves 6 to 8.

## Barley Pilaf

This slow-cooking dish, steamed with mushroom liquid, is worth the wait.

½ cup (¼ lb.) butter
1¾ cup pearl barley
2 medium-sized onions, chopped
2 medium cans (4 oz. each) sliced or button mushrooms
1 cup mushroom liquor and water
4 cups regular-strength chicken broth, or 6 chicken bouillon cubes dissolved in 4 cups boiling water
½ cup toasted slivered almonds (optional)

Melt half the butter in a heavy frying pan. Pour in the barley and cook slowly until it turns a golden brown, stirring frequently; spoon into a large buttered casserole. Put 2 tablespoons more of the butter into the frying pan; add chopped onions and sauté until clear; add to the barley. Melt the remaining 2 tablespoons butter; add drained mushrooms and sauté for 5 minutes; add to barley and onion.

Add enough water to reserved mushroom liquor to make 1 cup liquid and combine with the chicken stock. Pour 2 cups of the liquid over the barley. Cover tightly and bake 45 minutes in a 350° oven; add 2 more cups of liquid and stir; bake, covered, another 45 minutes. Stir in remaining cup of liquid and bake, covered, 30 minutes longer. Add almonds when you stir in the last cup of liquid. Serves 8 to 10.

## Sesame Wheat Pilaf

½ cup sesame seed
1 medium-sized onion, chopped
¼ pound small whole mushrooms or large mushrooms, sliced
¼ cup butter (⅛ lb.) or bacon drippings
2 cups quick-cooking cracked wheat (bulgur)
2 cans (10½ oz. each) condensed beef broth (bouillon)
¾ cup water
1 tablespoon chopped parsley
1 whole clove garlic

Toast sesame seeds by placing them on a baking sheet in a 350° oven for about 5 minutes, or until golden and crunchy.

Sauté onions and mushrooms in butter or bacon drippings over medium-high heat until onions are golden brown and mushroom liquid evaporates; use a frying pan that has a tight-fitting lid. Add cracked wheat and sesame seed; cook and stir until wheat is coated with fat. Add bouillon, water, parsley, and garlic cut in half and speared on a toothpick. Stir until blended.

Cover, reduce heat to low, and simmer slowly until the wheat is tender, about 15 to 20 minutes. Remove garlic; serve. Makes 6 to 8 servings.

*Note:* You can substitute 3 cups regular-strength chicken broth for the bouillon and water. You can use 1 can (6 or 8 oz.) whole or sliced mushrooms instead of fresh; drain and add after onions brown.

## Noodles Romanoff

1 package (8 oz.) egg noodles
  Boiling, salted water
1 cup large-curd cottage cheese
1 small clove garlic, minced or mashed
1 teaspoon Worcestershire
1 cup (½ pt.) sour cream
¼ cup grated onion
¼ teaspoon liquid hot-pepper seasoning
½ cup grated Parmesan cheese

Cook noodles in boiling, salted water until just tender; drain. Combine noodles with cottage cheese, garlic, Worcestershire, sour cream, onion, and liquid hot-pepper seasoning.

Turn into a buttered casserole

and top with grated cheese.

Bake uncovered in a 350° oven for 25 minutes, or until heated through. Makes 8 servings.

## Noodles with Cabbage

You'll enjoy the contrasting textures of tender noodles and buttery, caraway-flavored cooked cabbage in this unusual pasta side dish. Serve it with any simple fish, poultry, or meat entrée.

4 cups shredded cabbage
1 teaspoon salt
6 tablespoons butter or margarine
2 teaspoons sugar
½ teaspoon caraway seeds
¼ teaspoon pepper
1 package (8 oz.) wide noodles
  Boiling salted water

Place cabbage in a large bowl and sprinkle with salt; let stand for 30 minutes. Squeeze cabbage, discarding liquid.

In a wide frying pan over medium-high heat, melt butter. Add cabbage, sugar, caraway seeds, and pepper. Cook, stirring occasionally, until cabbage is tender-crisp (about 5 minutes). Keep warm.

Cook noodles in a large kettle of boiling salted water until just tender; drain. Toss with cabbage mixture just before serving. Makes 6 servings.

## Macaroni Mousse

1½ cups milk
1 cup soft bread crumbs
¼ cup (⅛ lb.) butter or margarine
1 red bell pepper or canned pimiento, finely chopped
1 tablespoon chopped parsley
1 teaspoon chopped onion
1 teaspoon salt
½ cup shredded American or mild Cheddar cheese
3 eggs, slightly beaten
1 cup uncooked elbow macaroni, cooked in salted water

Scald milk; add bread crumbs, butter, red pepper or pimiento, parsley, onion, salt, and cheese; blend well. Stir in eggs, then add well-drained cooked macaroni.

Pour into a greased 2-quart bak-

ing dish, set in a shallow pan of hot water, and bake in a 350° oven for about 1 hour, or until firm. Serves 6.

## Macaroni & Cheese

2 cups cooked macaroni
  Salt and pepper to taste
1 teaspoon dry mustard
1 cup milk
1 cup (or more) shredded American or mild Cheddar cheese

Combine macaroni, salt, pepper, and mustard dissolved in the milk. Stir in the cheese, reserving enough to sprinkle generously over the top; mix well.

Turn into a greased 1½-quart casserole, top with remaining cheese, and bake uncovered in a 350° oven 30 to 40 minutes. Serves 3 or 4.

## Fresh Egg Noodles

Use this basic noodle recipe to make wrappers for cannelloni or for thin noodles to serve with Italian sauces such as Sauce Suprême (next page) or Pesto (page 118). Experiment with noodles in casseroles as well.

About 1 cup (or more) unsifted regular all-purpose flour
6 egg yolks
  Olive oil
⅛ teaspoon salt
  Salted water

Pat flour in a firm mound on a board and make a well in the center. In the well, place egg yolks, 1 teaspoon olive oil, and salt. Moving your fingertips in a circle, break yolks and gradually work in flour. Use as much flour (about 1 cup) as needed to form a firm dough.

*(Continued on next page)*

Knead dough on a lightly floured board until very smooth and elastic, about 10 to 15 minutes (surface should spring back when lightly touched). Cover and let rest 5 minutes.

Divide dough in 4 equal parts. Roll each into a paper-thin rectangle a little larger than 9 by 10 inches.

**To Prepare Cannelloni Noodles.** Cut each 9 by 10 rectangle into four 4½ by 5-inch rectangles. Cover until all dough is cut to make a total of 16 noodles. Uncooked noodles can be stacked between double thicknesses of waxed paper and refrigerated overnight, or frozen.

To cook, bring about ½-inch salted water to boil in a large, shallow pan; add 1 tablespoon olive oil. Cook noodles without overlapping about 2 minutes, or just until tender but not soft. Lift out with a spatula and drain on cloth. Cooked noodles can be stacked between double thicknesses of waxed paper and refrigerated overnight.

**To Prepare Thin Noodles.** Dust each 9 by 10 rectangle with flour and place on lightly floured waxed paper. Let dry uncovered a few minutes. Roll up the 9-inch side to form a pinwheel of dough. Slice off pinwheels about ¼-inch wide.

Uncoil pinwheels and lay noodle strips on floured waxed paper to dry, about 30 minutes. You can freeze or refrigerate a day or so, wrapped airtight.

To cook, bring a large kettle of salted water to a boil; add 1 tablespoon olive oil. Add noodles a few at a time, swirling the water to separate, and boil just until tender to the bite, but not soft. Dress with butter or sauce.

## Pasta with Sauce Suprême

Although this is one of the quickest sauces you can make for any of the Italian "macaroni" shapes, it also is one of the most delicious—for first-course or side dishes, or even a main dish.

The sauce is good with ordinary spaghetti or macaroni, but especially glorious with special shapes (often available frozen), such as tortellini, ravioli, or gnocchi. Tagliarini or wide egg noodles are also suitable. If you use fettucine (available frozen), the result is a deluxe version of the dish called Fettucine served by many restaurants.

You also can use Fresh Egg Noodles (recipe on page 71).

¼ cup (⅛ lb.) butter
1½ cups whipping cream
½ teaspoon nutmeg, freshly grated if possible
4 to 5 cups hot or cold cooked, drained pasta (see preceding suggestions)
1 egg yolk (1 tablespoon)
¾ cup freshly grated Parmesan cheese
Grated nutmeg and grated Parmesan cheese

Melt butter with cream and ½ teaspoon nutmeg in a wide frying pan. Stir in the cooked pasta and bring quickly to boiling; stir gently from time to time. Let boil rapidly 1 to 2 minutes, then blend a little hot sauce with the egg yolk.

Remove pan from heat and stir in the egg yolk mixture and the ¾ cup Parmesan cheese, blending thoroughly. Serve at once, with additional nutmeg and Parmesan. Makes 4 main-dish or 6 to 8 side-dish servings.

## Tomato Sauce for Spaghetti

2 cloves garlic, halved
2 tablespoons olive oil or salad oil
1 can (1 lb. 12 oz.) pear-shaped tomatoes
⅛ teaspoon seasoned pepper or pepper
½ teaspoon each basil and oregano
Salt to taste
Optional: 2 to 3 cups cooked shrimp, scallops, or clams (directions follow)
½ cup chopped fresh parsley
½ to 1 pound spaghetti, cooked
Grated Parmesan or Romano cheese

In a heavy frying pan, sauté the garlic in oil until golden; discard garlic. Drain liquid from tomatoes into the pan, crush the tomatoes, and add to pan with the pepper, basil, and oregano.

Simmer gently, uncovered, for 30 minutes. Raise heat at end of cooking time to thicken sauce, if needed. Add salt to taste.

Add the cooked shellfish (if used) and parsley to sauce; cook just until heated through, about 5 minutes. Serve over spaghetti and pass the cheese at the table. Makes 4 to 6 servings.

**Shrimp Sauce.** Use about ¾ pound shelled, cooked small shrimp. Or buy about 1 pound medium-sized or large shrimp in shells; cook in simmering, seasoned water for 5 to 8 minutes, depending on size; cool, shell and devein, if needed; then cut into bite-sized pieces.

**Clam Sauce.** Use 2 cans (7½ oz. *each*) minced or chopped clams. Drain juices from cans into pan with the tomatoes (increase heat at end of cooking to thicken sauce). Add clams and heat.

**Scallop Sauce.** Simmer 1 to 1½ pounds scallops in seasoned water for 7 to 10 minutes. Drain and cut each scallop in about 4 pieces; add to sauce and heat.

## Yorkshire Pudding

This traditional accompaniment to roast beef is equally good as a breakfast dish if made with butter.

1⅓ cups unsifted regular all-purpose flour
½ teaspoon salt
3 eggs, well beaten
1½ cups milk
⅓ cup beef drippings or butter

Measure the flour into a bowl, sprinkle the salt over it, and stir to distribute evenly. Add the eggs, then the milk gradually, beating just until smooth with a rotary beater.

Melt drippings or butter in a 9 by 13-inch baking pan or 11 by 13-inch broiler pan. (Or, if you have roasted beef, use the roasting pan.) If you use butter, heat it until it turns golden brown.

Pour the batter into the hot fat. Bake in a 400° oven about 40 to 45 minutes or until the crust is a deep brown. Cut in squares; serve at once. Serves 6 to 8.

**Herbed Version.** Add 1 tablespoon minced parsley and ¼ teaspoon *each* crumbled rosemary and crumbled thyme to the flour.

# Breads, Pancakes & Coffee Cakes

## Basic Bread with Variations

For this recipe, you will need two metal or glass bread pans (either 5¼ by 9¼-inch size or 4½ by 8½), unless you make a loaf variation which can be baked on a baking sheet. Use a bowl of about 4-quart size for mixing; heavy pottery is best because it holds heat well.

Heat regular milk just below the boiling point to scald, then cool to about 105° for dry yeast or 95° for compressed yeast.

*Milk Substitutes.* You may mix 1 cup evaporated milk, which needs no scalding, with 1 cup very hot water—the resulting temperature is usually about right. Or dissolve ¼ cup dry skim milk in 1⅞ cups (2 cups minus 2 tablespoons) warm water.

To make one loaf rather than two, halve all ingredients except yeast and water (still use 1 package yeast dissolved in ¼ cup warm water).

¼ cup warm water
1 package yeast, active dry or compressed
2 cups scalded milk (cool to 105° or 95°)
2 tablespoons melted butter or margarine, or salad oil
2 teaspoons salt
2 tablespoons sugar
6 to 6½ cups regular all-purpose flour

*Step 1.* Pour ¼ cup water into bowl; add yeast and stir until dissolved. Stir in the milk, then add the melted butter, salt, and sugar; stir until well blended.

*Step 2.* Sift flour and measure. Stir in 3 cups flour, 1 cup at a time. Add fourth cup flour, and beat until dough is smooth and elastic (rest when you get tired). Mix the fifth cup flour in to make a stiff dough.

*Step 3.* Measure sixth cup flour, sprinkle about half of it on board. Turn out dough onto heavily floured area of board. Keep coating of flour on dough as you begin to knead.

*Step 4.* With floured hands, fold dough toward you with fingers; push firmly away with heel of your hand. Add more flour to board as it's kneaded in—until the dough no longer sticks. Kneading is finished when non-sticky dough is smooth and satiny.

*Step 5.* Put dough in greased bowl, grease top lightly. Cover bowl and set in warm place (about 80°) to rise.

*Step 6.* Let dough rise until almost doubled (about 1½ hours at 80°). Test by inserting two fingers about ½ inch into risen dough—if indentations remain, the dough is ready to shape.

*Step 7.* Punch dough down; squeeze out air bubbles with your hands; shape into a smooth ball. Grasp in center of ball and squeeze

dough to divide into equal portions for the 2 loaves.

*Step 8.* Form each loaf by squeezing dough to press out air bubbles; shape into a smooth oval. Turn over in one hand; with other hand, pinch seam lengthwise down center to seal; turn ends of oval in and pinch a seam at each end to seal.

*Step 9.* Put shaped loaves in greased pans, seams down. Cover; let rise in a warm place until almost doubled (about 45 minutes). Put in 375° oven (350° if you use glass pans).

*Step 10.* Bake until nicely browned and just starting to pull away from pan sides (about 45 minutes). Remove from oven; turn loaves out of pans to cool before slicing or wrapping.

**Variations.** Below and on the next page, we offer 20 different breads you can make with the preceding Basic Bread recipe. For delicious white and dark breads, simply follow the step-by-step directions, adding or substituting ingredients as explained in the variations. All steps have been numbered.

### WHITE BREAD VARIATIONS

**Egg Braid.** In Step 1, break 2 eggs into a 2-cup measure; beat in milk to make 2 cups, and use this mixture in place

*. . . Basic Bread with Variations (cont'd.)*

of all milk. In Step 8, divide the dough for each loaf into 3 parts; roll each into a strand. Braid each trio of strands together, pinching ends to seal. In Step 9, let rise on a lightly greased baking sheet. Brush with slightly beaten egg before baking. Bake at 375° for 30 to 35 minutes or until nicely browned.

**Tomato Caraway Snack Loaf.** In Step 1, use 2 cups warm tomato juice in place of milk; add 1 tablespoon caraway seed. In Steps 7 through 9, divide dough into 4 equal parts. Roll each into a long, thin loaf, about 14 inches long; let rise on lightly greased baking sheets. Brush with slightly beaten egg, and sprinkle each loaf with about 1 teaspoon caraway seed before baking. Bake at 375° for 25 to 30 minutes, or until lightly browned.

**Onion Bread.** In Step 1, use 1 can (10½ oz.) onion soup and enough warm water to make 2 cups liquid in place of all milk; omit sugar, use only 1 teaspoon salt, and add 1 tablespoon instant minced onion. In Steps 8 and 9, shape each loaf into a ball and place in a greased 1-quart round casserole; bake same as basic loaves.

**French Bread.** In Step 1, use water in place of milk; omit shortening. In Steps 8 through 10, shape into two oblong loaves; let rise on a lightly greased baking sheet. Brush with water and make diagonal slashes in top with a sharp knife before baking. Place in a 400° oven—with shallow pan of hot water in oven bottom—until crusty and brown, about 45 minutes.

*Note:* A recipe for Sourdough French Bread is on page 76.

**Diet Bread.** In Step 1, use all water, or ¼ cup powdered skim milk stirred into 1⅞ cups (2 tablespoons less than 2 cups) water, in place of milk. Omit the shortening, salt, and sugar.

**Poppy Seed Bubble Loaf.** In Steps 7 through 10, pinch off pieces of dough (after it's punched down) to make tiny balls about 1 inch in diameter. Melt 4 tablespoons butter. Measure ¼ cup poppy seed. Dip top of each ball first into butter, then into poppy seed, and pile all the balls in one lightly greased (10-inch) tube pan, seed side up; let rise. Bake at 375° about 55 minutes.

**Cinnamon Swirl Loaf.** In Steps 8 and 9 roll out dough for each loaf into a

rectangle about 6 by 16 inches. Mix 4 tablespoons sugar with 4 tablespoons cinnamon; sprinkle half evenly over top of each rectangle. Beginning with a narrow side, roll each tightly into a loaf; seal ends and bottom by pinching together to make seam. Let rise in 2 baking pans (5¼ by 9¼-inch size).

**Orange-Raisin-Nut Bread.** In Step 1, use 2 cups warm orange juice instead of milk; add 1 tablespoon grated orange peel, 1 cup seedless raisins, and ½ cup chopped walnuts.

**Herb Breads.** If you want to make two kinds, in Step 4 divide dough into two parts; knead each part separately, kneading a different herb into each. Select from these herbs, using the following amounts for each half of the dough: 1 tablespoon dill weed; 1 tablespoon savory; 1½ teaspoons basil; 1½ teaspoons oregano; 1½ teaspoons thyme; or 2¼ teaspoons marjoram.

## DARK BREAD VARIATIONS

When you substitute other flours, follow this order for mixing with the liquid ingredients: The first, second, and sixth (or last) cups of flour should be all-purpose white or whole wheat. The other flours can be the third, fourth, and fifth cups you add.

Because the finished loaves of bread are smaller and more compact than white bread, you'll have more attractively shaped loaves if you use medium-sized bread pans (4½ by 8½ inches or 3¾ by 7½ inches) instead of the standard 5¼ by 9¼-inch pans.

**Medium Rye.** Use 2 cups rye flour and 4 cups all-purpose.

**Swedish Orange Rye.** Use 2 cups rye flour and 4 cups all-purpose. In Step 1, add 2 tablespoons grated orange peel and 1 tablespoon caraway, anise, *or* fennel seed.

**Dark Rye.** Use 3 cups rye and 3 cups all-purpose flour. In Step 1, omit sugar; instead of all milk, use ½ cup light or dark molasses with 1½ cups milk.

**Light Rye.** Use 1 cup rye flour and 5 cups all-purpose. This has greater volume than the darker breads, and is best baked in the standard 5¼ by 9¼-inch bread pans.

**100% Whole Wheat.** Use all whole wheat flour. In Step 1, omit sugar; use

½ cup honey, molasses, or maple syrup with 1½ cups milk instead of all milk.

**50% Whole Wheat, Graham, or Cracked Wheat.** Use 3 cups of any of these flours, with 3 cups all-purpose. Use brown sugar instead of granulated sugar, if you prefer.

**Fruit-Nut Graham.** Make 50% Graham Bread. In Step 7, knead in 1 cup chopped mixed glacéed fruit or chopped pitted dates and 1 cup chopped nuts. After loaves are baked, glaze while still warm with ½ cup sifted powdered sugar mixed with 1 tablespoon water.

**Dark Mixed Grain.** For flour use ½ cup wheat germ, ½ cup buckwheat flour, 1 cup rye, and 4 cups whole wheat. Omit sugar; use ½ cup dark molasses with 1½ cups milk instead of all milk.

**Pumpernickel.** For flour use 1 cup whole bran cereal, 2 cups rye flour, and 3 cups whole wheat. In Step 1, add 1 tablespoon caraway seed.

**Oatmeal.** Use 4 cups all-purpose flour and 2 cups oat flour (found in health food stores, or make it by whirling rolled oats in electric blender until fine).

**Soy-Graham.** Use 1 cup soy flour, 2 cups graham, and 3 cups all-purpose.

# Refrigerator Bread

Prepare the recipe for Refrigerator Rolls on page 77, following instructions until dough is ready to shape.

Then, take two-thirds of the dough; knead slightly to release air bubbles and make smooth. Shape into a smooth oval. Turn over in one hand; with the other hand, pinch seam in center, turn ends, seal. Place in a greased 5 by 9-inch loaf pan, seam down.

Cover and let rise until almost doubled before baking. (Use remaining dough to fill small molds or miniature bread pans about one-third full, or to make about 8 dinner rolls.)

Brush with the egg yolk and water mixture described in roll recipe. Bake in a 350° oven about 45 minutes. (Small rolls and loaves take 25 minutes.) The crust will be nicely browned.

# Pueblo Bread

Lop-eared loaves of bread baked in clay ovens are traditional with the Pueblo Indians. This recipe tells you how to form and cut the dough to produce the authentic "crazy" shape. A pan of water in the oven with the baking loaves develops the hard crust that occurs naturally in Pueblo outdoor ovens.

2 tablespoons butter, margarine, or shortening
1 cup hot water
2 teaspoons each salt and sugar
½ cup warm water (lukewarm for compressed yeast)
1 package yeast (active dry or compressed)
  About 5 cups unsifted regular all-purpose flour

Measure butter into a small bowl, add hot water, salt, and sugar; stir occasionally until fat melts. In the meantime, blend warm water with yeast in another small bowl.

Measure 4 cups of the flour into a large bowl, making a well in the center. When water with fat is cooled to lukewarm, combine with yeast mixture and pour into flour well. Blend ingredients thoroughly.

Measure the remaining 1 cup flour onto a board, spreading part of it into a medium-heavy layer; turn dough out onto this area. Knead dough vigorously for 15 minutes, gradually working in a little of the flour at a time until all is absorbed by dough (if dough still feels a little sticky, add a little flour to board to prevent sticking). At the end of 15 minutes the dough should be smooth and velvety feeling with no flour on surface.

Place dough in a deep bowl, cover, and set in warm place and let rise until doubled in size. Knead again on a very lightly floured board to remove air.

Divide dough in 2 equal portions; shape each into a ball and flatten slightly. To shape each loaf, roll the ball of dough out on a lightly floured board to make a circle 8 inches in diameter.

Fold circle *almost* in half (like a giant Parkerhouse roll); the center of the top circular edge should set back about 1 inch from the center of the bottom edge.

Make 2 slashes all the way down through folded dough (forming 3 equal sections) from the curved side; but do not slash all the way to the fold—stop 1½ inches short of it. Set each loaf in a greased 9-inch pie pan, spreading slashes apart and letting ends of folded side extend up rim of pan.

Cover shaped loaves lightly and let rise in a warm place until about doubled in size. Bake in a 350° oven for 1 hour or until richly browned. Place a small pan of water in the oven with the loaves; do not put directly beneath baking bread. Serve hot or cold. Makes 2 loaves.

# Rich Batter Bread

This recipe received the most votes of all the favorite *Sunset* recipes mentioned by readers. No wonder. The recipe has many fun and foolproof aspects.

The tall, round loaves are light, moist, and fine textured. They rise and bake in coffee cans, which also act as containers both for storing the dough if you freeze it before baking and for keeping baked bread fresh. The plastic can lids not only aid storage, but also indicate—by popping off—when the bread has risen properly. The batter requires no kneading and only has to rise once.

1 package active dry yeast
½ cup warm water
⅛ teaspoon ground ginger
3 tablespoons sugar
1 can (13 oz.) undiluted evaporated milk
1 teaspoon salt
2 tablespoons salad oil
4 to 4½ cups unsifted regular all-purpose flour
  Butter or margarine

Dissolve yeast in water in a large mixer bowl; blend in ginger and 1 tablespoon of the sugar. Let stand in a warm place until mixture is bubbly, about 15 minutes. Stir in the remaining 2 tablespoons sugar and the milk, salt, and salad oil. With mixer on low speed, beat in flour 1 cup at a time, beating very well after each addition. Beat in last cup of flour with a heavy spoon; add flour until dough is very heavy and stiff but too sticky to knead.

Place dough in a well-greased 2-pound coffee can, or divide into 2 well-greased 1-pound coffee cans.

Cover with well-greased plastic lids. Freeze if you wish.

To bake, let covered cans stand in warm place until dough rises and pops off the plastic lids, 45 to 60 minutes for 1-pound cans, 1 to 1½ hours for 2-pound cans. (If frozen, let dough stand in cans at room temperature until lids pop; this takes 4 to 5 hours for 1-pound cans, 6 to 8 for the 2-pound size.) Discard lids and bake in a 350° oven for 45 minutes for 1-pound cans, 60 minutes for 2-pound cans. Crust will be very brown; brush top lightly with butter.

Let cool for 5 to 10 minutes on a cooling rack, then loosen crust around edge of can with a thin knife, slide bread from can, and let cool in an upright position on rack. Makes 1 large or 2 small loaves. Try the following variations.

**Light Wheat Bread.** Use basic recipe but use 1½ cups whole wheat flour and 3 cups all-purpose flour. Replace sugar with honey.

**Corn-Herb Batter Bread.** To yeast mixture, add 2 teaspoons celery seed, 1½ teaspoons ground sage, and ⅛ teaspoon marjoram. Substitute ½ cup yellow cornmeal for ½ cup of the flour.

**Raisin-Nut Batter Bread.** To yeast mixture, add 1 teaspoon cinnamon and ½ teaspoon nutmeg. Stir ½ cup *each* raisins and chopped walnuts into batter with final addition of flour.

# French Bread à la Zonie

1 long loaf French bread (sourdough preferred)
½ to 1 pound sharp Cheddar cheese, finely shredded
½ cup finely minced parsley
1 or 2 cloves garlic, minced or mashed
  Juice of ½ lemon
  Salt
  Pepper
  Melted butter and olive oil

Split the loaf of bread lengthwise, then slice the halves crosswise just to the crust but not through it.

Mix the cheese, parsley, garlic, lemon juice, salt, and pepper; beat in enough melted butter and olive oil to make a creamy, spreadable mixture. Spread this paste on the cut surfaces of the bread and let stand for an hour or two.

Just before serving, place on a baking sheet and heat thoroughly in a 375° oven, then brown lightly under the broiler.

## Sourdough Starter

The authentic sourdough of pioneers in the West and Alaska is a simple combination of milk and flour kept in a warm place until it begins to bubble from bacterial fermentation. The organisms responsible are present in milk.

To make the starter, place 1 cup milk in a glass jar or crock (nothing metal) and allow to stand at room temperature for 24 hours. Stir in 1 cup flour. Leave uncovered in a warm place (80° is ideal) for two to five days. Once it has a good sour aroma and is full of bubbles, it is ready to use. A good place is near the pilot light on a gas range; do not place it too close because too much heat will stop the fermentation. If it starts to dry out, stir in enough tepid water to bring it back to the original consistency.

If you are unsuccessful in making a starter, it may be because the necessary bacteria were not present in the milk or because the temperature was not high enough to sustain the fermentation.

Try to maintain about 1½ cups starter. Each time you use part, replenish it with equal amounts of milk and flour. Leave at room temperature several hours or overnight until full of bubbles again, then cover and store in the refrigerator.

The starter is best if you use it once a week. If you do not use it for two or three weeks, discard about half and replenish as described. Given good care a starter becomes more flavorful with age. If you don't plan to use the starter for several weeks, freeze it. Leave at room temperature for 24 hours after thawing.

A double leavening action exists in sourdough recipes: from the reaction of acid (directly related to the sourness) with soda, and from the bacterial action in the starter. The more sour your starter, the more soda you must add. Begin by using the suggested amount; don't increase or decrease it more than 50 per cent. You will also find that the rising times will vary with temperature.

A recipe for Sourdough French Bread follows. A recipe for Sourdough English Muffins is on page 80.

## Sourdough French Bread

Plan on 24 hours from start to finish for this sourdough bread.

1½ cups warm water
1 cup sourdough starter (see preceding instructions)
4 cups unsifted regular all-purpose flour
2 teaspoons salt
2 teaspoons sugar
2 cups unsifted regular all-purpose flour (more or less)
½ teaspoon soda (or more)

Combine water, starter, the 4 cups flour, salt, and sugar. Mix well, place in a non-metallic container, and leave at room temperature about 18 hours, or until sponge has doubled in size. Stir in 1 cup of the remaining flour which has been mixed with the soda; the resulting dough will be very stiff. Turn dough out onto a floured board and knead, adding remaining 1 cup flour as needed. Knead until smooth, at least 8 minutes, until the dough cannot absorb any more flour.

Shape into two oblong loaves or one large round loaf. Place on a *lightly* greased cookie sheet, cover, and place in a warm place for 3 to 4 hours, or until nearly doubled in bulk. Just before baking, brush with water; make diagonal slashes in the top with a sharp knife or a single-edge razor. Place a shallow pan of hot water in the bottom of the oven. (For a more tender crust, do not place pan of water in oven, and brush unbaked loaf with salad oil or butter instead of water.)

Bake in a 400° oven until crust is a medium dark brown (about 45 minutes for the oblong loaves, 50 minutes for the large round loaf). For a heavier and tougher crust, remove loaf from oven 10 minutes before it is done; brush with salted water and return to a 425° oven for the remaining time.

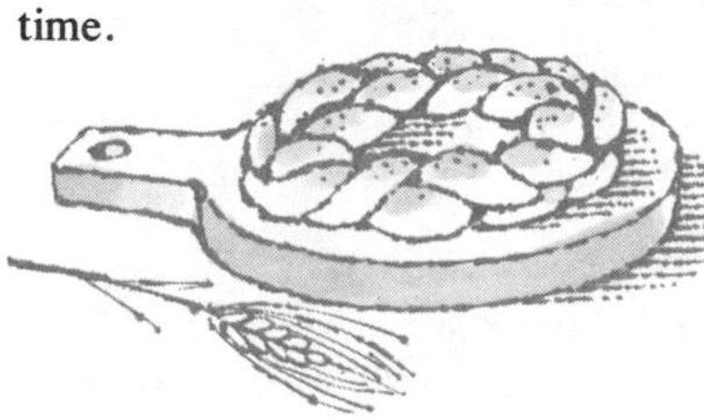

## Irish Soda Bread

4 cups unsifted regular all-purpose flour (or use 2 cups whole wheat flour and 2 cups regular flour)
1 teaspoon salt
3 teaspoons baking powder
1 teaspoon soda
¼ cup sugar (optional)
⅛ teaspoon cardamom or coriander (optional)
¼ cup (⅛ lb.) butter or margarine
2 cups currants or seedless raisins (optional)
1 egg
1¾ cups buttermilk (or regular milk plus 5 teaspoons vinegar)

Combine in a large bowl the flour, salt, baking powder, soda, sugar and spice, if used. Add butter or margarine, and cut in with a pastry blender or two knives until crumbly. Mix in currants if used. Beat egg slightly and mix with buttermilk; add to dry ingredients and stir until blended. Turn out on a floured board and knead until smooth, 2 or 3 minutes.

Divide dough in half, and shape each into a round loaf; place each loaf in an 8-inch cake or pie pan. Press down until dough fills pans. With a sharp knife, cut crosses on tops of loaves, about ½ inch deep in the middle. Bake in a 375° oven for 35 to 40 minutes. Serve warm or cold. Makes 2 loaves.

## Cornmeal Bread

Compared to usual cornbread recipes this one is exceptionally moist, light, and fine grained—almost cakelike in texture. It is also sweeter than most.

Any leftover pieces can be split open, buttered, and toasted under the broiler. Serve with honey, marmalade, or apple butter.

½ cup (¼ lb.) butter or margarine
⅔ cup sugar
2 eggs
1 cup buttermilk
½ teaspoon baking soda
1 cup yellow cornmeal
1 cup all-purpose flour
½ teaspoon salt

In a 3-quart pan, melt butter over medium heat. Remove from heat and stir in sugar. Add eggs and beat until well blended. Combine buttermilk and soda and stir into butter mixture. Add cornmeal, flour, and salt; mix just until blended.

Pour batter into a greased 8-inch square baking pan. Bake in a 375° oven for 30 minutes, or until bread begins to pull away from sides of pan. Cut into squares and serve warm. Makes 6 to 8 servings.

## Golden Spoon Bread

If you have had trouble making spoon bread which does not fall, you will like this recipe. The bread is delicate, but surprisingly stable.

Spoon bread, of course, has the name it does because you serve it with a spoon.

2 cups milk
2 tablespoons butter or margarine
1 teaspoon sugar
1 teaspoon salt
⅔ cup yellow cornmeal
4 eggs, separated

Put milk, butter, sugar, and salt in a saucepan; bring to a boil. Add corn-meal very gradually, stirring to pre-vent lumping, and cook over low heat, stirring constantly, for 3 to 5 minutes, or until thick; remove from heat and let cool slightly.

Stir in beaten egg yolks; beat egg white stiff and then fold into batter. Turn into a greased 1-quart casserole with straight sides, and bake in a 375° oven for about 30 to 35 minutes, or until firm enough for a wooden pick inserted in the middle to come out clean. Serve from the baking dish at once. Serves 4.

## Mexican Spoon Bread

A layer of green chiles and Cheddar cheese awaits you in this corn-rich bread.

1 can (1 lb.) cream-style corn
¾ cup milk
⅓ cup salad oil or melted shortening
2 eggs, slightly beaten
1 cup cornmeal
½ teaspoon soda
1 teaspoon salt
1 can (4 oz.) California green chiles, seeded and chopped
1½ cups shredded Cheddar cheese

Mix all ingredients except chiles and cheese in order given (wet ingredients first, then dry ones).

Pour half of batter into greased 9 by 9-inch square baking pan; sprinkle with green chiles and half the cheese. Spread remaining batter on top and sprinkle with remaining cheese.

Bake 45 minutes in a 400° oven. Cool just enough to set a little before cutting into serving-size pieces. Serves 8 to 10.

## Quick Croissants

This recipe became an instant hit be-cause it provides a remarkably simple way to make flaky pastry without hav-ing to butter, fold, roll, and chill the dough many times—the way French bakers traditionally do it.

Also, you can mix the dough as much as 4 days before baking. And you can freeze the baked rolls. After shaping, let the croissants rise at room temperature before baking.

1 package yeast, active dry or com-pressed
1 cup warm water (lukewarm for compressed yeast)
¾ cup evaporated milk, undiluted
1½ teaspoons salt
⅓ cup sugar
1 egg
5 cups unsifted all-purpose flour
¼ cup (⅛ lb.) butter or margarine, melted and cooled
1 cup (½ lb.) firm butter or mar-garine, at refrigerator tem-perature
1 egg, beaten with 1 tablespoon water

In a bowl, let yeast soften in water. Add milk, salt, sugar, egg, and 1 cup of the flour. Beat to make a smooth batter, and blend in melted butter; set aside.

In a large bowl, cut the 1 cup firm butter into remaining 4 cups flour until

butter particles are the size of dried kidney beans. Pour yeast batter over top and carefully turn the mixture over with a spatula to blend just until all flour is moistened. Cover with clear plastic film, and refrigerate until well chilled—at least 4 hours or up to 4 days.

Remove dough to a floured board, press into a compact ball, and knead about six turns to release air bubbles. Divide dough into four equal parts. Shape one part at a time, leav-ing remaining dough, wrapped in plas-tic film, in refrigerator.

**To Shape Croissants.** Roll one part of the dough on a floured board into a circle, 17 inches in diameter. Using a sharp knife, cut the circle into 8 equal pie-shaped wedges.

For each croissant, loosely roll wedges toward the point. Shape each roll into a crescent and place on an ungreased baking sheet with the point down; allow at least 1½ inches of space around each croissant.

Cover lightly, and let rise at room temperature in a draft-free place. (Do not speed the rising of the rolls by placing them in a warm spot.) When almost doubled in bulk (about 2 hours), brush with egg and water mix-ture. Bake at 325° for about 35 min-utes, or until lightly browned; serve warm. Makes 32.

Freeze the rolls if you like, tightly wrapped. To reheat, arrange rolls in single layer on baking sheet, and bake, uncovered, in a 350° oven for about 10 minutes.

## Refrigerator Rolls

You can keep this dough in the re-frigerator up to 4 days to bake fresh rolls whenever you wish.

1 cup milk
½ cup sugar
1 teaspoon salt
½ cup (¼ lb.) butter or margarine
1 package yeast, active dry or com-pressed
¼ cup warm water (lukewarm for compressed yeast)
3 eggs, slightly beaten
4¾ cups unsifted all-purpose flour
1 egg yolk mixed with 1 tablespoon water

Scald milk and pour over sugar, salt, and butter in a large bowl. Let cool to lukewarm. Soften yeast in the water and blend into milk and sugar mixture with the beaten eggs. Gradually stir in flour to make a soft dough; cover and let rise in warm place until it begins to puff up, about 30 minutes. Punch down, cover with clear plastic film and refrigerate 2 to 3 hours.

Punch down again, knead on lightly floured board just until smooth, about 1 minute; wrap in plastic bag or clear plastic film; refrigerate again, at least 4 hours (or as long as 4 days). Dough is then ready to shape.

Divide dough in half, then divide each half into 12 equal pieces. Form each piece into a smooth ball. Arrange 8 of the smooth balls into each of three greased 8 or 9-inch baking pans, spacing 1 inch apart. (At this point, you can cover pans with plastic wrap and refrigerate 3 to 4 hours if you wish.) Cover and let rise in a warm place (80°) until almost doubled before baking.

Brush with egg yolk and water mixture. Bake in a 350° oven about 25 minutes or until lightly browned. Makes about 2 dozen rolls.

## Italian Bread Sticks

1 package yeast, active dry or compressed
⅔ cup warm water (lukewarm for compressed yeast)
2 tablespoons each salad oil and olive oil
1 teaspoon salt
1 tablespoon sugar
About 2¼ cups unsifted regular all-purpose flour
1 egg, beaten
Poppy or sesame seed (optional)

Dissolve yeast in water; add oil, salt, sugar, and 1 cup of the flour. Beat until smooth. Add enough of the remaining flour to make a stiff dough. Turn out on a floured board and knead until smooth and elastic (about 5 minutes), using additional flour as needed. Place dough in buttered bowl, cover with damp towel, and let rise in warm place (about 80°) until doubled in bulk (about 1 hour).

Punch dough down; divide in half. Cut each half into 24 equal-sized pieces; roll each, using palms of hands, into 6 or 8-inch lengths. Place parallel on greased baking sheets about ½ inch apart. Brush with egg

and sprinkle with poppy or sesame seed, if desired. Let rise in warm place until almost doubled (about 30 minutes). Bake in a 325° oven for 30 minutes or until golden. Makes 4 dozen.

## Old-fashioned Cream Scones

Sprinkled with a little sugar just before baking, these biscuitlike wedges are the perfect place for lots of butter and your favorite jam.

2 cups unsifted regular all-purpose flour
1 tablespoon baking powder
2 tablespoons sugar
½ teaspoon salt
¼ cup (⅛ lb.) butter or margarine
2 eggs, beaten (reserve 1 tablespoon egg white for brushing on top)
⅓ cup whipping cream
2 teaspoons sugar

In a bowl combine the flour, baking powder, the 2 tablespoons sugar, and salt. With a fork, cut in the butter until mixture resembles fine crumbs. Stir in the eggs and cream to make a stiff dough.

Turn out onto a lightly floured board and knead lightly until dough sticks together. Divide into two parts. Roll each part out to make a circle about 6 inches in diameter and about 1 inch thick. With a knife, cut each circle into quarters, making even wedges.

Arrange on an ungreased baking sheet about 1 inch apart. Brush tops of scones with the reserved egg white and sprinkle with the 2 teaspoons sugar. Bake in a 400° oven for 15 minutes or until golden brown. Serve immediately. Makes 8 large scones.

**Orange Cream Scones.** Add 2 to 3 teaspoons grated orange peel and ¼ teaspoon vanilla when you add liquid.

## Monkey Bread

No one knows why this recipe from old Bohemia has the name it does.

3½ cups regular all-purpose flour
1½ packages yeast, active dry or compressed
¼ cup warm water (lukewarm for compressed yeast)
¾ cup milk, scalded and cooled to warm (lukewarm for compressed yeast)
¼ cup sugar
1 teaspoon salt
½ cup (¼ lb.) butter or margarine, melted and cooled
Melted butter

Sift flour and measure. In a large bowl, dissolve yeast in warm water. Stir in milk, sugar, salt, butter or margarine, and flour. Beat well, cover, and let rise in a warm place (80°) until almost double in bulk (about 1 hour).

Punch down and roll out on a lightly floured board to ¼-inch thickness. Cut in diamond shaped pieces about 2½ inches long. Dip each piece in melted butter and arrange pieces overlapping in a 9-inch ungreased ring mold—mold should be half full. Let rise until almost double in bulk.

Bake in a 400° oven for 30 minutes, or until golden brown. Serve warm; pull bread apart to eat. Serves 12.

## Hamburger Buns

2 packages yeast, active dry or compressed
½ cup warm water (lukewarm for compressed yeast)
2 cups milk, scalded and cooled
1 cup (½ lb.) butter or margarine, melted and cooled
¼ cup sugar
4 teaspoons salt
4 eggs, slightly beaten
9½ cups unsifted all-purpose flour
1 egg
1 teaspoon water
Sesame, celery, caraway, or poppy seeds or dried onion flakes

Dissolve yeast in the ½ cup warm water. Combine milk, butter, sugar, salt, the 4 eggs, and 4 cups of flour in a large bowl. Beat well with an electric mixer about 2 minutes.

Beat in remaining flour by hand to make a soft dough. Turn out on a lightly floured board and knead until smooth and elastic, about 10 minutes. Place dough in a greased bowl, cover, and let rise in a warm place until doubled in bulk, about 1½ hours. Then punch dough down and shape it.

Lightly grease 24 foil pans, each about 4 inches in diameter. Form smooth-topped balls of dough about 2 inches in diameter. Place dough in pans, pressing to flatten. Beat the 1 egg with the 1 teaspoon water; brush buns. Sprinkle each with 1 teaspoon seeds or onion flakes. Set pans on baking sheets; let dough rise in warm place until almost doubled in bulk, about 30 minutes.

Bake in a 375° oven for 12 to 15 minutes, or until lightly browned. Cool 5 minutes, then turn out on racks. Wrap when cool; freeze if you wish. Makes about 24.

## Baking Powder Biscuits

The following amounts will make 14 biscuits cut with a 1¾-inch cutter. See end of recipe for quantity of ingredients to make 7-biscuit or 21-biscuit batches.

    2  cups regular all-purpose flour
    4  teaspoons baking powder
    ½  teaspoon salt
    ¼  cup shortening
    ¾  cup milk
       Flour

Sift flour, measure, and sift again with the baking powder and salt. Cut in shortening with a pastry blender or two knives until the mixture has the texture of cornmeal. Add milk and stir lightly with a fork, just until the dough holds together well.

Turn dough out onto a lightly floured board, sprinkle lightly with flour, and gently fold a few times, just until the surface is no longer sticky. Roll or pat dough ¾ inch thick and cut with a floured cutter.

Arrange biscuits on an ungreased baking sheet, touching if you want them to have soft sides or apart for crusty sides. Bake on the center rack of a 450° oven for 12 to 15 minutes, until lightly browned and still slightly moist when broken apart. Makes 14 biscuits.

**For 7 Biscuits.** Use 1 cup flour, 2 teaspoons baking powder, ¼ teaspoon salt, 2 tablespoons shortening, and 6 tablespoons milk.

**For 21 Biscuits.** Use 3 cups flour, 2 tablespoons baking powder, ¾ teaspoon salt, 6 tablespoons shortening, and 1 cup plus 2 tablespoons milk.

### BISCUIT VARIATIONS

Here are some variations on the biscuit theme.

**Tomato.** Use tomato juice in place of the milk.

**Cheese.** Add ½ cup shredded American or Cheddar cheese to flour mixture.

**Cheese-frosted.** Place biscuits close together in pan. Melt ¼ pound shredded soft, nippy cheese and ½ cup (¼ lb.) butter or margarine together in a double boiler; blend well and pour over biscuits just before baking.

**Orange.** Add 1 tablespoon grated orange peel to flour mixture. Use half orange juice and half water for liquid. Bake. While still warm, cover tops with a frosting of powdered sugar blended with enough orange juice to be spreadable.

**Whole Wheat.** Use ⅔ cup whole wheat and 1⅓ cups all-purpose flour.

**Drop.** Use 1 cup milk to make a very soft dough. Drop into greased muffin pans, or on a lightly greased baking sheet or pie pan.

**Soda.** For leavening, use 2 teaspoons baking powder and ¼ teaspoon soda. Use buttermilk (or regular milk mixed with 2 teaspoons vinegar) for liquid.

**Herb.** Add ½ cup finely chopped chives, fresh parsley, or watercress to the dry ingredients.

**Pigs in Blankets.** Roll biscuit dough ⅛-inch thick. Cut in squares large enough to wrap each around a 2-inch piece of frankfurter. Place on an ungreased baking sheet and bake in a 375° oven for 20 minutes.

**Turnovers.** Roll biscuit dough ⅛-inch thick. Cut into squares of any desired size. Place a spoonful of egg, ham, chicken, or tuna sandwich filling in the center of each square. Fold opposite corners together to form a triangle; press together to seal. Place on an ungreased baking sheet; bake in a 400° oven for 15 minutes.

## Spicy Mandarin Orange Muffins

    1  can (11 oz.) mandarin orange
          segments
    1½ cups all-purpose flour
    1¾ teaspoons baking powder
    ½  teaspoon each salt and nutmeg
    ¼  teaspoon allspice
    ½  cup sugar
    ⅓  cup shortening
    1  egg, slightly beaten
    ¼  cup milk
    ¼  cup (⅛ lb.) butter or margarine,
          melted
    ¼  cup sugar mixed with ½ teaspoon
          cinnamon

Drain the mandarin oranges well and spread out on paper towels while you mix the batter.

Sift flour, measure, then sift with the baking powder, salt, nutmeg, allspice, and sugar into a bowl. Cut in the shortening until it is in fine particles. Combine the egg and milk and add all at once; mix just until the flour is moistened. Add drained orange segments and mix lightly until evenly distributed.

Spoon into large greased muffin pan, filling cups about ¾ full. Bake in a 350° oven for 20 to 25 minutes, or until browned. Remove from pans and while hot, dip tops in melted butter, then roll in the cinnamon-sugar. Makes about 1 dozen muffins.

## Basic Flour Muffins

    2  cups regular all-purpose flour
    3  tablespoons sugar
    1  tablespoon baking powder
    ½  teaspoon salt
    1  egg
    ¼  cup melted butter (cooled) or salad
          oil
    1  cup milk

Sift and measure flour. Sift with sugar, baking powder, and salt into a bowl. Make a well in the center. Beat egg with butter and stir into milk. Pour all at once into flour well. Stir *just* to moisten ingredients, with about 12 to 15 full circular strokes that scrape the bottom of the bowl; batter will still look lumpy. (Overbeating makes tough, coarse textured muffins.)

Grease muffin cups or line with baking cup liners; fill ⅔ full with batter. Bake in a 425° oven for about 25 minutes or until well browned. Makes 10 muffins, ½-cup size.

**Variations.** About ½ cup chopped nuts *or* ½ cup chopped dried fruit may be added to the dry ingredients.

## Sourdough English Muffins

  ½ cup sourdough starter (see instructions on page 76)
  1 cup milk
 2¾ cups unsifted regular all-purpose flour
  1 tablespoon sugar
  ¾ teaspoon salt
  ½ teaspoon soda
    About 3 tablespoons cornmeal

In a large mixing bowl, combine starter, milk, and 2 cups of the flour; mix together with a large spoon, cover loosely, and set aside at room temperature for about 8 hours or overnight. Mix ½ cup of the flour, the sugar, salt, and soda; sprinkle over dough; thoroughly mix in. Turn this very stiff dough out onto a board floured with the remaining ¼ cup flour; knead for 2 to 3 minutes or until no longer sticky—add flour if necessary.

Roll dough out to a ¾-inch thickness. Use a 3-inch cutter (a 7-oz. tuna can with ends removed makes a good cutter) to cut out 12 muffins. Place muffins 1 inch apart on a cooky pan or waxed paper which has been sprinkled with cornmeal. Sprinkle more cornmeal over top. Cover with a cloth or waxed paper; set aside in a warm place to rise—about 45 minutes.

Bake on a lightly greased electric griddle set at 275°, or in a frying pan over medium heat, for 8 to 10 minutes per side; turn once. Serve warm from the griddle, or split and toast. Makes 12 muffins.

## Bacon Corn Muffins

  6 slices bacon, coarsely chopped
  1 cup regular all-purpose flour
  2 teaspoons baking powder
  ½ teaspoon each salt and soda
  ⅓ cup sugar
  1 cup yellow cornmeal
  1 egg
  1 cup buttermilk

Cook bacon slowly until browned; drain, reserving 2 tablespoons of the drippings. Crush bacon until crumbly.

Sift flour, measure, and resift with the baking powder, salt, soda, and sugar into a bowl containing the cornmeal. Mix well.

Beat egg lightly with buttermilk and reserved bacon drippings. Stir crushed bacon (if you wish, reserve about 1 tablespoon for topping) and milk mixture into dry ingredients *just* until adequately combined.

Fill greased 2½-inch muffin pans ⅔ full; sprinkle reserved bacon over tops. Bake in a 425° oven for 15 to 18 minutes, or until golden brown. Makes 1 dozen muffins.

## Murray's Water Bagels

  1 package active dry yeast
    Water
  3 teaspoons salt
  3 tablespoons sugar
  6 cups regular all-purpose flour
  1 tablespoon sugar

Dissolve yeast in 1½ cups water, which should be at room temperature. Add salt and the 3 tablespoons sugar; stir to dissolve. Sift flour, measure, add. Knead dough on lightly floured board 10 minutes. Let rise in greased bowl 15 minutes.

Punch flat and form square of dough about 1 inch thick. Use a sharp knife to cut into 12 equal strips. Roll each strip between the fingers until it is about ½ inch in diameter. Join ends to form into doughnut shape by either of two methods: Wrap loosely around three fingers, overlap ends a little, and squeeze together; or form on board by overlapping ends and squeezing together with thumb and forefinger. Work each into uniform shape. Cover all with a towel and let rise 20 minutes.

Place 1 gallon of water in a deep pot, add 1 tablespoon sugar, and bring to a boil. Keep water just under the boiling point and add bagels one at a time; cook 4 or 5 at once. They will sink, then come to the top. Simmer each one for 7 minutes, remove from water with a fork, and place uncovered on a towel to cool.

Place on ungreased baking sheet, not touching. Bake in a 375° oven for 30 to 35 minutes, or until they are brown. Makes 12 bagels 4 inches in diameter.

## Swedish Flatbread

These fragile, crisp rounds which look like oversized crackers may be stored in an airtight container for two or even three weeks.

 2¾ cups unsifted all-purpose flour
  ¼ cup sugar
  ½ teaspoon each soda and salt
  ½ cup (¼ lb.) butter or margarine
  1 cup buttermilk

In a bowl, blend flour with sugar, soda, and salt. Cut in butter until mixture resembles fine crumbs. Stir in buttermilk, using a fork, until mixture holds together adequately.

Shape into a ball with your hands and break off small pieces to make balls an inch in diameter; separate on a floured board. Roll out each ball on floured board to make a round 4 to 5 inches in diameter, turning it over occasionally to prevent sticking. Space rounds slightly apart on ungreased baking sheets. Bake in a 400° oven for 5 minutes, or until lightly browned; check frequently. Cool on wire racks. Store in airtight containers until ready to serve. Serve cold or reheat them.

To reheat, place in a 350° oven for 2 to 3 minutes. Makes about 6 dozen.

## Popovers

When *Sunset Magazine* home economists researched the problems of what makes popovers pop, they came to the conclusion that many old wives' tales exist. Popovers do not need special treatment or special pans.

Popovers perform satisfactorily in a variety of cup-shaped containers—lightweight or heavy, shiny or dull. Preheating the pans is not necessary. Overbeating will actually cause the popovers to rise less. Lowering oven temperature during baking no longer has any effect because modern ovens are so well insulated the temperature does not fall quickly.

However, inaccurate measurement of ingredients or opening the oven door while popovers bake can cause them to fall flat.

- 1 cup regular all-purpose flour
- ¼ teaspoon salt
- 1 tablespoon sugar (optional)
- 1 tablespoon melted butter or salad oil
- 1 cup milk
- 2 large eggs or about ½ cup slightly beaten egg

Sift and measure flour into a bowl. Mix in the salt and sugar. Add oil, milk, and eggs, and beat with a hand beater (or electric beater at medium-high speed) until very smooth, scraping bowl frequently with a rubber spatula; this takes about 2½ minutes.

Grease baking cups with shortening or butter. Fill about one-third or one-half full with the batter. Bake on center rack in a 400° oven for about 40 minutes, or in a 375° oven for 50 to 55 minutes, or until well browned and firm to touch. Remove from pans and serve hot.

Makes 12 popovers baked in ⅓-cup size pans, 10 popovers baked in ½-cup size pans; or 8 or 9 popovers baked in 5 or 6-ounce ovenproof glass cups.

If you like the interior of the popovers to be especially dry, loosen from pan but leave sitting at an angle in cups; prick popovers' sides with a skewer and let stand in the turned-off oven, door slightly ajar, for 8 to 10 minutes.

Baking at 400° gives a richly browned shell with a fairly moist interior; at 375° it will be lighter in color, drier inside.

## Cheese Puffs

Drop these cheesy wonders into soups and salads, or serve as snacks.

- ½ pound American cheese, shredded
- ½ cup (¼ lb.) butter or margarine
- 1 cup unsifted regular all-purpose flour

Blend all ingredients together smoothly with fingers or pastry blender. Roll into small balls about the size of marbles. Place on an ungreased cooky sheet and bake in a 350° oven for 15 to 20 minutes. Serve immediately. Makes 6½ dozen.

*Note:* Unbaked cheese balls may be frozen. There is no need to thaw before baking.

## Crisp Cracker Flatbread

Soda crackers
Ice water
Salt

Place crackers in a shallow pan of ice water for exactly 8 minutes. Remove with a slotted spatula, draining as well as possible without breaking the crackers.

Lay crackers ½-inch apart on a baking sheet, sprinkle with salt, and bake in a 350° oven for 40 to 45 minutes, or until brown and crisp. Serve hot.

## Swiss Egg Braids

The same sweet, egg-rich dough may be used to make three different kinds of bread. Each kind is made of braided ropes of dough and baked on an ordinary metal baking sheet—no special pans are needed.

- 1 cup milk
- ½ cup sugar
- 1 teaspoon salt
- 2 packages yeast, active dry or compressed
- ½ cup warm water (lukewarm for compressed yeast)
- 5 cups unsifted all-purpose flour
- ½ cup (¼ lb.) butter or margarine, melted and cooled to lukewarm
- 3 eggs, slightly beaten

Scald milk and pour over sugar and salt in a large bowl. Let cool to lukewarm. Blend yeast with water

and let stand until softened; add to milk and sugar mixture. Beat in 2 cups of flour to make a smooth, thick batter. Cover and let stand in a warm place 45 minutes, or until light and foamy.

Add butter and eggs; blend thoroughly. Stir in 2½ cups of the remaining flour to make a soft dough. Sprinkle last ½ cup flour on board, then turn dough out onto the floured board; cover and let stand 10 minutes. Knead dough until it is smooth and satiny (this will take about 8 minutes).

Place in greased bowl; turn dough over to grease top. Cover and let rise in a warm place until doubled in bulk, about 1 hour and 45 minutes. Punch down. Shaping and baking directions follow.

**Swiss Egg Braids.** Divide dough in half, cover, and let stand 10 minutes. Then divide each half into thirds. Roll each portion of dough between hands to form a strand 12 inches long, 1¼ inches in diameter. Place 3 strands on board; braid together. Pinch ends together and tuck under loaf. Place on greased baking sheet. Repeat process to make second braid. Cover and let rise in warm place until nearly double, about 1 hour and 15 minutes. Brush with 1 egg yolk slightly beaten with 1 tablespoon water. Bake in a 350° oven for about 35 minutes or until golden brown. Cool on wire racks. Makes 2 loaves.

**Giant Cinnamon Braid.** Set aside ⅓ of the dough for the top braid. Divide the remaining dough into 3 equal portions. Roll each portion between hands to form a strand 12 inches long, and 1¾ inches in diameter. Mix ½ cup sugar and 1 tablespoon cinnamon on a large sheet of waxed paper. Roll each strand of dough in the mixture to coat all sides. Place the three strands on clean sheet of waxed paper; braid together. Pinch ends together and tuck under. Place on greased baking sheet.

Repeat process to make smaller braid with reserved dough, making 3 strands each 12 inches long and 1 inch in diameter. Place on top of larger braid, pressing in lightly. Cover and let rise until almost doubled in bulk, about 1 hour and 15 minutes. Brush loaf with 1 egg yolk beaten with 1 tablespoon water.

Bake in a 350° oven for about 45 minutes or until pick inserted in center comes out clean. (Cover loosely with foil if top begins to get too brown.) Cool on wire rack. Makes 1 loaf.

**Fruit-filled Rings.** While preparing dough, add 1 cup chopped candied fruits, 2 tablespoons vanilla, and 1 teaspoon rum flavoring with the butter and the eggs.

Before shaping dough, divide it in half, cover, and let stand 10 minutes. Divide each half into thirds. Roll each portion of dough between hands to form a strand 20 inches long, 1 inch in diameter. Place 3 strands on board; braid together. Form braid into a ring; pinch ends together. Place on greased baking sheet. Repeat process to make second ring. Cover and let rise in warm place until nearly double, about 1 hour and 15 minutes. Brush with 1 egg yolk beaten with 1 tablespoon water. Bake in a 350° oven for about 35 minutes or until golden brown.

Let cool to warm and top with this glaze: Mix together 1 tablespoon soft butter or margarine and 1 cup sifted powdered sugar. Add ½ teaspoon vanilla and 1½ tablespoons heavy cream; beat until blended and smooth. Makes 2 rings.

# Christmas Brioche

This tender, sweet bread has been called "Christmas" because the dough can be slapped, pounded, snipped, and twisted into innumerable holiday shapes from Santas to reindeer. However, you can also form your own designs of bunnies, pumpkins, or simple flat, round loaves. The "snowflake" design described here actually is attractive for any season of the year.

1 package yeast, active dry or compressed
¼ cup warm water (lukewarm for compressed yeast)
½ cup (¼ lb.) soft butter
⅔ cup sugar
2 teaspoons vanilla
2 tablespoons grated orange peel
½ teaspoon salt
3 whole eggs
3 egg yolks
½ cup milk, scalded and cooled
About 5¼ cups unsifted regular all-purpose flour
Beaten egg white

Mix yeast with warm water and set aside to soften. With a mixer, cream the butter, sugar, vanilla, orange peel,

and salt until fluffy. Beat in eggs and yolks, a few at a time, blending well. Then add yeast and milk and gradually mix in 4½ cups of the flour; you may have to work in the last portion of flour with your hands or a spoon.

Turn dough onto a heavily floured (about ¾ cup) board and knead until smooth and quite elastic, about 15 minutes. Add more flour if necessary.

Butter a large bowl; turn dough over in it to coat surface. Cover and let rise in a warm place for about 1½ hours or until doubled in bulk.

*Snowflake Design:* Turn dough onto a lightly floured board and knead into a smooth ball. Pinch off a lump of dough about 3 inches in diameter to use for decorating and reshape both pieces into smooth balls. Flatten large ball with hands to a ½ to ¾-inch-thick circle on buttered foil or a 14-inch pizza pan.

Invert a bowl (about half the diameter of the dough circle) in the center of the dough circle. Make about 20 evenly spaced cuts with floured kitchen scissors around the dough in sunburst or petal fashion, from the outside of the circle in to the bowl. Twist each of the 20 "petals" tight (several twists each). Remove the bowl.

Slip foil (if pan is not used) onto rimless baking sheet (one sheet or two baking sheets overlapping).

To decorate, form little pieces of dough from small ball into teardrop shapes by pulling surface of dough to underside, so base is pointed. With a floured finger poke holes into the center of the large cake of dough (where the bowl rested); nest teardrops in them.

Let dough rise, uncovered, in a warm place until well puffed, 30 to 45 minutes. Brush surface with beaten egg white. Bake in a 325° oven for 45 to 50 minutes or until richly browned. Serve hot, or let cool on a wire rack and wrap airtight.

The loaf keeps well for a week at room temperature; freeze for longer storage. To reheat, place uncovered loaf on a baking sheet in a 325° oven for 25 minutes; pull apart—*do not cut*—to serve. Makes 1 large loaf.

# Yeast Sweet Rolls with Variations

With this basic dough, you can make Hot Cross Buns, Cinnamon Rolls, or Glazed Orange Rolls.

About 4 cups regular all-purpose flour
¼ cup (⅛ lb.) butter or margarine
1 teaspoon salt
¼ cup sugar
1 cup milk, scalded
1 package yeast, active dry or compressed
¼ cup warm water (lukewarm for compressed yeast)
1 egg, slightly beaten
Softened butter

Sift the flour and set aside. Place the butter, salt, and sugar in a large bowl; add the scalded milk and allow to cool to lukewarm, stirring to dissolve the sugar and salt and to melt the butter. Soften the yeast in the warm water and add, along with the beaten egg, to the cooled milk mixture.

Stir in 3½ cups of the flour, 1 cup at a time, beating vigorously to blend. Scrape dough from the sides of the bowl and brush the top of the dough and the sides of the bowl with softened butter.

Cover dough and let rise in a warm place (80°) about 2 hours, or until almost doubled in bulk. Then turn out on a well-floured board and knead lightly, adding flour until the dough is no longer sticky (do not use more than ¼ to ½ cup flour on the board). Suggestions follow for shaping and baking.

**Hot Cross Buns.** When you prepare the basic dough, incorporate with the flour ½ teaspoon cinnamon, ⅛ teaspoon nutmeg, and ½ cup dried fruits (currants, chopped candied orange peel, or chopped mixed candied fruits). Follow rest of basic recipe.

Shape risen dough into 2 dozen round buns. Place apart on greased baking sheets, cover, and let rise in a warm place (80°) until almost double in size. Slash the tops of each with a sharp knife to make a cross. Bake in a 425° oven about 10 to 14 minutes.

While still warm, fill in the crosses with a frosting made by blending ½ cup powdered sugar, ⅛ teaspoon vanilla, and about 2 teaspoons milk (enough to make a creamy icing). Makes 2 dozen.

**Inside-out Cinnamon Rolls.** Roll out 1 recipe of the basic dough to a rectangle 10 by 24 inches and ¼-inch thick; spread with softened butter (about 3 tablespoons). Sprinkle with ¾ cup brown sugar and about 2 teaspoons cinnamon. Cut into strips about 10 inches long and 1 inch wide, and roll each separately into a snail shape, with the sugar side out.

Place rolls 1 inch apart on a greased baking sheet and sprinkle tops with the excess sugar that fell off the dough. Cover and let rise in a warm place (80°) until almost doubled in bulk.

Bake in 350° oven for about 20 minutes. Makes about 2 dozen.

**Glazed Orange Rolls.** Prepare a filling by creaming together ½ cup (¼ lb.) softened butter, 1 cup sugar, and the grated peel of 2 medium-sized oranges.

Roll out one recipe of the basic sweet dough to a rectangle 10 by 24 inches and ¼-inch thick; spread the filling evenly over the dough. Roll dough up as for a jelly roll (roll 24-inch side) and chill. Cut the chilled dough into 1-inch-thick slices, and place in buttered muffin pans or 1 inch apart on greased baking sheets.

Cover and let rise in a warm place (80°) until almost doubled in bulk. Bake in a 425° oven about 10 to 14 minutes. Serve warm "as is" or topped with the following glaze. Makes 2 dozen.

*Orange glaze:* Simmer together ½ cup sugar, ¼ cup light corn syrup, and ¼ cup water for about 10 minutes; add the grated peel of 1 orange.

# Cardamom Fruit Bread

- 1¼ cups milk
- ½ cup sugar
- 1½ teaspoons salt
- 1 teaspoon ground cardamom
- ½ cup (¼ lb.) butter or margarine
- 2 packages yeast, active dry or compressed
- ½ cup warm water (lukewarm for compressed yeast)
- 1 egg, slightly beaten
- 5½ cups unsifted regular all-purpose flour
- 1 cup chopped candied fruits
- ¾ cup seedless raisins
  Candied whole cherries
- 1 egg white, slightly beaten

Scald milk and pour over sugar, salt, cardamom, and butter in a large bowl. Cool to lukewarm. Soften yeast in water; stir into milk mixture. Beat in egg and 2 cups of the flour to make a smooth batter. Cover and let stand 20 minutes.

Mix together the candied fruit, raisins, and 2 tablespoons of the flour; blend into batter. Stir in enough of the remaining flour to make a soft dough; turn out onto lightly floured board and knead until smooth, about 5 minutes.

Place in greased bowl, turn dough to grease top, cover, and let rise in warm place until doubled, about 1 hour 45 minutes. Punch down, and divide dough into four equal portions.

To shape each loaf, take one portion of the dough and divide into four equal parts; form each part into a loaf-shaped roll 3 inches long. Place these four rolls side by side in a 3½ by 7½-inch loaf pan. Press one whole candied cherry in the center of each of the four parts.

Cover and let rise in warm place until almost doubled, about 1 hour 30 minutes. Brush with egg white. Bake in a 325° oven for 45 minutes, or until inserted pick comes out clean. Makes 4 small loaves.

(To bake fruit bread in 5 by 9-inch loaf pans, divide dough in half then divide each half into four equal parts. Shape each part into a loaf-shaped roll 4½ inches long. Place these four rolls side by side into each of two loaf pans. Increase baking time to 55 minutes.)

# Carrot Bread

- 4 eggs
- 2 cups sugar
- 1¼ cups salad oil
- 3 cups unsifted regular all-purpose flour
- 2 teaspoons baking powder
- 1½ teaspoons soda
- ¼ teaspoon salt
- 2 teaspoons cinnamon
- 2 cups finely shredded raw carrots

Beat the eggs, and add the sugar gradually, beating until thick. Add the oil gradually and continue beating until thoroughly combined. Stir in the flour, baking powder, soda, salt, and cinnamon until mixture is smooth. Stir in the carrots until blended well.

Turn into two well-greased 5 by 9-inch loaf pans or four well-greased 1-pound cans, filling them no more than ⅔ full. Bake the bread in a 350° oven for 1 hour for large loaf or 45 minutes for small loaves, or until a cake tester comes out clean.

# Sun River Banana Bread

- 2¼ cups regular all-purpose flour
- 1 teaspoon baking powder
- ½ teaspoon soda
- ½ teaspoon salt
- ½ cup coarsely chopped nuts
- ⅓ cup shortening
- ⅔ cup sugar
- 2 eggs
- ⅔ cup mashed, fully ripened bananas
- ¼ cup buttermilk or water

Sift flour, measure, and sift again with the baking powder, soda, and salt. Add the nuts.

In another bowl, cream shortening and sugar until light and fluffy. Beat in eggs, one at a time. Blend in banana pulp. Add flour mixture and liquid alternately, beating until smooth. Pour into a well-greased and floured loaf pan. Bake on the center rack in a 350° oven about 1 hour. Remove from pan and cool on rack. Makes 1 loaf.

# Confetti Nut Bread

- 1 egg
- 1 cup granulated sugar
- ⅓ cup brown sugar, firmly packed
- 2 tablespoons salad oil
- 2½ cups regular all-purpose flour
- 1 teaspoon baking powder
- ¼ teaspoon salt
- 1 teaspoon soda
- 1 cup water
- 1 cup chopped mixed candied fruit
- 1 cup broken nut meats

Beat egg; gradually add sugars. Stir in salad oil. Sift flour and measure. Reserve ¼ cup flour to mix with fruit and nuts.

Sift remaining flour again with baking powder, salt, and soda. Add water alternately with dry ingredients to egg mixture. Add fruit and nuts that have been thoroughly dredged in the ¼ cup of flour so that each piece of fruit will remain separate.

*(Continued on next page)*

Place batter in a well-greased and floured loaf pan and bake in a 350° oven 1 hour. Remove from pan and cool on rack. Makes 1 loaf.

## Prune Bread

    2   cups boiling water
    2   cups dried prunes, pitted and
          coarsely chopped
    2   teaspoons soda
    2   tablespoons melted butter
    1¼  cups sugar
    1   egg
    1   teaspoon vanilla
    4   cups regular all-purpose flour
    2   teaspoons baking powder
    1   teaspoon salt
    1   cup chopped walnuts

Pour boiling water over chopped, uncooked prunes; add soda, and allow to stand.

In another bowl, cream butter, sugar, and egg thoroughly; stir in vanilla.

Sift flour, measure, and sift again with baking powder and salt. Add to butter mixture alternately with water from prunes. Stir in prunes and nuts.

Spoon into two 9 by 5-inch greased loaf pans. Bake in a 300° oven for 1 hour, or until the bread is golden brown. Makes 2 loaves.

## French Pancakes (Crêpes)

An inventive cook, or even merely a foresighted one, will keep packages of these thin pancakes in the freezer. They can be filled with something so simple as sugared fresh fruit for dessert, or turned into an elegant entrée stuffed with seafood in curry or Newburg sauce.

    3   eggs
    1   cup milk
    ¾   cup flour
    1   tablespoon sugar
    ¼   teaspoon salt

In a small mixing bowl, beat the eggs well; mix in the milk until smooth. Sift flour, measure, and sift again with the sugar and salt. Add the dry ingredients to the egg mixture and beat with an electric mixer or rotary beater into a smooth batter. Set aside in a cool place for at least 1 hour.

Pour about 2 tablespoons batter for each crêpe onto a lightly buttered, heated 6 to 8-inch pan over medium heat. Turn once, baking until golden-brown on both sides. Makes 16 or more crêpes.

**To Freeze.** Make stacks of from 6 to 12 crêpes, wrap tightly in foil, and freeze. To thaw, set in a warm place on a wire rack for 2 to 3 hours or place the foil-wrapped crêpes in a 175° oven for 15 to 20 minutes.

## Quick Stollen

Vanilla sugar, the perfumed, sparkling topping for stollen, must be made ahead: Bury a split vanilla bean in 1 cup sugar and cover container tightly. Let stand for 2 or 3 days at room temperature.

    2½  cups unsifted regular all-purpose
          flour
    2   teaspoons baking powder
    ¾   cup sugar
    ½   teaspoon salt
    ¼   teaspoon mace
    ⅛   teaspoon cardamom
    ¾   cup ground blanched almonds
    ½   cup (¼ lb.) cold butter
    1   cup cottage cheese, whirled
          smooth in a blender or forced
          through a wire strainer
    1   egg
    ½   teaspoon vanilla
    ¼   teaspoon almond extract
    2   tablespoons rum (or 1½ table-
          spoons water and ½ teaspoon
          rum flavoring)
    ½   cup each currants and golden
          raisins
    ¼   cup chopped candied lemon peel
    3   tablespoons melted butter
    2   tablespoons vanilla sugar (see
          preceding directions)

Combine flour, baking powder, sugar, salt, mace, cardamom, and almonds. Cut in butter with a pastry blender until mixture resembles coarse crumbs.

Blend cottage cheese, egg, vanilla, almond extract, rum, currants, raisins, and lemon peel; stir into flour mixture until all ingredients are moistened. Mold dough into a ball, place on a floured board, and knead 6 to 10 turns or until dough is smooth.

Roll dough out on a floured board to form an oval about 8½ by 10 inches. With rolling pin lightly crease dough just off center, parallel to the

10-inch side. Brush dough with 1 tablespoon of the melted butter. Fold smaller section over the larger.

Place on an ungreased baking sheet which is covered with brown paper. Bake in a 350° oven for about 45 minutes or until crust is well browned and bread tests done in center. Brush with remaining butter; sprinkle with vanilla sugar.

Serve warm, or cool on a wire rack. Wrap airtight to mellow for 2 to 3 days, or freeze. To reheat, wrap loaf in foil and place in a 350° oven for 30 minutes. Makes 1 loaf.

## Baked German Pancake

The giant-sized version of this pancake is called German; the individual ones baked in smaller pans were dubbed Dutch Babies by an old-time Seattle restaurant. Present these show-off pancakes at a party brunch.

    3   eggs
    ½   cup regular all-purpose flour
    ½   teaspoon salt
    ½   cup milk
    2   tablespoons melted butter
        Lemon wedges
        Powdered sugar
        Melted butter

Using a French whip or fork, beat eggs until blended. Sift flour; measure, and sift again with salt. Add flour and salt to eggs in 4 additions, beating after each addition, just until mixture is smooth. Add milk in 2 additions, beating slightly after each. Lightly beat in melted butter.

Generously butter bottom and sides of unheated 9 or 10-inch heavy frying pan. Pour batter into frying pan and bake in a 450° oven for 20 minutes. Reduce oven temperature to 350° and bake 10 minutes more. Slip onto heated plate; serve immediately. Offer lemon wedges, powdered sugar, and melted butter. Makes 2 to 3 servings.

**Dutch Babies Variation.** Prepare batter as for German pancake, but bake differently: Generously butter three 5 or 6-inch baking pans (little pie pans or frying pans). Fill each with ⅓ of the mixture. Bake in a 400° oven for 20 minutes; reduce heat to 350° and bake for 10 minutes more. Makes 3 servings.

## Cornmeal Mountain Buttermilk Pancakes

    1 egg
 1¼ cups buttermilk (or regular milk
       plus 4 teaspoons vinegar)
    1 tablespoon molasses
  ¼ cup melted shortening
    1 cup unsifted regular all-purpose
       flour
    1 teaspoon salt
  ½ teaspoon soda
    2 teaspoons baking powder
  ½ cup yellow cornmeal

Beat together the egg, milk, molasses, and shortening. Add the flour, sifted with the salt, soda, and baking powder; add cornmeal, stir just to blend.

Bake on a moderately hot greased griddle. Makes about 16 pancakes 4 inches in diameter.

## Plain Crispy Waffles

    2 eggs, separated
    2 teaspoons baking powder
  ½ teaspoon salt
    1 tablespoon sugar
    1 cup milk
    3 tablespoons salad oil
 1⅓ cups unsifted regular all-purpose
       flour

Beat egg whites until stiff.

In another bowl, blend the egg yolks with the baking powder, salt, and sugar. Pour in the milk and oil; mix. Add the flour gradually, beating just until smooth. Fold in the beaten egg whites. Bake in waffle iron according to manufacturer's instructions. Makes 4 waffles.

## Light 'n' Crisp Buttermilk Waffles

    1 cup unsifted regular all-purpose
       flour
  ½ cup yellow cornmeal
    1 cup rolled oats
    2 tablespoons baking powder
  ½ teaspoon salt
    2 eggs
  ½ cup melted bacon drippings or
       other shortening, cooled
    3 cups buttermilk

Put all dry ingredients into a bowl, break in the eggs, add the bacon drippings, and stir in the buttermilk.

Let the batter stand about 15 to 30 minutes, until it almost doubles in quantity (because of the large amount of baking powder). Bake waffles in a waffle iron according to manufacturer's instructions. Makes about 12.

## Baked Orange Doughnuts

Doughnuts don't have to be deep-fried to taste good. Here, a 10-minute baking in the oven brings out a nice orange flavor.

    2 packages yeast, active dry or
       compressed
  ½ cup warm water (lukewarm for
       compressed yeast)
    1 cup milk, scalded and cooled to
       lukewarm
    6 tablespoons butter or margarine,
       melted and cooled
    1 cup sugar
    2 teaspoons salt
 1½ tablespoons grated orange peel
    2 eggs
    5 cups unsifted regular all-purpose
       flour
  ½ cup (¼ lb.) butter, melted
  ½ cup sugar mixed with 2 table-
       spoons cinnamon

Dissolve yeast in warm water. In large mixer bowl, combine milk, the 6 tablespoons butter, 1 cup sugar, salt, orange peel, eggs, yeast mixture, and 2 cups of the flour. Beat with electric mixer on high speed about 3 minutes. Gradually beat in remaining flour with a wooden spoon. Turn dough out onto lightly floured board and knead until smooth, about 10 minutes. Place dough in greased bowl, cover, and let rise in a warm place until doubled, about 1½ hours.

Punch dough down. Roll out on floured board with rolling pin to ¼-inch thickness. Lift dough from board, turn over, and let rest 1 to 2 minutes. Then cut with doughnut cut-

ter or use a 3-inch biscuit cutter and cut hole with a 1½-inch cutter. Place cut-out doughnuts on greased baking sheet. Let rise about 30 minutes in a warm place (80°) until almost doubled.

Bake in a 350° oven about 10 minutes or until lightly browned. Brush at once with the ½ cup melted butter and sprinkle with cinnamon-sugar. Makes about 2½ dozen.

## Yellowstone Park Doughnuts

    3 large eggs, separated
    1 cup sugar
 4½ cups regular all-purpose flour
    5 teaspoons baking powder
    1 teaspoon salt
    1 cup milk
    1 teaspoon nutmeg, or vanilla or
       lemon extract
    3 tablespoons melted shortening
       Salad oil or shortening for deep
       frying
       Granulated or powdered sugar
       (optional)

Beat the egg whites until stiff and dry, then beat in the yolks, one at at time. Beat in the sugar gradually. Sift the flour, measure, and sift again with the baking powder and salt; add to the egg mixture alternately with the milk, beating well after each addition. Add the flavoring and the melted shortening.

Turn dough onto a lightly floured board, roll out ½-inch thick, and cut with a doughnut cutter. Heat oil to 380°. Drop in a few doughnuts at a time, and turn frequently until well puffed and golden. Remove with a slotted spoon and drain on paper toweling. When cool, roll in sugar, if desired. Makes 3 dozen.

## Crumb Coffee Cake Superb

This recipe, obtained sometime back in the 1920's from a cook at an inn in Brownsville, Washington, has remained a favorite of present-day cooks—with a minor change or two in the ingredients and method.

A similar recipe, without the nuts and raisins, later appeared—titled Moonshine Gingerbread. You'll serve this good-morning cake with a smile.

*(Continued on next page)*

2 cups regular all-purpose flour
1 cup sugar
½ teaspoon each ginger and cinnamon
¼ teaspoon nutmeg
½ cup (¼ lb.) butter or margarine
½ cup raisins
½ cup chopped nuts (optional)
1 egg, beaten
¾ cup buttermilk (or regular milk plus 2 teaspoons vinegar)
1 teaspoon baking powder
½ teaspoon soda

Sift flour, measure, and sift again with the sugar and spices into a bowl. Cut in the butter until the mixture is crumbly like cornmeal. Take out 1 cup of this crumbly mixture and set aside. Stir the raisins and nuts into the remaining crumbly mixture.

Mix together the egg, milk, baking powder, and soda; stir into the flour and butter mixture containing raisins and nuts, just until well mixed.

Spread half of the reserved crumbs (½ cup) in the bottom of a greased 8 by 8-inch baking pan. Pour in the thick batter, spread evenly, then sprinkle the remaining crumbs (½ cup) over the top. (Or just sprinkle all the 1 cup crumbs on the top.) Bake in a 375° oven for 40 minutes. Cool in the pan. Makes 9 servings.

## Jam Swirl Coffee Cake

⅔ cup each butter or margarine and sugar
2 cups unsifted regular all-purpose flour
2 teaspoons baking powder
½ teaspoon each salt, soda, and cinnamon
¼ teaspoon nutmeg
2 eggs
⅔ cup buttermilk (or regular milk plus 2 teaspoons vinegar)
⅓ cup seedless raspberry, strawberry, or boysenberry preserves

In a large bowl, cream together butter and sugar. Add ¾ cup of the flour and blend until mixture resembles crumbs. Remove ⅔ cup for topping; reserve.

To the remaining crumb mixture add baking powder, salt, soda, cinnamon, nutmeg, and eggs; beat until smooth. Add remaining 1¼ cup flour alternately with buttermilk, beating after each addition just until blended.

Spread batter in a greased 9-inch-square baking pan.

Drop teaspoonfuls of the berry preserves over the top of the batter. Cut through the batter with a knife to marble the preserves through the cake. Work reserved mixture between fingers until it resembles coarse crumbs. Sprinkle over top of batter.

Bake in a 375° oven for 35 minutes, or until a pick inserted in center comes out clean. Makes 9 servings.

## Cinnamon-Sour Cream Coffee Cake

1 cup (½ lb.) butter
1¼ cups sugar
2 eggs
1 cup (½ pt.) sour cream
2 cups regular all-purpose flour
½ teaspoon soda
1½ teaspoons baking powder
1 teaspoon vanilla
¾ cup finely chopped walnut meats combined with 1 teaspoon cinnamon and 2 tablespoons sugar

In the large bowl of your electric mixer, combine the butter, sugar, and eggs. Beat until the mixture is light and fluffy. Blend in the sour cream.

Sift flour, measure, and sift with soda and baking powder into the creamed mixture; add vanilla. Blend well.

Spoon half of the batter into a 9-inch tube pan or 10-inch bundt pan which has been buttered and floured (batter will be quite thick). Sprinkle half of cinnamon-nut mixture over batter. Spoon in remaining batter and top with rest of nut mixture.

Place in a cold oven, set oven at 350°, and bake about 55 minutes. Cut pieces in pan to serve warm or cool. Makes 8 to 10 servings.

## Pecan-Sour Cream Coffee Cake

½ cup (¼ lb.) butter or margarine
1 cup granulated sugar
3 eggs
2 cups regular all-purpose flour
1 teaspoon baking powder
1 teaspoon soda
¼ teaspoon salt
1 cup sour cream
½ cup golden raisins
Pecan Topping (recipe follows)

In the large bowl of your electric mixer, cream together butter and sugar. Add eggs, one at a time, beating well after each addition.

Sift flour, measure, and sift again with baking powder, soda, and salt; add to creamed mixture alternately with sour cream, making about 3 equal additions of each and blending after each addition. Sprinkle raisins over the top and stir in.

Spread mixture in a greased baking pan (13 by 9 by 2 inches). Sprinkle with pecan topping. Bake in a 350° oven (325° for a glass pan) about 30 minutes or until it tests done. Cut in squares and serve either warm or cold. Makes 12 servings.

**Pecan Topping.** Mix ¾ cup firmly packed brown sugar, 1 tablespoon flour, and 1 teaspoon cinnamon; cut in 2 tablespoons butter or margarine until mixture has the consistency of cornmeal. Mix in 1 cup chopped pecans.

## Swiss-style Cereal (Müsli)

This unusual Swiss breakfast cereal has the double virtues of being extremely nutritious, yet as irresistible as hot buttered popcorn.

1 cup each whole filberts and whole blanched almonds
3 cups quick-cooking rolled oats
¾ cup sweetened wheat germ
1 cup dried currants
⅔ cup finely chopped dried apricots
¾ cup firmly packed brown sugar
Milk or cream
Fruit such as sliced bananas or strawberries, or canned mandarin oranges (optional)

Spread filberts on a rimmed baking sheet, and the almonds on another. Bake in a 350° oven for 5 to 8 minutes, or until very lightly browned; shake pans occasionally. Let nuts cool; rub filberts in your hands to loosen as much of the brown exterior as possible, then blow or fan off this chaff. Chop filberts and almonds coarsely.

Blend nuts with oats, wheat germ, currants, apricots, and sugar. Store in a tightly closed container at room temperature. Serve in bowls with milk or cream; top with fruit, if you like. Makes about 8 cups or about 16 servings.

# Desserts & Sweets

## Desserts

### Rich Lemon Sauce

You can buy good chocolate, caramel, or fruit sauces, but a good lemon sauce must be freshly made. This is especially fine on Best-ever Gingerbread (page 95) or Persimmon Pudding (page 90).

¼ cup (⅛ lb.) butter or margarine
1 cup sugar
2 tablespoons flour
1¼ cups boiling water
½ teaspoon grated lemon peel
   Dash of nutmeg (optional)
1½ tablespoons lemon juice

In a saucepan, blend the butter, sugar, and flour; gradually add boiling water. Add lemon peel and nutmeg. Boil 3 minutes. Remove from heat and stir in the lemon juice. Makes 1½ cups.

### Favorite Soft Custard or Custard Sauce

1 whole egg, or 2 egg yolks, slightly beaten
¾ cup milk, scalded
2 tablespoons sugar
   Dash of salt
¼ teaspoon vanilla, or other flavorings such as nutmeg, Sherry, or rum

Blend egg, milk, sugar, and salt in the top of a double boiler. Cook, stirring constantly, over hot water until the custard coats a metal spoon.

Remove from heat and flavor with vanilla or other flavoring. Cool quickly. Makes ¾ cup.

### Spiced Mexican Custard (Jericalla)

2 cups milk
2 sticks whole cinnamon, each 3 or 4 inches long
½ cup sugar
3 eggs, beaten

Combine milk, cinnamon sticks, and sugar in a saucepan and, stirring, bring to a boil. Cover and chill overnight.

Set 4 small baking dishes (each at least ⅔ cup size) in a baking pan and surround with hottest tap water to about half the depth of the dishes. Remove dishes, put the pan of water in the oven, and set the oven temperature at 350°.

When oven has reached that temperature, again heat the milk mixture to scalding, stirring. Set cinnamon aside and beat hot milk into the eggs with a fork. Pour an equal portion of mixture into each baking dish and set the dishes in the hot water bath.

Bake at 350° for 25 to 30 minutes, or until the centers of the custards jiggle only slightly when a dish is

shaken gently. At once remove custards from water, using a wide spatula or kitchen tongs. Chill custards and serve in the baking dishes. (If you like, rinse cinnamon sticks, drain, and break in half. Set a piece atop each jericalla.) Makes 4 servings.

### Cream Puffs

The early cream puff recipes printed in *Sunset Magazine* were patterned along the classic methods.

Then, in the 1960's, some inquisitive home economists joined the staff and thoroughly researched the cream puff situation. They made hundreds to discover what method would produce the lightest, most sure-fire puffs. This recipe is the winner among all tested.

You can use it to make tiny puffs for dessert or appetizers (depending on your choice of filling), or éclairs.

1 cup flour
1 cup water
¼ teaspoon salt
1 teaspoon sugar
½ cup (¼ lb.) butter or margarine
4 eggs (⅞ cup)
   Filling (ice cream, sweetened whipped cream, or French Pastry Cream—recipe follows)

Sift and measure the flour. Put water, salt, sugar, and butter into a pan and heat until butter is melted. Bring mixture to a full rolling boil over high heat, add the flour all at once, remove pan from heat, and stir until mixture becomes a smooth, very thick paste that clings together and comes away from the sides of the pan.

Stir in the eggs, one at a time, until paste is smooth and shiny (paste may seem thin when you begin to add the eggs, but it will thicken as you continue to stir). Let paste cool about 15 minutes before shaping and baking.

You can refrigerate the paste at this point and bake it later. After removing from refrigerator, let stand at room temperature about 30 minutes before baking.

Shape cream puffs with a pastry bag or with a tablespoon. To make 12 puffs, use ¼ cup for each puff, placing them 3 inches apart on a greased baking sheet. Bake in a 400° oven for 35 to 45 minutes or until puffs are golden and lightweight. Split while hot to keep shell crisp.

*Just* before serving, fill each puff with about ½ cup filling. To fill all 12, you'll need 6 cups filling. Dust with powdered sugar.

**Petite Puffs (Variation).** Shape cream puffs with pastry bag or a spoon, using 2 tablespoons paste for each (this will make 36 puffs). Place 2 inches apart on a greased baking sheet. Bake in a 400° oven for 25 to 35 minutes or until puffs are golden and lightweight. Split and fill when cool.

*For dessert,* fill each with about 2 tablespoons filling—a total of 4 to 5 cups filling. Use about 3 puffs for each serving.

*For cocktail appetizers,* fill with about 2 tablespoons of your favorite fish, chicken, or meat-salad sandwich filling. You'll need 4 to 5 cups filling.

**Éclairs (Variation).** Shape with a pastry bag or tablespoon using about ¼ cup of the paste for each (this will make 12). Make each éclair about 1 by 4 inches long and place 2 to 3 inches apart on a greased baking sheet. Bake in a 400° oven for 35 to 45 minutes or until golden and lightweight. Split while hot.

Just before serving, fill each with ⅓ to ½ cup filling—a total of 6 cups. Sprinkle the éclairs with powdered sugar or frost with melted sweet milk chocolate (to frost 12 éclairs melt a 14-ounce bar of chocolate).

**French Pastry Cream.** In a pan, cream together 1 tablespoon butter and ¾ cup sugar until mixed; add a dash salt and ½ cup all-purpose flour; beat in 4 eggs until mixture is light.

Heat 2 cups milk to boiling and beat gradually into the sugar and flour, keeping the mixture as smooth as possible. Cook over low heat, stirring vigorously (preferably with a whip or egg beater) for 5 minutes or until mixture boils and thickens. Stir in one of the following flavorings: 1 teaspoon vanilla; *or* 6 tablespoons kirsch, anisette, or crème de cacao; *or* 4 squares melted unsweetened chocolate; *or* 1 tablespoon instant coffee powder with 1 teaspoon vanilla; *or* 1 diced banana; *or* ½ cup shredded coconut. Cool before using. Makes 3 cups.

## Zabaglione

Use the leftover egg whites to make Meringue Shells (recipe on page 92) or Snow Cake (page 96).

    8  egg yolks
    3  to 4 tablespoons sugar
    ½  cup Dry Sauterne, Dry Semillon,
       Malvasia Bianca, Marsala,
       Madeira, or sweet Muscatel

In a round-bottom pan or top of a double boiler, beat together egg yolks, 3 tablespoons of the sugar, and the wine. Place the round-bottom pan over direct heat (gas, electric, or denatured alcohol flame), or set the double boiler over gently simmering water.

Whip mixture constantly with a wire whip until it is thick enough to retain briefly a slight peak when whip is withdrawn; it takes about 5 minutes, more or less.

Taste, and add the remaining sugar if desired. Pour into stemmed glasses and serve at once. Serves 6 to 8.

## Favorite Baked Custard

Serve this dairy delight with pride.

    6  eggs, slightly beaten
    ½  cup sugar
    ¼  teaspoon salt
    1  teaspoon vanilla or other flavoring
    1  quart (4 cups) milk, scalded
       Cinnamon or nutmeg

Blend the eggs, sugar, salt, and flavoring; strain into the milk; mix well. Pour into 6 or 8 greased custard cups or a 1½-quart baking dish. Set in a pan of hot water deep enough for the water to come as high on the outside of the containers as the custard is on the inside. Sprinkle with cinnamon or nutmeg, if desired.

Bake in a 350° oven about 45 minutes for custard cups, or about 1 hour for a baking dish. Test doneness by gently pushing the center of the custard toward one side with the back of a spoon. If it breaks to form a crevice about ⅜ to ½-inch deep, the custard is done. If only the top pulls away and the custard is soupy, it is not done. Serves 6 to 8.

## Fresno Pudding

A brown sugar sauce marbles this oven-baked pudding full of raisins. Serve it warm as a welcome-home dessert.

    1    cup unsifted regular all-purpose
         flour
    ⅔    cup sugar
    1½   teaspoons baking powder
    ¼    teaspoon salt
    1    cup seedless raisins
    ½    cup milk
    2    cups water
    1    cup brown sugar, firmly packed
    2    tablespoons butter or margarine
         Whipping cream

Sift flour, sugar, baking powder, and salt together into a mixing bowl. Stir in raisins, then the milk; stir just to blend well. Pour batter into a greased 9-inch-square baking pan.

Heat together the water, brown sugar, and butter, stirring until sugar is dissolved. Pour the syrup over batter in the baking dish. (Don't worry if the syrup seems too thin—the batter will rise through it and mix to make a delicious sauce.)

Bake in a 350° oven for 30 to 40 minutes. Serve warm with cream. Makes 6 to 8 servings.

## Chocolate Buttercream

Served by itself, this uncooked buttercream is like a rich French *pot de crème*.

¾ cup (⅜ lb.) butter
1 cup sugar
4 ounces unsweetened chocolate, melted and cooled
2 teaspoons vanilla
4 eggs

Cream butter; add sugar, chocolate, and vanilla, and cream well. Add eggs; beat about 3 minutes, until mixture is light in color, smooth, and thick. (If it gets dark and runny from overbeating, chill mixture, then rebeat.) Refrigerate or freeze until you need to use. After storing, beat again with an electric mixer if you want it lighter and fluffier.

**Flavor Variations.** Add 2 teaspoons grated orange peel *or* instant coffee powder. For other flavors, omit the vanilla and add one of the following: 4 tablespoons light rum, ¼ teaspoon peppermint extract, 2 to 3 tablespoons crème de menthe, crème de cacao, Cointreau, *or* coffee-flavored liqueur.

**Chocolate Pots de Crème.** Make half the chocolate buttercream and spoon into little pots made for the French pots de crème, or use Oriental tea cups or small dessert dishes. Top each serving with chopped nuts or chopped candied ginger. Chill thoroughly. Makes 6 to 8 servings.

**Chocolate Pie.** Make a chocolate crumb crust by mixing together 1 cup chocolate wafer cooky crumbs, ¼ cup sugar, and 3 tablespoons soft butter. Press firmly into a 9-inch pie pan and bake in a 350° oven about 7 minutes. Cool.

Make 1 recipe chocolate buttercream and spoon into the cooled shell; chill. Garnish with whipped cream or ice cream; serve small portions. To lighten the texture of the pie, you can fold the chocolate buttercream into 1 cup heavy cream, whipped. Makes 8 to 10 servings.

**Chocolate-filled Orange Cake.** Prepare 1 package (1 lb. 3 oz.) yellow butter cake mix as package directs, adding 2 teaspoons grated orange peel to the batter. Grease and lightly flour four 9-inch cake pans. Divide batter among four pans; bake in a 350° oven for 15 minutes, or until cake springs back when lightly pressed. Cool in pans about 5 minutes, then turn out on wire racks.

Make 1 recipe chocolate buttercream. To assemble cake, spread ¼ of the buttercream filling on each layer. Carefully stack layers and refrigerate. (When chilled, wrap cake and freeze, if you wish.) To serve, frost sides of cake with sweetened whipped cream. Garnish top with thin twisted orange slices. Refrigerate. Makes about 12 servings.

## Mocha Soufflé

This chocolate soufflé has an intriguing flavor addition—coffee.

4 tablespoons cornstarch
1¼ cups milk
¾ cup sugar
2 tablespoons butter
4 ounces semisweet chocolate
2 tablespoons instant coffee powder
2 tablespoons water
4 eggs, separated
2 egg whites
⅛ teaspoon salt
¼ teaspoon cream of tartar

Lightly butter a 2½-quart soufflé dish. Cut a 12-inch-wide sheet of foil 4 inches longer than the circumference of the soufflé dish. Fold into thirds, lengthwise. Butter it lightly. Place buttered side of foil inward around dish, extending 2½ inches above the rim. Double-fold the ends to seal tightly.

Mix cornstarch and part of the milk in a saucepan. Mix in remaining milk and ½ cup of the sugar. Stirring, bring to a boil and cook until thickened. Dot with the butter.

Melt chocolate with instant coffee and water over hot water. Transfer the sauce mixture to a bowl and mix in the egg yolks, one at a time. Then beat in the chocolate mixture.

You can do this ahead and chill. Later, stirring, heat to lukewarm, then fold in egg whites prepared as follows:

Beat the 6 egg whites until foamy, add salt and cream of tartar, and beat until soft peaks form. Gradually beat in the remaining ¼ cup sugar, beating until stiff peaks form.

Fold ¼ of the meringue into chocolate sauce base until smoothly blended; then fold in the rest.

Spoon mixture into prepared dish. Bake in a 375° oven 30 minutes for a slightly saucelike center (top of soufflé should ripple in center only when shaken), or 35 minutes for a soufflé that is more evenly set (center should feel set when pressed). Serve at once to 6 people.

## Chocolate Angel Cake Dessert

2 packages (6 oz. each) semisweet chocolate pieces
2 tablespoons sugar
3 eggs, separated
2 cups (1 pt.) heavy cream, whipped
1 small angel food cake (8 oz.)

Melt chocolate chips with sugar over hot water. Remove from heat, add beaten egg yolks, and cool 5 minutes. Beat egg whites stiff; fold beaten whites and whipped cream into chocolate mixture.

Break angel food cake into bite-size pieces; sprinkle a layer in the bottom of a buttered 8 by 12 by 2-inch baking dish, using about one half of the cake. Cover with a layer of the chocolate mixture. Dot this with the rest of the cake pieces; top with the remainder of the chocolate mixture.

Chill overnight. Cut in small squares to serve. Serves 14 to 16.

## Chocolate Sundae Pudding

1 cup regular all-purpose flour
2 teaspoons baking powder
½ teaspoon salt
2 tablespoons unsweetened cocoa
⅔ cup sugar
½ cup milk
½ cup chopped walnuts
2 tablespoons melted butter or margarine
1 teaspoon vanilla
Topping (recipe follows)
1 cup boiling water
Whipping cream

Sift flour, measure, and sift again with baking powder, salt, cocoa, and sugar into a mixing bowl. Add the milk, nuts, butter, and vanilla; blend well. Pour the mixture into a greased 9-inch-square baking pan.

*(Continued on next page)*

Spread topping evenly over the first mixture. Pour 1 cup boiling water over all. Do not stir.

Bake in a 350° oven for 50 minutes to 1 hour, or until slightly crusty on top and firm. A pudding will form on top, with a fudge sauce layer below. Serve hot with plain or whipped cream. Serves 6.

**Topping:** Combine ¼ cup granulated sugar, ½ cup brown sugar, 3 tablespoons unsweetened cocoa, ¼ teaspoon salt, and 1 teaspoon vanilla.

## Angel Lemon Delight

     3  eggs, separated
     1  cup sugar
     ¼  cup flour
     ⅛  teaspoon salt
     2  tablespoons melted butter or
          margarine
        Juice of 2 lemons
        Grated peel of 1 lemon
    1½  cups milk

Beat egg whites until they form stiff peaks. In another bowl, mix sugar, flour, and salt; stir in melted butter, lemon juice, lemon peel, well-beaten egg yolks, and milk; beat with a rotary beater until smooth and creamy. Fold in stiffly beaten egg whites. Turn mixture into 8 buttered custard cups, or into a buttered 1-quart casserole, and set in a shallow pan of hot water.

Bake in a 350° oven, about 45 minutes for custard cups or 1 hour for a casserole. Serve warm or cold. Serves 6 to 8.

## Angel Pie

Angel Pie immediately became a favorite when the recipe first appeared in *Sunset Magazine* several decades ago. The egg white shell and lemon filling are as light as a feather.

     4  eggs, separated
     ½  teaspoon cream of tartar
        Pinch of salt
    1½  cups sugar
        Grated peel of 2 lemons
     3  tablespoons lemon juice
     1  cup (½ pt.) whipping cream

Beat egg whites until frothy, sprinkle in cream of tartar and salt, and beat until stiff. Beat in 1 cup of the sugar, 2

tablespoons at a time. The mixture should be glossy and stand in stiff peaks when all the sugar has been added.

With the back of a tablespoon, spread meringue in a well-greased 9-inch pie pan, pushing it high on the sides so that it resembles a pie shell. Bake in a 300° oven for 40 minutes. Cool on a rack.

Beat egg yolks and the remaining ½ cup sugar in the top of a double boiler until light. Stir in lemon peel and juice and cook over hot water until thick, stirring constantly. Chill. Whip cream and fold into chilled lemon mixture. Fill meringue shell with lemon filling; chill for several hours. Serves 6 to 8.

## Persimmon Pudding

     1  cup persimmon purée (instructions
          follow)
     2  teaspoons soda
     1  egg, beaten
     ½  cup milk
     1  teaspoon lemon juice
     ½  teaspoon vanilla
     1  tablespoon melted butter or mar-
          garine
     1  cup regular all-purpose flour
     1  cup sugar
     1  teaspoon cinnamon
        Dash salt
     ½  cup each chopped pecans and
          raisins
        Rich Lemon Sauce (recipe on
          page 87)

To make persimmon purée, use a spoon to scoop the flesh from the skin of fresh persimmons; whirl in blender until smooth or press through a food mill. Make the purée just before use (it turns brown with long standing).

Stir together the persimmon purée and 1 teaspoon of the soda; reserve. In a large bowl combine egg, milk, lemon juice, vanilla, and butter. Sift flour, measure, and sift again with sugar, cinnamon, salt, and remaining

1 teaspoon soda. Add to egg mixture alternately with persimmon purée, blending well after each addition. Mix in pecans and raisins.

Pour batter into a greased and floured 8-inch square pan. Bake in a 350° oven for 55 minutes or until browned. Let cool in pan 5 minutes, then cut in squares. Serve with lemon sauce. Makes 9 servings.

## Baked Apples with Orange Sauce

     6  large, firm cooking apples
     1  cup sugar
    1½  cups water
     ¾  cup strained orange juice
     1  tablespoon grated orange peel

Core apples and peel about one-third down from top; place in casserole or deep pan, peeled side up. Boil ¾ cup of the sugar and the water together for 5 minutes; pour over apples.

Cover and bake in a 400° oven until tender, 30 to 40 minutes. Sprinkle remaining sugar over apples; place, uncovered, under broiler until brown.

Drain syrup from apples; add orange juice and rind, and boil for 10 minutes. Pour syrup over apples, chill, and serve plain or with cream. Serves 6.

## Pear or Apple Crisp

     4  Anjou or Bartlett pears, or 5 cook-
          ing apples (Winesap, Golden De-
          licious, or Pippin)
     1  teaspoon cinnamon
     ¼  teaspoon nutmeg
     1  teaspoon to 1 tablespoon lemon
          juice (depending on tartness of
          fruit)
     ½  cup water
     1  cup sugar
     ¾  cup unsifted regular all-purpose
          flour
     ½  cup (¼ lb.) butter or margarine
        Whipping cream

Peel and slice the pears or apples into a buttered 9-inch-square baking pan, sprinkle with the spices, and add the lemon juice and water.

Mix the sugar and flour, and work in the butter to make a crumbly mixture. Spread this over the fruit.

Bake uncovered in a 350° oven about 1 hour, or until the fruit is tender and the crumbly crust is lightly browned. Serve warm with cream. Serves 4.

*Note:* Drained canned pears may be substituted. Reduce baking time to 30 minutes.

## Plums in Port

Large slice of orange, ½-inch thick
6 whole cloves
4 cups whole purple prune plums, each slashed on one side to the pit
1 cup Tinta or Ruby Port
½ cup sugar
1 whole stick cinnamon

Cut orange in quarters and stud with the cloves. Combine in a saucepan with plums, Port, sugar, and cinnamon. Bring to a boil and simmer, uncovered, about 10 minutes or until fruit just begins to soften. Cool, remove cinnamon, then chill. Makes 6 to 8 servings.

## Cherry Dessert

2 cans (1 lb. 5 oz. each) prepared cherry pie filling
½ teaspoon cinnamon
¼ teaspoon almond extract
1 package (about 9 oz.) white or yellow one-layer cake mix
½ cup (¼ lb.) butter, melted
½ cup sliced almonds

Combine pie filling, cinnamon, and extract; spread in a 9 by 13-inch baking pan. Sprinkle cake mix over the top; drizzle with butter; sprinkle with almonds.

Bake in a 375° oven for about 35 minutes. Makes 8 to 10 servings.

## Strawberries with Sour Cream Dip

1 cup (½ pt.) sour cream
1 teaspoon lemon peel
1 teaspoon lemon juice
½ cup powdered sugar
24 whole strawberries

Beat sour cream, lemon peel, lemon juice, and powdered sugar with a rotary beater until light. Place in a bowl; surround with strawberries. Serves 4.

## Caramel Pears

3 fresh Bosc or Anjou pears
1½ cups each sugar and water
2 tablespoons lemon juice
2 teaspoons vanilla
Salt
2 tablespoons butter or margarine
2 tablespoons toasted, chopped almonds
½ cup canned or bottled caramel ice cream topping
Sweetened whipped cream

*Note:* If you use the Anjou variety, choose slightly under-ripe pears.

Peel and halve the pears; remove seed pockets and stems. In a wide shallow pan, combine the sugar, water, lemon juice, and vanilla; bring to a boil. Drop the pears into boiling liquid, and poach 5 to 8 minutes or until pears are just slightly tender when pierced. Drain pears; discard syrup. Sprinkle cut sides of pears lightly with salt; place cut side down in a 9-inch baking pan.

Just before serving, melt the butter or margarine and pour over pears; place under broiler, about 5 inches from heat, and broil 1 to 2 minutes. Turn cut sides up, and place 1 teaspoon almonds into the hollowed portion of each pear half. Spoon the caramel topping over pears. Return to broiler for 1 minute. Serve warm with whipped cream. Makes 6 servings.

## Rhubarb Crisp

3 cups diced rhubarb (½-inch pieces)
¾ cup sugar
1 egg, well beaten
2 tablespoons flour
¼ teaspoon mace
¼ cup (⅛ lb.) butter or margarine
⅓ cup brown or granulated sugar
⅔ cup unsifted regular all-purpose flour
Whipping cream (optional)

Thoroughly mix the rhubarb, the ¾ cup sugar, egg, 2 tablespoons flour, and mace. Spread in a 9-inch-square pan.

Work together with finger tips or fork until crumbly the butter, the ⅓ cup brown or granulated sugar, and ⅔ cup flour. Press down over rhubarb.

Bake in a 375° oven for 30 minutes, or until rhubarb is tender. Cut in squares and serve warm with cream. Serves 4.

## Fruit Fritters

Powdered sugar and syrup, sweetened whipped cream, vanilla ice cream, or lemon sauce are each good accompaniments for hot, crisp fritters.

Serve the cooled Melba Sauce with the fritters of your choice.

Fresh fruit, prepared according to directions which follow
2 cups flour
3 teaspoons baking powder
1 teaspoon sugar
⅛ teaspoon salt
1¼ cups milk
3 tablespoons salad oil
3 egg whites
Salad oil for deep frying
Melba Sauce (optional)

Pineapple or apples should be peeled, cored, and sliced ¼-inch thick (pears are best cut in wedges). Peeled bananas are sliced diagonally in 3 pieces. Small clusters of seedless or seeded grapes may be dipped and fried. Cut melon 1-inch thick and then in 2 or 3 inch pieces.

Batter will coat about 1 pineapple, or about 20 fruit pieces.

Sift flour, measure, and sift into mixing bowl with baking powder, sugar, and salt. Combine milk and oil, and stir into sifted dry ingredients. Beat egg whites until stiff but not dry, and fold into flour mixture. Allow to stand 15 minutes before dipping fruits.

Drain prepared fruits well on paper toweling. Dip into batter to coat, allow excess batter to drip off, and drop into heated oil (375°). Fry a few at a time until golden; drain. Serve at once, with sauce if you like. Makes 5 to 6 servings.

**Melba Sauce.** Force 1 package (10 oz.) thawed frozen red raspberries through a wire strainer; measure juice and add water to make 1 cup. In a small saucepan, combine ¼ cup sugar and 2 teaspoons cornstarch. Add raspberry juice and cook, stirring, until thick. Cool. Makes 1 cup.

## Fresh Fruits in Watermelon or Pineapple Shells

Watermelons or pineapples make the most attractive containers for mixtures of fresh fruits.

*To prepare watermelon*, cut a lengthwise slice from the top and scoop out the meat with a melon-ball cutter. Cut the edge of the shell in scallops or notches. Combine some of the melon balls with some of the following: pineapple cubes, halved strawberries, grapes, pitted sweet cherries, sliced peaches, halved and seeded plums, sliced pears, or other melons cut in balls. Sprinkle with rum, brandy, Sherry, orange-flavored liqueur, or kirsch to flavor. Fill shell with fruit and chill. Garnish with mint sprigs.

*To prepare pineapple*, cut a lengthwise slice off the pineapple's side, leaving on the spiny leaves. Use a grapefruit knife to hollow out shell. Cut fruit into cubes and sweeten if necessary. Combine with other fruits cut in cubes or slices. Good choices are papayas, mangoes, bananas, oranges, tangerines, unpeeled apples, and strawberries. Rum and orange-flavored liqueur are suitable flavorings to sprinkle on. Flaked coconut may also be added.

## Meringue Shells

These shells keep indefinitely stored airtight, ready to be filled with ice cream and sauce or whipped cream and fruits.

  4  egg whites (½ cup)
  ½  teaspoon cream of tartar
  ¾, 1, or 1¼ cups granulated sugar
      (depending on sweetness you
      want)
  1  teaspoon vanilla extract or other
      extract flavoring to taste

Combine egg whites with cream of tartar in a clean, dry, fat-free bowl that holds at least 6 cups below the top curve of the electric-mixer beater. Beat whites at highest speed until frothy, then add the sugar *very* gradually, 1 tablespoon about every minute. When all the sugar is incorporated, add the vanilla and beat 1 or 2 minutes more. The whites should hold *very* stiff, sharp peaks.

On greased, flour-dusted baking sheets, shape the meringue and bake according to the directions that follow.

**Individual Meringue Shells.** The basic recipe will make 8 to 10 shells. Allow about ½ cup meringue for each. Spread with a spoon or pipe with cake decorator into a 3-inch solid disk about ½-inch thick. Build up a rim around the outer edge about 1½ inches high. Bake in a 250° oven for 1 hour. Turn off heat and dry in oven for 3 to 4 hours. Cool.

**Large Meringue Shell.** Spread or pipe a little more than half the basic recipe into a 12-inch disk. Make a border of the remaining meringue on the outer edge. Bake shell in a 250° oven for 1½ hours. Turn off heat and dry in oven for 3 to 4 hours. Cool.

## Chocolate Fondue

Who could possible refuse this luscious chocolate and fruit dessert?

 12  ounces (1 bar) milk chocolate, or
      12 ounces semisweet baking
      chocolate
  ¾  cup whipping cream
  3  tablespoons Cointreau, brandy, or
      rum
  2  medium-sized bananas
 1½  cups strawberries, halved apricots, cherries, or grapes
 1½  cups fresh pineapple cubes
  6  slices pound cake, angel food, or
      sponge cake, about ¾-inch
      thick

Place chocolate and cream in the top of a double boiler; set over hot (not boiling) water and heat, stirring, until chocolate melts and blends with cream. Stir in Cointreau. Transfer to a small pan and place either over a candle warmer or electric food warmer. Or use a small chafing dish with a hot water bath. (Be careful not to overheat chocolate sauce or it may scorch.)

Cut bananas into ½-inch sections and arrange on a tray with the hulled strawberries and pineapple cubes. Cut cake into 1-inch squares and add to the tray. Place tray beside the hot chocolate sauce and accompany with bamboo skewers or fondue forks, to be used for spearing foods and then dipping them into the sauce. Makes 6 to 8 servings.

## Frozen Chocolate Cooky Cups

Chocolate and peppermint join forces in this potent and elegant dessert. The servings are small, but very rich.

  1  cup (½ lb.) butter or margarine
  2  cups sifted powdered sugar
  4  squares (4 oz.) unsweetened
      chocolate, melted
  4  eggs
  ¾  teaspoon peppermint flavoring
  2  teaspoons vanilla
  1  cup vanilla wafer crumbs (about
      half of a 7-oz. box)
      Whipped cream
      Maraschino cherries

Using an electric mixer, if possible, beat together the butter and powdered sugar until light and fluffy. Add the melted chocolate and continue beating thoroughly. Add the whole eggs, and beat again until fluffy. Then beat in the peppermint and vanilla.

Sprinkle about half of the cooky crumbs in each of 18 cupcake pan liners. Spoon the chocolate mixture into the liners, then top with the remaining crumbs. Freeze until firm. When ready to serve, top each with whipped cream and a bright red cherry. Makes 18 small, but rich servings.

## Vanilla Ice Cream

This crank-freezer ice cream is best made with a vanilla pod, but extract can be substituted. Peach and chocolate-flake versions can be made.

  3 - inch piece of vanilla bean pod or
      1½ teaspoons vanilla
 1½  cups milk
  1  tablespoon cornstarch
  ¼  teaspoon salt
  ¾  cup sugar
  4  egg yolks
 1½  cups whipping cream

Split vanilla pod and scrape seeds into milk; drop in the pod. Scald. Combine cornstarch, salt, sugar, and slightly beaten egg yolks, and mix well. Beat in a little of the scalded milk, then combine the two mixtures and cook over a low heat or in a double boiler, stirring constantly, until thick and smooth. (Add vanilla if vanilla bean was not used.) Chill, then stir in cream.

Pour into freezer can, not more

than two-thirds full, and chill thoroughly (in freezer or refrigerator). Assemble, freeze, using 1 part ice cream (rock) salt to 8 parts crushed ice. Turn until crank is hard to move, about 15 minutes for 2-quart size. Drain off ice water, carefully remove lid of freezer container, lift out dasher.

Serve at once. Or pack ice cream into can, cover can with waxed paper or foil, and replace top. Add ice and salt (1 part salt to 4 parts ice) until can is covered, then cover with newspapers or burlap and let stand for an hour or two. Makes 1 generous quart.

**Peach Version.** Substitute ¾ teaspoon almond extract for the vanilla, and add 1½ tablespoons lemon juice and 1½ cups fresh ripe peeled peaches, mashed through a strainer or whirled in a blender with the cream. Makes 1½ quarts.

**Chocolate-flake Version.** Reduce sugar to ½ cup. Add 1 cup shaved sweet or semisweet chocolate (use a potato peeler or grater). Makes 1¼ quarts.

## Trader Vic's Ice Cream

This is a "showmanship" dessert. You flame the sauce in front of your guests and pour it flaming over ice cream.

¾ cup Jamaica rum
6 tablespoons apricot preserves
1 quart vanilla ice cream
   Sliced bananas or other fresh fruit (optional)

Blend rum with preserves in a chafing dish or 2-quart glass saucepan. Scoop ice cream onto dessert plates and ring with fruit, if used.

Heat sauce until warm, bring to the table, touch a match to it, and stir vigorously while it burns. When flame starts to die, pour over ice cream. Serves 6.

## Cherries Jubilee

This dessert has an elegant reputation, but is no more difficult to prepare than a hot fudge sundae (that is, a very elegant hot fudge sundae).

1½ quarts vanilla ice cream
2 cans (1 lb. each) dark Bing cherries
⅓ cup currant jelly
2 tablespoons cornstarch
2 tablespoons water
⅓ cup kirsch (cherry brandy)
   Sweetened whipped cream and grated milk chocolate (optional)

Let ice cream soften slightly and pack into a metal mold, or scoop ice cream into large balls; freeze.

Drain the syrup from the cherries into a saucepan. Add currant jelly. Heat to boiling and stir in a blend of the cornstarch and water; cook, stirring, until thickened. Add cherries and heat through. Refrigerate until serving time.

Dip mold into hottest tap water for about 10 seconds, then invert onto chilled serving plate. Return plate with unmolded ice cream to freezer.

At serving time, reheat cherry sauce and take molded ice cream from freezer. Warm kirsch in a small pan. At the table, ignite kirsch and spoon flaming over the hot cherry sauce; serve over the ice cream. Accompany with whipped cream and chocolate, if you wish. Serves 8.

## Grasshopper Torte

1¼ cups half-and-half (light cream)
2½ cups firmly packed whole marshmallows (about 36)
½ cup green crème de menthe
⅓ cup white crème de cacao
   Few drops green food coloring
2 egg whites
3 tablespoons sugar
1½ cups whipping cream
   Chocolate Crust (recipe follows)
   Semisweet chocolate curls

Measure half-and-half into a small pan, add marshmallows and cook, stirring, until marshmallows are melted. Set pan in cold water and stir until mixture is cooled. Blend in crème de menthe, crème de cacao, and about 6 drops food coloring. Chill mixture until it begins to thicken.

Beat egg whites until stiff, then gradually beat in the sugar and continue whipping until whites hold short, distinct peaks. In a large bowl, whip cream until stiff. Thoroughly fold marshmallow mixture and whites into cream. Pour into pan with removable bottom or spring-released sides which you have lined with chocolate crust. Cover and freeze until firm (8 hours or longer).

Remove pan sides. The easiest way to remove the sides is to dip a towel in hot water, wring dry, and wrap around pan. Let stand 30 seconds. Then remove the towel, run a knife blade around the edge of the torte, and take away the pan sides. Set torte on serving dish. Garnish with chocolate curls made by shaving a bar of chocolate with a vegetable peeler. Serves 12 to 16.

**Chocolate Crust.** Mix 1 cup finely crushed chocolate-flavored-wafer cooky crumbs with 2 tablespoons melted butter, and pat crumbs evenly over bottom of an 8 or 9-inch pan (at least 2 inches deep) with removable bottom or spring-released sides.

## Mandarin Dessert

1 package (3 oz.) orange-flavored gelatin
¾ cup hot water
1 can (6 oz.) frozen orange juice
1 pint vanilla ice cream
1 can (11 oz.) mandarin oranges, drained

Dissolve gelatin in water and add frozen orange juice. Allow ice cream to stand at room temperature until soft enough to stir; combine with gelatin mixture. Add mandarin oranges and spoon into a 1-quart mold; refrigerate overnight. Makes 4 or 5 servings.

## Pineapple Sherbet

2 eggs, separated
¾ cup sugar
1 can (about 8 oz.) crushed pineapple
2 tablespoons lemon juice
2 cups buttermilk
1 teaspoon unflavored gelatin (part of an envelope)
1 tablespoon water

Combine egg yolks, ½ cup of the sugar, pineapple (including the syrup), lemon juice, and buttermilk in a blender; whirl until blended. (Or beat with rotary beater.) Soften gelatin in water; stir over hot water until dissolved; blend into buttermilk mixture.

Pour into a 2-quart container and freeze until firm around the outer edges of the container, about 1½ hours.

Beat the egg whites until soft, moist peaks form; gradually beat in the remaining ¼ cup sugar until whites hold firm peaks. Break the partially frozen sherbet into chunks, pour into a chilled bowl, and beat until fluffy. Then fold into egg-white mixture. Freeze until firm. Makes about 1½ quarts.

## Lemon-Orange Ice

After a barbecue on a hot summer's night, spoon up this refreshing citrus ice for an evening cooler.

1½  cups sugar
1½  cups water
 2  teaspoons unflavored gelatin
⅓  cup cold water
 1  cup boiling water
 1  cup strained lemon and orange juice (about 3 lemons and 2 oranges)
    Lemon extract, if desired
 2  egg whites, beaten

Boil the 1½ cups sugar and 1½ cups water together rapidly for 10 minutes to make a syrup. Measure 1⅓ cups of the syrup; reserve.

Soften gelatin in the cold water; then dissolve in the boiling water. Add fruit juice, syrup, and a few drops of lemon extract. Freeze until mushy.

Put mixture into a bowl; add egg whites; beat until smooth and fluffy. Freeze until firm. Serves 6 to 8.

# Cakes

## Seven-minute Frosting

1  egg white
3  tablespoons water
⅛  teaspoon cream of tartar (or 1 teaspoon vinegar)
¾  cup sugar
   Dash of salt
1  teaspoon vanilla, or other flavoring

Put all ingredients, except vanilla or other flavoring, in the upper part of a double boiler. Stir to blend, then set aside 15 minutes or longer.

Set over boiling water and beat vigorously and constantly with a rotary or electric beater just until mixture stands in peaks. (This takes anywhere from 3 to 7 minutes.)

Remove from heat and stir a minute or two. Flavor with vanilla or any flavoring you like.

## Favorite Orange Refrigerator Cake

You save time in preparing this dessert if you buy the sponge cake layers. Most bakeries have them.

2  eight-inch sponge cake layers
3  eggs, separated
½  cup sugar
1  tablespoon cornstarch
   Dash of salt
1  cup orange juice
5  teaspoons lemon juice
1  cup whipping cream
   Preserved orange slices or fresh orange sections for garnish

Slice each cake layer in half horizontally, making 4 layers in all. Beat egg whites until stiff, but not dry. In the top part of the double boiler, mix together the sugar, cornstarch, and salt; stir in orange juice, lemon juice, and slightly beaten egg yolks. Cook over hot water, stirring constantly, until thickened; remove sauce from heat.

Fold beaten egg whites into the orange sauce while it is still hot. Spread hot filling between the cake layers (use a spatula to spread excess filling onto sides of cake until all has been absorbed into the cake). If layers slip while filling, hold in place with skewers.

Refrigerate overnight. Several hours before serving time, whip cream and sweeten to taste. Frost top and sides of cake. Refrigerate until time to serve. Then garnish top of cake with preserved orange slices or orange segments. Makes 8 to 10 servings.

## Elegant Cheesecake

1  cup zwieback crumbs
2  tablespoons sugar
¼  teaspoon cinnamon
3  tablespoons melted butter
3  large packages (8 oz. each) cream cheese, softened
½  teaspoon salt
3  tablespoons light rum, or 1 tablespoon vanilla
4  egg whites
1  cup sugar
2  cups (1 pt.) sour cream
2  tablespoons sugar
⅛  teaspoon salt

Mix together the crumbs, 2 tablespoons sugar, cinnamon, and melted butter. Press in an even layer into the bottom of an 8 or 9-inch pan with spring-released sides or removable bottom.

Mix cream cheese, the ½ teaspoon salt, and rum together until soft and creamy. Beat the egg whites until they form soft peaks, then gradually beat in the 1 cup sugar to make a meringue. Fold egg white mixture into the cheese until well blended. Turn into the crumb-lined pan. Bake in a 350° oven about 25 minutes.

Remove from oven; increase oven temperature to 450°. Combine sour cream with sugar and the ⅛ teaspoon salt; spread over top of cake. Return to oven for 4 to 5 minutes, until cream is set. Remove from oven and cool until cold. Remove sides from pan. Serves 12.

## Cheesecake Anne

This light, crustless cheesecake is a favorite of the home economists who develop and perfect recipes for *Sunset Magazine*.

Elegant Cheesecake (above) is a

more traditional type with crumb crust and rich texture.

3 large packages (8 oz. each) cream cheese
6 eggs, separated
1 cup sugar
2 tablespoons flour
1 cup sour cream
1 teaspoon each lemon juice and vanilla

Beat cream cheese with egg yolks until smooth. Beat in sugar, flour, sour cream, lemon juice, and vanilla. Whip egg whites until they hold short distinct peaks, then fold gently into cheese mixture.

Pour batter into an ungreased 8 or 9-inch cheesecake pan (one with removable bottom or spring-released sides).

Bake in a 325° oven for 1 hour and 10 minutes, or until center of cake no longer appears soft.

Let cool at room temperature at least 2 hours before cutting, or chill before serving if you prefer a creamier consistency. Makes 12 servings

## Lemon Cake Dessert

1 package (3 oz.) lemon-flavored gelatin
1½ cups granulated sugar
3 cups packaged biscuit mix
4 eggs
¾ cup salad oil
¾ cup water
1½ cups sifted powdered sugar
½ cup lemon juice

Into the large bowl of your electric mixer, put the gelatin, granulated sugar, biscuit mix, eggs, salad oil, and water. Beat at slow speed until the ingredients are combined, then beat at medium speed for 5 minutes.

Pour into a greased and floured 13 by 9-inch baking pan and bake in a 350° oven for 35 to 40 minutes, or until cake tests done.

Combine the powdered sugar with the lemon juice. Remove cake from oven, allow to cool about 5 minutes, then use a fork to pierce the cake all over. Pour lemon mixture evenly over the top of cake. Cool. Serve plain or with a dollop of sweetened whipped cream or a scoop of vanilla ice cream. Makes 12 servings.

## Sponge Cupcakes

Use these airy little cupcakes as a base for strawberry shortcake or with fresh fruits for light desserts.

2 eggs, separated
¼ teaspoon salt
½ cup sugar
1 teaspoon lemon juice
½ teaspoon grated lemon peel
½ cup regular all-purpose flour

In the large bowl of your electric mixer, beat the egg whites with salt until stiff. Gradually add the sugar, about 1 tablespoon at a time, beating after each addition until glossy.

In another bowl beat the egg yolks with the lemon juice and peel until thickened. Fold the egg yolk mixture into beaten whites.

Sift the flour, measure, and sift again over top of egg mixture and carefully fold together until well blended.

Spoon into large muffin cups, either greased or with paper liners, filling them about ⅔ full. Bake in a 400° oven for about 10 to 12 minutes. Serve warm or cold. Makes 10 to 12.

## Sandtorte (Sand Cake)

Of all the cakes mentioned as favorites by *Sunset Magazine* readers, this one received the most mentions. You'll want to bake it a day before serving and sprinkle it with sifted powdered sugar.

1 cup (½ lb.) soft butter
3 cups sugar
6 eggs
1 cup (½ pt.) sour cream
3 cups all-purpose flour
¼ teaspoon baking powder
1½ teaspoons vanilla
Powdered sugar

In the large bowl of an electric mixer, cream the butter and blend in the sugar. Add the eggs, one at a time, beating well after each addition. Blend in sour cream.

Sift the flour, measure, and sift again with the baking powder. Add the flour mixture in 4 or 5 parts to first mixture, blending well each time. Add vanilla.

Pour the batter into a well-

buttered mold (2 or 2½-quart) or into a buttered 9-inch tube pan. Bake in a 350° oven for about 1 hour 25 minutes, or until it tests done when you insert a wooden skewer or toothpick.

When the cake is done, remove from the oven, let stand for 5 minutes, then invert on a cooling rack. Allow to cool completely, then wrap tightly in plastic film or foil and leave for about 24 hours at room temperature before serving. Before you cut it, sprinkle the top lightly with sifted powdered sugar. Slice into wedges. Makes about 16 servings.

## Best-ever Gingerbread

Everyone has a favorite gingerbread topping—perhaps whipped cream, ice cream, or sauce. Those who believe lemon sauce is a necessity may use the Rich Lemon Sauce recipe on page 87.

1 cup sugar
¼ teaspoon salt
1 teaspoon ginger
½ teaspoon cinnamon
½ teaspoon cloves
1 cup salad oil
1 cup molasses
2 teaspoons baking soda
1 cup boiling water
2½ cups unsifted regular all-purpose flour
2 eggs, well beaten

In a bowl, combine the sugar, salt, ginger, cinnamon, and cloves. Stir in the salad oil, then the molasses, mixing well. Mix the soda into the boiling water and immediately stir into the mixture. Gradually blend in the flour, to prevent lumping. Then mix in the eggs.

Turn into a greased 9 by 13-inch pan and bake in a 350° oven about 40 to 45 minutes. Makes 12 servings.

# Snow Cake

Although its ingredient list sounds like you are making an angel food cake, Snow Cake will have an even pound-cake texture, sponge-cake bounce, and vanilla butter-cake flavor. Dust it generously with powdered sugar before serving.

- 1 cup egg whites (about 8 whites)
- 1 cup sugar
  Dash of salt
- 1 teaspoon vanilla
- 1 cup all-purpose flour
- 1 teaspoon baking powder
- ½ cup (¼ lb.) butter, melted and cooled
  Powdered sugar

In the large bowl of your electric mixer, whip the egg whites until frothy; with mixer at highest speed, gradually add the sugar and beat until mixture will stand in stiff, but not dry, peaks; then beat in the salt and vanilla.

Sift flour, measure, then sift again with baking powder into the egg whites, folding until well blended. Fold in the melted and cooled butter until evenly blended, and turn mixture into a tube-type cake mold (about 2-quart size) that is buttered well and dusted with sugar.

Bake in a 350° oven for 1 hour or until cake bounces back when touched lightly. (This cake does not rise.) Remove from pan and cool on rack. Dust well with powdered sugar before serving.

*Note:* For a cake of the best quality, use egg whites that are as fresh as possible. However, leftover whites you freeze work almost as well. Just fill freezer containers with the raw egg whites, cover, and freeze. Thaw and warm to room temperature before using.

# Buttermilk Pound Cake

- ½ cup (¼ lb.) butter or margarine
- 2½ cups sugar
- 4 eggs
- 3 cups regular all-purpose flour
- ¼ teaspoon soda
- 1 cup buttermilk
- 2 teaspoons vanilla
- 1 teaspoon almond extract
  Grated peel of 1 large orange and 1 small lemon

In a large mixing bowl, beat butter or margarine until creamy. Gradually add sugar, beating until mixture is light and fluffy. Beat in eggs, one at a time, beating well after each addition.

Sift flour, measure, and sift again with soda. Beat into creamed mixture alternately with buttermilk mixed with vanilla, almond extract, and grated orange and lemon peel (begin and end with dry ingredients). Pour into a greased and floured 10-inch tube cake pan.

Bake in a 350° oven for 1 hour or until toothpick inserted comes out clean. Cool in pan 5 minutes; turn out onto wire rack. Makes 12 to 14 servings.

# Crazy Chocolate Cake

If you are looking for a cake you can mix together in a jiffy, here it is. For an equally simple frosting, try the Chocolate Buttercream on page 89.

- 1½ cups unsifted regular all-purpose flour
- 1 cup sugar
- 3 tablespoons unsweetened cocoa
- 1 teaspoon soda
- ½ teaspoon salt
- 6 tablespoons salad oil
- 1 tablespoon vinegar
- 1 teaspoon vanilla
- 1 cup cold water

Sift flour with sugar, cocoa, soda, and salt into an ungreased 9-inch-square baking pan. Make three depressions. Distribute the oil among the depressions, then the vinegar and vanilla. Pour the cold water over all.

Using a slotted pancake turner, mix all the ingredients. Use the turner both to stir and to scrape the bottom and corners of the pan so that all is thoroughly mixed. Don't worry if a few small lumps remain in batter.

Bake in a 350° oven for 30 to 35 minutes, or until a toothpick inserted comes out clean. Cool in the pan on a rack. Serves 9.

# Chocolate-filled Orange Cake

Use a mix to make this cake filled with Chocolate Buttercream (recipe and cake instructions on page 89).

# Chocolate Pound Cake

- 1 cup (½ lb.) butter or margarine
- 2½ cups sugar
- 5 eggs
- 3 cups regular all-purpose flour
- ½ teaspoon each salt and baking powder
- ½ cup unsweetened cocoa
- 1 cup milk
- 1 teaspoon vanilla

Cream butter until light and fluffy. Add sugar gradually, creaming well. Beat in eggs, one at a time. Sift flour, measure, then sift twice again with salt, baking powder, and cocoa. Mix in dry ingredients alternately with milk, beating just until blended. Stir in vanilla. Turn into a greased and floured 10-inch tube pan.

Bake in a 325° oven for 1 hour and 40 minutes, or until a toothpick inserted comes out clean. Let cool on rack, then turn out. Makes 12 to 14 servings.

# Caramel-frosted Filbert Roll

- 5 eggs, separated
- ¾ cup granulated sugar
- ⅓ cup graham cracker crumbs
- 1 teaspoon baking powder
- 1 teaspoon vanilla
- ⅛ teaspoon each salt and cream of tartar
- 1 cup lightly packed ground filberts (whirl in blender or use nut grinder)
- 1 cup (½ pt.) whipping cream
- 2 tablespoons powdered sugar
  Caramel Frosting (recipe follows)
- 2 tablespoons coarsely chopped filberts

Beat egg yolks until light and lemon-colored. Gradually add all but 2 tablespoons of the granulated sugar and beat until thick. Mix in crumbs, baking powder, and vanilla.

Beat egg whites until foamy, add salt and cream of tartar, and beat until stiff. Beat in the remaining 2 tablespoons sugar. Fold egg whites into the yolk mixture alternately with the ground nuts.

Butter a 10 by 15-inch jelly roll pan, line bottom with waxed paper; butter again. Pour in batter and smooth evenly with a spatula. Bake in a 350° oven for 20 minutes, or until the top of cake springs back when touched lightly.

Let stand 5 minutes, then turn out onto a large muslin cloth which is lightly dusted with powdered sugar. Lightly roll up in the cloth and let cool on a rack.

For filling, whip cream and powdered sugar until stiff. If desired, flavor with vanilla. Unroll cool cake and spread whipped cream filling evenly over it. Roll up cake and place seam side down on a serving dish.

Frost the roll with Caramel Frosting and garnish with chopped filberts. Chill. Makes 8 servings.

**Caramel Frosting.** Melt ¼ cup (⅛ lb.) butter in a small pan and stir in ½ cup firmly packed brown sugar. Bring to a full rolling boil and cook over low heat, stirring constantly, for 2 minutes. Pour in 2 tablespoons milk and cook, stirring, until it comes to a full boil.

Remove from heat and let cool until lukewarm. Gradually add ¾ cup powdered sugar and beat until smooth.

# French Cooky Cake

This cake requires no cooking.

1 cup (½ lb.) soft butter
1 teaspoon grated orange peel
3 cups sifted powdered sugar
2 egg yolks
¼ cup ground sweet chocolate
1 teaspoon instant coffee powder
2 teaspoons hot water
1 package (7 to 9 oz.—24 to 30 cookies) Petit Beurre, tea biscuits, or shortbread cookies
3 tablespoons hot or cold coffee
1 or 2 tablespoons ground sweet chocolate for topping

With a rotary beater, cream butter, orange peel, and powdered sugar until fluffy. Beat in egg yolks, one at a time, whipping until mixture is very smooth and light. Blend the ¼ cup chocolate and coffee powder with 2 teaspoons hot water, then add to the butter mixture and mix thoroughly.

Divide cookies into 3 equal stacks. Arrange the first stack side by side on a flat serving dish to form a rectangle or square. Sprinkle with 1 tablespoon coffee, and spread with a little less than ⅓ of the buttercream mixture. Arrange second stack of cookies on the buttercream, sprinkle with another 1 tablespoon coffee, and spread with a little less than ⅓ of the buttercream. Place the third stack of cookies over this layer; moisten evenly with 1 more tablespoon coffee. Frost tops and sides of rectangle with remaining buttercream (or reserve a small amount for decoration).

Lightly dust the 1 or 2 tablespoons chocolate over the top of the cake; decorate, if you wish, with puffs of the reserved buttercream. Chill at least 3 hours or overnight before serving; cover after buttercream gets firm. Cut in squares or rectangles to serve. Makes 8 to 12 servings.

# Karidopita (Greek Nut Cake)

To grind the nuts, whirl them in a blender or use one of the grinders made for this purpose.

½ cup (¼ lb.) soft butter
1 cup sugar
3 eggs, slightly beaten
¼ cup milk
2 cups regular all-purpose flour
2 teaspoons baking powder
1 teaspoon cinnamon
¼ teaspoon each salt and ground cloves
2 cups ground walnuts
Honey Syrup (recipe follows)

Cream the butter until light and fluffy; gradually beat in sugar. Stir in the eggs and the milk; blend thoroughly.

Sift flour; measure and sift again with baking powder, cinnamon, salt, and cloves. Slowly blend flour into the creamed mixture. Stir in walnuts, and blend well.

Pour into a greased 10-inch tube pan. Bake in a 350° oven for 35 minutes, or until cake tests done. Remove from oven; cool in pan 10 minutes. Remove from the pan. Prick the surface of the cake with a fork, and baste several times with honey syrup until cake is soaked. Makes 12 servings.

**Honey Syrup.** In a pan, mix together 1 cup *each* sugar and water. Bring the mixture to a boil and stir in 2 tablespoons honey. Simmer, stirring occasionally, for about 5 minutes. Remove from heat, and allow the syrup to cool before pouring it over the cake.

# Hungarian Dobos Torte

It takes much time to make this classic cake, but it keeps 7 to 10 days in the refrigerator. Prepare the cake at least a day before you serve it.

5 eggs, separated
1½ cups sifted powdered sugar
2 tablespoons flour
1⅔ cups (half of a 1-pound package) sweet ground chocolate
¾ cup strong, hot coffee
1¼ cups soft butter or margarine
Caramel Topping (recipe follows)
Chocolate Frosting (recipe follows)

Beat egg whites until stiff but not dry. In another bowl beat egg yolks with an electric mixer; slowly add powdered sugar; continue beating until thick and satiny. Beat in flour. Fold this mixture into the beaten egg whites.

Grease and flour the *bottom sides* of *inverted* 8-inch layer pans *or* the removable bottoms of cake pans. For each layer (12 in all) use about ⅓ cup batter, spreading evenly to about ½ inch from the edge.

Bake in a 375° oven for 5 to 6 minutes, or until golden brown. Remove layers from pans with a spatula immediately after taking from the oven; cool layers on wire racks before stacking. (Handle carefully. They are brittle if cool.)

Make a filling by blending the ground chocolate and hot coffee until smooth. Allow to cool to lukewarm. Stir in soft butter until completely blended. (*Do not whip.*) Refrigerate until ready to spread on cooled cake layers.

Before you assemble the torte, select and reserve the best layer for the top. Spread each of the remaining layers with enough filling to cover (about 3 tablespoons); stack. Reserve remaining filling for sides.

**Caramel Topping.** Heat ½ cup sugar over medium heat, stirring often, until it melts and becomes light amber (watch it carefully). Place the torte layer you reserved on waxed paper, carefully cover it with the hot liquid caramel, spreading to the outer edge. Place this layer on top of the stack. Spread remaining filling on all sides.

Heat the blade of a wooden-handled knife or spatula (don't use your best one) in the flame of a gas range or on an electric element. Use the hot knife blade to cut through the caramel layer, marking 12 wedge-shaped servings. Pipe on Chocolate Frosting with cake decorator to trim top edge. Refrigerate overnight or longer. Makes 12 servings.

**Chocolate Frosting.** Cream 3 tablespoons soft butter with ¾ cup sifted powdered sugar. Blend in until smooth 1 tablespoon light cream and ¼ cup sweet ground chocolate. Makes about ¾ cup.

# Black Forest Cherry Cake

- 1 **can (1 lb.) sour pitted cherries**
- ¾ **cup kirsch (cherry brandy)**
- 1 **oz. unsweetened chocolate**
- 1 **package (about 1 lb. 2 oz.) yellow cake mix**
- ½ **cup (¼ lb.) butter**
- 4 **cups sifted powdered sugar Few drops red food coloring**
- 1 **envelope unflavored gelatin**
- 3 **cups whipping cream**
- ½ **oz. semisweet chocolate**
- 12 **maraschino cherries with stems**

Drain sour cherries thoroughly and cut in half. Pour over them ¼ cup of the kirsch; cover, and let stand at least 4 hours. Grease and flour four 9-inch round cake pans. Melt the unsweetened chocolate over hot water (or use the liquid unsweetened chocolate product for baking). Prepare cake mix following package directions, using eggs and water called for on the package.

Spoon half of the batter into two of the prepared cake pans, smoothing the top evenly. Blend melted chocolate into the remaining half of the batter and spread batter into the other two cake pans. Bake in a 350° oven for 12 to 14 minutes, or until the top springs back when touched lightly. Cool slightly, then turn out of pans. When cold, cut each layer in half horizontally, making 8 thin layers.

Make a cherry buttercream by draining the kirsch from the cherries and measuring it (you should have ¼ cup). Cream the butter until light and blend in 3½ cups of the powdered sugar alternately with the kirsch drained from the cherries. Add enough red food coloring to tint a pale pink; set aside.

Soften gelatin in ¼ cup of the kirsch; place over hot water and heat until dissolved; cool. Whip cream until thick. Gradually beat in the liquid gelatin, the remaining ¼ cup kirsch, and the remaining ½ cup powdered sugar, beating until stiff peaks form; set aside.

To assemble cake, place 1 split chocolate layer on a cake plate, cover with ⅓ of the cherry buttercream, and ⅓ of the sour pitted cherries. Cover with a split yellow cake layer and a layer of the whipped cream ⅓ inch thick. Repeat process in the same order twice again (chocolate layer, cherry buttercream, and cherries, yellow layer, whipped cream). Finish with the fourth chocolate layer (you omit the fourth yellow cake layer). Cover top and sides of cake with remaining whipped cream and garnish with curls of semisweet chocolate (made by shaving bar of chocolate with a vegetable peeler) and maraschino cherries.

Chill until ready to serve (as long as several days). If you want to freeze the cake, leave cherries off and add later. Makes 14 to 16 servings.

# Pineapple Upside-down Cake

- ¼ **cup (⅛ lb.) butter or margarine**
- ½ **cup brown sugar, firmly packed**
- 1 **can (1 lb. 4 oz.) sliced pineapple**
- 3 **eggs**
- 1 **cup granulated sugar**
- 1 **cup regular all-purpose flour**
- 1 **teaspoon baking powder**
- ¼ **teaspoon salt**

Melt the butter in a heavy 10-inch frying pan which can be placed in the oven. Add the brown sugar and cook very slowly, stirring constantly, for about 10 minutes, or until bubbly over entire surface. Cover with the drained pineapple slices (reserve syrup) and cool.

Beat the eggs with the granulated sugar until light and fluffy; add ¼ cup of the reserved pineapple syrup. Sift flour, measure, and sift again with baking powder and salt; fold into the egg mixture. Pour over pineapple in frying pan. Bake uncovered in a 350° oven for about 45 minutes. While still warm, loosen cake with a spatula and turn out on a serving plate. Serves 6 to 8.

# Stanford Hospital Prune Cake

Although details are lost of the origin of this recipe which first appeared in *Sunset Magazine* in the late '40s, the hospital is still in Palo Alto, California, and the cake is still a favorite.

It makes a good coffee cake, as well as dessert.

- ½ **cup butter (¼ lb.) or shortening**
- 2 **cups sugar**
- 6 **eggs, separated**
- 3 **cups regular all-purpose flour**
- 2 **teaspoons each baking powder and soda**
- 1 **teaspoon each salt, cinnamon, and ground cloves**
- ½ **teaspoon nutmeg**
- 2¼ **cups finely chopped moist-pack pitted prunes**
- ½ **cup chopped nuts**
- ½ **cup buttermilk (or regular milk mixed with 1½ teaspoons vinegar)**
- 1 **tablespoon lemon juice Sweetened whipped cream**

Cream the butter and sugar well. Add the egg yolks, and beat smooth. Sift the flour, measure, then sift with the baking powder, soda, salt, and spices. Coat the prunes and nuts with some of the flour mixture; reserve.

Add remaining flour mixture a little at a time, alternately with the milk, to the butter mixture, beating smooth. Then mix in the lemon juice, prunes, and nuts. Beat egg whites stiff and fold into the batter.

Pour into three greased and floured 9-inch round layer cake pans. Bake in a 375° oven about 30 minutes, or until a toothpick inserted comes out clean.

Serve warm, cut in wedges, with sweetened whipped cream on top; or put layers together with whipped cream. Serves 12 to 16.

## Glazed Pineapple-Carrot Cake

2 cups regular all-purpose flour
1½ cups sugar
1 teaspoon soda
2 teaspoons cinnamon
½ teaspoon salt
3 eggs
½ cup salad oil
¾ cup buttermilk
2 teaspoons vanilla
1 can (about 8 oz.) crushed pineapple, well drained
2 cups finely shredded carrots
1 cup chopped almonds or pecans
1 cup flaked coconut
Buttermilk Syrup (recipe follows)

Sift flour; measure and sift with sugar, soda, cinnamon, and salt into a bowl. Beat eggs together with the oil, buttermilk, and vanilla. Add to dry ingredients all at once and mix until smooth. Mix in pineapple, carrots, nuts, and coconut.

Pour into a lightly greased and floured 9 by 13-inch baking pan. Bake in a 350° oven for 45 minutes, or until center springs back when lightly touched. Remove cake from oven and lightly prick it all over with a fork.

Slowly pour hot Buttermilk Syrup over cake. Serves 12.

**Buttermilk Syrup.** In a saucepan combine ⅔ cup sugar, ¼ teaspoon soda, ⅓ cup buttermilk, ⅓ cup butter or margarine, and 2 teaspoons light corn syrup. Bring to boiling over medium heat; boil 5 minutes. Remove from heat and add ½ teaspoon vanilla.

## Butter Kuchen (Fruit Picture Cake)

Undoubtedly this cake of German origin has become popular because it is such a marvelous way to display the beauties of fresh fruit in season.

½ cup (¼ lb.) soft butter
½ cup sugar
3 eggs
½ teaspoon vanilla
1 cup unsifted all-purpose flour
Fruit topping and additional flavorings as suggested

In the small bowl of your electric mixer, cream butter with sugar until smoothly blended. Beat in eggs, one at a time, beating thoroughly after each addition. Stir in the vanilla and flour and mix well.

Butter and flour an 11-inch round shallow pan (a tart pan with removable bottom is the most desirable shape, although you can use a fixed-bottom pan). Spread the batter evenly in the pan and arrange fruit over the surface according to directions following.

Bake cake in a 375° oven for 40 minutes, or until cake feels firm when touched in the center. Let cake cool at least 30 minutes on a wire rack. Remove pan rim, if possible, and serve cake warm; or cool completely and serve cold. Makes 10 to 12 servings.

**Plum Topping.** Cut 14 to 16 Italian plums (fresh prunes or purple plums) in halves and remove pits. Arrange halves, cut side up, over the surface of the unbaked Butter Kuchen, placing them close together. Sprinkle fruit evenly with 2 to 3 tablespoons sugar, then bake and cool as directed. About 30 minutes before you want to serve the cake, dust the surface liberally with powdered sugar.

**Pear Topping.** Add to the Butter Kuchen batter along with the vanilla, ¼ teaspoon anise seed, ½ teaspoon anise extract, and 1 teaspoon grated lemon peel. Pour the batter into the pan as directed. Cut 3 large Bartlett pears in halves lengthwise, core and stem; then slice off the rounded back of each pear half and cut each of these pieces in half lengthwise, too. Arrange large pear slices on the cake batter, then fit the little pieces in between the large slices. Sprinkle pears with 2 tablespoons lemon juice, ½ teaspoon anise seed, and then 2 to 3 tablespoons sugar. Bake as directed.

**Nectarine Topping.** Peel 3 large nectarines, and then cut from the pits in thin slices (or pit and slice if freestone). Mix fruit with ¼ teaspoon nutmeg; arrange the slices neatly, overlapping concentrically on the surface of the Butter Kuchen batter. Sprinkle evenly with 1½ to 2 tablespoons sugar. Bake as directed for the Butter Kuchen. While still warm, brush top of cake lightly with 2 tablespoons warm orange marmalade.

**Peach-Almond Topping.** Whirl ¾ cup almonds in a blender to consistency of fine powder (or grind through the fine blade of a food chopper), then blend thoroughly with 2 tablespoons soft butter, 4 tablespoons *each* all-purpose flour and brown sugar, and ¼ teaspoon almond extract until mixture is crumbly. Set aside while you prepare the cake.

Peel, halve, and pit 4 large peaches and cut each half in quarters. Arrange the fruit in rows on the Butter Kuchen batter. Sprinkle fruit evenly with 2 tablespoons sugar. Bake for 30 minutes.

Remove kuchen from oven and quickly make a border on the cake of the prepared almond mixture. Return kuchen immediately to the oven and continue to bake 10 minutes more, or until cake feels firm when lightly touched in the center.

## Gumdrop Fruit Cake

4 cups unsifted regular all-purpose flour
1 teaspoon cinnamon
¼ teaspoon each ground cloves and nutmeg
1¼ teaspoons soda
¼ teaspoon salt
1 package (15 oz.) golden raisins
1 to 2 pounds gumdrops (do not use grape or licorice-flavored ones)
1 cup (½ lb.) butter or margarine
1 cup coarsely chopped pecans
2 cups sugar
2 eggs, well beaten
1 can (1 lb.) apple sauce
1 teaspoon vanilla

Sift flour with the cinnamon, cloves, nutmeg, soda, and salt. Coat the raisins with some of the flour mixture.

Put some of the flour mixture on a board and coat the gumdrops with it. Working on the floured board, cut the gumdrops into small pieces (the flour keeps them from sticking to each other).

Melt 1 tablespoon of the butter in a small saucepan. Sauté the pecans in the butter until they are golden brown and crisp. Cool, then coat in some of the flour mixture.

Cream the remaining butter and sugar together until well blended and fluffy. Combine the eggs, apple sauce, and vanilla.

Add apple sauce mixture and flour mixture alternately to the creamed butter and sugar. Stir in raisins, gumdrops (including any flour from the cutting board), and nuts.

Have ready three 7⅜ by 3⅝ by 2¼-inch loaf pans, which have been greased and then lined with greased brown paper. Pour the thick batter into these. Bake in a 300° oven about 2 hours, or until a toothpick inserted comes out clean and the cakes are golden brown. Makes 3 small loaf cakes.

## Old-English Fruit Cake

This is a solid, dark cake with just enough batter to hold the fruits and nuts together.

    2  cups (1 lb.) butter
    1  pound brown sugar
   12  eggs, separated
    4  cups regular all-purpose flour
    2  teaspoons each cinnamon, mace,
       and cloves
    1  teaspoon each allspice, nutmeg,
       and salt
    1  pound mixed candied fruit
    1  pound candied cherries
    1  pound seeded raisins
    1  pound seedless raisins
    1  pound currants
    1  pound pitted dates, cut in pieces
   ½  pound diced citron (optional)
    1  pound broken walnuts
    1  cup rum or brandy
   ½  cup double-strength coffee
       Grated peel and juice of 3
         medium-sized oranges
       Grated peel and juice of 1 lemon
       Brandy or rum

Cream together butter and sugar until light and fluffy. Add well-beaten egg yolks and stir vigorously until smooth and creamy.

Sift flour, measure, and sift with spices. Combine candied fruit, cherries, seeded raisins, seedless raisins, currants, dates, citron, and walnuts, and mix lightly with 1 cup of the spiced flour. Add remaining flour to batter, blending alternately with mixture of rum, coffee, and fruit peel and juices. Add fruit and nut mixture and mix well.

Beat egg whites until they hold stiff peaks, then fold into batter.

Butter 4 loaf pans (5 by 9-inch size), line with brown paper, and butter again. Spoon in batter. Bake in a 250° oven for about 3 hours, 30 minutes, or until a toothpick inserted in center of cakes comes out clean.

Have a shallow pan of water in bottom of oven.

Set cakes in pans on wire racks to cool; remove from pan. Wrap each cake in a cloth moistened in brandy. Wrap individually in 2 layers of foil, sealing to make airtight. Age at least 1 month. Chill before slicing. Makes 4 cakes.

## Cookies

## Ribbon Cakes

These festive cookies are baked in an unusual way to produce stripes of jelly across them. Because they keep six weeks tightly covered, they are excellent to make ahead for Christmas. The recipe came from Finland.

    3  cups unsifted regular all-purpose
       flour
    1  cup sugar
    1  teaspoon baking powder
    1  cup (½ lb.) soft butter or margarine
    2  whole eggs plus 1 egg white
   ½  teaspoon vanilla
    1  cup jelly or jam (plum, blackberry,
       or raspberry jelly, or apricot jam)
    2  tablespoons sugar

In a large bowl, mix together flour, the 1 cup sugar, and baking powder. Blend in butter with hands or pastry blender until like cornmeal. Add eggs and vanilla; work into a stiff dough.

Divide into two balls, one twice the size of the other. On a heavily floured board (¼ to ½ cup flour), roll out the larger ball to ⅛-inch thickness; place in a cooky pan (11 by 15½ inches), smoothing out to edges and patching corners. Spread jelly over the top.

Roll out remaining dough to ⅛-inch thickness and cut in ½-inch-

wide strips; place diagonally across jelly ½ inch apart. Sprinkle the 2 tablespoons sugar over the top.

Start baking in a 375° oven. The edges will be done first. When edges start to brown (about 20 minutes), take pan from oven; cut off and remove about a 3-inch strip all around the edges. Return pan to oven for 10 minutes; remove. Cut into about 1 by 2-inch rectangles. Makes about 7 dozen cookies.

## Graham Cracker Brownies

    2  eggs
   ½  cup granulated sugar
   ½  cup brown sugar, firmly packed
       Dash of salt
   14  graham crackers, crushed fine
   ½  cup chopped nuts
   ½  teaspoon vanilla

Beat eggs until light. Mix sugar, salt, graham cracker crumbs, and nuts; add to beaten egg, mixing well; add vanilla.

Spread mixture evenly in a greased 8-inch-square pan and bake in a 350° oven for 25 to 30 minutes. While still warm, cut into strips about 1 inch wide and 2 inches long. Makes 2½ dozen.

## Chocolate-Mint Layer Cookies

These are a rich chocolate-mint brownie.

    2  ounces unsweetened chocolate
   ½  cup (¼ lb.) butter or margarine
    2  eggs
    1  cup sugar
   ½  cup unsifted regular all-purpose
       flour
   ½  cup sliced unblanched almonds
       Mint Cream (recipe follows)
       Chocolate Glaze (recipe follows)

Melt chocolate and butter together over hot water. In a bowl, beat together eggs and sugar until ivory-colored; add flour, nuts, and chocolate-butter mixture; stir until combined.

Pour the batter evenly into a greased and flour-dusted 9-inch-square pan. Bake in a 350° oven for 25 minutes, or until toothpick inserted in center comes out clean; let cool in pan.

Spread Mint Cream evenly over chocolate layer; cover and chill until firm, about 1 hour. Drizzle Chocolate Glaze over mint topping; cover and chill until firm; cut into bite-sized squares. Makes about 36 cookies.

**Mint Cream.** Beat together until smooth 1½ cups sifted powdered sugar, 3 tablespoons soft butter, 2 tablespoons half-and-half (light cream), and ¾ teaspoon peppermint extract.

**Chocolate Glaze.** Melt together over hot water 2 ounces sweet chocolate and 2 tablespoons butter or margarine.

## Oatmeal Shortbread

1½ cups unsifted regular all-purpose flour
⅔ cup quick-cooking rolled oats
1 cup (½ lb.) butter or margarine
⅔ cup brown sugar, firmly packed

Combine all the ingredients in a mixing bowl and mix with your fingers until well blended and crumbly. Press firmly and evenly into a lightly buttered pan (10 by 15 inches).

Bake in a 300° oven for about 45 minutes. Cut into squares or bars while still warm, then cool in pan. Makes about 3 dozen 2-inch squares.

## German Cookies

There's a sardonic touch to the name of these cookies. During World War II, mothers baked these to mail overseas because they could survive a six-week journey, arriving moist and tasty. They became German only if captured en route.

4 eggs
1 package (1 lb.) dark brown sugar
2½ cups regular all-purpose flour
1 teaspoon cinnamon
½ teaspoon cloves
Dash of salt
1 cup chopped walnuts
1 cup powdered sugar
¼ cup water

Beat eggs and sugar together until creamy. Sift flour, measure, then sift again with cinnamon, cloves, and salt

into egg mixture. Add chopped walnuts. Mix well. Spread on a greased 12 by 18-inch rimmed cooky pan.

Bake in a 375° oven for about 20 minutes. Immediately spread a glaze of the powdered sugar mixed with water over top. Cool, then cut into 2 by 3-inch (or smaller) strips. Makes about 5 dozen.

## Dream Bars

Of all the cookies which have made a hit with young and old, Dream Bars are far and away the leader. This is one of the top dozen all-time favorite *Sunset* recipes.

They are really more a candy than cooky—very rich and sweet.

½ cup (¼ lb.) butter or margarine
½ cup brown sugar, firmly packed
1 cup unsifted regular all-purpose flour
2 eggs
1 cup brown sugar, firmly packed
1 teaspoon vanilla
2 tablespoons flour
½ teaspoon salt
1 teaspoon baking powder
1½ cups shredded coconut
1 cup chopped nuts
Orange Butter Frosting (recipe follows)

Mix butter, the ½ cup brown sugar, and the 1 cup flour with fingers or fork into a crumbly mass; pat into an 8 by 12-inch baking pan, covering the bottom evenly. Bake in a 375° oven for 10 minutes. Set aside to cool.

Beat the eggs, the 1 cup brown sugar, and vanilla together. Mix the 2 tablespoons flour, salt, and baking powder. Sprinkle over the coconut and nuts; mix to coat. Add to the egg-sugar mixture and blend. Pour mixture onto the baked crust, spread evenly, and bake in a 375° oven for 20 minutes. Cool slightly. Use a sharp knife to cut into bars about ¾ inch wide and 2 inches long while still warm; frost with Orange Butter Frosting. Makes 4 dozen.

**Orange Butter Frosting.** Cream ¼ cup (⅛ lb.) soft butter or margarine thoroughly with 2 cups sifted powdered sugar. Add 1 teaspoon vanilla and 1 teaspoon (or more to taste) grated orange peel. Work in about 2 tablespoons orange juice, enough to make the mixture pliable and a little softer than you want the finished frosting.

## Frosted Coffee Bars

This recipe which first made a hit in the 1930's has remained relatively unchanged, except that cooks now probably tend to make the coffee with instant coffee powder.

½ cup shortening
1 cup brown sugar, firmly packed
1 egg
½ cup strong hot coffee
1⅔ cups regular all-purpose flour
½ teaspoon each baking powder, soda, cinnamon, and salt
½ cup seedless raisins
¼ cup chopped walnuts
1½ cups sifted powdered sugar
1 tablespoon soft butter or margarine
1 teaspoon vanilla
About 3 tablespoons strong hot coffee

Cream shortening with sugar; blend in egg, then the ½ cup coffee. Sift flour, measure, and sift again with the baking powder, soda, cinnamon, and salt; mix well with first mixture. Stir in the raisins and walnuts.

Spread batter in a greased cooky pan (11 by 16 inches) and bake in a 375° oven for about 15 minutes. Cool in pan.

Spread with thin icing made by blending the powdered sugar, butter, vanilla, and 3 tablespoons coffee (add more coffee if needed). When icing is set, cut into squares. Makes 20 cookies about 2 inches square, or 12 dessert-sized servings about 3 inches square.

## Pumpkin Bars

½ cup (¼ lb.) butter or margarine
1 cup brown sugar, firmly packed
1 egg
½ cup canned pumpkin
1½ cups unsifted regular all-purpose flour
1 teaspoon cinnamon
½ teaspoon each ground ginger, allspice, and soda
½ cup chopped dates or raisins
½ cup chopped walnuts, pecans, or filberts
Orange Glaze (recipe follows)

In the large bowl of your electric mixer, cream together the butter and sugar. Add the egg and pumpkin and beat well. Blend the flour with the spices and soda and sift into creamed mixture. Add dates and nuts; mix well.

Spread evenly in a greased 11 by 16-inch baking pan. Bake in a 350° oven until the cake begins to pull away from the sides of the pan—16 to 18 minutes. Spread with Orange Glaze. Cool and cut into bars or squares. Makes about 3 dozen 2-inch squares.

**Orange Glaze.** Blend 1 cup unsifted powdered sugar with 5 teaspoons orange juice concentrate *or* with 1 teaspoon grated orange peel and 3 teaspoons orange juice.

# English Toffee Cookies

These are a special favorite because they are thin and crisp with flavor like toffee candy and because you can make a large quantity of them easily.

1 cup (½ lb.) butter or margarine
1 cup sugar
1 egg, separated
2 cups regular all-purpose flour
1 teaspoon cinnamon
1 cup chopped pecans or walnuts

Cream the butter or margarine and sugar together until smooth. Add the egg yolk, and mix in thoroughly. Sift the flour, measure, and sift again with the cinnamon. Add flour to the creamed mixture, using your hands to blend together lightly but thoroughly.

Spread in an even layer over the entire surface of a greased cooky sheet (10 by 15 inches). Work with your palms to smooth the surface. Beat the egg white slightly; spread on top to completely cover. Sprinkle the chopped nuts over all, pressing them into the dough.

Bake in a 275° oven for 1 hour. Cut in 1½-inch squares while still hot. Cool. Makes about 6 dozen.

# Date Pinwheel Cookies

1 cup chopped dates
2 cups brown sugar, firmly packed
½ cup water
⅔ cup shortening
2 eggs
1 teaspoon vanilla
4 cups regular all-purpose flour
1 teaspoon soda
¼ teaspoon cream of tartar
½ teaspoon salt

Make filling: In a saucepan combine dates, ½ cup of the brown sugar, and water; simmer about 8 minutes, or until mixture thickens, stirring constantly. Remove from heat and cool.

Cream shortening and the remaining sugar until light, then beat in eggs and vanilla.

Sift flour, measure, and sift again with the soda, cream of tartar, and salt. Stir flour mixture into shortening mixture gradually to make a stiff dough. Divide in half. Roll out each portion on a lightly floured board, making a rectangle about 8 by 10 inches and ¼-inch thick. Spread with half the cooled date filling, then roll up like a jelly roll.

Wrap in waxed paper and chill thoroughly, preferably 12 hours or overnight.

Cut slices ¼-inch thick with a sharp knife; place on an ungreased baking sheet. Bake in 400° oven for 8 to 10 minutes. Makes 7 to 8 dozen.

# Chewy Chocolate Chip Bars

Buttery pastry (recipe follows)
2 eggs
1 cup firmly packed brown sugar
1½ teaspoons vanilla
2 tablespoons all-purpose flour
1 teaspoon baking powder
½ teaspoon salt
1 cup finely chopped nuts
1 package (6 oz.) semisweet chocolate baking chips

Make the buttery pastry. Pat the pastry in an even layer over the bottom of a greased 9 by 13-inch baking pan. Bake in a 350° oven for 10 minutes. Let cool.

In a small bowl, beat together the eggs. Add the brown sugar and beat

until blended. Mix in the vanilla, flour, baking powder, salt, and nuts. Spread evenly over the first layer. Sprinkle chocolate chips evenly over top.

Bake in a 350° oven for 25 minutes or until lightly browned. Let cool and cut in bars. Makes 24 to 36 pieces.

**Buttery pastry.** In a small bowl beat together ½ cup butter or margarine with ½ cup firmly packed brown sugar until creamy. Mix in 1 cup all-purpose flour.

# Twice-baked Italian Cookies

Toasted until hard and crunchy, these anise-flavored slices are delicious when served with wine for dunking.

2 cups sugar
1 cup (½ lb.) butter, melted
4 tablespoons anise seed
¼ cup anise-flavored liqueur
3 tablespoons Bourbon, or 2 teaspoons vanilla and 2 tablespoons water
2 cups coarsely chopped almonds or walnuts
6 eggs
5½ cups regular all-purpose flour
1 tablespoon baking powder

Mix sugar with butter, anise seed, anise liqueur, Bourbon (or vanilla and water), and nuts. Beat in the eggs. Sift and measure flour and sift again with baking powder into the sugar mixture; blend thoroughly. Cover and chill the dough for 2 to 3 hours.

On a lightly floured board, shape dough with your hands to form flat loaves that are about ½ inch thick and 2 inches wide, and as long as your cooky sheets. Place no more than 2 loaves, parallel and well apart, on a buttered cooky sheet (one without rims is best). Bake in a 375° oven for 20 minutes.

Remove from oven and let loaves cool on pans until you can touch them, then cut in diagonal slices that are about ½ to ¾ inch thick. Lay slices on cut sides close together on cooky sheet and return to the oven (375°) for 15 minutes more or until lightly toasted. Cool on wire racks and store in airtight containers. Makes about 9 dozen.

## Almond Butter Cookies

2 cups regular all-purpose flour
1 teaspoon baking powder
⅛ teaspoon salt
1 cup (½ lb.) butter or margarine
1 cup sugar
2 egg yolks
½ teaspoon lemon extract
¾ teaspoon each vanilla and almond extract
    About 4 ounces whole, blanched almonds, toasted in a 350° oven for 15 minutes

Sift flour, measure, and sift again with the baking powder and salt; set aside. Cream butter and sugar together until light and fluffy. Add egg yolks, one at a time, beating well after each is added. Blend in lemon, vanilla, and almond extract. Gradually add flour, mixing well.

Pinch off pieces of dough and form into 1-inch balls. Set on an ungreased baking sheet about 2 inches apart, and press a toasted almond in center of each. Bake in a 300° oven 15 to 20 minutes, until edges just begin to brown. Cool 5 minutes, then remove to racks. Makes about 4½ dozen.

## Ginger Ball Cookies

¾ cup shortening
1 cup sugar
1 egg, well beaten
4 teaspoons molasses
2 cups regular all-purpose flour
2 teaspoons soda
1 teaspoon each ground cinnamon and ginger
½ teaspoon ground cloves
¼ teaspoon salt
    Granulated sugar

Cream shortening with sugar in a large mixing bowl. Mix in egg and molasses. Sift and measure flour; sift again with the soda, cinnamon, ginger, cloves, and salt. Stir the dry ingredients into the mixture in the bowl. Mix well. Shape dough into one-inch balls and roll each one in granulated sugar.

Place at least 4 inches apart on a greased cooky sheet, and bake in a 375° oven for about 12 minutes. Remove from pan to cool. Makes about 4 dozen.

## Orange-Nut Refrigerator Cookies

In 1948 when this recipe was first published, cooks would have had to grind the nuts or chop them by hand for these cookies. Now most will use their blender to pulverize the nuts in seconds.

1 cup (½ lb.) soft butter or margarine
½ cup firmly packed brown sugar
½ cup granulated sugar
1 egg
2 teaspoons grated orange peel
3 cups regular all-purpose flour
½ teaspoon soda
½ teaspoon salt
½ cup finely minced walnuts

Mix together butter and sugars until blended; add egg and beat until fluffy. Stir in orange peel. Sift flour, measure, and mix with the soda, salt, and nuts; add in small portions to butter mixture, mixing well after each addition. Divide dough in half and shape each into a roll 7 inches long and 2½ inches in diameter. Wrap in waxed paper; chill until firm.

Cut into slices about ⅛ inch thick. Bake on greased cooky sheets in a 375° oven for 12 minutes, or until edges are very lightly browned. Makes about 7 dozen.

## Dutch Ginger Thins

1¼ cups regular all-purpose flour
½ cup sugar
½ cup (¼ lb.) firm butter or margarine
1 egg, separated
¼ teaspoon vanilla
¼ cup well-drained, sliced preserved ginger (sliced ⅛-inch thick)
1 teaspoon preserved ginger syrup

Sift flour and measure; mix in the sugar. Cut in the butter or margarine.

Beat the egg yolk slightly and stir into the mixture along with the vanilla. Work dough with hands until smooth.

Roll out on a floured board to about ⅛-inch thickness; cut with a 2½-inch scalloped or round cutter. Place on ungreased baking sheets.

Press a ginger slice into each cooky center. Beat egg white with ginger syrup; brush cookies with mixture.

Bake in a 375° oven for 10 to 12 minutes, until lightly browned. Makes about 2 dozen.

## After-school Cookies

Any cooky containing peanut butter, raisins, and oats is sure to be in great demand after school.

1½ cups seedless raisins
    Boiling water
1 cup (½ lb.) butter or margarine
2 cups sugar
½ cup peanut butter (creamy or chunk-style)
3 eggs, well beaten
3 cups regular all-purpose flour
½ teaspoon salt
¾ teaspoon soda
2 teaspoons cinnamon
5 tablespoons milk
2 teaspoons vanilla
1¼ cups quick-cooking rolled oats

Pour boiling water over the raisins, let stand 5 minutes, then drain and pat dry with paper towels.

Cream butter and sugar together thoroughly. Blend in the peanut butter. Add the beaten eggs and mix well. Sift flour, measure, and sift with the salt, soda, and cinnamon. Blend flour into the creamed mixture along with the milk. Stir in vanilla, rolled oats, and raisins.

Drop by teaspoonfuls about 2 inches apart on an ungreased cooky sheet. Bake in a 375° oven about 15 minutes. Makes about 8 dozen medium-sized cookies.

## Brown Sugar Christmas Thins

These caramel-flavored, crisp cookies are perfect for cutting into all sorts of Christmas shapes. Even 4-year-olds can have a lot of fun rolling and cutting them.

1 package (1 lb.) brown sugar
1 pound soft butter or margarine
1½ teaspoons vanilla
4½ cups unsifted regular all-purpose flour

Cream sugar, butter, and vanilla until fluffy, then work in flour; mix at slow speed or use a spoon or your hands. Shape into a smooth ball; cover and chill as long as a week. Let dough come to room temperature before rolling.

Pinch off a small lump of dough, shape into a ball, then flatten and roll very thin on a well-floured pastry cloth or board.

Cut in desired shapes and place on ungreased baking sheets. Bake at 300° for about 15 minutes (more or less depending upon thickness of cookies) or until slightly browner than raw dough. Cool cookies briefly on baking sheet, then transfer to wire racks to cool completely. Package airtight; they stay very crisp. Makes about 15 dozen cookies, each ⅛-inch thick and 2½ inches in diameter.

## Favorite Peanut Butter Cookies

3½ cups regular all-purpose flour
1 teaspoon soda
1 cup (½ lb.) butter or margarine
1 cup peanut butter
1 cup brown sugar, firmly packed
1 cup granulated sugar
2 eggs
1 teaspoon vanilla

Sift the flour, measure, and sift again with the soda.

Cream the butter; gradually cream in the peanut butter, then the brown sugar, then the granulated sugar. Beat in the eggs, one at a time; add vanilla. Work in the sifted dry ingredients.

Form into balls the size of large marbles and place 2 inches apart on a lightly greased baking sheet. Press balls down slightly with a fork, marking crisscrosses on top of each with the fork tines.

Bake the cookies in a 375° oven for 10 to 12 minutes, or until golden brown. Makes 7 dozen.

## Meringue Cookies

2 egg whites
Dash salt
1 cup sugar
1 cup chopped walnuts
1 cup chopped dates
1 teaspoon vanilla

Using a rotary beater, beat egg whites stiff in the upper part of a double boiler. Add salt and gradually beat in sugar. Put over boiling water and continue beating until the mixture gets sugary around the edges. Add walnuts, dates, and vanilla; stir well. Drop by small teaspoonfuls onto a well-buttered baking sheet.

Bake in a 250° oven for almost an hour, or until they are set and firm so that they can be removed without breaking. Cool on a rack, then store tightly covered. Makes 1½ to 2 dozen.

## Cornflake Macaroons

2 egg whites
1 cup sugar
2 tablespoons melted butter or margarine
1 teaspoon vanilla, or ½ teaspoon maple flavoring
⅔ cup shredded coconut
⅔ cup chopped walnuts
½ teaspoon salt
4 cups cornflakes

Beat the egg whites until stiff, then gradually beat in the sugar. Add the other ingredients in order given. Form into 36 small clusters an inch apart on greased baking sheets. Bake in a 375° oven about 15 minutes. Makes 3 dozen.

## German Oatmeal Lace Cookies

⅔ cup quick-cooking rolled oats
¼ cup flour
¼ teaspoon each salt, cloves, and ginger
½ cup sugar
½ cup (¼ lb.) butter
2 tablespoons whipping cream

In a small frying pan, combine all the ingredients and cook over medium heat, stirring, until mixture begins to bubble. Remove from heat; mix well.

Drop dough, 1 level teaspoon at a time (measure to make sure cookies turn out the same size), well apart onto a lightly greased cooky sheet, allowing 3 or 4 cookies to each sheet.

Bake in a 375° oven for 5 to 7 minutes or until cookies are evenly browned. Remove from oven and let stand until cookies are firm enough to lift from pan with a spatula (less than a minute), but are still soft enough to shape. (If you want flat cookies, leave them on pans until firm, then cool on wire racks.)

To shape cookies, wrap around metal pastry tubes or cones that are ½ inch or larger in diameter (or fashion forms from several thicknesses of heavy foil). Or drape cookies over horizontally suspended wooden spoon handles or a broomstick. Place cookies on wire racks to cool completely; then remove forms. Store airtight. Makes about 3 dozen.

## Billy Goats

The woman who contributed this recipe more than three decades ago wrote that she didn't know why this recipe had such a peculiar name.

2 cups regular all-purpose flour
¼ teaspoon soda
2 teaspoons baking powder
1 teaspoon cinnamon
¼ teaspoon ground cloves
1 cup coarsely chopped walnuts
1 pound pitted dates, chopped
½ cup (¼ lb.) soft butter or margarine
1 cup sugar
2 eggs, separated
2 tablespoons buttermilk or sour cream
½ teaspoon vanilla

Sift flour; measure and sift again with the soda, baking powder, cinnamon, and cloves. Mix in nuts and dates.

Cream the butter with the sugar and beat in the egg yolks, buttermilk, and vanilla. Beat the egg whites until stiff.

Combine the flour mixture and the butter-sugar mixture, blending well. Using a fork, break up the stiff batter and carefully mix in the beaten egg whites.

Drop by teaspoon-sized spoonfuls onto a baking sheet ½-inch apart. Bake in a 375° oven about 12 minutes, until browned. Makes 6½ dozen.

## No-Bake Choco-Nut Drop Cookies

3 cups quick-cooking rolled oats
5 tablespoons unsweetened cocoa
½ cup chopped nuts
½ cup shredded coconut
2 cups sugar
½ cup milk
½ cup (¼ lb.) butter or margarine

In a bowl combine the oats, cocoa, nuts, and coconut. In a pan put sugar, milk, and butter or margarine; bring just to a boil, stirring to combine. Pour over the rolled oats mixture. Mix lightly until blended.

Drop from a teaspoon onto waxed paper or foil. Let stand until firm, about 10 minutes. Makes about 4 dozen cookies.

## Rosettes

You need a special rosette iron to make these crisp-fried crullers of Scandinavian origin. Serve like cookies, or omit sugar and lemon extract to make them for patty shells.

Be sure to preheat the iron in the fat before making each rosette, or it will not come loose easily.

2 eggs
2 teaspoons sugar
¼ teaspoon salt
1 cup milk
1 tablespoon lemon extract
1 cup regular all-purpose flour
  Shortening or salad oil for deep frying
  Powdered sugar

Beat together until well mixed (but not foamy) the eggs, sugar, milk, salt, milk, and lemon extract. Sift flour, measure, and beat into liquid ingredients until smooth (batter should be like thick cream). Let stand 2 hours.

Heat shortening or salad oil to 370°. For each rosette, preheat the iron in fat about 1 minute; dip hot iron just to rim in the batter (don't let batter come over top edge of iron or it will be hard to remove). Lower iron into fat for 30 seconds, or until golden brown. Remove from fat, and loosen with fork; drain.

Store in airtight container to keep crisp. Sprinkle with powdered sugar before serving. Makes about 40.

## Pies

## Standard Pastry

2 cups regular all-purpose flour
½ teaspoon salt
⅔ cup shortening
¼ cup ice-cold water

Sift flour, measure, and sift with salt into bowl. Add shortening and cut into flour with pastry blender (or two knives, cutting parallel) until pieces are about the size of large peas. Add water by tablespoonfuls, sprinkling over the top. Toss with a fork to moisten evenly.

Turn out on waxed paper and press together. Wrap well if you want to chill before rolling. Makes 1 double-crust, 9-inch pie or 2 pie shells.

**Hot Water Pastry Variation.** Place shortening in a bowl; sprinkle with salt. Use hot instead of cold water; pour hot water over shortening and stir lightly with a fork. Add flour all at once and stir until moisture is absorbed. Gather together and press into a ball. Wrap in waxed paper if you want to chill before rolling.

**Tips on Rolling and Baking.** For best results, use a canvas cover on your pastry board and a stocking cover on your rolling pin. You will use less flour and there will be no sticking.

For each crust, use half the pastry. Press into a ball and flatten lightly. Start rolling out pastry from the center, using light, quick motions. Lift and turn the pastry as you roll. Avoid letting the rolling pin go over the edges of the pastry, as this makes it thinner along the edge than in the center. The ideal thickness for pastry is about ⅛ inch. A slightly thicker

pastry may be used for the bottom of fruit pies.

Fit the pastry into the pan loosely. Don't stretch it; pat it gently into place.

*For a 1-crust pie or baked pie shell*, trim edge of pastry with scissors, leaving about a 1-inch overhang. Fold this edge under neatly. Pinching with the thumb and forefinger, flute the doubled pastry to make a high, decorative rim. If pastry is to be used in recipe calling for a baked pastry shell, prick shell well with a fork and bake in a 425° to 450° oven for 10 to 12 minutes, or until lightly browned.

*For a 2-crust pie*, trim edge of bottom crust to fit rim of pan. Fill and lay top crust loosely over the filling; trim edge of top crust with scissors, leaving about a ½-inch overhang. Tuck overhang in between edge of bottom crust and rim of pan. Flute edges between thumb and forefinger, or press with a floured fork. Slit top crust in several places.

## Flaky Pie Crust

This recipe, which many cooks who have had trouble making good pie crust prefer, makes enough for two double-crust pies or four baked pie shells. It freezes well, so you can keep baked pie shells in your freezer ready to fill.

3 cups regular all-purpose flour
1 teaspoon salt
1¼ cups shortening
1 egg, well beaten
1 tablespoon vinegar
4 tablespoons water

Sift flour, measure, and sift into a bowl with the salt. Add the shortening and use a pastry blender or two knives to cut it into the flour until coarse crumbs are formed.

In a small bowl combine the beaten egg with the vinegar and water; drizzle over the flour mixture. Mix lightly until the flour is all moistened and holds together in a ball (add a few drops additional water, if needed).

To make pie shells, divide into 4 pieces, roll out each piece on a lightly floured board, and fit into four 9-inch pie pans. Prick each well with a fork. Bake in a 425° oven for 12 minutes, or until lightly browned.

# Press-in Butter Pastry

This pastry differs considerably from conventional pie pastry. It doesn't shrink or change shape when baked.

- 2 cups unsifted all-purpose flour
- 4 tablespoons sugar
- ¾ cup (⅜ lb.) butter
- 2 egg yolks

Mix flour and sugar together. Add butter and crumble it into the flour with your fingers until mixture is mealy in texture and there are no large particles. Stir in the egg yolks with a fork until well blended, then work dough with your hands until it holds a smooth, noncrumbly ball (the heat of your hands softens butter and makes the dough stick together).

To shape, press the pastry into pan or pans, pushing it firmly to make an even layer. Allow about 1 teaspoon dough for tart pans 2 inches wide and about ¼ inch deep; about 2 tablespoons dough for tart pans 3 inches wide and 1 inch deep; about 1 cup dough for a 9-inch pie pan (shaping dough up to, but not onto pan rim); and about 1½ cups dough for an 11-inch tart pan.

Bake pastry in 300° oven for 20 or 30 minutes or until pastry is lightly browned; the larger pastries take more time to brown than the small ones do. Let pastry cool in pan; invert smaller tarts and tap lightly to free, then turn right side up. If you wish to remove pastry from pie pan, carefully invert on wire rack; then, supporting with a serving dish, turn cupped side up. The 11-inch tart pastry can be taken from pan only if supported by a removable metal bottom. Makes 2 cups dough.

# Crumb Crust

- 1½ cups finely crushed graham cracker crumbs
- ⅓ cup sugar
- ⅓ to ½ cup melted butter or margarine

Combine crumbs with sugar and blend in melted butter or margarine. Press firmly onto bottom and sides of a 9-inch pie pan. Chill for 1 hour, or bake in a 350° oven for about 10 minutes to set the crust. The baked crust will be firmer.

Cooky Crust. Substitute either vanilla or chocolate wafer crumbs, or gingersnaps, for graham crumbs. Omit sugar.

# Cherry or Blueberry Cream Cheese Pie

Of all the favorite *Sunset* pies, this one seems to be the all-time, top-ranking favorite. The same filling in a plain crust has been published by the name of French Cherry Pie.

- 1 small package (3 oz.) cream cheese
- ½ cup powdered sugar
- ½ teaspoon vanilla
- 1 cup whipping cream
  Butter-crumb Crust (recipe follows) or 1 baked 9-inch pastry shell
- 1 can (1 lb. 5 oz.) prepared cherry pie filling (or 1 can blueberry pie filling with 1 tablespoon lemon juice)

Beat together until smooth the cream cheese, powdered sugar, and vanilla. Whip the cream until stiff and carefully fold into the cream cheese mixture. Turn into the prepared pie shell, spreading evenly. Spoon the pie filling evenly over top. Chill thoroughly before serving. Makes 6 to 8 servings.

**Butter-crumb Crust.** Blend together 1 cup unsifted all-purpose flour, 2 tablespoons powdered sugar, and ½ cup (¼ lb.) butter just until crumbly. Turn into a buttered 9-inch pie pan, and pat evenly on bottom and sides of pan. Prick well with a fork. Bake in a 425° oven for 8 to 10 minutes, or until lightly browned. Cool before filling.

# Apple Pie

- 8 medium-sized tart apples
- 1 to 1½ tablespoons lemon juice
- ¾ to 1 cup sugar
- 1 tablespoon flour
- ½ teaspoon nutmeg or cinnamon or whole cloves
- 2 tablespoons butter or margarine
  Pastry for a double-crust, 9-inch pie
  Milk or half-and-half (light cream)
  Sugar

Peel apples, slice very thin, then sprinkle with lemon juice. Combine sugar, flour, and spice; mix well with apples. Let stand while preparing pastry. (Some prefer to let the apples stand overnight.)

Place fruit in a 9-inch pie pan lined with pastry, letting the apples heap a little in the center. Pour in juice left in bowl. Dot with butter.

Roll out top crust, cut out design in center (such as an apple), and adjust on top of apples. Flute edge to seal well. Brush top lightly with milk to glaze. Sprinkle with sugar for sparkle.

Bake in a 450° oven 10 minutes, then reduce heat to 350° and continue baking 30 to 40 minutes longer, or until apples are tender. Makes 1 pie (6 to 8 servings).

# Lattice-top Sweet Cherry Pie

- 5 cups pitted, halved fresh sweet cherries (Bing or Royal Anne)
- ¼ cup lemon juice
- ⅛ teaspoon almond extract
- ½ cup granulated sugar
- ⅓ cup light brown sugar, firmly packed
  Dash salt
- 3½ tablespoons quick-cooking tapioca
  Pastry for double-crust, 9-inch pie
- 1 tablespoon butter or margarine

Combine cherries, lemon juice, almond extract, granulated and brown sugar, salt and tapioca. Mix together and let stand while you make the pastry.

Roll out pastry for bottom crust and fit into a 9-inch pie pan. Roll out the remaining pastry and cut in 10 strips, ¾ inch wide and about 12 inches long.

Fill pastry shell with cherry mixture and dot with butter. Arrange strips of dough over the cherries to form a lattice top. Crimp and seal edges of pastry. Bake in a 450° oven for 10 minutes; reduce temperature to 350° and bake 30 minutes. Serves 6 to 8.

## Fresh Berry Tarts

No tart pans are needed; the fruit is arranged on a flat cooky crust.

½ package (3 oz. size) strawberry, raspberry or cherry-flavored gelatin (about 4 tablespoons)
¾ cup boiling water
   Cooky Crust (recipe follows)
2 cups sliced fresh strawberries, whole raspberries, or halved, pitted fresh cherries
1 cup heavy cream, whipped, and slightly sweetened, for garnish

Dissolve the gelatin in the boiling water. Chill until syrupy. Spread about ⅓ of it over the cooled crust. Arrange fruit on top of the gelatin (if berries are tart, sprinkle with 2 to 3 tablespoons sugar). Brush or spoon remaining gelatin evenly over the fruit. Chill until set.

To garnish and serve, cut into three lengthwise strips, each 3 inches wide. Line edge of each strip with the whipped cream; spoon it on evenly, or force through a cake decorator. Cut each strip into 3-inch squares to serve. Store in refrigerator. Makes 12 servings.

Cooky Crust. Cream together ½ cup (¼ lb.) butter or margarine and ½ cup sugar until light. Beat in 1 egg and 1 tablespoon grated orange peel until mixture is light and lemon colored. Sift all-purpose flour, measure 1 cup, and sift again with ½ teaspoon baking powder. Add dry ingredients gradually to the creamed mixture, beating until smooth.

Line a 9 by 12-inch baking pan with waxed paper. Butter the waxed paper and spread dough evenly onto it. Bake in a 375° oven for 15 to 20 minutes or until lightly browned. Cool thoroughly. (The crust may be made ahead and frozen, if you like.)

## Upside-down Cobbler

You can make this pie with various kinds of fruits or berries, either canned or fresh. If you use fresh ones, first poach them in water, with sugar to taste. To make the pie, you need about 1½ to 2 cups fruit (drained) cut in small pieces, or berries—and about ⅔ to 1 cup sweetened liquid. A 1-pound can will contain the proper proportions.

When you sprinkle on sugar just before baking the pie, use some judgment about the amount. Use as much as ½ cup for *very* tart fruit or berries. Canned berries need about ¼ cup. Canned fruit (such as peaches or pears) or fruit cocktail needs only 1 or 2 tablespoons.

¼ cup (⅛ lb.) soft butter or margarine
½ cup sugar
1 cup unsifted regular all-purpose flour
2 teaspoons baking powder
⅛ teaspoon salt
½ cup milk
1 can (1 lb.) fruit, cut in small pieces, or berries (or amounts of cooked fruit and liquid suggested in preceding paragraphs)
   Sugar to taste (1 tablespoon to ½ cup—see preceding paragraphs)
   Whipping cream

Cream butter and sugar until smooth and well blended. Sift the flour with baking powder and salt. Add flour mixture a little at a time alternately with the milk, beating just until the thick batter is smooth. Spread the batter evenly in a greased 9-inch-square baking pan (it will rise to the top while baking).

Pour berries or fruit and their liquid over batter. Sprinkle with sugar suggested (based on sweetness of fruit and liquid).

Bake in a 350° oven about 1 hour, or until crust is golden brown. Serve warm with plain or whipped cream. Serves 6.

## Fresh Peach Cream Pie

1 large package (8 oz.) cream cheese
¼ cup sugar
2 tablespoons Cointreau or orange juice concentrate
½ cup whipping cream
9-inch pastry shell, baked and cooled
3 cups sliced peeled peaches
⅓ cup orange marmalade

With an electric mixer, beat cream cheese, sugar, and Cointreau or orange juice concentrate until smooth; gradually add the cream, beating until mixture is light and fluffy. Spoon into pie shell; chill at least 30 minutes.

Just before serving arrange peaches over filling, overlapping

slices slightly. Heat orange marmalade just until melted; carefully spoon over peaches. Serve at once. Makes about 8 servings.

## Pineapple Cheese Pie

4 packages (3 oz. each) cream cheese
2 eggs
½ cup sugar
½ teaspoon vanilla
1 large can (1 lb. 13 oz.) pineapple chunks
   Baked Crumb Crust (facing page)
1 cup (½ pt.) sour cream
3 tablespoons sugar
1 teaspoon vanilla

Beat cream cheese, eggs, the ½ cup sugar, and the ½ teaspoon vanilla together until fluffy. Stir in well-drained pineapple chunks. Turn into crust.

Bake in a 375° oven for 20 minutes. Mix together the sour cream, the 3 tablespoons sugar, and the 1 teaspoon vanilla; spread over top of pie. Return to oven and bake 5 minutes longer. Cool before serving. Serves 6.

## Chocolate-topped Rum Pie

1 envelope unflavored gelatin
¼ cup cold water
4 eggs, separated
1 cup sugar
½ teaspoon salt
½ cup hot water
⅓ cup rum
9-inch pastry shell, baked and cooled
6 tablespoons butter
6 tablespoons powdered sugar
1½ ounces unsweetened chocolate, melted
1 egg yolk

Soften gelatin in the cold water.

In the top of a double boiler, beat the 4 egg yolks slightly and stir in ½ cup of the sugar and the salt; gradually stir in the ½ cup hot water. Cook over hot water, stirring constantly, until the mixture thickens. Remove from heat and mix in softened gelatin, stirring until gelatin is dissolved.

Cool slightly, pour in rum, and beat well. Refrigerate until the custard starts to congeal.

Beat egg whites until stiff and

gradually beat in the remaining ½ cup sugar. Fold into chilled rum custard. Spoon into pastry shell; chill until firm.

Cream together the butter and powdered sugar until light and fluffy. Stir in melted chocolate. Add the 1 egg yolk and beat well. Spread on pie. Chill again. Serves 6.

# Chocolate Pie

Uncooked Chocolate Buttercream (recipe on page 89) makes an excellent pie. (Instructions for making a pie are with the recipe, including instructions for a crumb crust.)

# Chocolate-Mint Pie

These fluffy layers of chocolate and mint make an elegant dessert.

    1  envelope unflavored gelatin
    ¾  cup sugar
    2  cups milk
    3  eggs, separated
    1  tablespoon cornstarch
    2  ounces unsweetened chocolate
    ½  cup whipping cream
    3  tablespoons crème de menthe or
         mint syrup
 9-inch pastry shell, baked and cooled
       Unsweetened chocolate for garnish

In the top of a double boiler, mix gelatin and ½ cup of the sugar. Stir in the milk gradually and set over boiling water until scalded. Beat egg yolks with cornstarch until foamy. Gradually stir in some of the hot milk mixture.

Return to double boiler and cook over boiling water, stirring until thickened. Chill until it starts to congeal.

Beat egg whites until stiff; gradually beat in remaining ¼ cup sugar. Beat cream until thick. Melt the 2 ounces of chocolate. Beat chilled custard mixture until fluffy; fold egg whites, then whipped cream into the custard.

Divide the mixture; fold melted chocolate into one half; blend mint into other half. Turn chocolate filling into the pie shell; chill 5 minutes. Top with mint filling. Chill thoroughly.

For garnish, use a vegetable peeler to shave chocolate curls from unsweetened chocolate. Makes 6 to 8 servings.

# Fresh Coconut Cream Pie

Heretofore, coconuts have been hard nuts to crack. But the method on page 120 (How to Crack a Coconut) for coping with the problem easily has let many a cook serve the joys of a fresh coconut pie more often.

    1  envelope unflavored gelatin
 1¾  cups milk
    ½  cup sugar
    2  tablespoons cornstarch
    ½  teaspoon salt
    2  eggs, separated
    2  tablespoons butter or margarine
    ½  teaspoon vanilla
    ⅛  teaspoon almond extract
    1  cup grated fresh coconut
 9-inch baked pastry shell
    ½  cup whipping cream
       Sugar

Soften gelatin in ¼ cup of the milk. Blend sugar, cornstarch, and salt in a medium-sized pan; gradually stir in remaining milk. Cook over low heat, stirring constantly, until mixture thickens and boils.

Remove from heat, beat egg yolks slightly, and stir a small amount of the hot liquid into the egg yolks. Add the egg yolk mixture to the remaining hot milk mixture, return to heat, and continue cooking, stirring constantly, for 2 minutes.

Remove from heat and blend in the softened gelatin, butter, and flavorings; cool until lukewarm. Beat egg whites until stiff but not dry; fold egg whites with ¾ cup of the coconut into the cooled custard. Pour into the pastry shell, and chill. Just before serving, whip cream; sweeten to taste, and spread over coconut filling. Garnish with remaining coconut. Makes 1 pie (6 to 8 servings).

# Lemon Cheese Pie

This pie is creamy like cheesecake.

 1¼  cups sugar
    ¼  cup cornstarch
    1  cup water
    1  teaspoon grated lemon peel
    ⅓  cup lemon juice
    2  eggs, separated
    ½  cup (half an 8 oz. package) sof-
         tened cream cheese
       Baked Lemon Crust (recipe fol-
         lows)

In a saucepan, combine 1 cup of the sugar with cornstarch. Stir in water, lemon peel and juice, and egg yolks, beaten. Cook, stirring, until thick. Remove; blend in softened cheese. Cool.

Beat egg whites to soft peaks; gradually beat in remaining ¼ cup sugar. Fold into lemon mixture. Turn into pie shell. Chill. Makes 6 to 8 servings.

**Lemon Crust.** Sift flour, measure 1 cup, and sift again with ½ teaspoon salt into a bowl. Cut in ⅓ cup shortening until fine. Combine 1 slightly beaten egg with 1 teaspoon grated lemon peel and 1 tablespoon lemon juice; sprinkle over flour mixture. Mix with a fork until the dough holds together. Roll out to fit a deep 9-inch pie pan. Flute edge, prick, bake in a 400° oven for 12 to 15 minutes. Cool.

# Lemon Meringue Pie

 1¼  cups sugar
    ¼  cup flour
    2  tablespoons cornstarch
    ⅛  teaspoon salt
    2  cups boiling water
    3  eggs, separated
    2  tablespoons grated lemon peel
    ⅓  cup lemon juice
    1  tablespoon butter or
         margarine
       Baked 9-inch pastry shell
    6  tablespoons sugar

Mix the 1¼ cups sugar, flour, cornstarch, and salt in double boiler; gradually stir in boiling water and cook over boiling water for about 10 minutes, or until mixture thickens. Beat egg yolks, add grated lemon rind, lemon juice, and butter. Stir into cooked mixture; place over boiling water and cook about 5 minutes longer, stirring constantly. Let cool slightly, then pour into baked pastry shell.

Make meringue: Beat egg whites until stiff, then add the 6 tablespoons sugar gradually, beating until mixture is quite stiff. Pile over cooled filling, spreading well to edge of pastry. Bake in a 325° oven for 20 minutes, or until lightly browned. Serves 6.

**Lime Meringue Pie.** Follow recipe for Lemon Meringue Pie, using lime juice and rind. Add a small amount of green vegetable coloring to filling.

## Orange Chiffon Pie

1 envelope unflavored gelatin
¾ cup sugar
   Dash of salt
1 cup hot water
3 eggs, separated
1 can (6 oz.) frozen orange juice
   concentrate
3 tablespoons lemon juice
9 or 10-inch pastry shell, baked and
   cooled
1 cup (½ pt.) whipping cream
   (optional)
¼ cup slivered almonds, toasted
   (optional)

In the top of a double boiler, mix together the gelatin, ½ cup of the sugar, and the salt. Stir in the hot water and cook over boiling water, stirring, until gelatin dissolves. Beat egg yolks slightly and stir in gelatin mixture. Return to double boiler; cook, stirring, until mixture coats the spoon.

Remove from heat, and stir in the orange juice concentrate and lemon juice; chill until it starts to congeal. Beat egg whites stiff; gradually beat in remaining ¼ cup sugar.

Combine two mixtures; spoon into pastry shell; chill. Top with the whipped cream and toasted almonds, if you wish. Serves 6 to 8.

## Pumpkin Chiffon Pie

This recipe lets you have your Thanksgiving pumpkin pie without having to eat all those calories, too. (The truth is you still get plenty of calories, but it just doesn't *seem* like it.)

   Ginger Cooky Crust (recipe
      follows)
1 envelope unflavored gelatin
¾ cup brown sugar, firmly packed
¼ teaspoon salt
1½ teaspoons pumpkin pie spice, or 1
      teaspoon Chinese "five spice"
3 eggs, separated
½ cup milk
¼ cup water
1½ cups canned pumpkin
⅓ cup granulated sugar
   Sweetened whipped cream
      (optional)

Prepare the crumb crust and refrigerate. Combine the gelatin, brown

sugar, salt, and spice mixture in a saucepan. Beat egg yolks slightly and stir in milk, water, and pumpkin; add to sugar mixture. Cook over medium heat, stirring constantly, to just below simmering point.

Set pan in ice water (or refrigerate); stir occasionally until mixture is cold and slightly thickened.

In a bowl, beat egg whites until thick; add granulated sugar, about 1 tablespoon at a time, and beat well after each addition. Beat until whites hold firm peaks. Fold gelatin mixture into the beaten egg whites.

Pour into crumb-lined pan and chill at least 4 hours, or overnight. Serve with whipped cream on each piece, if you wish. Makes a 9-inch pie.

**Ginger Cooky Crust.** Combine 1¼ cups fine gingersnap cooky crumbs with 3 tablespoons sifted powdered sugar. Stir in 3 tablespoons melted butter. Press lightly into the bottom and sides of a 9-inch pie pan.

## Pecan Pie

2 eggs, separated
½ cup brown sugar, firmly packed
⅛ teaspoon salt
½ teaspoon cinnamon
1 tablespoon flour
¼ cup (⅛ lb.) butter or margarine,
   melted
½ teaspoon vanilla
1 cup dark corn syrup
¾ cup coarsely chopped pecans
½ cup pecan halves
9-inch unbaked pastry shell

Beat egg yolks with a rotary beater. Add brown sugar, salt, cinnamon, flour, melted butter, vanilla, and syrup, beating well to blend.

Beat egg whites until stiff but not dry; fold into egg yolk mixture; add the ¾ cup of coarsely chopped pecans. Pour filling into pie shell; arrange pecan halves on top in an attractive pattern.

Bake in a 350° oven about 45 minutes, or until the center of the pie is set (test by shaking gently). Cool. Makes a 9-inch pie (about 8 rich servings).

## Mincemeat-Cream Cheese Pie

4 packages (3 oz. each) cream cheese
2 eggs
½ cup sugar
   Grated peel of 1 lemon
1 tablespoon lemon juice
2 cups mincemeat
   Baked 9-inch pastry shell
1 cup sour cream
2 tablespoons sugar
½ teaspoon vanilla
   Lemon slices

Beat together cream cheese, eggs, ½ cup sugar, lemon peel, and lemon juice with an electric mixer until very smooth. Spoon mincemeat into pastry shell. Pour cheese mixture evenly over mincemeat.

Bake in a 375° oven for 20 minutes. Mix together sour cream, the 2 tablespoons sugar, and vanilla. When pie has baked the 20 minutes, remove from oven and spread sour cream mixture evenly over top. Return to oven for 10 minutes.

Then chill pie before cutting and serving. Garnish with twisted lemon slices and lemon leaves (if available). Makes 8 servings.

---

# Candies & Sweets

---

## Almond Toffee

2¼ cups sugar
1 teaspoon salt
½ cup water
1¼ cups (½ lb. plus ¼ cup) butter
1½ cups chopped blanched almonds
1 cup finely chopped walnuts
6 ounces milk chocolate, melted

Combine sugar, salt, water, and butter in a large heavy pan; bring to a boil. Add half the almonds and cook, stirring constantly to prevent scorching, until mixture reaches 300° (hard crack stage). Remove from heat. Stir in the remaining almonds and half the walnuts.

Pour the candy into a well-buttered 10 by 15-inch jelly-roll pan;

*. . . Almond Toffee (cont'd.)*

let stand in a cool place until the toffee hardens.

Remove toffee from pan, spread melted chocolate over the top, and sprinkle with the remaining walnut meats. When the chocolate is firm, break the toffee apart by tapping with an ice pick or knife at intervals across the surface. Makes about 4 dozen pieces.

## Glacéed Fruit

These are bite-sized fruits coated with a clear, crackling sugar shell.

Berries, cherries, tiny figs or apricots, clusters of several seedless grapes, and tangerine or orange segments can be used. Dry fruit well.

⅔ cup light corn syrup
1 cup water
2 cups sugar
Fruits (suggestions precede)

Combine syrup, water, and sugar in a deep saucepan and cook over highest heat, stirring until sugar is dissolved. Boil rapidly until temperature reaches 290° (just about hard-crack stage).

Remove syrup from heat and dip fruit *immediately and quickly.* Hold stemmed fruit by the stem; hold other fruit between two forks. Place fruits apart on a lightly oiled or non-stick baking sheet.

When the bubbling of the hot syrup subsides, set pan in a bowl and pour enough boiling water into the bowl to come above the syrup level. (When the coating becomes too thick, return syrup to direct heat and stir until it is thinned.)

Fruits will keep, uncovered and cool, for up to 2 hours. Syrup will glaze about 40 medium-sized strawberries.

## Panocha Rocky Roads

1 cup granulated sugar
1 cup brown sugar, firmly packed
¼ teaspoon salt
½ cup strong coffee
¼ cup whipping cream
1 tablespoon corn syrup
2 tablespoons butter or margarine
¼ to ½ teaspoon maple flavoring
1 cup chopped nuts
10 large marshmallows, quartered

In a large saucepan, mix the sugars, salt, coffee, cream, and corn syrup. Stir constantly while bringing to a boil, then boil steadily, without further stirring, until a little of the syrup dropped into cold water forms a soft, waxy ball (236° on a candy thermometer).

Remove from the heat, add the butter and flavoring, and let stand while preparing a square or oblong pan (about 7 by 11 inches or 8 by 8 inches) by buttering it lightly and scattering over it the nuts and marshmallows. When the candy has cooled almost to lukewarm, beat hard until it is thick and creamy, then pour it over the nuts and marshmallows. When cold, cut into 18 squares.

## Popcorn Balls

2 quarts (8 cups) salted, popped corn
⅔ cup molasses
⅔ cup sugar
2 tablespoons butter or margarine
2 tablespoons vinegar
½ cup water
¼ teaspoon soda

Pick over the corn, discarding all hard kernels. Combine molasses, sugar, butter, vinegar, and water in a saucepan; boil gently, without stirring, until a little of the mixture becomes brittle when tested in cold water (270° on a candy thermometer). Remove from heat and stir in soda. Pour syrup over corn, mixing thoroughly. Let stand 5 minutes, then shape into balls. Makes 6 to 8 balls.

## Candied Citrus Peels

Peel from 4 grapefruit or 8 oranges or 12 limes or 12 lemons (or an equivalent mixture)
Cold water
2 cups sugar
1 cup water
Sugar

Cut peel into thin strips. Place in saucepan and cover with cold water; slowly bring to a boil. Drain. Repeat boiling and draining process 5 times.

Make a syrup of 2 cups sugar and 1 cup water. Add peels. Boil until syrup is very thick and mostly absorbed. Spread peels on cake rack to cool. Roll in additional sugar. Spread on waxed paper or a cake rack to dry.

## Spiced Walnuts

1 cup walnut halves
Salad oil or shortening for deep frying
1 teaspoon salt
½ teaspoon cinnamon
¼ teaspoon each nutmeg, cloves, and allspice
½ cup sugar

Fry nuts in hot deep fat (360°) about 5 minutes, or until golden brown. Drain on absorbent paper; drop into a paper bag containing a mixture of the salt, spices, and sugar. Shake bag to coat nuts well. Makes 1 cup.

## Western Nut Brittle

1½ cups sugar
¼ cup water
¼ cup (⅛ lb.) butter
½ teaspoon soda
½ teaspoon salt (if nuts are unsalted, use ¾ teaspoon)
1 cup coarsely chopped nuts (roasted or unroasted)
1 teaspoon vanilla

In a saucepan stir together sugar and water; add butter. Bring to a boil and cook rapidly, stirring occasionally until mixture begins to turn golden, then stirring frequently to prevent burning.

When temperature reaches 310° (hard crack stage), remove candy from heat and blend in soda mixed with salt. Stir into foaming mixture the nuts and vanilla; pour immediately onto a buttered marble slab or a large, rimmed, buttered baking sheet.

Let cool just until you can touch it. With buttered hands, pull candy as thin as possible, letting ribbons form, and break into pieces (work from edge of candy towards the center). Store in an airtight container. Makes about ¾ pound.

# Drinks & Punches

## Coffee for a Crowd

If a quantity coffee-maker is not available, here is a simple way to brew clear coffee in a single large kettle.

    1   egg, shell and all
    1¼  pounds regular-grind coffee
    1   cup cold water
    9   quarts cold water

Thoroughly mix egg, broken shell, and coffee together; add 1 cup water. Tie coffee mixture in a large cheesecloth bag, allowing room for coffee to expand.

   Immerse coffee bag in a large pot containing the 9 quarts water. Bring to a boil. Remove from heat and let coffee stand about 4 or 5 minutes. Remove coffee bag and stir; keep hot. Makes 48 servings.

   *Note:* You may start by boiling the water. Then add the bag of coffee, bring to a boil again, stir, and remove from the heat. Cover and let stand 10 minutes; remove bag and keep coffee hot.

## Café Brulot

       Peel of 1 orange, cut in a spiral
    4  sticks whole cinnamon, 3 inches
          long
   20  whole cloves
    1  cup warmed brandy or Cognac
   14  lumps sugar
   1⅔ cups hot, strong coffee

Put orange peel, spices, warm brandy, and sugar in a large, attractive, heatproof bowl.

Bring to table; tip bowl and touch lighted match to edge of liquid to set aflame. Use a ladle to stir the mixture constantly while it burns, about 2 minutes. Slowly pour in the hot coffee. Ladle at once into after-dinner-sized coffee cups. Makes 8 small cups coffee.

## Caffé Espresso

You must have special Italian-roast coffee and an espresso machine (or you can prepare a reasonable facsimile using a *macchinetta,* sometimes called Neopolitan or *caffettiera,* or a pressurized Domus espresso pot. Follow the manufacturer's directions. Serve in demitasse cups with raw or regular sugar; cream is never served.

**Espresso Romano.** Pour espresso coffee into small, stemmed, heatproof glasses and garnish with a twist of lemon peel.

**Cappuccino.** Combine espresso coffee with an equal amount of milk heated on an espresso steam valve. Or quickly pour coffee into an equal amount of hot milk, and stir until foamy. Serve in slender cups, sprinkled with cinnamon.

## Turkish Coffee

You must use the special pulverized Turkish or Greek coffee sold in cans or jars. The coffee is traditionally made in a special pot with a handle, called a *cezve* or *ibrik,* but a very small saucepan or syrup-warmer can

be substituted. The coffee is always served in demitasse cups.

   To make coffee for 4 people, measure 4 demitasse cups of cold water into the pot. Add 4 teaspoons sugar (or as much as 8 teaspoons). Place over low heat and gradually bring to a boil. Stir in 4 tablespoons coffee.

   *Very* slowly bring to a boil, during which froth will form. Pour a little of the froth into each cup. Repeat the frothing-up process one or two more times; pour coffee over froth. Properly made coffee is completely covered with a layer of froth. Makes 4 cups.

## Café au Lait

Purchase French-roast coffee and make in a drip pot or with coffee filters. Or brew American coffee extra strong.

   Combine the hot coffee with an equal amount of hot milk. The French use two pots, one held in each hand, to pour the coffee and milk simultaneously into each cup.

## Irish Coffee

This drink is served by so many San Francisco restaurants that it probably should be renamed. For each serving, use these ingredients.

    2  teaspoons sugar
       Hot, strong coffee
    2  tablespoons (1 oz.) Irish whiskey
       Softly whipped cream

*(Continued on next page)*

Put sugar in a warmed wine glass; fill glass about two-thirds full of hot coffee. Stir to dissolve sugar. Stir in the Irish whiskey and top with whipped cream. Makes 1 serving.

## Mexican Chocolate

You can use this recipe to make regular hot chocolate; just leave out the spice.

- 6 cups milk
- ¾ teaspoon cinnamon
- 6 ounces coarsely chopped sweet cooking chocolate
- ½ cup heavy cream, whipped
- 2 tablespoons sugar
- 6 whole cinnamon sticks

Heat milk with the ¾ teaspoon cinnamon until steaming. Add chopped chocolate and stir until melted. Beat with a rotary mixer until mixture is frothy.

Have ready heavy cream, whipped stiff with the sugar. Pour hot chocolate into cups and top each with a spoonful of the cream. Drop a cinnamon stick in each cup, if you wish. Makes 6 servings.

## Fruited Iced Tea

- 2 oranges
- 2 lemons
- 1 cup sugar
- 2 quarts (8 cups) water
- 2 tablespoons tea leaves
  Fresh mint

Squeeze juice from oranges and lemons. Combine fruit juices, orange and lemon rinds, sugar, and water in a saucepan; simmer for 10 minutes; strain. Add tea leaves to hot liquid, cover, and steep for 5 minutes; strain and chill.

Pour over cracked ice in tall glasses, and garnish with sprigs of mint. Serves 8.

## Sparkling Iced Tea

Tea can turn unpleasantly cloudy as it cools. Here are ways to brew sparkling, clear tea.

**Cold-water Method.** This method requires time for the tea to flavor the water. Put 4 to 8 tea bags into a quart jar and fill the jar with cold water. Refrigerate for 12 to 18 hours, until the tea is the strength you desire. This tea will be clear and cold.

Or, for quicker brewing, set the jar outside in the sunshine for 3 to 4 hours instead of in the refrigerator.

**Hot-water Method.** Bring 1 quart of water to a rolling boil in a saucepan. Remove from heat and immediately add ⅓ cup loose tea or 15 tea bags. Stir and then let sit 5 minutes. Stir and strain into a pitcher holding an additional quart of cold water. Do not refrigerate. Pour over ice in glasses.

## Orange Sangría

- 1 medium-sized orange
- ¼ cup sugar
- 2 cups freshly squeezed orange juice
- 1 bottle (4/5 qt.) dry red wine
- ½ cup Cointreau (or other orange-flavored liqueur)

Cut the orange in half. Cut 1 or 2 thin slices from one half, cut them into quarters, and save for garnish. With a vegetable peeler, thinly cut off the thin outer peel of the other half of the orange. In a bowl, using a spoon, bruise the peel with the sugar to release the flavorful oils; then stir in the orange juice, wine, and orange-flavored liqueur. Cover and chill; after the first 15 minutes, remove the orange peel.

Serve Sangría in a bowl or from a pitcher, garnished with the quartered orange slices. Add ice cubes to the individual servings, if you like. Makes 6 cups, or 12 servings of ½ cup each.

## Champagne Fruit Punch

- 1 bottle (4/5 qt.) Sauterne, well chilled
- 1 bottle (4/5 qt.) Champagne, chilled
- 2 bottles (1 qt. each) grapefruit soda, chilled
- 2 cups washed, stemmed strawberries

In a punch bowl containing a block of ice, stir together until blended the Sauterne, Champagne, and grapefruit soda. Drop in strawberries. Ladle some of the punch into each punch glass or Champagne glass, and add a strawberry to each serving. Makes 30 servings of ½ cup each.

## Minted Fruit Punch

- 1 cup sugar
- ½ cup water
- ½ cup grapefruit juice
  Juice of 6 oranges (save the peel of half an orange)
  Juice of 6 lemons
- ¼ cup crushed pineapple
- ½ cup crème de menthe
  Rind of ½ cucumber
- 1 quart ginger ale

Heat sugar and water together until sugar is dissolved. Add the fruit juices, pineapple, crème de menthe, cucumber rind, and the peel of ½ orange. Chill for several hours. Remove cucumber and orange peel. Add ginger ale; pour over ice in tall glasses. Serves 10 to 12.

## Success Punch

- 1 dozen lemons
- 3 oranges
- 2½ cups sugar
- 4 cups water
- 2 cans (46 oz. each) pineapple juice
- 1 can (46 oz.) grapefruit juice
- 2 quarts sparkling water or club soda
  Mint sprigs
  Sliced fruit (such as oranges or pineapple) for garnish

Slice lemons and oranges, including juices, into saucepan and heat to boiling. Mash with potato masher or wooden spoon while heating. Remove from heat; add sugar and water; stir to dissolve sugar. Strain, discarding fruit pulp; cool.

Combine liquid with the canned fruit juices; pour over block of ice in punch bowl. Add sparkling water; stir punch just to blend. Garnish with mint and fruit. Makes 2 gallons, or 64 servings of ½ cup each.

# Grapefruit Punch with Ginger

The zesty, intriguing flavor of this punch is due to several Oriental ingredients—Japanese green tea and fresh ginger root.

1 bottle (1 qt.) grapefruit soda
2 cups boiling water
1 tablespoon green tea leaves
2 tablespoons sugar
3 tablespoons thawed frozen orange juice concentrate (undiluted)
1-inch piece of fresh ginger root

Several hours or the night before serving, freeze half of the grapefruit soda into cubes; recap soda. Pour the boiling water over the tea leaves; steep 5 minutes. Strain; stir in the 2 tablespoons sugar; cover and chill thoroughly.

To make punch, pour orange juice concentrate into a 2-quart pitcher. Using a garlic press or fine wire strainer, press juice from the ginger into pitcher (about ½ teaspoon juice). Pour in tea and grapefruit-soda ice cubes; stir in remaining 2 cups chilled soda. Makes about 7 six-ounce servings.

## Mulled Cider

2 quarts (8 cups) cider
½ to 1 cup brown sugar
1 stick whole cinnamon, 1 inch long
6 whole cloves
1 teaspoon whole allspice
  Nutmeg

Place cider in saucepan; add sugar and spices. Simmer for 15 minutes; strain. Serve hot in mugs with a dash of nutmeg. Serves 8.

## Mock Champagne Cocktail

This non-alcoholic punch has a bubbly, tart quality reminiscent of a Champagne cocktail.

½ cup sugar
½ cup water
½ cup grapefruit juice
¼ cup orange juice
2 cups ginger ale, chilled
3 tablespoons grenadine syrup
  Lemon peel

Combine sugar and water in a saucepan; boil slowly for 10 minutes, stirring only until sugar is dissolved; cool. Mix sugar-water syrup, grapefruit juice, and orange juice; chill thoroughly.

Just before serving, add ginger ale and grenadine; stir to mix. Serve in Champagne or sherbet glasses and put a twist of lemon peel in each glass. Serves 8.

## Frothy Eggnog Punch

14 eggs, separated
1¼ cups sugar
1 quart milk
1 cup (½ pt.) whipping cream
1 cup (½ pt.) each light rum and brandy

Beat egg yolks until smooth. Combine with ¾ cup *each* of the sugar and milk in a large saucepan; place over a medium-low heat; cook, stirring until it thickens to a soft custard (about 12 minutes), cool.

Beat egg whites until frothy; add remaining ½ cup sugar and beat until they form soft peaks; spoon into cooled custard. Whip the cream in the same bowl. Add whipped cream and remaining 3¼ cups milk to beaten whites and custard; gently mix together.

Refrigerate for several hours or overnight. Just before pouring into punch bowl, stir in the rum and brandy. Serves 15 to 20.

## Ice Cream Fizz

Select a large 12 to 14-ounce glass (a stemmed oversize sundae glass or iced tea glass is suitable). Use these quantities for each serving:

2 tablespoons bottled berry syrup or sundae topping
1 heaping tablespoon whipped cream
2 tablespoons sparkling water or club soda
2 scoops ice cream
¼ cup sparkling water or club soda

Pour berry syrup or sundae topping into the large glass and add whipped cream. Stir to blend. Pour in the 2 tablespoons soda water and stir to make a smoothly blended fizz.

Add ice cream and then the ¼ cup soda water, letting soda hit the side of the glass rather than the ice cream (or ice crystals will form). Serve with straws.

*Note:* Flavor combinations are endless, but these are favorites—raspberry syrup and 1 scoop *each* raspberry sherbet and vanilla ice cream; blackberry syrup and wild blackberry ice cream; strawberry syrup and strawberry ice cream; boysenberry syrup and raspberry sherbet.

## Swedish Punch

2½ cups cranberry juice cocktail
  Brown sugar or raw sugar to taste (optional)
2 whole cinnamon sticks, each about 3 inches long
6 whole cardamom pods, crushed
⅛ teaspoon ground allspice
1 tablespoon butter
  Wedges of fresh, unpeeled grapefruit, studded with whole cloves

Combine cranberry juice, sugar, cinnamon, cardamom, and allspice. Refrigerate overnight to blend flavors, if you wish.

Bring to boil. Simmer 5 minutes. Strain. Add butter, stirring until melted. Pour into serving cups, and decorate rims of the cups with wedges of grapefruit, each studded with several whole cloves. Serve hot. Makes 5 or 6 servings.

## Ginger Milk Shake

Use preserved ginger root (the kind bottled in syrup) to make these quick drinks in a blender. The pieces of ginger should be a half-inch or so long.

Serve the smooth and frothy liquid to a special foursome.

10 small pieces preserved ginger
1 tablespoon preserved ginger syrup
1 quart vanilla ice cream
2 cups milk

In a 5-cup blender container, combine the ginger, syrup, and ¼ of the ice cream. Whirl very smooth.

Add the rest of the ice cream and the milk. Whirl on high speed just until blended. Serves about 4.

# Sauces & Relishes

## Blender Mayonnaise

2   tablespoons lemon juice
½   teaspoon salt
1   teaspoon prepared mustard
1   egg
1   cup salad oil (or part olive oil)

Combine the lemon juice, salt, mustard, egg, and ¼ cup of the oil in the blender. Whirl at high speed until smooth. Remove top and slowly pour in the remaining oil, and continue to whirl until thick −2 to 3 minutes. Makes about 1½ cups.

## Trader Vic's Mayonnaise Special

This "handmade" mayonnaise, a recipe from the famous restaurant chain, has a richer texture than that made in a blender. Because you add vinegar at the end of the process, you can season to just the degree of tartness you prefer.

2   egg yolks
1   teaspoon dry mustard
    About 2 cups salad oil
1   teaspoon salt
    Freshly ground black pepper
    Red wine vinegar

In a bowl, blend the egg yolks and mustard thoroughly. Beating with a spoon or wire whip, drip in the oil a few drops at a time, beating or stirring vigorously. Continue dripping in the

oil *very* gradually until the emulsion takes hold, then you can add the oil a little more generously each time you pour. If the mixture gets too thick to work, add a dash of vinegar. Add no more than 2 cups oil, less if you like the consistency.

When you have reached the desired volume, stir in 1 teaspoon salt and freshly ground black pepper. Season with vinegar to the degree of tartness you like. Makes about 2 cups.

**Variations.** Olive oil makes a richer mayonnaise; some cooks like to use one-fourth or one-half olive oil. White vinegar is milder in flavor and lemon juice is tarter; interesting results can be obtained from using part lemon juice and part vinegar. Other additions can give a boost to flavor, such as 1 teaspoon sugar, a little paprika, a dash of cayenne, or a small amount of grated lemon peel.

## Mayonnaise Variations

With homemade or purchased mayonnaise, you can prepare a variety of seasoned sauces which are good for dressing salads, serving with seafood cocktails, or accompanying meats and fish.

**Tartar Sauce.** (This familiar fish sauce has a mayonnaise base.) To 1 cup mayonnaise, add 1 tablespoon *each* of the following (finely chopped): onion, capers, pimiento-stuffed olives, pickle, and parsley. Or, for a short-cut, add drained sweet pickle relish.

**Rémoulade Sauce.** This is another good seafood sauce. To 1 cup mayonnaise, add 2 or 3 chopped shallots or green onions, 2 minced anchovy fillets, 1 teaspoon chopped capers, 2 teaspoons chopped dill pickle, and 1 tablespoon minced parsley.

**Avocado Mayonnaise.** To ½ cup mayonnaise, add the smoothly mashed pulp of 1 medium-sized avocado. Season to taste with salt and lemon juice. Serve with fruit or vegetable salads.

**Mustard Mayonnaise.** Into ¾ cup mayonnaise, blend 2 to 3 tablespoons prepared mustard; add salt and lemon juice to taste. Delicious with cold meats.

**Watercress Mayonnaise.** Blend 1 cup mayonnaise with 1 cup finely chopped watercress. Use as a vegetable or green salad dressing.

**Anchovy Mayonnaise.** Into 1 cup mayonnaise, blend 4 teaspoons anchovy paste. Or whirl mayonnaise in the blender with 4 anchovy fillets. Use with fish, vegetable, and green salads.

**Horseradish Mayonnaise.** Into 1 cup mayonnaise, blend 2 tablespoons horseradish. Use with seafood salads.

**Green Mayonnaise.** To ¼ cup mayonnaise, add ½ cup sour cream, 2 teaspoons lemon juice, ⅛ teaspoon crumbled dried tarragon, ¼ teaspoon salt, 1 mashed or puréed garlic clove, and ¼ cup *each* finely chopped watercress, spinach, and parsley (be sure the greens are dry before chopping). Chill. Use with shellfish cocktails and green salads.

**Chutney Mayonnaise.** This is good with fruit salads. If you make mayonnaise in the blender, whirl 2 to 4 tablespoons coarsely chopped chutney with 1 cup mayonnaise in the blender. Or chop chutney very, very fine and stir into mayonnaise, with a little of the chutney juice.

**Curry Mayonnaise.** To 1 cup mayonnaise, add ¾ teaspoon grated orange peel and 1 to 2 teaspoons curry powder. For a small amount of garlic flavor, place 1 large clove garlic, slightly crushed, in the mayonnaise; let stand 30 minutes and discard the garlic. Or season with a very small amount of puréed garlic. Use with fruit salads or as a dip for fresh pineapple spears.

## Blender Béarnaise

Make Blender Hollandaise (see this page), but with the following changes: Use tarragon vinegar in place of the lemon juice and add 3 tablespoons chopped parsley with the vinegar. If you want a more distinct tarragon flavor, add 1 or 2 teaspoons crumbled dried tarragon along with the parsley.

## Double-boiler Hollandaise

You may prefer this curdle-proof recipe because it utilizes whole eggs, rather than just the egg yolks as most Hollandaise recipes do.

Serve over asparagus, green beans, broccoli, or cabbage wedges; or as a dipping sauce for artichokes.

½ cup (¼ lb.) butter or margarine
2 eggs
1 tablespoon lemon juice
⅛ teaspoon cayenne
¼ teaspoon salt
¼ cup hot water

Melt butter in top of double boiler. Beat eggs until blended, and gradually pour the hot butter over the eggs, beating constantly with a wire whip.

Return butter-egg mixture to top of double boiler and, stirring, cook over hot water until thickened.

Add lemon juice, cayenne, salt, and hot water and stir until blended. Makes 1 cup sauce.

## Blender Hollandaise

3 egg yolks, at room temperature
1½ tablespoons lemon juice
¾ cup (⅜ lb.) butter or margarine
1 tablespoon hot water
½ teaspoon salt
Dash of cayenne
1 teaspoon prepared mustard

Combine egg yolks and lemon juice in the blender. Melt butter and heat until it bubbles—don't brown. Add 1 tablespoon hot water to egg yolks and lemon juice; turn blender on high speed and immediately pour in the hot butter in a steady stream. (This takes about 5 seconds.)

Add salt, cayenne, and mustard; whirl until well blended—about 30 seconds. Makes about 2 cups sauce.

**Hollandaise with Cucumber or Shrimp.** Either of these variations is good with fish. After you have made the sauce, stir into it 1 tablespoon *each* chopped parsley and chives. Then add either 1 cucumber (peeled, seeded, and chopped) *or* 1 can (about 5 oz.) shrimp, which have been rinsed and drained.

## Brown Lemon Butter

Among the many foods which this simple sauce enhances are artichokes, broccoli, asparagus, green beans, liver, hamburger steak, broiled beefsteak, fried or poached eggs, and fish (pan-fried, baked, or broiled).

½ cup (¼ lb.) butter or margarine
3 tablespoons lemon juice
Dash of Worcestershire
1 tablespoon minced parsley (optional)

Heat the butter slowly until it turns a golden, nutty brown. Cool slightly and add the lemon juice, Worcestershire, and parsley if used; pour hot over food or serve in a small bowl.

**Black Butter Variation.** You get a different flavor in the sauce if you heat the butter longer—not really until

black and burned, but a very dark brown. Vinegar instead of lemon juice is good with black butter—you can use as much as ½ cup per ½ cup of butter.

## Lemon Butter

This is excellent with broiled fish; it also is good mixed with hot boiled potatoes, carrots, or turnips.

½ cup (¼ lb.) butter
2 tablespoons lemon juice
½ teaspoon salt
1 tablespoon minced parsley
Dash of cayenne

Cream the butter thoroughly and then cream in the other ingredients.

## Crumb-Butter Topping

This topping will dress up plain vegetables (particularly broccoli, asparagus, and green beans), sautéed mushrooms, or cooked noodles.

1 cup fine dry bread crumbs
¼ cup (⅛ lb.) butter or margarine, melted
Choice of seasonings: minced parsley, chives, or onion; shredded cheese; sieved or chopped hard-cooked egg

Either buy bread crumbs or prepare them this way: With a rolling pin, roll crisp dry bread slices between sheets of waxed paper or in a plastic bag until fine. Or crush and whirl the dried bread in the blender to make fine crumbs.

Mix crumbs with melted butter. If you want to brown them, spread on a shallow baking pan and put in a 300° oven. Stir often for 10 minutes, or until browned. Add your choice of seasonings. Sprinkle crumbs over the food just before serving.

# White Sauce

With our basic recipe for White Sauce—valuable in any cook's repertoire—you can make a raft of delicious variations just by making some simple changes. Use the sauce to dress vegetables or to create main dishes, either from leftovers or from first-time-around ingredients.

¼ cup (⅛ lb.) butter or margarine
¼ cup unsifted all-purpose flour
2 cups milk
   Salt and pepper to taste
   Dash of nutmeg (optional)

In a saucepan, melt butter and stir in flour until well blended and bubbly (do not let butter brown). Remove from heat. Gradually stir in milk. Cook, stirring constantly, until mixture is thickened and smooth. Add salt, pepper, and nutmeg to taste. (If you don't want to risk lumping, cook the mixture in a double boiler. Less stirring and attention is necessary.) Makes 2 cups.

**Variations.** Substitute bacon drippings for all or part of the butter. Season with Worcestershire, onion or garlic salt, Sherry, white wine, mustard, or paprika. Interesting additions are chopped parsley, capers, sliced or chopped olives, chopped hard-cooked eggs, anchovies, small shrimp, or crab meat.

**Béchamel Sauce.** For the milk, substitute 1 cup regular-strength chicken broth and 1 cup half-and-half (light cream).

**Mornay (Cheese) Sauce.** Add ¼ cup grated Parmesan cheese, ¼ cup shredded Swiss cheese, and a dash of cayenne to 2 cups of Béchamel Sauce (see preceding variation). Heat, stirring constantly, just until cheese is melted. Good with seafood and vegetables.

**Aurora (Tomato) Sauce.** Add ½ cup canned tomato purée and 1 tablespoon paprika to 2 cups Béchamel Sauce (see preceding variation). Good with eggs, chicken, and sweetbreads.

**Mushroom Sauce.** Cook ½ cup chopped onions and 1 cup chopped fresh mushrooms in 1 tablespoon butter in a covered saucepan until vegetables are wilted and juicy. Combine with 1 cup Béchamel Sauce and heat, stirring. Add 1 teaspoon minced parsley. Good with most meats.

# Spicy Seafood Cocktail Sauce

1 cup chile sauce
½ teaspoon Worcestershire
4 drops liquid hot-pepper seasoning
⅓ cup lemon juice

Mix all ingredients just until blended. Cover and chill. Makes 1⅓ cups sauce.

# Horseradish Sauce

½ cup whipping cream
1 tablespoon prepared horseradish
1 teaspoon sugar
½ teaspoon lemon juice

Whip cream until stiff, and fold in horseradish, sugar, and lemon juice. Chill for several hours. Serve with beef or tongue. Makes about 1 cup.

# Vinaigrette Sauce

Serve as a sauce for cold meat, or use as a flavorful dressing for sliced tomatoes, chilled broccoli, or chilled asparagus.

1 hard-cooked egg, finely chopped
1 teaspoon finely chopped onion
1 tablespoon each finely chopped red and green pepper
½ cup salad oil
3 tablespoons vinegar
½ teaspoon each salt and paprika
⅛ teaspoon black pepper

Mix all the ingredients and allow to stand, if possible, for an hour. Shake well before using. Makes 1 cup.

# Mustard Sauce

2 tablespoons each dry mustard, sugar, water, and white wine vinegar
1 tablespoon butter
1 teaspoon cornstarch
1 egg, beaten
½ cup whipping cream

Mix together in a small saucepan the dry mustard, sugar, water, and vinegar. Add the butter and cornstarch. Stirring constantly, cook until sauce comes to a full rolling boil and is thick and clear. Stir sauce into the beaten egg, return to pan, and cook, stirring constantly, 2 or 3 minutes longer, until thick—do not let boil. Chill.

Whip the cream until stiff and fold in just before serving. Makes 1½ cups.

# English Mustard

Mix equal parts of dry mustard and sugar with a dash of salt. Add just enough cold water to make a stiff paste, then slowly stir in vinegar until mixture is of the desired consistency.

# Chinese Mustard

Combine 4 tablespoons dry mustard with 2 tablespoons water and 1 tablespoon soy sauce; cover and let stand several hours to blend flavors.

# Curry Sauce

This sauce can be used to convert cooked meat, seafood, hard-cooked eggs, or cooked vegetables into a tasty dish. It also can accompany Appetizer Meatballs (recipe on page 8.)

¼ cup (⅛ lb.) butter or margarine
1 large onion, chopped
1 clove garlic, minced or mashed
2 tablespoons curry powder
¼ cup flour
1 tablespoon cornstarch
2 teaspoons sugar
½ teaspoon salt
   Dash of cayenne
2 cups regular-strength chicken broth
1 cup whipping cream

Melt butter or margarine in a heavy pan; add chopped onion and sauté until limp. Stir in garlic and curry powder; cook about 1 minute more. Add flour, cornstarch, sugar, salt, and cayenne; stir over low heat until blended and bubbly.

Gradually stir in chicken broth and whipping cream; cook over low heat, stirring, until thickened. Makes about 3 cups sauce.

# Teriyaki Sauce

Although this sauce was designed to accompany the Appetizer Meatballs recipe on page 8, it makes an excellent marinade or baste for beef or chicken kebabs, a hot dip for batter-fried shrimp, or a sauce for broiled steak.

- 2 tablespoons cornstarch
- ⅓ cup soy sauce
- ¼ cup sugar
- 1 clove garlic, minced or mashed
- 2 teaspoons minced fresh ginger, (or ½ teaspoon ground ginger)
- ¼ cup dry white wine (optional)
- 2 cups regular-strength beef broth (or 2¼ cups, if wine is omitted)

In a pan, blend together the cornstarch, soy sauce, sugar, garlic, and fresh or ground ginger. Stir in wine, if used, and the beef broth. Cook, stirring, until thickened. Makes about 2½ cups.

## Sweet & Sour Sauce

This sauce was designed to accompany the Appetizer Meatballs recipe, page 8.

But you can also use it with cooked shrimp, pieces of cooked chicken, turkey, or roast pork, or crisp fried won ton to make a Chinese-style main dish. You can easily cut the recipe in half to make a smaller amount of sauce. For dunking bite-size goodies, pour the sauce into small dishes.

- 2 cans (about 14 oz. each) pineapple chunks, drained (reserve syrup)
- 1¼ cups regular-strength chicken broth
- ¼ cup brown sugar
- ¾ cup vinegar
- 1 tablespoon each soy sauce and catsup
- ¼ cup cornstarch
- 1 cup thinly sliced green onions
- 3 green peppers, seeded and cut in 1-inch squares

Combine pineapple syrup with chicken broth, brown sugar, vinegar, soy sauce, catsup, and cornstarch. Cook, stirring, until thickened. At this point, you can refrigerate the sauce as much as a day ahead.

Shortly before you want to use the sauce, heat it slowly, stirring until bubbly. Add onions and green peppers. Cook 1 minute longer. Remove from heat and add pineapple chunks. Makes about 2½ cups liquid sauce (plus vegetables and fruit).

## Stroganoff Sauce

This sauce can be used with the Appetizer Meatballs recipe on page 8, or to convert leftover meats into a main dish. Butter-browned mushrooms, either fresh ones you prepare yourself or canned ones, may also be added.

You could also add slices of leftover cooked beef to the sauce, before you add the sour cream, to make a quick family main dish.

A recipe for Beef Stroganoff baked in the oven is on page 25.

- ¼ cup (⅛ lb.) butter or margarine
- 1 small onion, minced
- ¼ cup all-purpose flour
- 2¼ cups regular-strength beef broth
- 1 cup (½ pt.) sour cream
- ½ teaspoon dill weed
- Salt and pepper

Heat butter or margarine in a heavy pan; add onion and sauté until onion is limp. Stir in flour and cook until blended and bubbly. Slowly stir in broth and cook, stirring, until thickened.

Mix in sour cream, ½ teaspoon dill weed, and salt and pepper to taste. Do not let sauce boil after sour cream has been added. (Reheat over low heat, stirring constantly, just to the boiling point.) Makes about 3½ to 4 cups.

## Cumberland Sauce

This sauce is excellent with duck, venison, mutton, and any full-flavored meat or game.

- Whole peel of 1 orange
- ½ cup currant jelly
- ⅓ cup orange juice
- ⅓ cup Port wine
- 2 tablespoons lemon juice
- 1 teaspoon dry mustard
- ½ teaspoon powdered ginger

Cover orange peel with cold water, bring to a boil, and drain. Scrape off any white membrane and cut peel into matchlike pieces, about ⅛-inch wide and ½-inch long.

Combine jelly, orange juice, and Port in a saucepan. Mix together lemon juice, mustard, and ginger and stir in. Heat, stirring, over low heat until jelly melts. Add peel to sauce. Serve hot in a sauce bowl. Makes about 1⅓ cups.

## Mint Sauce for Roast Lamb

Instructions for roasting lamb appears on page 35.

- ¼ cup finely chopped fresh mint
- ¼ cup sugar
- Dash of salt
- 1 cup hot cider vinegar

Mix mint, sugar, and salt; stir in vinegar. Cool before serving. Makes 1 cup.

## Circle J Ranch Barbecue Sauce

Prepare this tangy sauce ahead for ribs, steak, or chicken.

- 1 clove garlic, minced
- 1 small onion, minced
- ¾ teaspoon prepared mustard
- 1 tablespoon grated fresh horseradish or prepared horseradish
- 1 teaspoon minced parsley
- ½ teaspoon each crumbled thyme and marjoram (or 1 teaspoon each minced fresh herbs)
- 3 cups water
- 2 tablespoons vinegar
- 1 tablespoon meat seasoning sauce or Worcestershire
- ½ cup catsup
- ⅔ cup butter
- 2 teaspoons sugar
- ¼ teaspoon chile powder
- ¼ teaspoon black pepper
- ¾ teaspoon salt
- Liquid hot-pepper seasoning to taste

Combine all ingredients and simmer uncovered for 45 minutes. Use the sauce for basting meat or fish, or dip chunks of hot cooked meat into the heated sauce before serving. Makes about 1 quart sauce.

## Sunset All-purpose Barbecue Sauce

This subtle sauce can be used with meat, fish, or chicken.

¼ cup salad oil
¼ cup Bourbon or Sherry
2 tablespoons soy sauce
1 teaspoon Worcestershire
1 teaspoon garlic powder
   Freshly ground black pepper to taste

Combine salad oil, Bourbon or Sherry, soy sauce, Worcestershire, garlic powder, and pepper. Pour over meat and marinate in refrigerator (turning occasionally).

Marinate roasts 24 to 48 hours; steaks, 4 hours; salmon or chicken, 2 hours. Also use as a basting sauce. Makes about ½ cup sauce.

## Pesto

The word "basil" comes from the Greek word for king, so it's no surprise that this aromatic sauce is fit for royal occasions.

Our blender recipe is easy to prepare. Use the paste as a sauce for Fresh Egg Noodles (recipe on page 71), spaghetti, or vegetables, or as a spread for French bread.

1 cup fresh basil leaves, firmly packed (see following suggestion for using dried basil)
3 to 6 cloves garlic
1 cup freshly grated Parmesan cheese
¼ cup pine nuts
   About ½ cup oil

Put basil, garlic, cheese, and pine nuts in a blender (or use a mortar). Whirl (or pound), adding olive oil drop by drop until the sauce has the consistency of mayonnaise. This sauce keeps several days refrigerated. Makes about 1 cup.

**Dried Basil Variation.** Dried basil can be substituted if fresh leaves are not available. Substitute ¼ cup dried basil (freshly purchased) and ¼ cup chopped parsley for the fresh basil. You might like to use less garlic (the sauce is not as bulky as that made with fresh leaves) and add up to 2 tablespoons lemon juice to compensate for flavor and moisture.

## Clarified Butter

Ordinary butter browns and burns very easily when you make omelets and pancakes, sauté fish, pan-fry meats, or baste roasting fowl. Yet there is a way of removing the elements of butter which burn so quickly (the process is called clarifying). Clarified butter keeps very well, making it worthwhile to prepare a pound at a time.

To clarify butter, put it in a saucepan and set over the lowest possible heat on your range for about one hour. When you see that clear butter has risen to the top and separated from a milky residue beneath, carefully skim off the clear butter and strain it through four layers of cheesecloth that have been dipped in cold water and wrung out. Store covered in the refrigerator.

## 3-Way Tomato Relish

This relish good with barbecued steaks is called "three-way" because you season portions of it to three varying degrees of hotness—meek, mild, and wild.

4 pound ripe medium-sized tomatoes (about 12)
3 large onions, peeled and chopped
2 cups each white vinegar and chopped celery
¾ cup sugar
¼ cup prepared horseradish
2 teaspoons each salt and dry mustard
½ teaspoon paprika
2 cloves garlic, minced or mashed
1 teaspoon basil
2 teaspoons whole mixed pickling spices
2 green peppers, seeded and chopped
3 small hot, dried red chiles, crushed

Peel tomatoes and chop coarsely. Place chopped tomatoes and their juices in a large deep pan (at least 5 quarts) with onions, vinegar, celery, sugar, horseradish, salt, mustard, paprika, garlic, and basil, along with the pickling spices tied in a square of cheesecloth.

Bring tomato mixture to a boil, reduce heat, and boil slowly, uncovered, for 1 hour; stir occasionally. Add green peppers and continue

cooking for 1½ hours longer, stirring frequently.

Remove seasoning packet and discard it. Ladle ⅓ of the sauce into a 1-pint jar. To remaining sauce add 2 of the dried hot chiles and continue cooking for 15 minutes more; ladle ½ of this mixture into another 1-pint jar. Add remaining chile to sauce still in the pan and cook the mixture for 15 minutes before placing in a third jar.

Label jars to indicate heat level of each portion of the relish. This will keep in the refrigerator for as long as a month, or may be frozen. Makes 3 pints.

## Mexican Tomato & Green Chile Sauce

This light and not-too-hot sauce makes a good topping for tacos, tostadas, and enchiladas.

6 medium-sized tomatoes
½ cup (or more) thinly sliced or diced canned California green chiles (seeds and pith removed)
⅓ cup minced onion
1 teaspoon salt
   Minced canned jalapeño chiles (or other hot chiles) to taste

Peel and finely chop the tomatoes. Mix with California green chiles, onion, salt, and as many jalapeño chiles as please your taste (about 1 jalapeño to each cup of sauce will make it noticeably hot). Makes 3 cups.

## Red Cabbage Relish

3 pounds red cabbage
¼ cup salt
1 cup cider vinegar
1 cup water
¼ cup mixed pickling spices

Shred the cabbage very thin, or chop finely. Put into a glass or pottery bowl (metal may discolor the cabbage) and mix well with the salt. Let stand 12 hours, or overnight.

In a saucepan combine vinegar, water, and spices; bring to a boil, then cool. Drain the cabbage fairly free of brine and pack into scalded glass jars, alternating with some of the spices and vinegar. The relish may be used after an hour. It keeps well in the refrigerator without sealing. Makes 2 quarts (you can easily cut the recipe in half if you want to make just 1 quart).

## Mustard Ring

The molded ring on page 18 can be served as a meat accompaniment.

## Tomato Chutney

1 tablespoon shortening or salad oil
1 small hot, dried red chile, crushed
½ teaspoon each cumin seed and mustard seed
¼ teaspoon nutmeg
4 medium-sized tomatoes (peeled and sliced ⅛-inch thick), or 1 can (1 lb.) whole tomatoes and juices
½ lemon
⅓ cup raisins (1½ oz. package) or currants
½ cup sugar

Melt shortening in a saucepan and add the crushed chile, whole cumin seed, mustard seed, and nutmeg. When seeds start to jump, add the tomatoes. Quarter lemon (or finely chop, including peel) and place on top.

Simmer, stirring frequently, for 15 minutes. Stir in the raisins and sugar. Simmer, stirring frequently, until very thick—about 30 minutes longer. Chill. This sauce is best made several days before use. If desired, pack hot in sterilized jars and seal. Makes about 1½ cups.

## Fresh Cranberry Ice

Several hours before dinner, scoop out balls of the cranberry ice, arrange in small serving dishes, and set back in freezer. Serve with turkey as a refreshing change from the usual relish.

4 cups (1 lb.) cranberries
2 cups sugar
3½ cups water
½ cup orange juice
¼ cup lemon juice

Put cranberries into a pan with sugar and water. Bring to boiling and simmer gently, stirring occasionally, for 10 minutes. Cool, then press through a wire strainer and discard pulp. Add orange and lemon juice. Pour in a loaf pan, cover with foil, and freeze. Makes about 1 quart.

## Favorite Raw Cranberry Relish

Although a number of versions of a ground raw cranberry relish have been designed, this one with oranges and apples has proved especially popular. Serve the tangy condiment with broiled chops, roast beef or pork, or game hens.

2 cups (½ lb.) cranberries
2 oranges
2 red apples
2 cups sugar

As you wash cranberries, discard any soft berries and stems. Peel the oranges (remove a thin layer of the yellow skin only from one of them and discard the white inner rind). Quarter and core the apples.

Put the cranberries, orange pulp, half the rind from the one orange (or more to taste), and apples through a food chopper, using the medium blade. Set a pan under the grinder to catch the juices. Mix sugar with the ground fruits and juices. Refrigerate a few hours before serving. Makes about 1 quart.

## Hot Gingered Papaya

Baked papaya is a delicious accompaniment and garnish for barbecued chicken, lamb, or pork. It also goes well with curry dishes. If you omit the cayenne, it can be served as a hot dessert.

2 firm ripe papayas
¼ cup (⅛ lb.) butter
2 tablespoons lime juice
½ teaspoon ground ginger
Dash cayenne pepper

Cut papayas in half lengthwise and scoop out seeds; arrange in a greased baking pan. Melt together the butter, lime juice, and ginger; spoon into the cavity of each papaya.

Bake in a 350° oven about 30 minutes, basting several times with the butter mixture. Serve hot with a dash of cayenne pepper. Serves 4.

## Ginger-buttered Fruit Kebabs

These kebabs, grilled over charcoal in a small brazier, make a beautiful and tasty garnish for roast turkey or chicken, or baked ham.

For each kebab, prepare a thick half slice of orange with peel, a red apple wedge, a thick diagonal slice of banana, and a fresh or canned pineapple chunk. Thread each on a small bamboo skewer. Grill 5 to 10 minutes or until lightly browned, basting frequently with Ginger Butter (recipe follows). Place on a dish over a candle warmer or an electric warming tray. Allow 1 fruit kebab for each serving.

**Ginger Butter.** In a small pan, slowly melt ½ cup (¼ lb.) butter; stir in 2 tablespoons sugar and 1 teaspoon ground ginger. Makes enough for 12 to 18 kebabs.

## Other Relishes

On page 123 are several relishes which you probably will want to make in quantity to seal in jars. However, you can make smaller batches.

## Aspic Glaze

Cold cooked foods are handsome served with an aspic glaze. The aspic coating keeps the food moist, particularly desirable for buffet service.

**Small Glazed Aspics.** Here is a list of foods suitable for glazing: poached whole trout and fish steaks or fillets (salmon and sole); cooked prawns, crab legs, or lobster slices; hard-cooked egg halves or deviled eggs; poached chicken breasts; and open-faced sandwiches.

Chill the cooked foods; pat dry if necessary. Arrange pieces on a rack over a tray to catch drips. Spoon over aspic stock (recipe follows); completely cover surface. (Stir aspic stock frequently to keep smooth.) Chill until set. Glaze should be ¹⁄₁₆-inch thick. If you like, repeat glazing.

Decorate as desired (instructions follow); chill until set. Glaze again and chill until set. Trim edges neatly and arrange on platter. Keep cold.

**Large Glazed Aspics.** Suitable foods include: poached salmon; poached chicken or turkey; cold meat loaves; boiled tongue, ham, or roast beef tenderloin.

Fill serving platter with a thin layer of aspic stock (recipe follows); chill until set. Place chilled, cooked food to be glazed on rack over tray (as for small aspics) and mask evenly with aspic stock; chill until set.

Position coated food on aspic-lined tray. Decorate (instructions follow); chill until set. Spoon aspic stock over food; chill once more until set.

**Quick Aspic Stock.** Soften 2 envelopes unflavored gelatin in ½ cup canned regular-strength chicken broth, condensed beef bouillon, or condensed consommé (fat removed). Simmer ⅓ cup dry white or dry red wine and ¼ cup Madeira or Sherry until reduced by one-half. Remove from heat; blend in 3 more cups broth and the softened gelatin.

To clarify, beat 2 egg whites until foamy, then, beat into stock. Heat, stirring continuously, until mixture comes to a boil. Stop stirring; cook until egg rises to top. Turn off heat and let stand 5 minutes. Bring to a boil twice more, at 5-minute intervals. (Liquid should be clear below egg.)

Line a colander with a cotton cloth dampened in hot water. Pour liquid through. If necessary, pour through the filter again. Makes 1 quart.

**Hints on Glazing.** Keep everything *cold* involved in their preparation (foods, molds, racks, spoons), right up until serving time.

The aspic stock must have the correct consistency—cool and syrupy, yet smooth and liquid, and thick enough to glaze evenly. The warm, slightly beaten white of an egg that is no longer fresh has approximately the same consistency.

To get the proper consistency quickly, set the bowl of aspic stock in crushed ice and stir until it is ready to use.

If the aspic gets too firm or lumpy, just melt over hot water again and make a fresh start.

**Decorating Aspics.** Almost any food that can be thinly sliced and has color can be used for decorating: white or yolk of hard-cooked egg (or slices of whole egg), olives, pimiento, radishes (both white and red parts), truffles, green pepper, or chive spears.

Cut decorations in fancy or geometric shapes, dip in aspic stock, and arrange on aspic-glazed foods. Chill.

# How to Crack a Coconut

Puncture the eyes at the end of the coconut and drain off the liquid. Put in a 350° oven for 30 minutes.

Place hot coconut on a hard surface and hit hard with a hammer; the coconut will readily come apart into large pieces. Pry out meat with an old table knife, remove brown skin with a potato peeler, rinse, and dry on paper towels.

One coconut will produce 3 to 4 cups grated meat. To grate in a blender, drop in about 1 cup of ½-inch cubes at a time.

# Coconut Milk

Coconut milk is specified in many interesting drink, curry, or dessert recipes. But the frozen or canned product often is difficult to find, or expensive.

You can make the milk easily from fresh or packaged coconut, particularly if you have a blender. Fresh milk is quicker to prepare than you might think if you use the easy-crack method of getting the meat out of a coconut described in the preceding recipe.

Remember that packaged coconut usually is sweetened; milk made from it should only be used in cases where sweetness is desirable.

**Fresh Coconut Milk Made in the Blender.** Drain and crack 1 coconut; taste to make sure it is free from any off flavors. Cut meat (no need to peel off brown husk) in ½-inch cubes. To each cup of meat, add ¾ cup hot liquid (hot water added to liquid drained from coconut) in the blender. Whirl for 20 to 30 seconds, then steep for 30 minutes. Strain through a double thickness of cheesecloth, squeezing out liquid. Makes about 2 cups.

**Milk from Packaged Coconut Made in the Blender.** Combine 2⅔ cups *each* packaged flaked coconut and cold milk; leave in refrigerator 1 hour. Whirl in blender for about 40 seconds. Strain through a double thickness of cheesecloth, squeezing out liquid. Makes at least 2 cups.

**Milk Made without a blender.** Mix 2 cups shredded coconut (fresh or packaged) with 2 cups half-and-half (light cream). Heat just below simmering point, then remove from heat and steep 30 minutes. Pour through a wire strainer or cheesecloth, pressing out all liquid. Makes 2 cups.

# Yogurt

The mild flavor is worth the wait.

**1 quart milk**
**¼ cup instant non-fat dry milk**
**2 tablespoons yogurt (your own or commercially made)**

Combine the milk and non-fat dry milk in a heavy pan; bring slowly to the boiling point, stirring. As soon as it boils, remove from heat and cool to about 115° (you can put the pan in a bowl of cold water to speed the cooling). If you don't have a thermometer, put a drop of milk on your wrist; it should feel warmer than lukewarm.

Blend a little of the warm milk with the yogurt until smooth, then stir the yogurt mixture into the warm milk. At this point the object is to maintain the milk at about 115° for 6 to 8 hours (if it goes below about 95°, the action stops). You can leave the milk in a bowl, if well covered, but it may be easier to handle if transferred to a prewarmed glass jar.

If you have a gas oven, the temperature inside with just the pilot light on may be about right—the temperature must never go over about 120° or your culture will be killed.

Most people simply wrap the container of warm milk in some good insulating material, such as a heavy wool blanket. Various insulated boxes and picnic bags work successfully, too; you can prewarm them by letting jars of very hot water stand in them while you are preparing the milk.

Be sure to place the insulated container of warm milk in a spot where the rate of cooling will be slow—on a high shelf, in a cupboard above a wall oven (turned on), in the car parked in the sun with windows closed, or near the hot water heater.

During the 6 to 8 hours it usually takes to make yogurt, the milk should not be disturbed. Makes 1 quart.

# Preserves & Pickles

## Use of Pectin

The jelly and jam recipes which follow can all be made without addition of commercial fruit pectin.

It is recommended that you follow the pectin manufacturer's recommendations and enclosed recipes for the use of that particular product (there have been changes in package sizes and products in the past few years).

## Quince-Apple-Cranberry Jelly

4   quinces
    Water
8   apples
4   cups (1 lb.) cranberries
    Sugar

Cut up the quinces, discarding the cores. Put in a large pan, cover with water, and cook over low heat for 40 minutes. Meanwhile, core apples and cut in pieces.

When the quinces have cooked 40 minutes, add the apples. After 10 minutes, add the cranberries and cook 10 minutes longer. Put the fruits in a jelly bag or 4 thicknesses of cheesecloth and let the juices drip through. Do not squeeze bag or jelly may be cloudy.

Use 4 cups of juice for each batch of jelly. Add an equal amount of sugar and boil rapidly until the jelly stage is reached (about 220° on a candy thermometer, or when liquid sheets from a metal spoon to form a large drop).

Skim and pour into hot, sterilized glasses. Seal according to manufacturer's instructions. Makes about 8 cups.

## Queen of Jams

3   pounds peaches (about 7 medium-sized)
3   pounds figs (about 3 dozen small)
½   cup water
5   pounds (11¼ cups) sugar
⅛   teaspoon ground cinnamon

Peel the peaches (and the figs, if you prefer), and cut them in small pieces. In a large pan, combine fruits and the water, and cook slowly until tender. Mash fruit with a potato masher, add the sugar and cinnamon, stirring, and cook slowly until almost as thick as desired. (The jam will thicken when cool; to test consistency, place a little on a saucer and chill quickly in a freezer.)

Pour into hot, sterilized jars; seal according to manufacturer's instructions. Makes about 10 cups.

## Plum Jam

Plums that have lots of sweet-tart flavor, such as Santa Rosa or Duarte, are especially good for plum jam. This recipe is also excellent with Queen Ann plums.

4   cups chopped pitted plums (put through coarse blade of food chopper)
3½  cups sugar

Combine in a pan the chopped plums and sugar; let stand 1 hour. Cook, stirring frequently, over low heat until thickened. (Check consistency by putting a little on a plate and chilling quickly in the freezer.) Pour hot into hot, sterilized jars; seal according to manufacturer's instructions. Makes about 4 cups.

## Persimmon Freezer Jam

Persimmon jam is made without boiling (boiling causes bitterness). It needs to be refrigerated and used within about two months. For longer storage, freeze, then use the defrosted jam within about two weeks.

4   cups persimmon purée (see following instructions)
3   cups sugar
2   tablespoons lemon juice
¼   teaspoon grated lemon peel

In a large pan combine persimmon purée and sugar. Cook over low heat, stirring constantly until thickened, about 20 minutes. Do not boil. Remove jam from heat and stir in lemon juice and lemon peel.

Pour into hot, sterilized jars to within ¼ inch of top. Adjust caps and seal. Store in refrigerator or freezer. Makes about 6 cups.

**Persimmon Purée.** Use a spoon to scoop the flesh from the skin of fresh persimmons; whirl in blender until smooth or press through a food mill. Use at once or freeze.

## Satsuma Plum & Raspberry Jam

6 cups pitted Satsuma plums, ground in food chopper
About 3 cups raspberries (about 2 boxes)
6 cups sugar

Cook plums and raspberries together for 20 minutes. Add the sugar and continue cooking until thick. (Check consistency by putting a little on a plate and chilling quickly in the freezer.)

Pour hot into hot, sterilized jars and seal according to manufacturer's instructions. Makes about 9 cups.

## Simplicity Apricot Jam

You can put up any sized batch of jam you like with this simple recipe:

Wash thoroughly ripe apricots, remove pits but do not peel, and cut the fruit into fairly small pieces. Measure fruit and cover with an equal measure of sugar. Let stand several hours or overnight for juices to form. Cook, stirring, until jam reaches the consistency you like best, considering that it will firm just a little when cool.

Pour hot jam into hot, sterilized jars and seal according to the manufacturer's instructions.

## Meyer Lemon Marmalade

About 6 medium-sized Meyer lemons
6 cups water
About 6½ cups sugar

Thinly slice lemons, discarding ends and seeds to make 3 cups lemon slices. Place in a bowl, pour on water,

cover, and let stand in a cool place overnight. Then bring lemon mixture to a boil; boil, uncovered, for 10 minutes. Remove from heat, cover, and let stand overnight again.

Measure the lemon-water mixture; add an equal amount of sugar. Bring mixture to a rapid boil, stirring until sugar dissolves. Lower heat, but continue cooking rapidly for about 45 minutes, or until marmalade sheets from a spoon when tested. Pour hot marmalade into hot, sterilized canning jars. Adjust lids to seal. Makes about 6 cups.

## Pineapple Orange Marmalade

1 large pineapple (about 5 lbs.)
1 large orange
3 tablespoons minced fresh ginger
3 cups sugar

Remove rind and core from pineapple; finely chop fruit. Finely chop unpeeled orange, discarding seeds.

In a heavy 5-quart kettle, combine pineapple, orange, ginger, and sugar. Bring to a gentle, rolling boil and cook, uncovered, stirring often, for 25 minutes, or until thickened.

Remove from heat and let cool. Pour into freezer containers or jars to within ½ inch of top. Cover and refrigerate up to 2 months or freeze. Makes about 3 pints.

## Perfect Amber Marmalade

There are marmalades and marmalades, but not all are as beautiful in color and as delicate in flavor as this one. Select thin-skinned fruit.

1 grapefruit
1 orange
1 lemon
Cold water
Sugar

Slice fruit very, very thin, discarding seeds and cores. Measure into a nonmetallic bowl, and for each cup of fruit add 3 cups of cold water. Let stand overnight.

Put the fruit and water in a pan and boil for exactly 10 minutes after it reaches boiling point. Again let it stand overnight. Measure again, heat,

add 1 cup of sugar for each cup of the fruit mixture, and boil steadily until the jelly stage is reached (liquid sheets from a metal spoon to form a large drop, or about 220° on a candy thermometer).

Pour hot into hot, sterilized glasses and seal according to manufacturer's instructions. Makes about 5 cups.

## Tomato Marmalade

Although yellow tomatoes such as the Jubilee or Sunray are preferred, you can use firm, small, tartly flavored red ones just as well.

1 pound (4 or 5) yellow tomatoes
1½ cups sugar
1 lemon, seeded and sliced very thin

Peel tomatoes and cut them into eighths. Put into a pan or bowl and cover with sugar; let stand overnight.

In the morning, drain off the syrup, reserving the pulp. Bring syrup to a boil; cook to 235° on the candy thermometer, or until a drop of the mixture in cold water makes a soft pliable ball (30 to 45 minutes). Add the tomato pulp and sliced lemon; cook until tomatoes are bright and transparent and mixture sheets from a metal spoon to form a large drop (about 20 minutes). Pour hot into hot, sterilized jars. Seal immediately according to manufacturer's instructions. Makes 2 cups.

## Baked Apple Butter

4 to 5 pounds (about 12 large) cooking apples
3 cups apple cider or apple juice
Brown sugar
Cinnamon, cloves, allspice, and nutmeg to taste

Wash and quarter the apples; remove stems and blemishes. Place in a large pan and add cider. Cover and cook the fruit gently until it is quite soft. Force through a colander or food mill; measure the pulp.

For every cup of fruit pulp, stir in about ½ cup of brown sugar, depending upon the sweetness of the apples, and spices to taste. (For 4 to 5 pounds apples, about 2 teaspoons cinnamon,

½ teaspoon cloves, 1 teaspoon allspice, and ¼ teaspoon nutmeg may be a combination which will please your tastes.)

Place fruit in a heavy baking pan and bake in a 275° to 300° oven until butter is thick and dark. (If desired, butter may be partially cooked on top of range, then placed in oven.) Pour hot into hot, sterilized glasses and seal. Makes 9 cups.

## Ginger Pears

8 pounds pears (about 32 small or 21 large)
½ pound fresh ginger root, thinly sliced
4 pounds (9 cups) sugar
4 lemons, seeded and thinly sliced

Peel, core, and thinly slice the pears into a bowl; add ginger root and sugar. Mix well and let stand overnight in the refrigerator. The next day add lemon and transfer into a large pan; bring to a boil and cook slowly, stirring, until amber (25 to 35 minutes).

Seal hot in hot, sterilized jars according to manufacturer's instructions. Makes about 12 cups.

## Cherry Conserve

2 pounds sweet cherries, pitted
1 orange
4 cups sugar
Juice of ½ lemon
1 cup seedless raisins
1 cup chopped almonds, filberts, or pecans

The cherries may be chopped, halved, or used whole. Seed the orange and slice very thin (or run through the food chopper). Mix the cherries, sliced orange, sugar, and lemon juice in a large pan; cook slowly, stirring, until the mixture is thick and transparent. (Check consistency by putting a little on a plate and chilling quickly in the freezer.) Add the raisins and nuts 5 minutes before removing from the heat.

Pack hot into hot, sterilized jars

and seal immediately according to manufacturer's instructions. Makes 6 cups.

## Berry Preserves

Strawberries and the other berries, if very tart, may need no lemon juice added at all. Very ripe berries (or those lacking tartness) probably require it for jelling and flavor improvement.

5 cups strawberries (crushed), whole blackberries, raspberries, or other berries
5 cups sugar
½ cup lemon juice

Combine washed berries and sugar in a 4-quart pan. Let stand several hours or overnight until juices form.

Bring to a boil, stirring gently just until sugar dissolves. Keep at a moderate rolling boil 10 minutes. Add lemon juice (½ cup for all but strawberries or very tart berries).

Return to heat and bring to a boil again. Begin to test for jelly stage (about 220° on a candy thermometer, or when liquid sheets from a metal spoon to form a large drop); this stage will probably be reached about 2 minutes after the preserves begin to boil again. Remove from heat and skim off white foam. Pour hot into hot, sterilized jars and seal according to manufacturer's instructions. Makes about 5 cups.

## Brandied Cherries

Brandied cherries make a fine sauce over vanilla ice cream.

3 pounds large black cherries, pitted
3 pounds (6¾ cups) sugar
Brandy

Place cherries in a large pan and cover with sugar. Let stand an hour or so until juices form. Cook slowly over low heat for about 20 minutes, or until the cherries are barely tender. Remove the fruit from the syrup, and if necessary, continue to cook the syrup until it is slightly thickened.

Measure and add ¼ cup of brandy for every cup of syrup. Pour over the cherries and seal at once in hot, sterilized jars. Makes about 12 cups.

## Prune Chutney

1 cup light brown sugar, firmly packed
1 cup granulated sugar
¾ cup white vinegar
¾ to 1½ teaspoons crushed red pepper
2 teaspoons salt
2 teaspoons mustard seed
2 large cloves garlic, thinly sliced
¼ cup thinly sliced onion
½ cup preserved or candied ginger, thinly sliced
1 cup white raisins
3½ cups halved and pitted plums or fresh Italian prunes

In a large kettle, combine the brown sugar, granulated sugar, and vinegar. Bring to a boil. Add the red pepper, salt, mustard seed, garlic, onion, ginger, and raisins; mix together well. Add the cut-up prunes and simmer until thickened (about 30 minutes), stirring frequently.

Pour hot into hot, sterilized jars. Seal immediately according to manufacturer's instructions. Makes 4 cups.

## Alaska Rhubarb & Onion Relish

No one knows why this old and unusual recipe is called "Alaska."

4 cups chopped rhubarb
4 cups chopped white onions
2 cups (1 pt.) cider vinegar
1 tablespoon salt
4 cups brown sugar
1 teaspoon each cloves, allspice, and cinnamon
Cayenne to taste (up to 1 teaspoon for a hot relish)

Combine all the ingredients and cook slowly until quite thick. Pour while hot into hot, sterilized jars and seal immediately according to manufacturer's instructions. Makes 8 cups.

## Pepper Relish

6 green bell peppers
6 red bell peppers
6 large onions, peeled
Boiling water
1 cup sugar
2 tablespoons salt
1 teaspoon celery seed
1½ cups cider vinegar

*(Continued on next page)*

Remove seeds, white pith, and stems from peppers. Put peppers and onions through the food chopper with a medium blade. Cover with boiling water and let stand 5 minutes; drain well. Add the sugar, salt, celery seed, and vinegar. Bring to the boiling point, and let boil 20 minutes.

Pour hot into hot, sterilized jars and seal according to manufacturer's instructions. Makes about 8 cups.

## Other Relishes

Recipes for relishes and chutneys which can be made in small quantity and do not need to be sealed in jars are on pages 118 and 119. Tomato Chutney (page 119) can be sealed if you like.

## Prize Bread-and-Butter Pickles

Coarse pickling salt is recommended because it does not contain additives which will discolor the pickles or alter the pickling process. But if you can't get it, ordinary uniodized table salt can be used.

- 1 gallon medium-sized pickling cucumbers, very thinly sliced
- 8 large onions, very thinly sliced
- 2 green peppers, seeded and cut in very thin strips
- ½ cup salt
- 5 cups sugar
- 1½ teaspoons ground turmeric
- ½ teaspoon ground cloves
- 2 tablespoons mustard seed
- 1 teaspoon celery seed
- 5 cups cider vinegar

Mix the cucumbers, onions, peppers, and salt and let stand 3 hours. Drain.

Combine the sugar, spices, and vinegar in a large kettle. Heat mixture scalding hot, stirring to dissolve sugar. Add drained vegetables and heat *just* to boiling. Seal at once in hot, sterilized jars according to manufacturer's instructions. Makes 24 cups.

## Zucchini Pickles

When zucchini plants become "over-bearing" or the squash are in bountiful supply, you can turn them into these crisp, mustard pickles.

- 10 cups thinly sliced zucchini
- 2½ cups cider vinegar
- 1½ cups sugar
- 1 tablespoon salt
- 2 teaspoons dry mustard
- 2 teaspoons ground turmeric
- ½ teaspoon celery seed
- ⅛ teaspoon powdered alum
- 2 large onions, thinly sliced

Thoroughly scrub the zucchini, but do not peel; cut in thin slices. In a large kettle, combine the vinegar with the sugar, salt, dry mustard, turmeric, celery seed, and alum. Add the thinly sliced zucchini and onion.

Bring to a boil and simmer for 15 to 20 minutes, or until the squash becomes semi-transparent. Pour the zucchini mixture into hot, sterilized jars; seal immediately. Makes 10 to 12 cups.

## Old-fashioned Pickled Peaches

When peaches are at their prime, take time to preserve them for winter meals with this 4-day process. The spices and brown sugar make for a rich-tasting and succulent pickle.

- 5 pounds firm clingstone peaches (about 12 medium-sized or 16 small)
- 2 cups cider vinegar
- 3½ cups granulated sugar
- 3 cups brown sugar, firmly packed
- 3 or 4 sticks whole cinnamon
- 2 tablespoons whole cloves

Peel peaches and put in a deep non-metallic vessel. Boil the vinegar, sugars, and spices until the sugar is dissolved. Pour boiling hot over the peaches, cover with a plate weighted down to hold the fruit under the liquid, and let stand 24 hours. Drain off the liquid, reheat, pour over the peaches again, and let stand another 24 hours. Repeat this step on the third day.

On the fourth morning, drain off the liquid (strain out the spices), boil it down to a fairly thick syrup, and in this simmer a few peaches at a time until they are tender but not soft. Pack hot peaches in hot, sterilized jars, cover with hot syrup, and seal jars according to manufacturer's instructions. Makes about 4 quarts.

## Sweet Watermelon Pickles

Of all the pickle, jam, and jelly recipes, this one seems to be the Number 1 favorite.

- 1 large watermelon with thick, firm rind
- 2 tablespoons salt
  Water
- 2 cups (1 pt.) cider vinegar
- 7 cups sugar
- 1 tablespoon whole cloves
- 2 or 3 sticks whole cinnamon
  Whole cloves

Remove all the pink flesh and peel off the hard green skin. Cut the rind in 1 or 1½-inch squares or into decorative shapes with a small cooky cutter (the pieces will shrink so don't make them too small).

Dissolve the salt in 1 gallon of cold water; soak the rind in this solution overnight, or 8 to 10 hours. Rinse with cold water and soak the rind in ice-cold water for 1 hour. Drain rind, place in a large pan, and cover with boiling water; simmer just until tender enough to be pierced easily with a toothpick. Drain thoroughly.

Prepare a syrup by combining the vinegar, sugar, and a cheesecloth bag containing the 1 tablespoon cloves and cinnamon sticks. Heat until the sugar is dissolved and the mixture boils. Add the rind and cook gently until the rind is clear and transparent. Remove the spice bag and let the rind stand in the syrup for 24 hours.

Insert a whole clove in the center of each piece of pickle and pack them attractively in small, hot sterilized jars. Heat the syrup to boiling, pour it over the pickles in the jars, and seal immediately according to manufacturer's instructions. Makes about 10 cups.

# Index

## Metric Conversion Table

| To change | To | Multiply by |
|---|---|---|
| ounces (oz.) | grams (g) | 28 |
| pounds (lbs.) | kilograms (kg) | 0.45 |
| teaspoons | milliliters (ml) | 5 |
| tablespoons | milliliters (ml) | 15 |
| fluid ounces (fl. oz.) | milliliters (ml) | 30 |
| cups | liters (l) | 0.24 |
| pints (pt.) | liters (l) | 0.47 |
| quarts (qt.) | liters (l) | 0.95 |
| gallons (gal.) | liters (l) | 3.8 |
| Fahrenheit temperature (°F) | Celsius temperature (°C) | 5/9 after subtracting 32 |